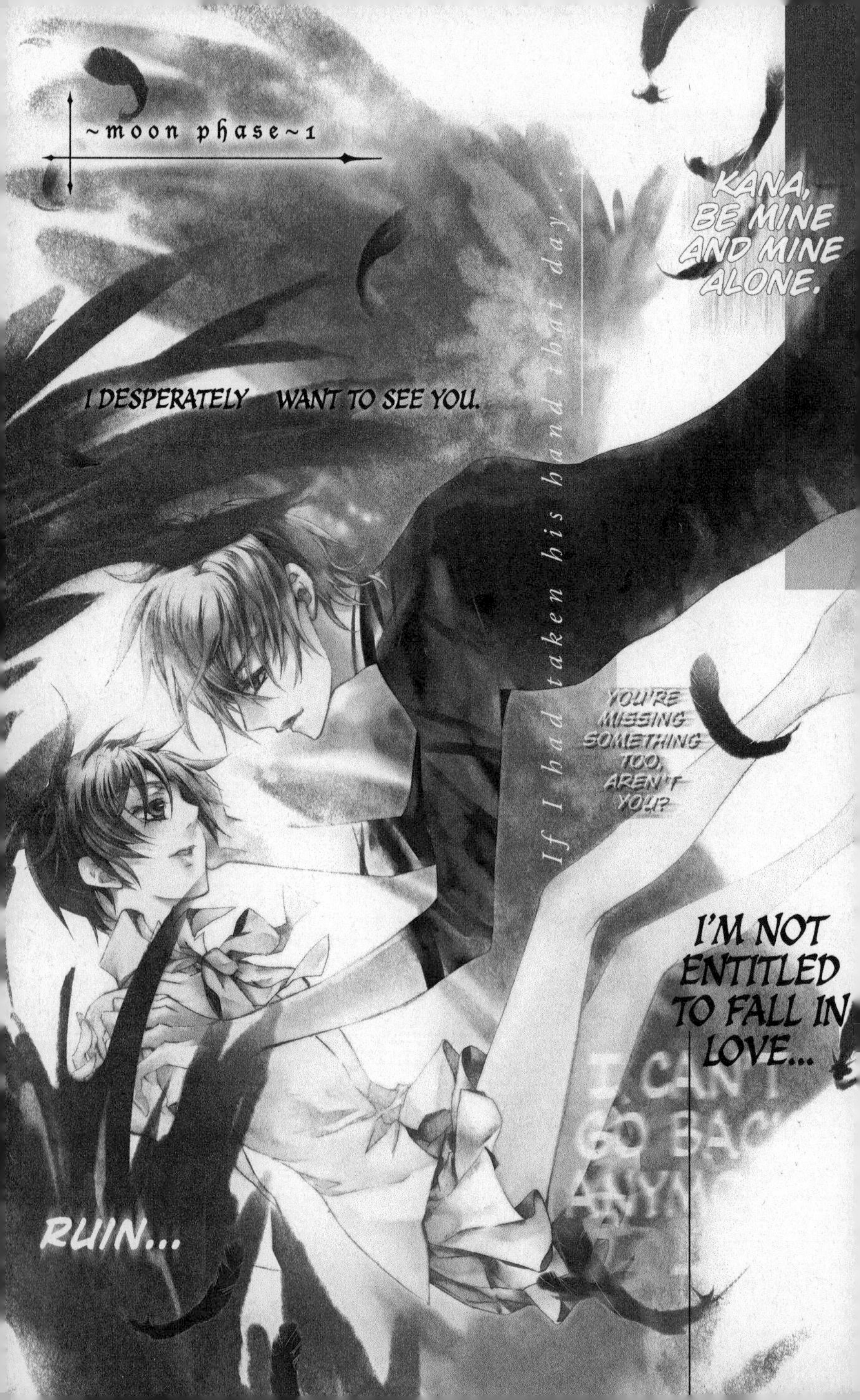
~moon phase~1
KANA, BE MINE AND MINE ALONE.
If I had taken his hand that day...
I DESPERATELY WANT TO SEE YOU.
YOU'RE MISSING SOMETHING TOO, AREN'T YOU?
I'M NOT ENTITLED TO FALL IN LOVE...
RUIN...

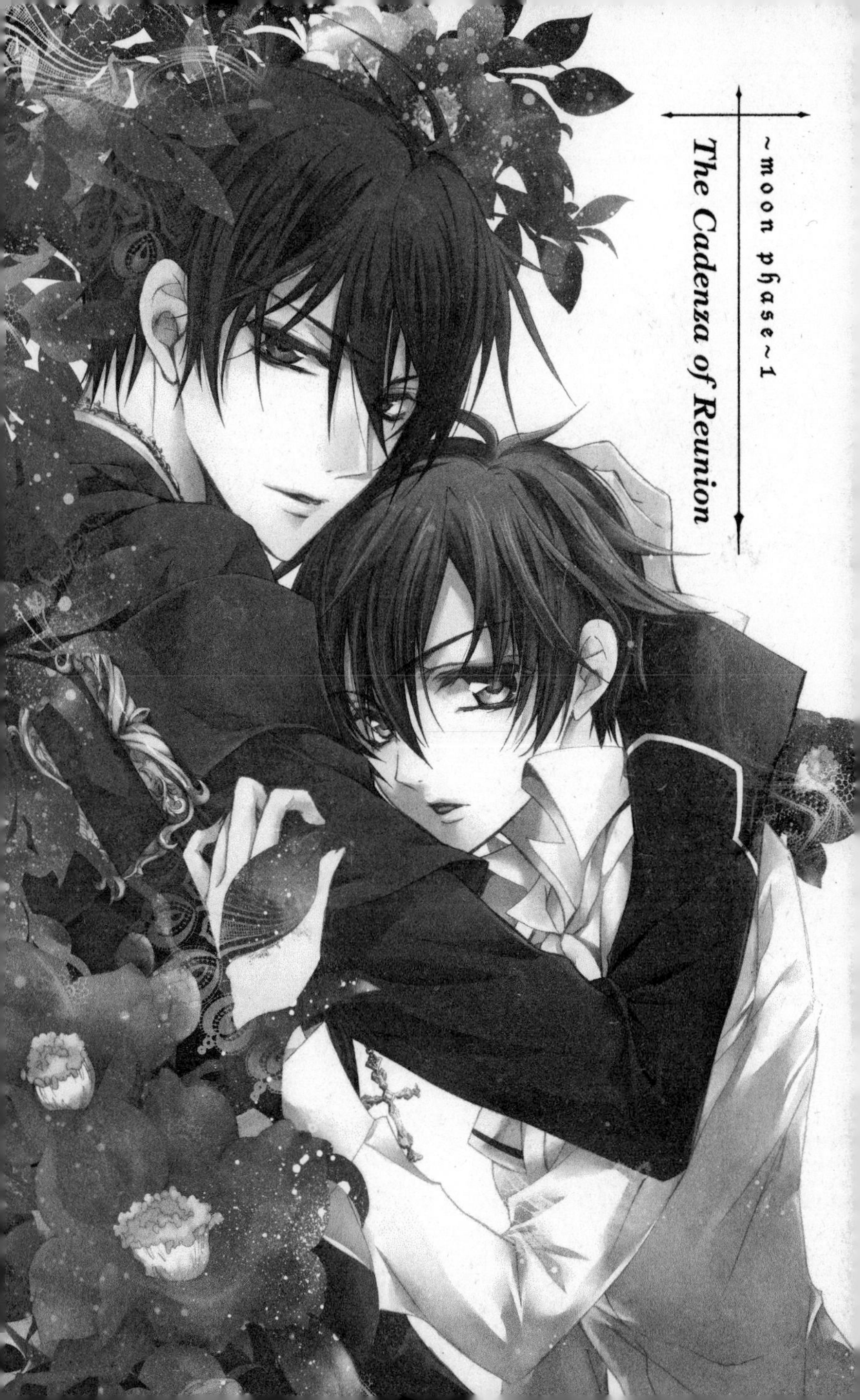
~moon phase~1
The Cadenza of Reunion

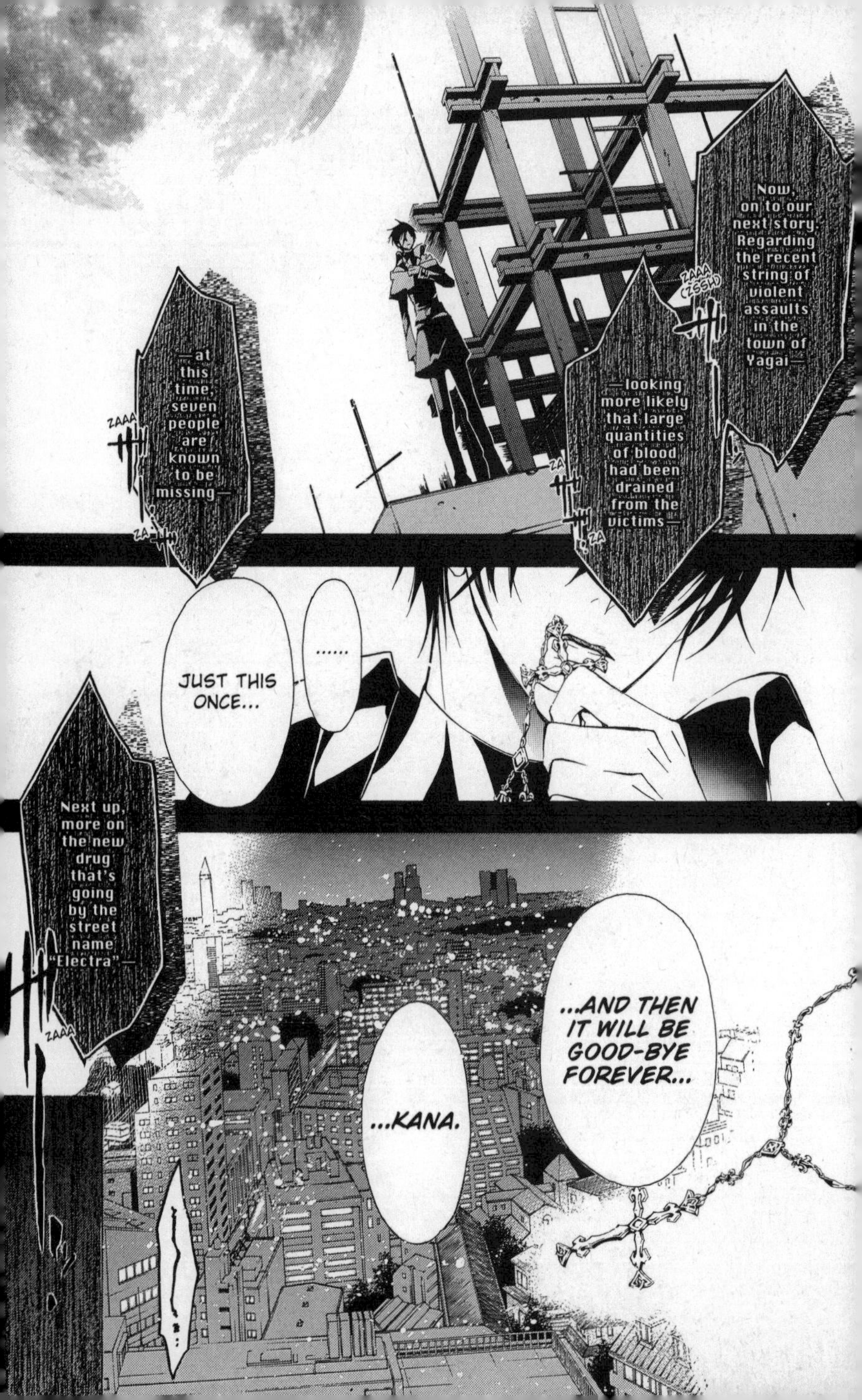
Now, on to our next story. Regarding the recent string of violent assaults in the town of Yagai—
ZAAA (ZSSH)
—looking more likely that large quantities of blood had been drained from the victims—
ZA
ZA
—at this time, seven people are known to be missing—
ZAAA
ZA
......
JUST THIS ONCE...
Next up, more on the new drug that's going by the street name "Electra"—
ZAAA
...AND THEN IT WILL BE GOOD-BYE FOREVER...
...KANA.

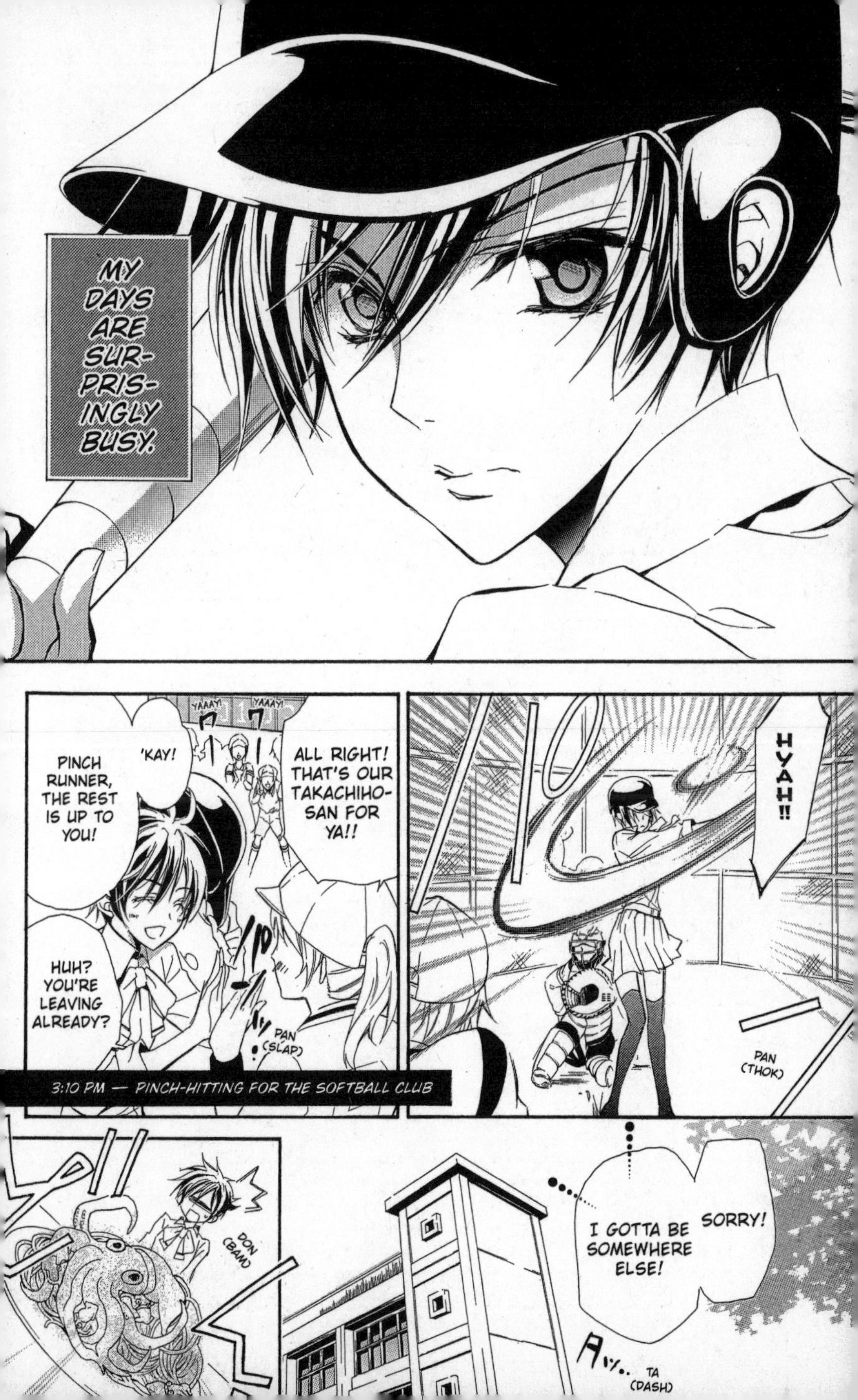
MY DAYS ARE SUR-PRIS-INGLY BUSY.
HYAH!!
PAN (THOK)
YAAAY! YAAAY!
ALL RIGHT! THAT'S OUR TAKACHIHO-SAN FOR YA!!
'KAY!
PINCH RUNNER, THE REST IS UP TO YOU!
PAN (SLAP)
HUH? YOU'RE LEAVING ALREADY?
3:10 PM — PINCH-HITTING FOR THE SOFTBALL CLUB
......
SORRY!
I GOTTA BE SOMEWHERE ELSE!
TA (DASH)
DON (BAM)

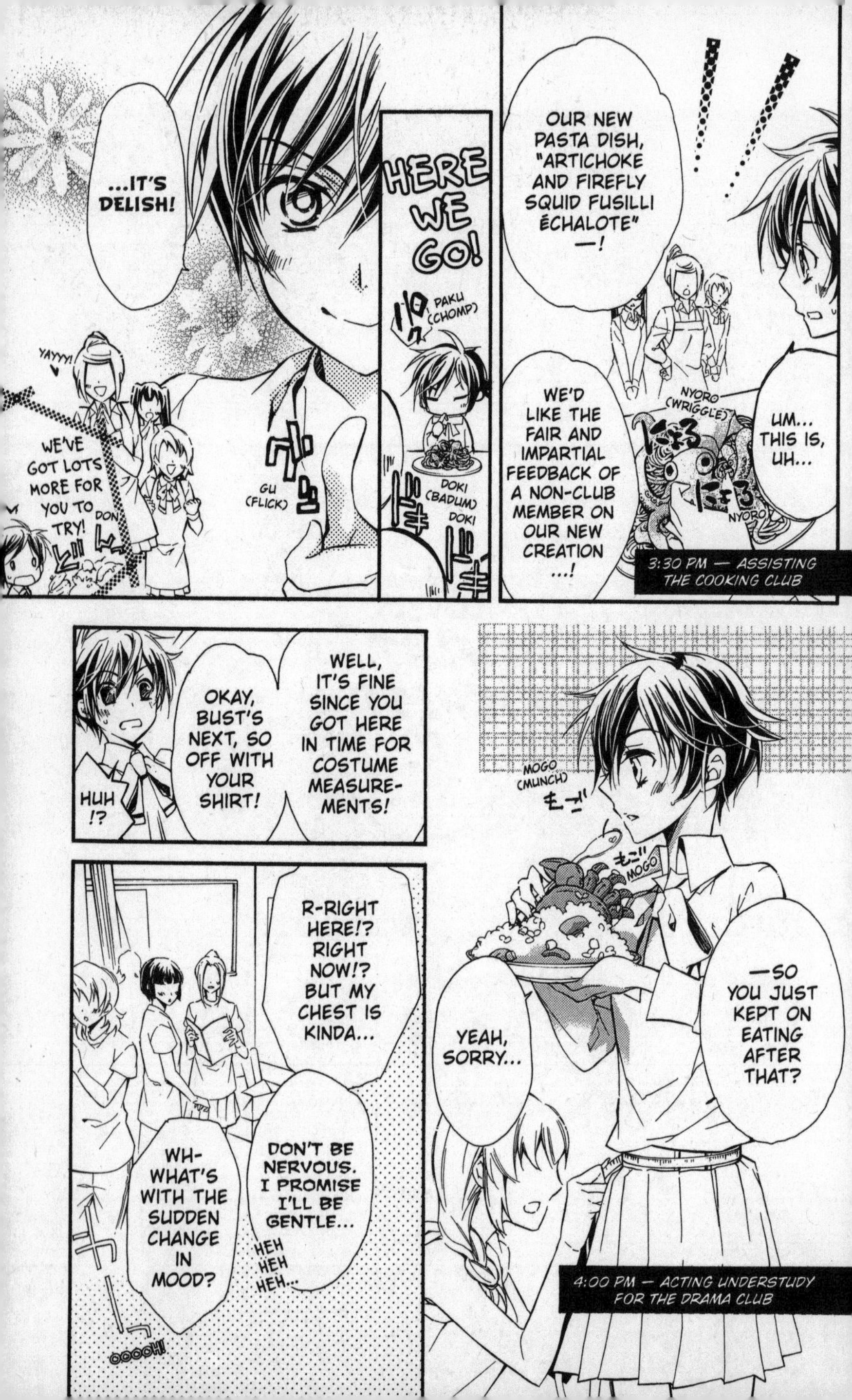

OUR NEW PASTA DISH, "ARTICHOKE AND FIREFLY SQUID FUSILLI ÉCHALOTE" —!
UM... THIS IS, UH...
WE'D LIKE THE FAIR AND IMPARTIAL FEEDBACK OF A NON-CLUB MEMBER ON OUR NEW CREATION ...!
NYORO (WRIGGLE)
NYORO
3:30 PM — ASSISTING THE COOKING CLUB
HERE WE GO!
PAKU (CHOMP)
DOKI (BADUM) DOKI
...IT'S DELISH!
GU (FLICK)
YAYYY!
WE'VE GOT LOTS MORE FOR YOU TO TRY!
DON
MOGO (MUNCH)
—SO YOU JUST KEPT ON EATING AFTER THAT?
MOGO
YEAH, SORRY...
4:00 PM — ACTING UNDERSTUDY FOR THE DRAMA CLUB
WELL, IT'S FINE SINCE YOU GOT HERE IN TIME FOR COSTUME MEASURE-MENTS!
OKAY, BUST'S NEXT, SO OFF WITH YOUR SHIRT!
HUH !?
R-RIGHT HERE!? RIGHT NOW!? BUT MY CHEST IS KINDA...
DON'T BE NERVOUS. I PROMISE I'LL BE GENTLE...
HEH HEH HEH...
WH-WHAT'S WITH THE SUDDEN CHANGE IN MOOD?
OOOOH!

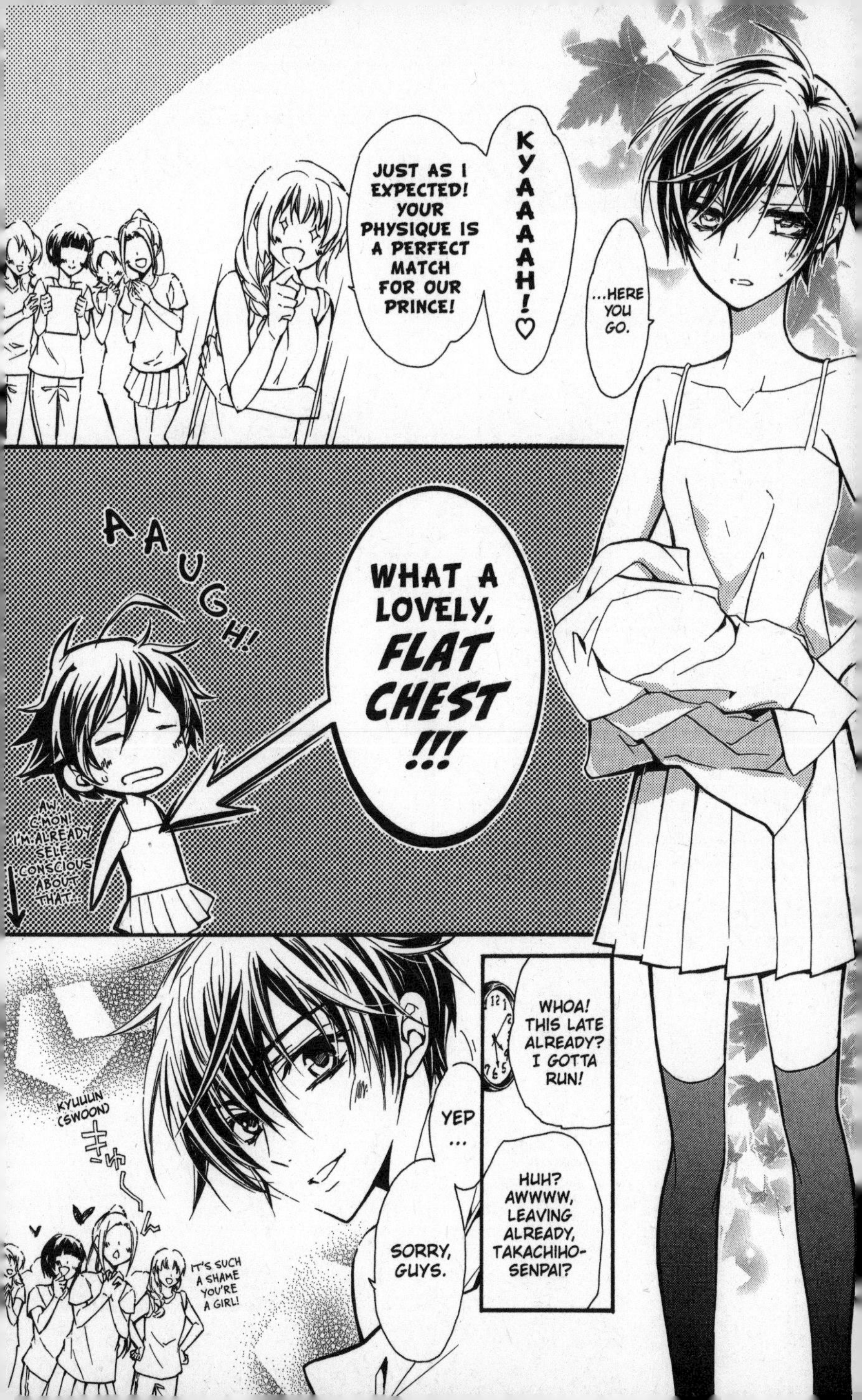
...HERE YOU GO.
KYAAAAAH!♡
JUST AS I EXPECTED! YOUR PHYSIQUE IS A PERFECT MATCH FOR OUR PRINCE!
WHAT A LOVELY, FLAT CHEST!!!
AAUGH!
AW, C'MON! I'M ALREADY SELF-CONSCIOUS ABOUT THAT...
WHOA! THIS LATE ALREADY? I GOTTA RUN!
HUH? AWWWW, LEAVING ALREADY, TAKACHIHO-SENPAI?
YEP...
SORRY, GUYS.
KYUUUN (SWOON)
きゅ〜ん
IT'S SUCH A SHAME YOU'RE A GIRL!

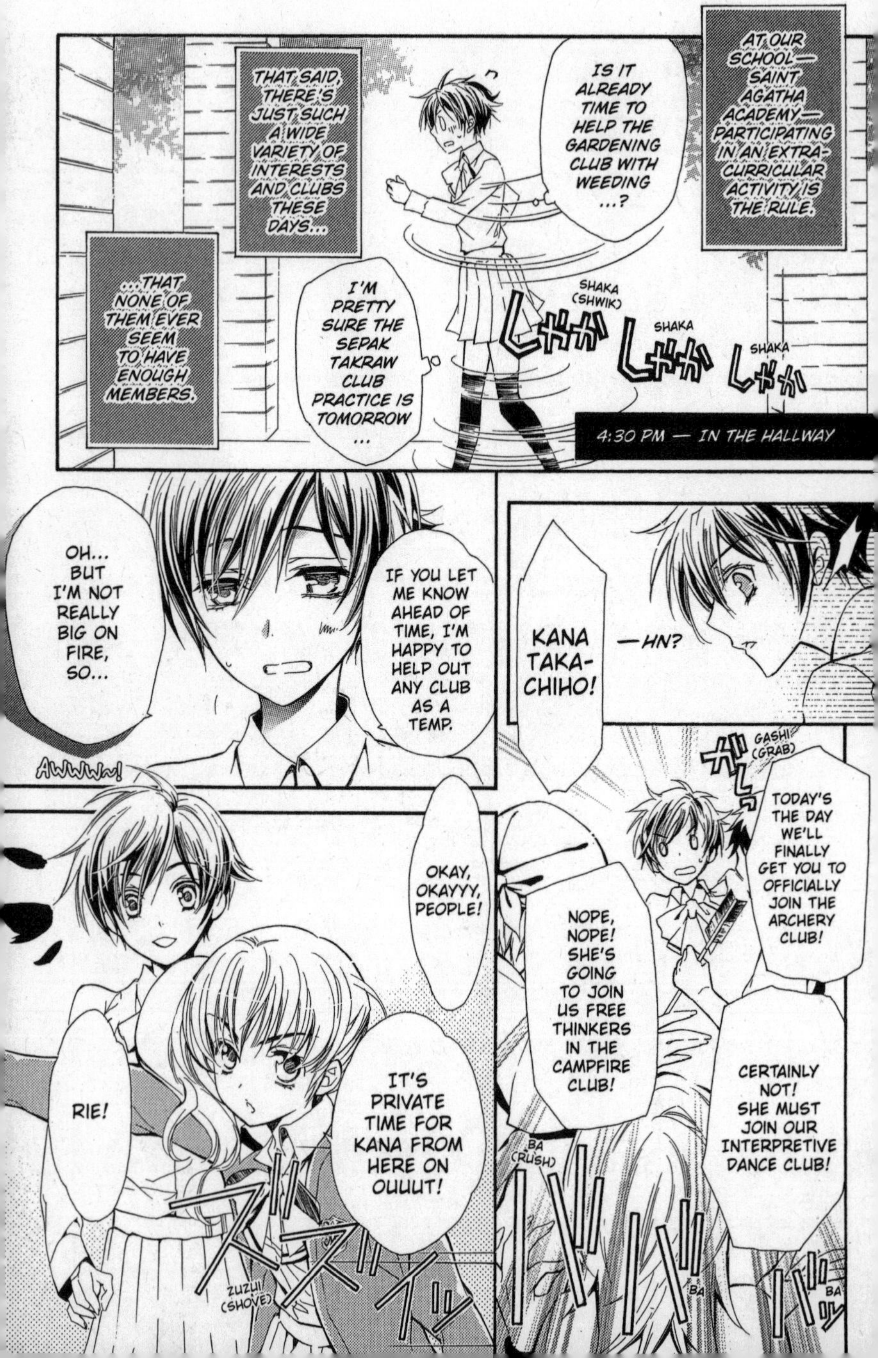
AT OUR SCHOOL—SAINT AGATHA ACADEMY—PARTICIPATING IN AN EXTRA-CURRICULAR ACTIVITY IS THE RULE.
IS IT ALREADY TIME TO HELP THE GARDENING CLUB WITH WEEDING ...?
THAT SAID, THERE'S JUST SUCH A WIDE VARIETY OF INTERESTS AND CLUBS THESE DAYS...
SHAKA (SHWIK)
SHAKA
SHAKA
I'M PRETTY SURE THE SEPAK TAKRAW CLUB PRACTICE IS TOMORROW ...
4:30 PM — IN THE HALLWAY
...THAT NONE OF THEM EVER SEEM TO HAVE ENOUGH MEMBERS.
KANA TAKA-CHIHO!
—HN?
GASHI (GRAB)
TODAY'S THE DAY WE'LL FINALLY GET YOU TO OFFICIALLY JOIN THE ARCHERY CLUB!
NOPE, NOPE! SHE'S GOING TO JOIN US FREE THINKERS IN THE CAMPFIRE CLUB!
CERTAINLY NOT! SHE MUST JOIN OUR INTERPRETIVE DANCE CLUB!
BA (RUSH)
BA
BA
IF YOU LET ME KNOW AHEAD OF TIME, I'M HAPPY TO HELP OUT ANY CLUB AS A TEMP.
OH... BUT I'M NOT REALLY BIG ON FIRE, SO...
AWWWW!
OKAY, OKAYYY, PEOPLE!
IT'S PRIVATE TIME FOR KANA FROM HERE ON OUUUT!
RIE!
ZUZUI (SHOVE)

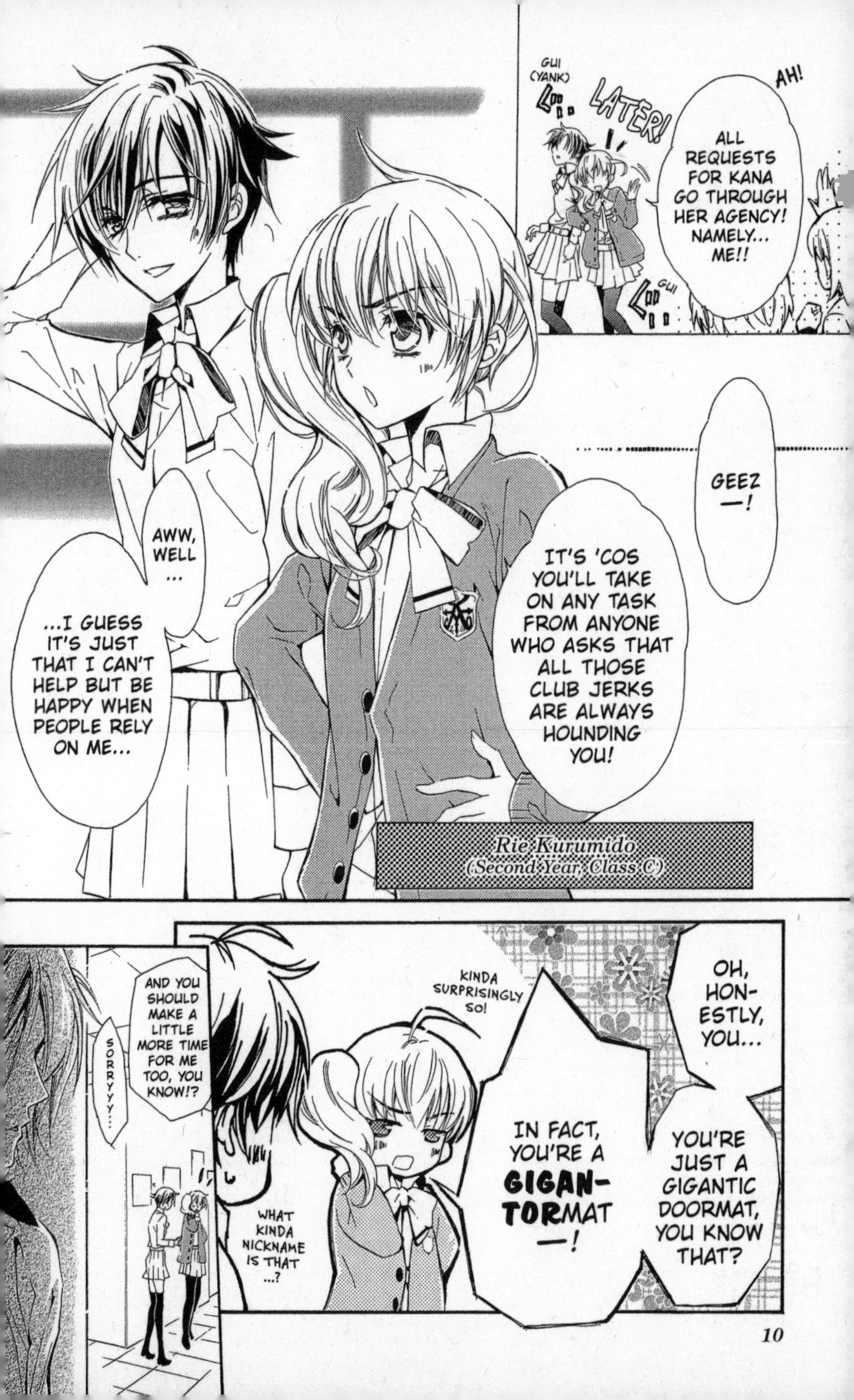
AH!
ALL REQUESTS FOR KANA GO THROUGH HER AGENCY! NAMELY... ME!!
LATER!
GUI (YANK)
GUI
GEEZ—!
IT'S 'COS YOU'LL TAKE ON ANY TASK FROM ANYONE WHO ASKS THAT ALL THOSE CLUB JERKS ARE ALWAYS HOUNDING YOU!
AWW, WELL...
...I GUESS IT'S JUST THAT I CAN'T HELP BUT BE HAPPY WHEN PEOPLE RELY ON ME...
Rie Kurumido
(Second Year, Class C)
OH, HON-ESTLY, YOU...
YOU'RE JUST A GIGANTIC DOORMAT, YOU KNOW THAT?
IN FACT, YOU'RE A **GIGAN-TOR**MAT—!
KINDA SURPRISINGLY SO!
WHAT KINDA NICKNAME IS THAT...?
AND YOU SHOULD MAKE A LITTLE MORE TIME FOR ME TOO, YOU KNOW!?
SORRYYY...

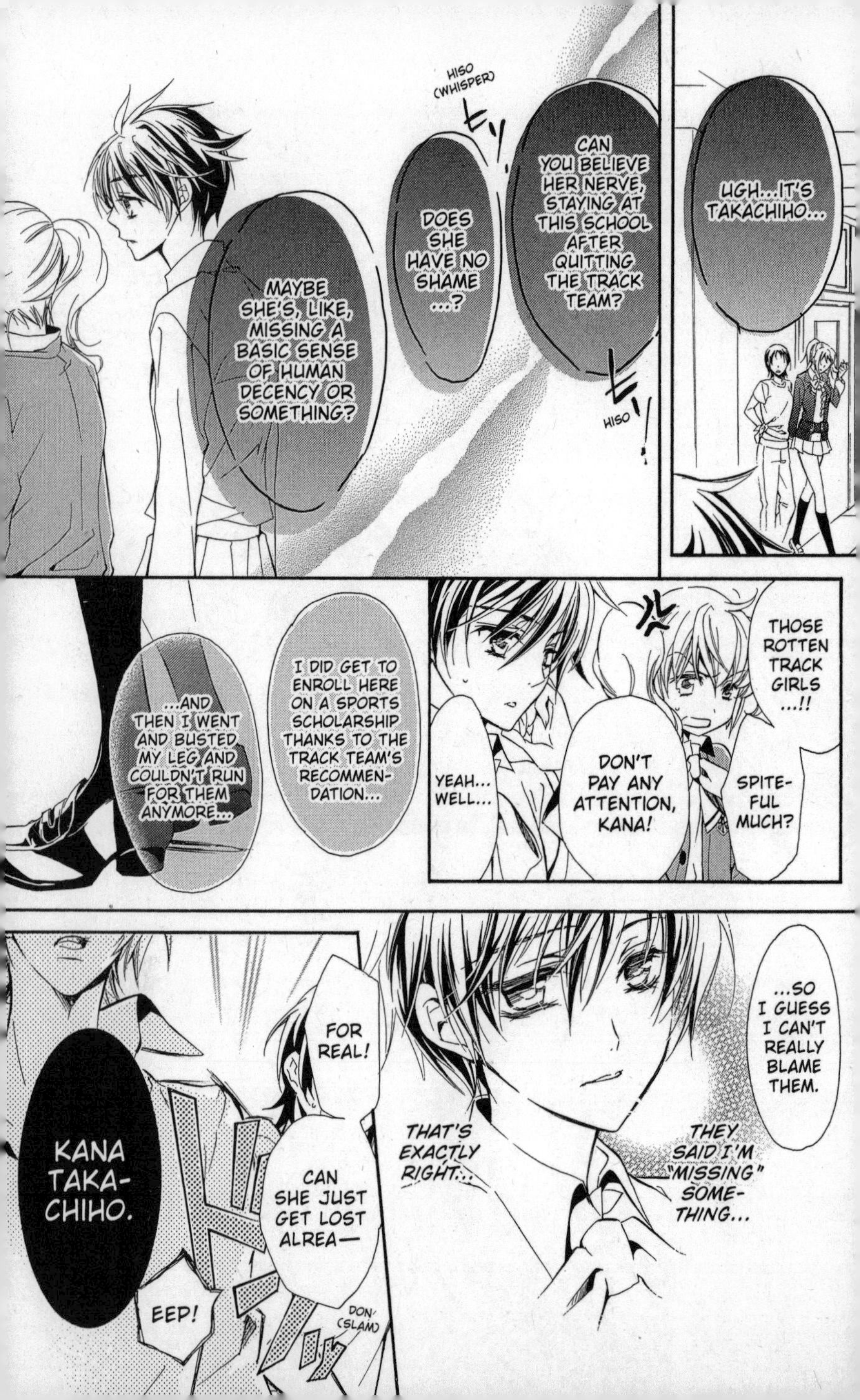
UGH...IT'S TAKACHIHO...
HISO (WHISPER)
CAN YOU BELIEVE HER NERVE, STAYING AT THIS SCHOOL AFTER QUITTING THE TRACK TEAM?
DOES SHE HAVE NO SHAME ...?
HISO
MAYBE SHE'S, LIKE, MISSING A BASIC SENSE OF HUMAN DECENCY OR SOMETHING?
THOSE ROTTEN TRACK GIRLS ...!!
SPITE-FUL MUCH?
DON'T PAY ANY ATTENTION, KANA!
YEAH... WELL...
I DID GET TO ENROLL HERE ON A SPORTS SCHOLARSHIP THANKS TO THE TRACK TEAM'S RECOMMEN-DATION...
...AND THEN I WENT AND BUSTED MY LEG AND COULDN'T RUN FOR THEM ANYMORE...
...SO I GUESS I CAN'T REALLY BLAME THEM.
THEY SAID I'M "MISSING" SOME-THING...
THAT'S EXACTLY RIGHT...
FOR REAL!
CAN SHE JUST GET LOST ALREA—
DON (SLAM)
EEP!
KANA TAKA-CHIHO.

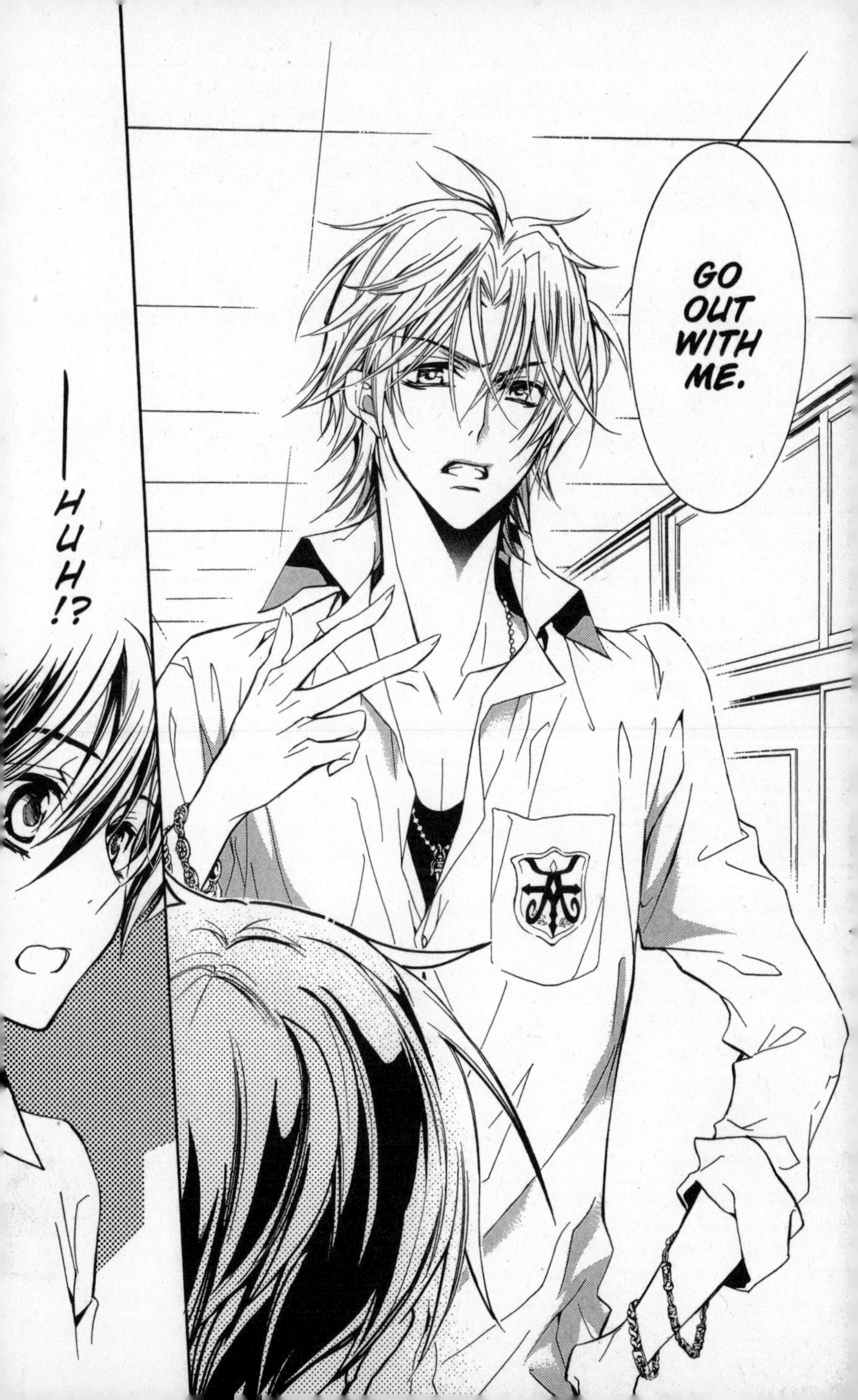
GO OUT WITH ME.
—HUH!?

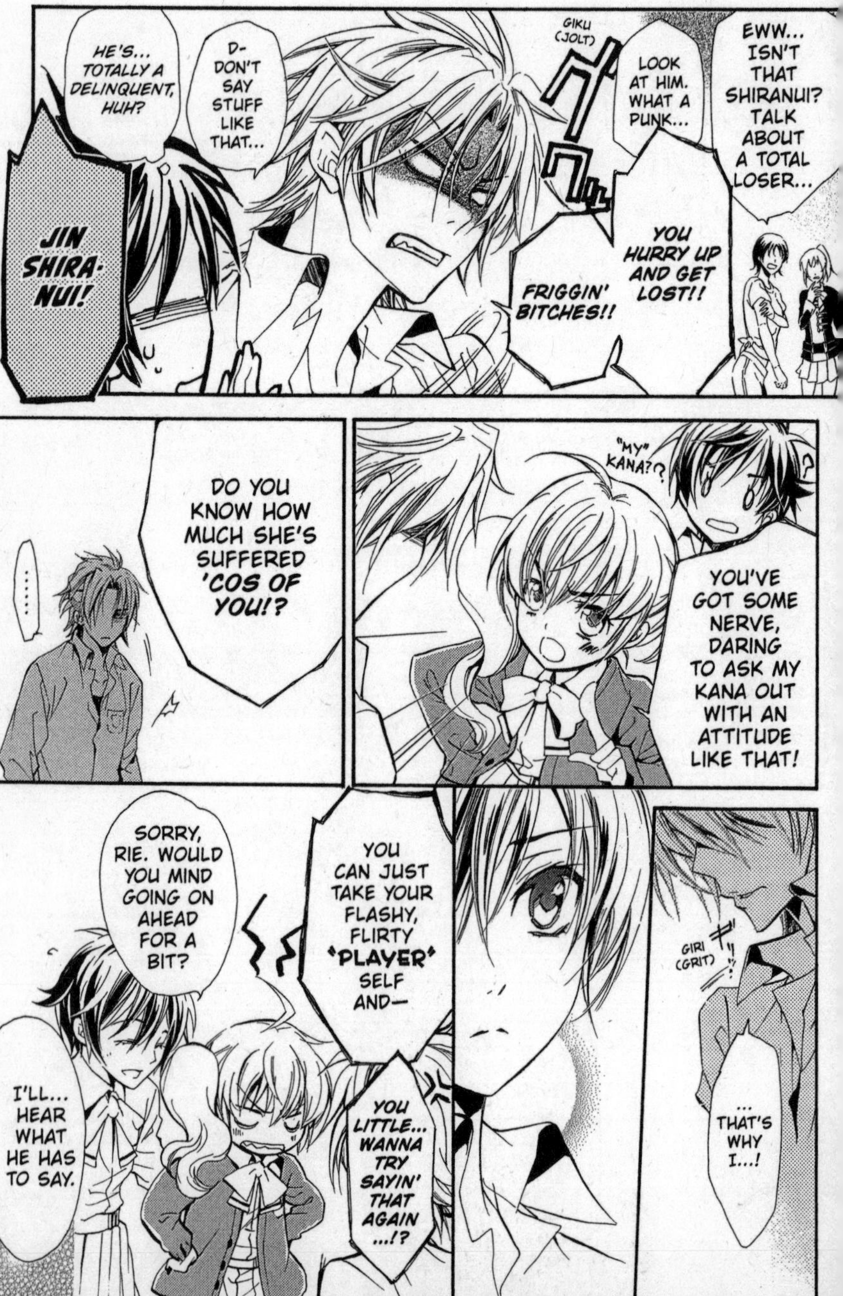
EWW... ISN'T THAT SHIRANUI? TALK ABOUT A TOTAL LOSER...
LOOK AT HIM. WHAT A PUNK...
GIKU (JOLT)
YOU HURRY UP AND GET LOST!!
FRIGGIN' BITCHES!!
D-DON'T SAY STUFF LIKE THAT...
HE'S... TOTALLY A DELINQUENT, HUH?
JIN SHIRA-NUI!
"MY" KANA?
YOU'VE GOT SOME NERVE, DARING TO ASK MY KANA OUT WITH AN ATTITUDE LIKE THAT!
DO YOU KNOW HOW MUCH SHE'S SUFFERED 'COS OF YOU!?
......
GIRI (GRIT)
...THAT'S WHY I...!
YOU CAN JUST TAKE YOUR FLASHY, FLIRTY "PLAYER" SELF AND—
SORRY, RIE. WOULD YOU MIND GOING ON AHEAD FOR A BIT?
YOU LITTLE... WANNA TRY SAYIN' THAT AGAIN ...!?
I'LL... HEAR WHAT HE HAS TO SAY.

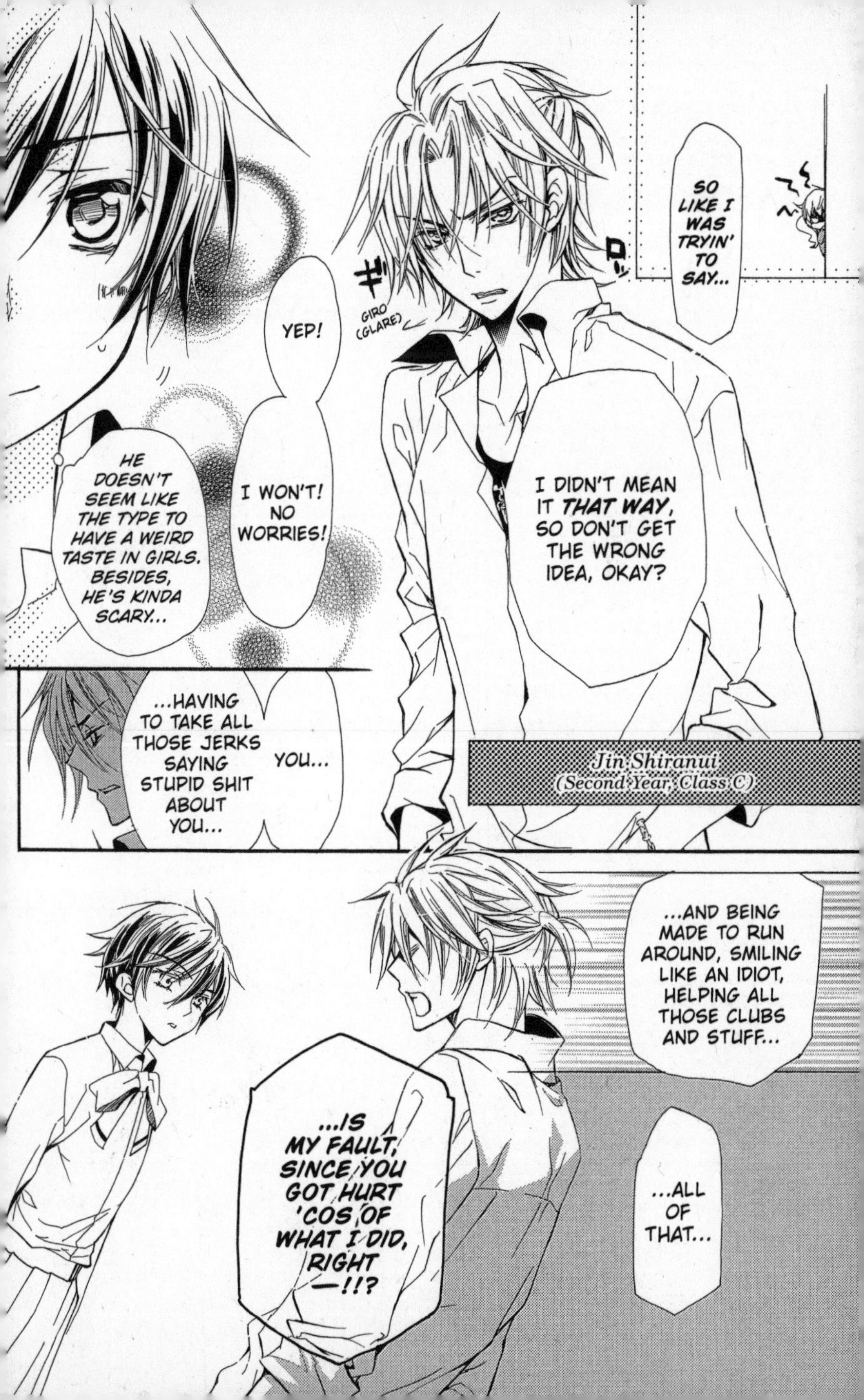

SO LIKE I WAS TRYIN' TO SAY...
I DIDN'T MEAN IT *THAT WAY*, SO DON'T GET THE WRONG IDEA, OKAY?
Jin Shiranui (Second Year, Class C)
GIRO (GLARE)
YEP!
I WON'T! NO WORRIES!
HE DOESN'T SEEM LIKE THE TYPE TO HAVE A WEIRD TASTE IN GIRLS. BESIDES, HE'S KINDA SCARY...
YOU...
...HAVING TO TAKE ALL THOSE JERKS SAYING STUPID SHIT ABOUT YOU...
...AND BEING MADE TO RUN AROUND, SMILING LIKE AN IDIOT, HELPING ALL THOSE CLUBS AND STUFF...
...ALL OF THAT...
...IS MY FAULT, SINCE YOU GOT HURT 'COS OF WHAT I DID, RIGHT—!!?

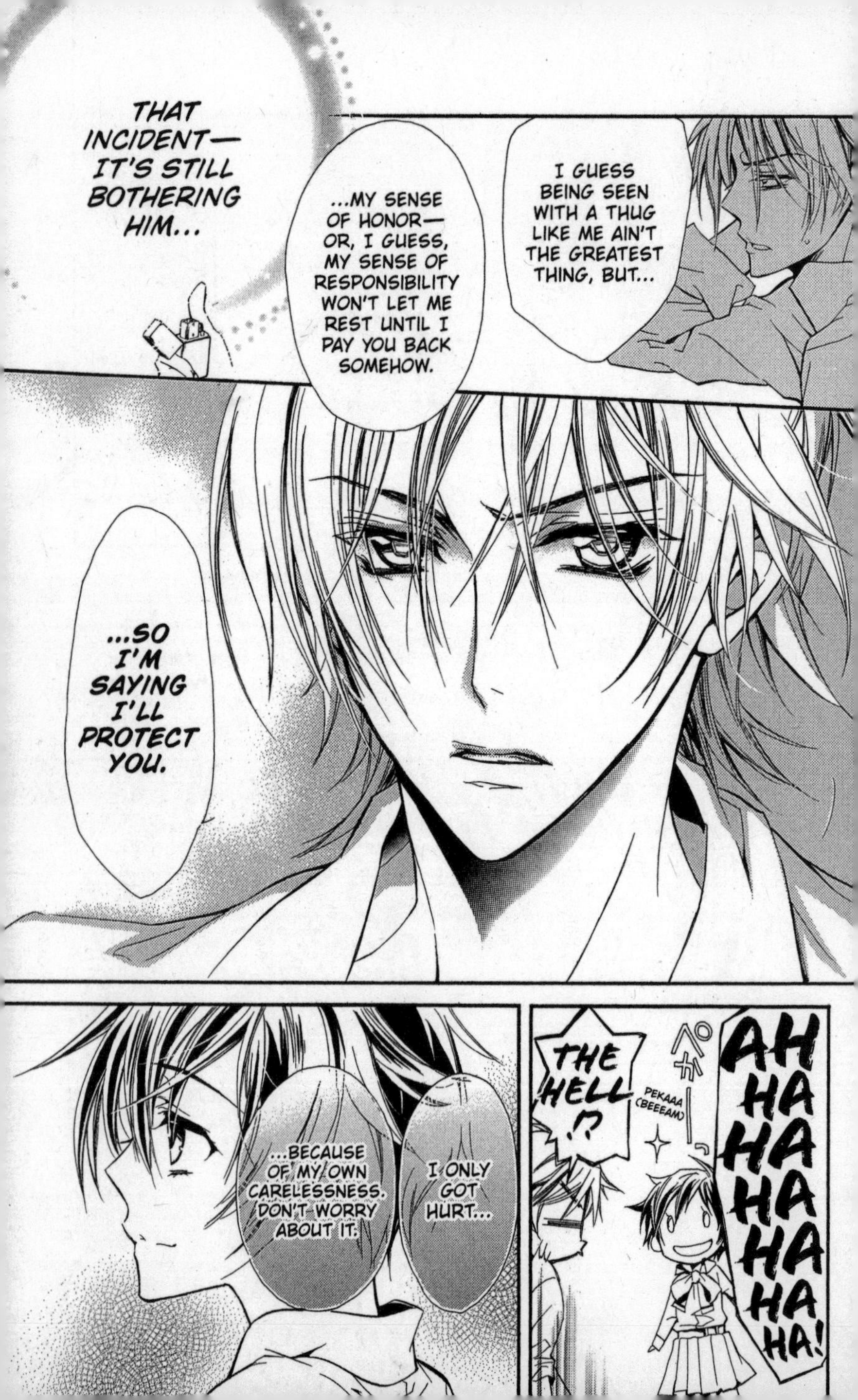
I GUESS BEING SEEN WITH A THUG LIKE ME AIN'T THE GREATEST THING, BUT...
...MY SENSE OF HONOR—OR, I GUESS, MY SENSE OF RESPONSIBILITY WON'T LET ME REST UNTIL I PAY YOU BACK SOMEHOW.
THAT INCIDENT—IT'S STILL BOTHERING HIM...
...SO I'M SAYING I'LL PROTECT YOU.
AH HA HA HA HA HA HA!
PEKAAA (BEEEAM)
THE HELL!?
I ONLY GOT HURT...
...BECAUSE OF MY OWN CARELESSNESS. DON'T WORRY ABOUT IT.

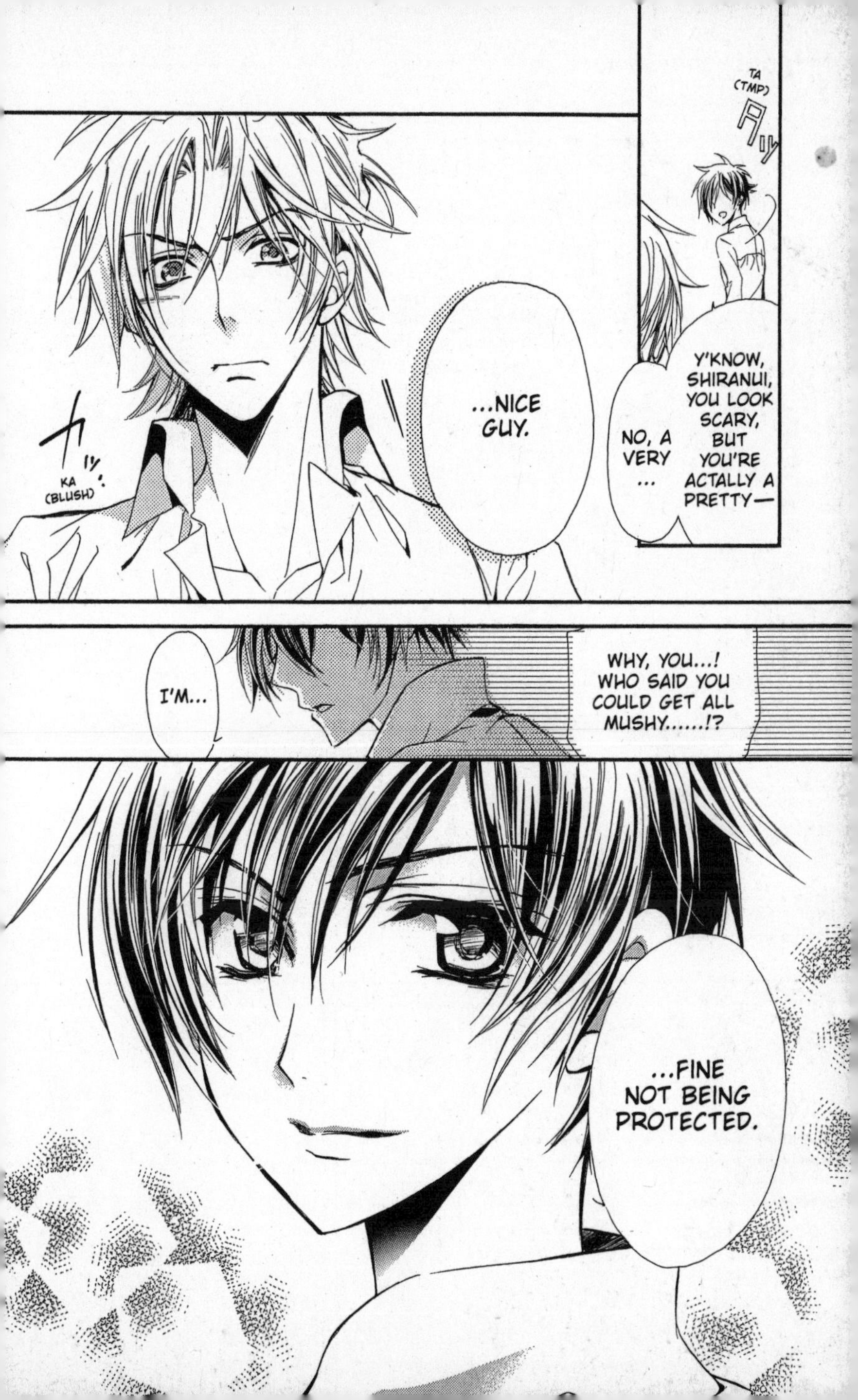
TA (TMP)
Y'KNOW, SHIRANUI, YOU LOOK SCARY, BUT YOU'RE ACTALLY A PRETTY—
NO, A VERY ...
...NICE GUY.
KA (BLUSH)
WHY, YOU...! WHO SAID YOU COULD GET ALL MUSHY......!?
I'M...
...FINE NOT BEING PROTECTED.

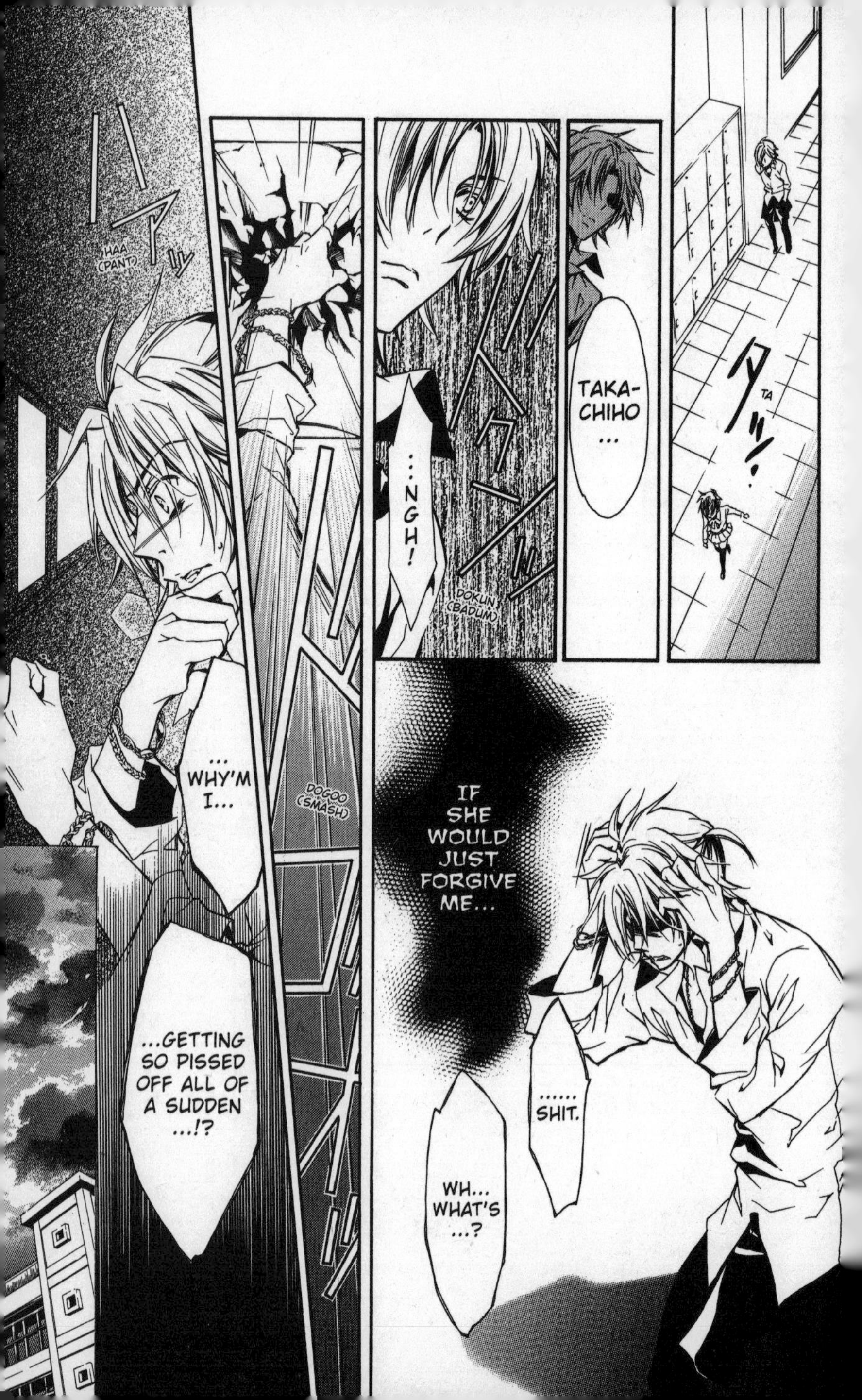
TA
TAKA-CHIHO ...
...NGH!
DOKUN (BADUM)
IF SHE WOULD JUST FORGIVE ME...
...... SHIT.
WH... WHAT'S ...?
DOGOO (SMASH)
HAA (PANT)
... WHY'M I...
...GETTING SO PISSED OFF ALL OF A SUDDEN ...!?

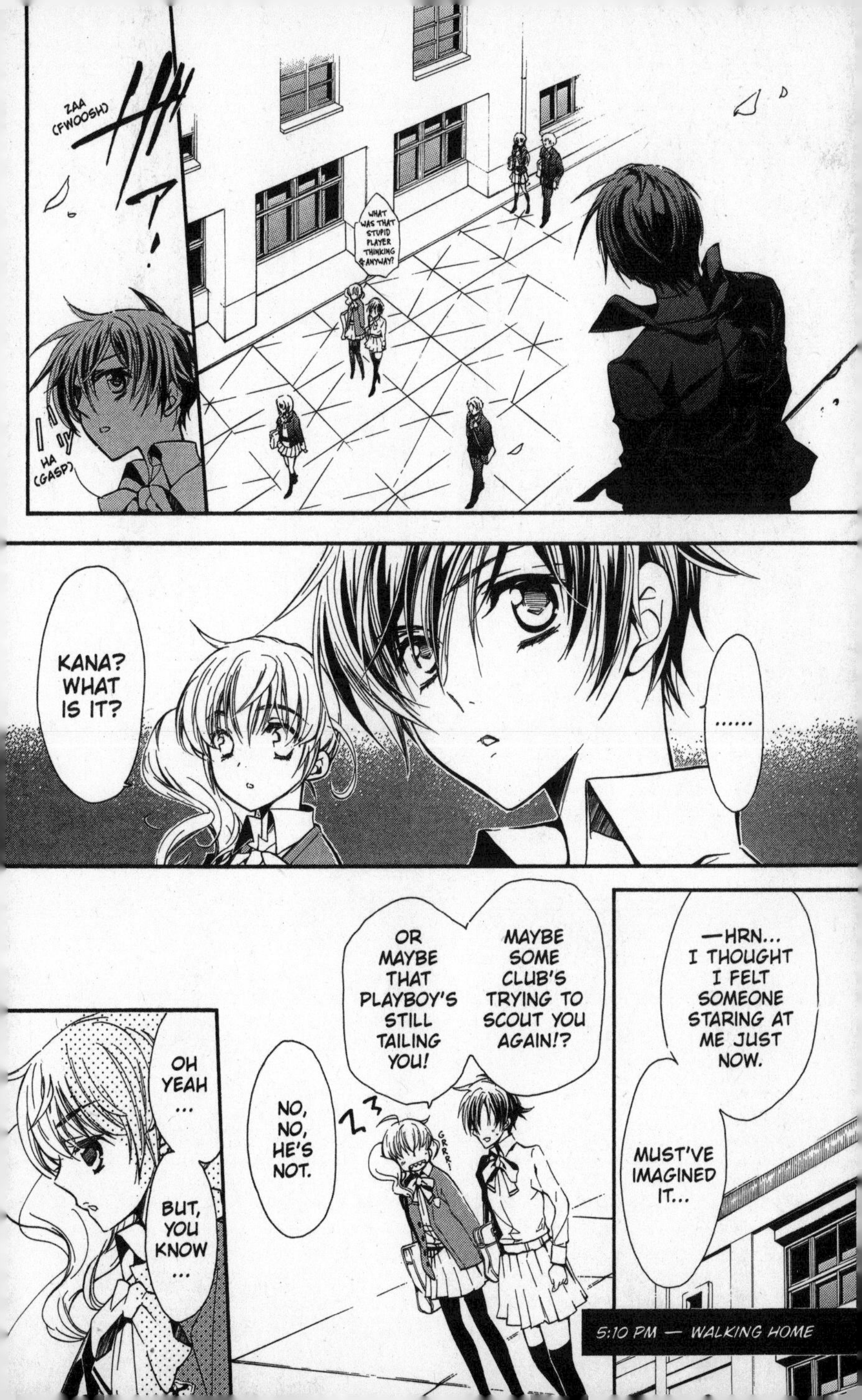
WHAT WAS THAT STUPID PLAYER THINKING ANYWAY?
ZAA (FWOOSH)
HA (GASP)
......
KANA? WHAT IS IT?
5:10 PM — WALKING HOME
—HRN... I THOUGHT I FELT SOMEONE STARING AT ME JUST NOW.
MUST'VE IMAGINED IT...
MAYBE SOME CLUB'S TRYING TO SCOUT YOU AGAIN!?
OR MAYBE THAT PLAYBOY'S STILL TAILING YOU!
GRRR!
NO, NO, HE'S NOT.
OH YEAH...
BUT, YOU KNOW...

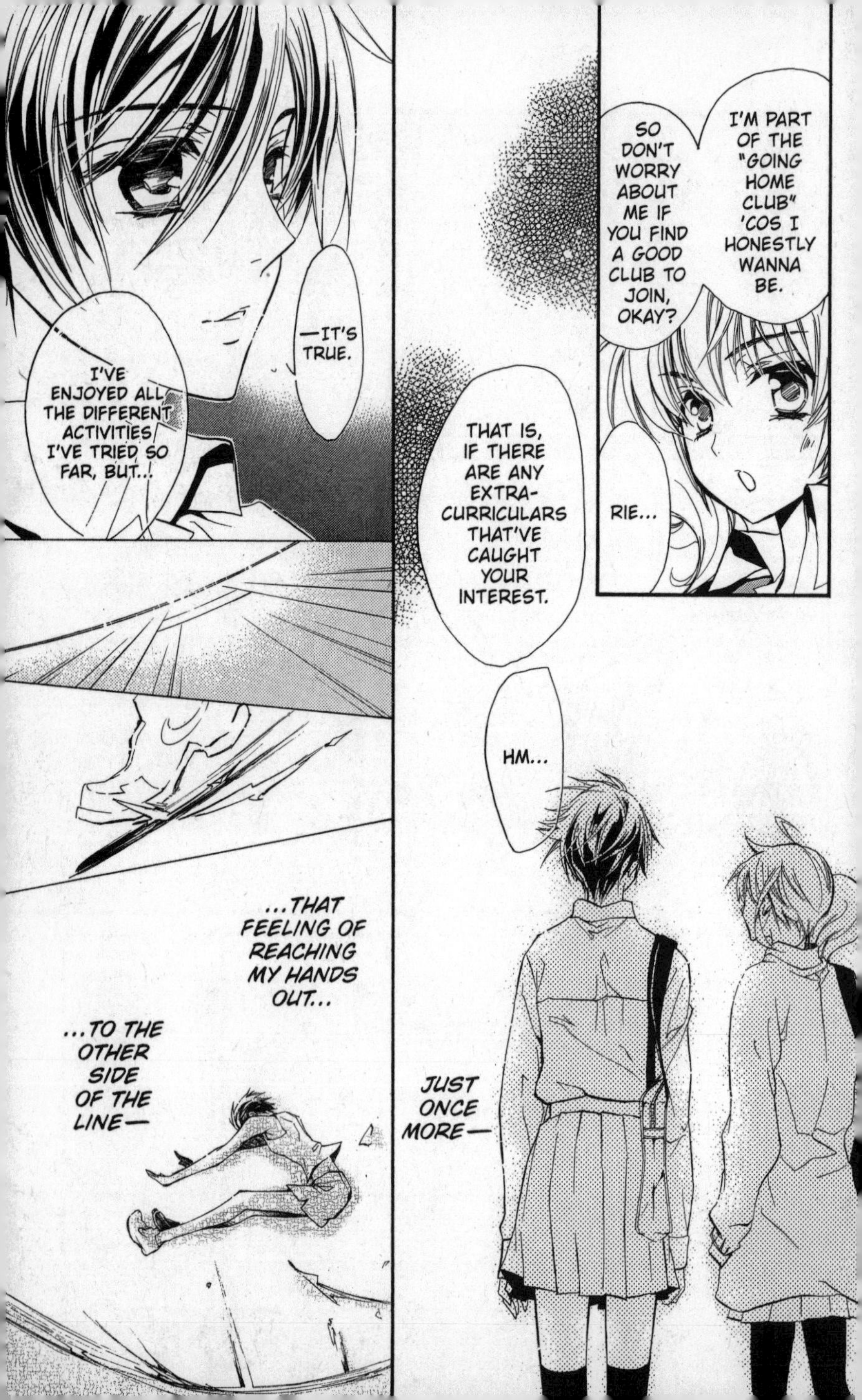
I'M PART OF THE "GOING HOME CLUB" 'COS I HONESTLY WANNA BE.
SO DON'T WORRY ABOUT ME IF YOU FIND A GOOD CLUB TO JOIN, OKAY?
RIE...
THAT IS, IF THERE ARE ANY EXTRA-CURRICULARS THAT'VE CAUGHT YOUR INTEREST.
HM...
JUST ONCE MORE—
—IT'S TRUE.
I'VE ENJOYED ALL THE DIFFERENT ACTIVITIES I'VE TRIED SO FAR, BUT...
...THAT FEELING OF REACHING MY HANDS OUT...
...TO THE OTHER SIDE OF THE LINE—

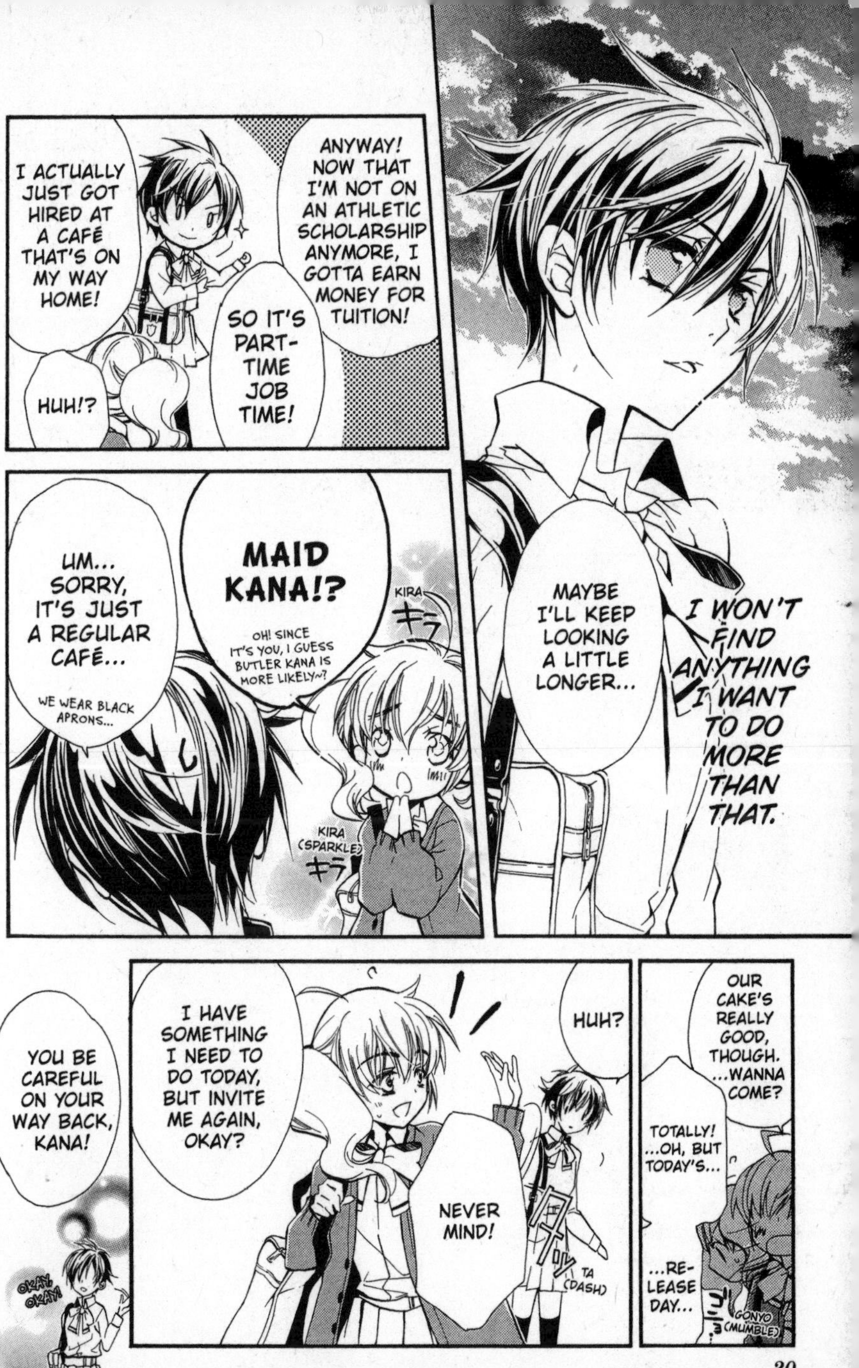
MAYBE I'LL KEEP LOOKING A LITTLE LONGER...
I WON'T FIND ANYTHING I WANT TO DO MORE THAN THAT.
ANYWAY! NOW THAT I'M NOT ON AN ATHLETIC SCHOLARSHIP ANYMORE, I GOTTA EARN MONEY FOR TUITION!
SO IT'S PART-TIME JOB TIME!
I ACTUALLY JUST GOT HIRED AT A CAFÉ THAT'S ON MY WAY HOME!
HUH!?
MAID KANA!?
KIRA
OH! SINCE IT'S YOU, I GUESS BUTLER KANA IS MORE LIKELY~?
UM... SORRY, IT'S JUST A REGULAR CAFÉ...
WE WEAR BLACK APRONS...
KIRA (SPARKLE)
OUR CAKE'S REALLY GOOD, THOUGH. ...WANNA COME?
TOTALLY! ...OH, BUT TODAY'S...
...RE-LEASE DAY...
GONYO (MUMBLE)
HUH?
I HAVE SOMETHING I NEED TO DO TODAY, BUT INVITE ME AGAIN, OKAY?
NEVER MIND!
TA (DASH)
YOU BE CAREFUL ON YOUR WAY BACK, KANA!
OKAY, OKAY!

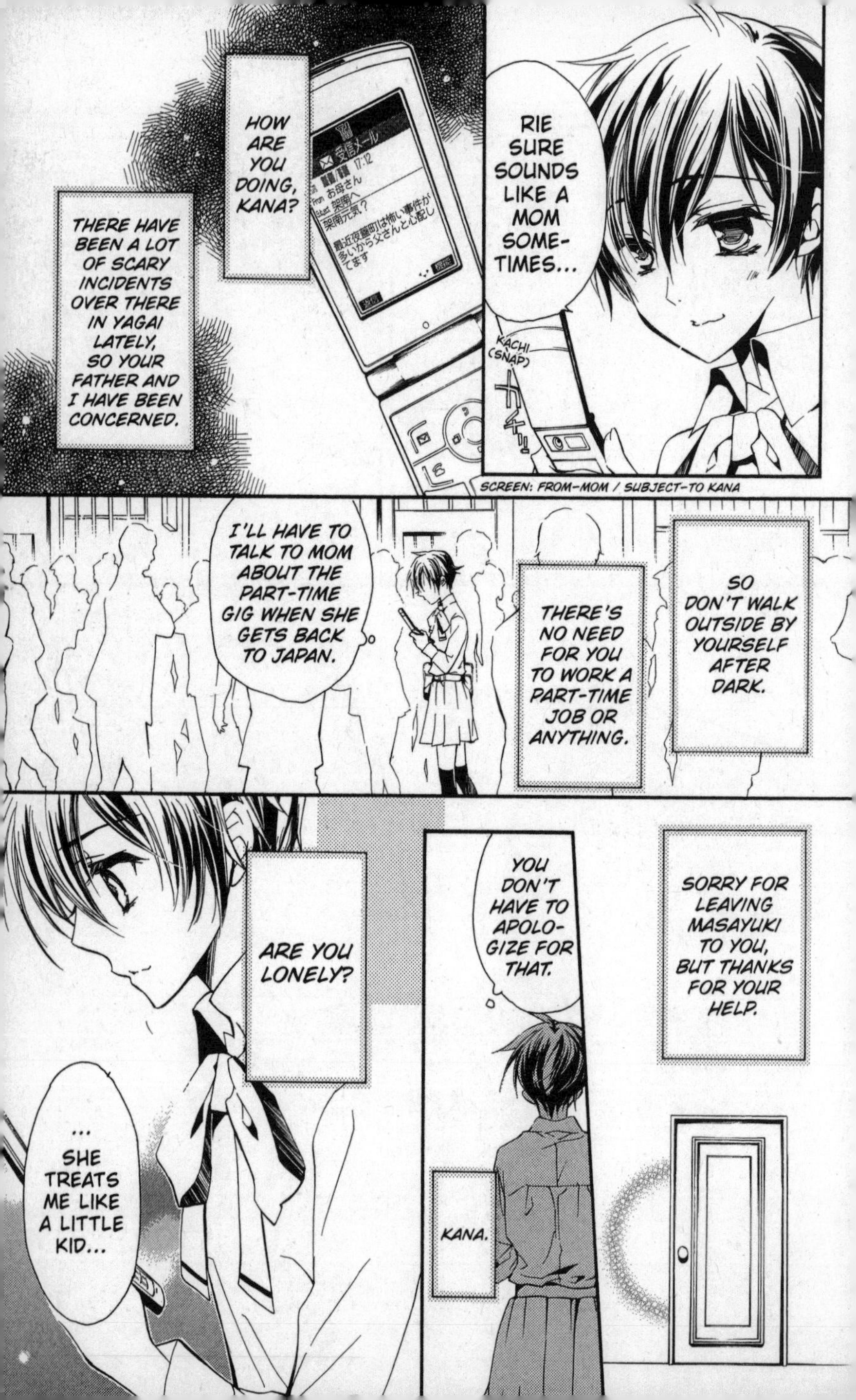
RIE SURE SOUNDS LIKE A MOM SOME-TIMES...
KACHI (SNAP)
HOW ARE YOU DOING, KANA?
THERE HAVE BEEN A LOT OF SCARY INCIDENTS OVER THERE IN YAGAI LATELY, SO YOUR FATHER AND I HAVE BEEN CONCERNED.
SCREEN: FROM-MOM / SUBJECT-TO KANA
SO DON'T WALK OUTSIDE BY YOURSELF AFTER DARK.
THERE'S NO NEED FOR YOU TO WORK A PART-TIME JOB OR ANYTHING.
I'LL HAVE TO TALK TO MOM ABOUT THE PART-TIME GIG WHEN SHE GETS BACK TO JAPAN.
SORRY FOR LEAVING MASAYUKI TO YOU, BUT THANKS FOR YOUR HELP.
YOU DON'T HAVE TO APOLO-GIZE FOR THAT.
KANA.
ARE YOU LONELY?
... SHE TREATS ME LIKE A LITTLE KID...

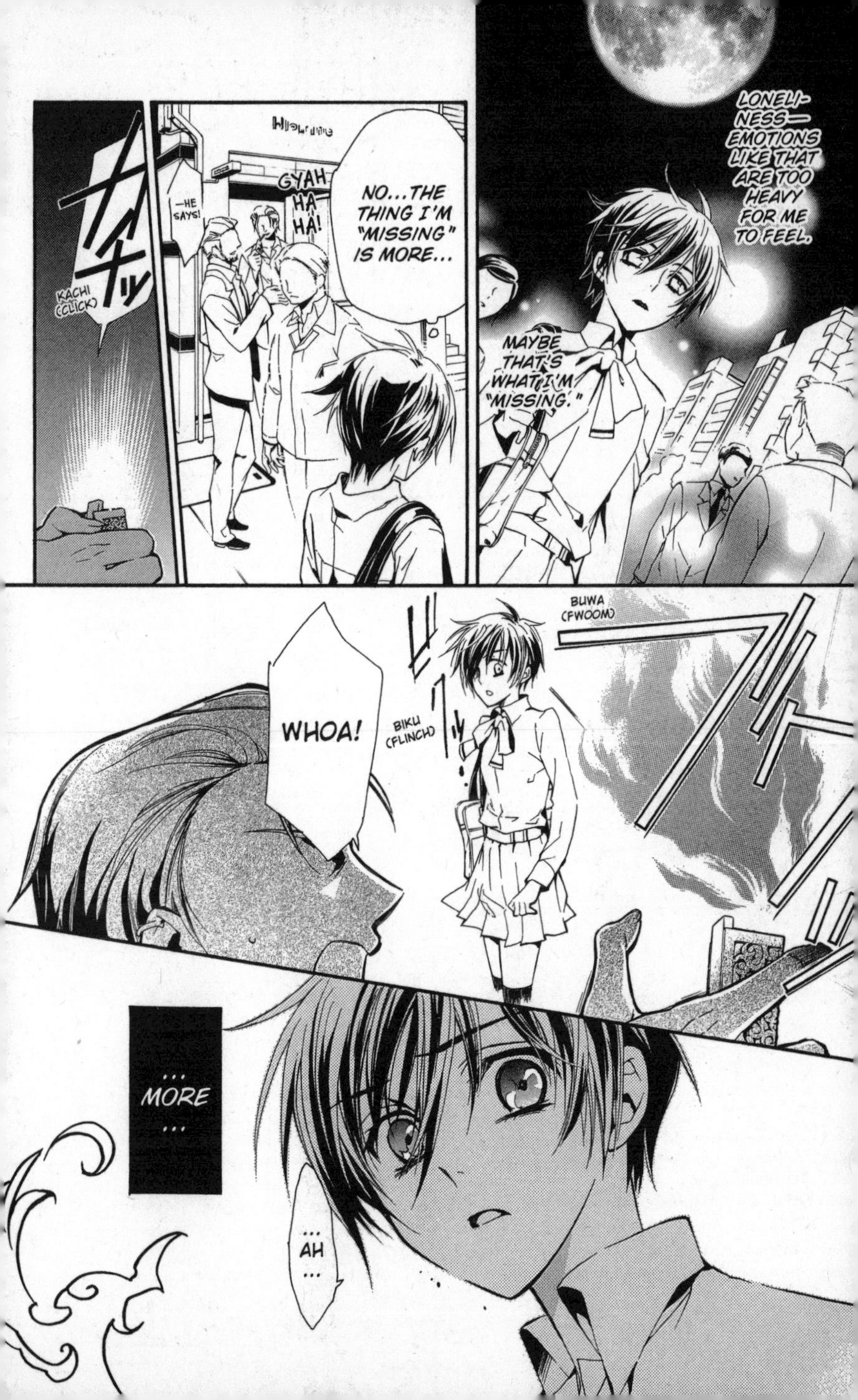
LONELI-NESS—EMOTIONS LIKE THAT ARE TOO HEAVY FOR ME TO FEEL.
MAYBE THAT'S WHAT I'M "MISSING."
NO...THE THING I'M "MISSING" IS MORE...
GYAH HA HA!
—HE SAYS!
KACHI (CLICK)
BUWA (FWOOM)
WHOA!
BIKU (FLINCH)
...MORE...
...AH...

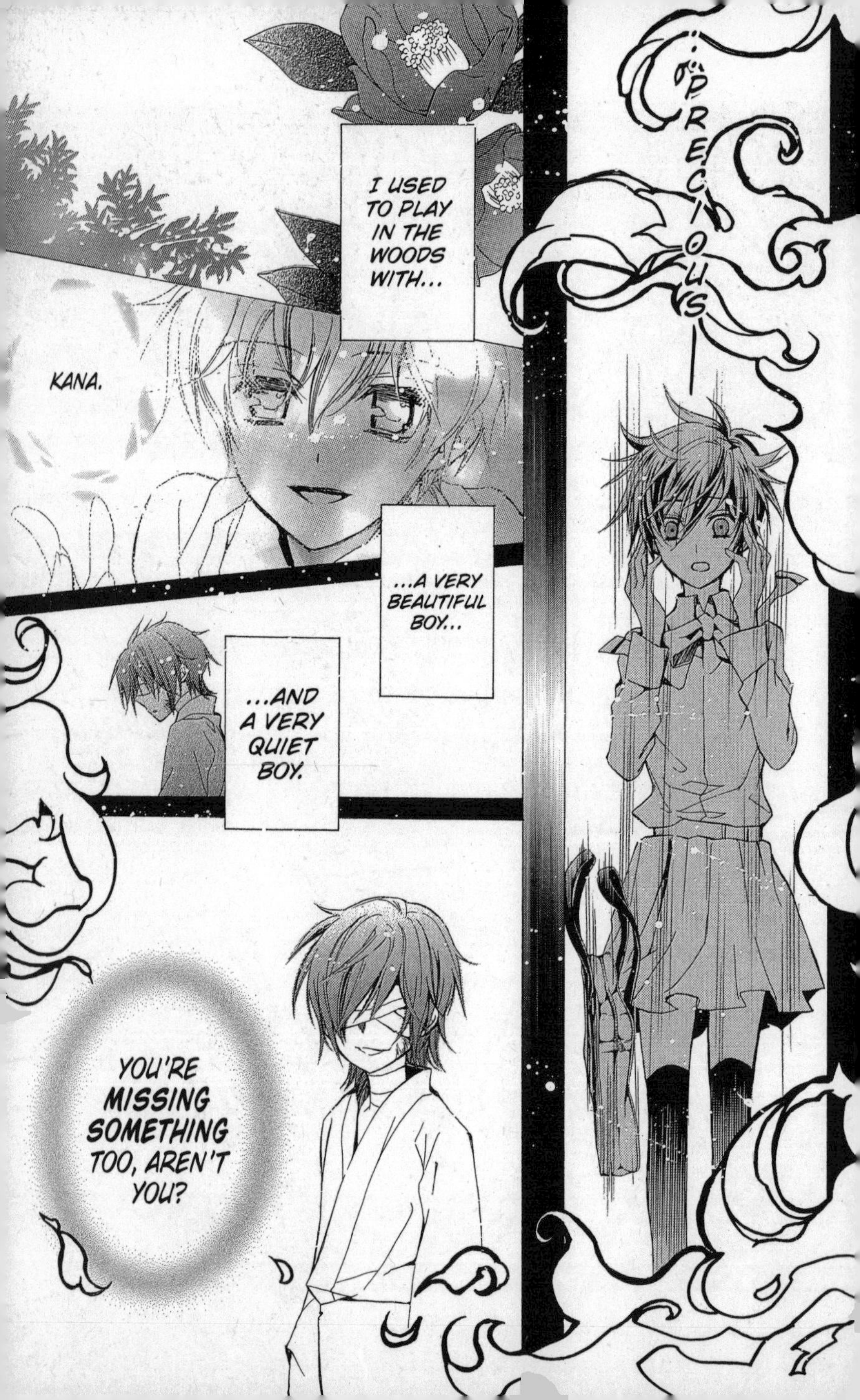
...PRECIOUS
I USED TO PLAY IN THE WOODS WITH...
KANA.
...A VERY BEAUTIFUL BOY...
...AND A VERY QUIET BOY.
YOU'RE MISSING SOMETHING TOO, AREN'T YOU?

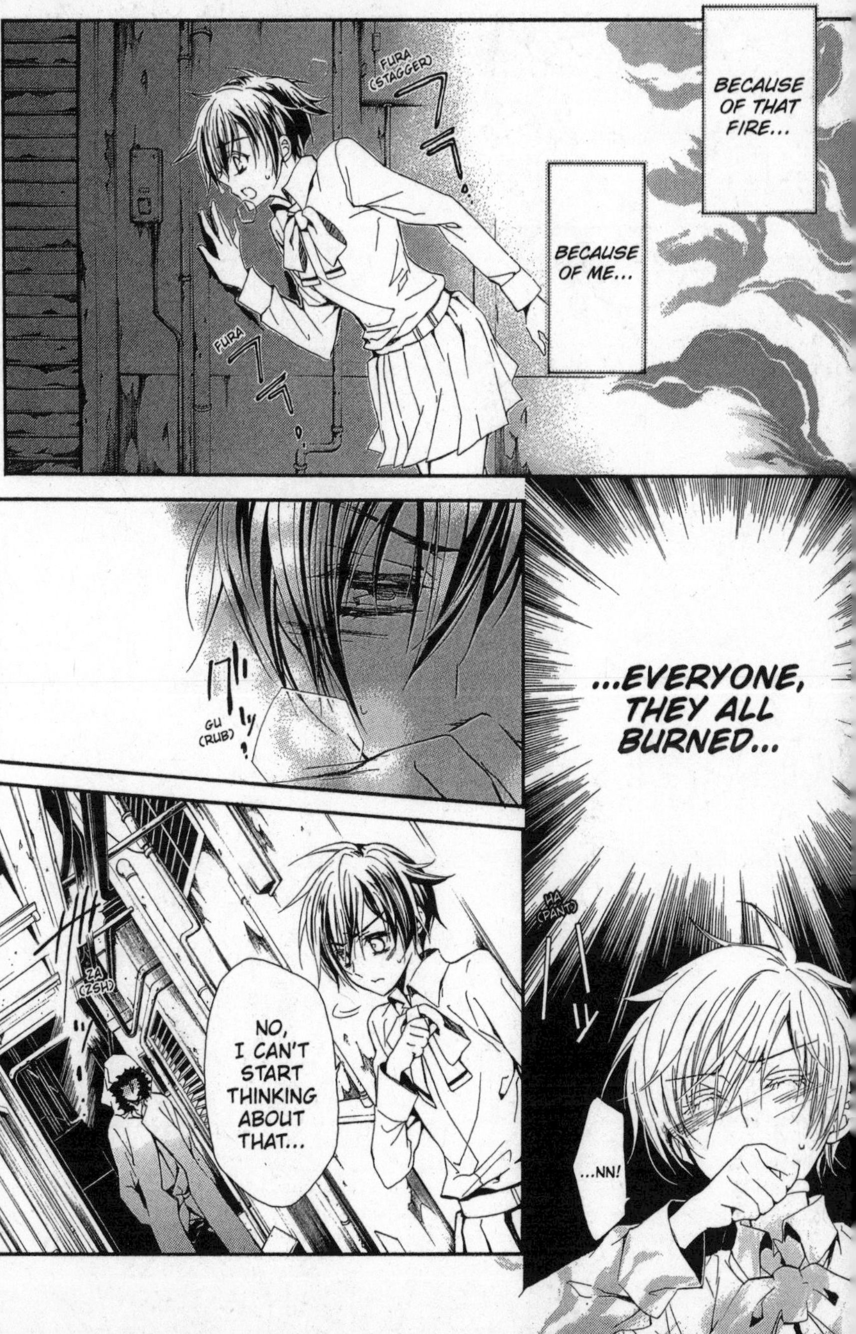
BECAUSE OF THAT FIRE...
BECAUSE OF ME...
FURA (STAGGER)
FURA
...EVERYONE, THEY ALL BURNED...
HA (PANT)
...NN!
GU (RUB)
NO, I CAN'T START THINKING ABOUT THAT...
ZA (ZSH)

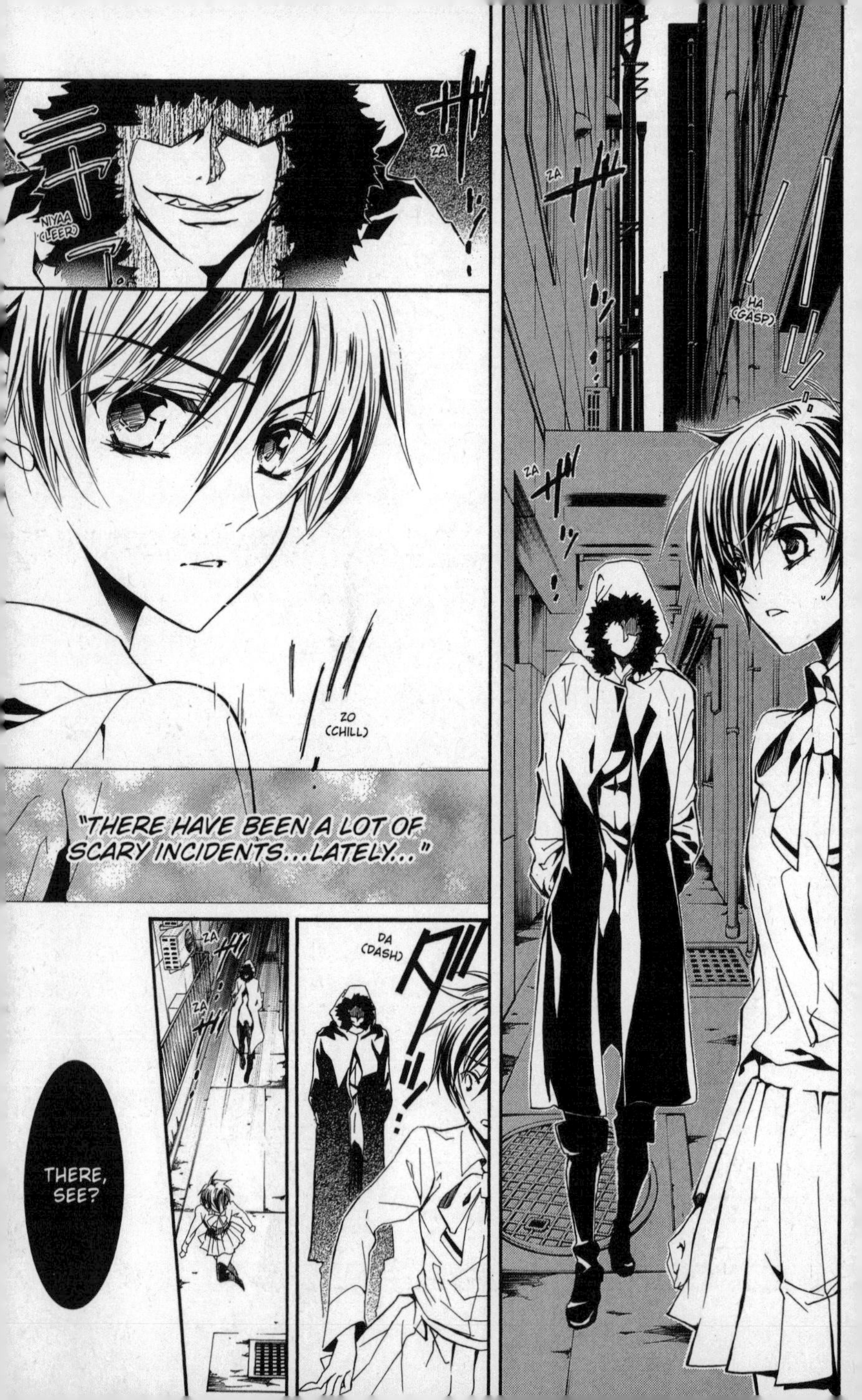
ZA
HA (GASP)
ZA
ZA
NIYAA (LEER)
ZO (CHILL)
"THERE HAVE BEEN A LOT OF SCARY INCIDENTS...LATELY..."
DA (DASH)
ZA
ZA
THERE, SEE?

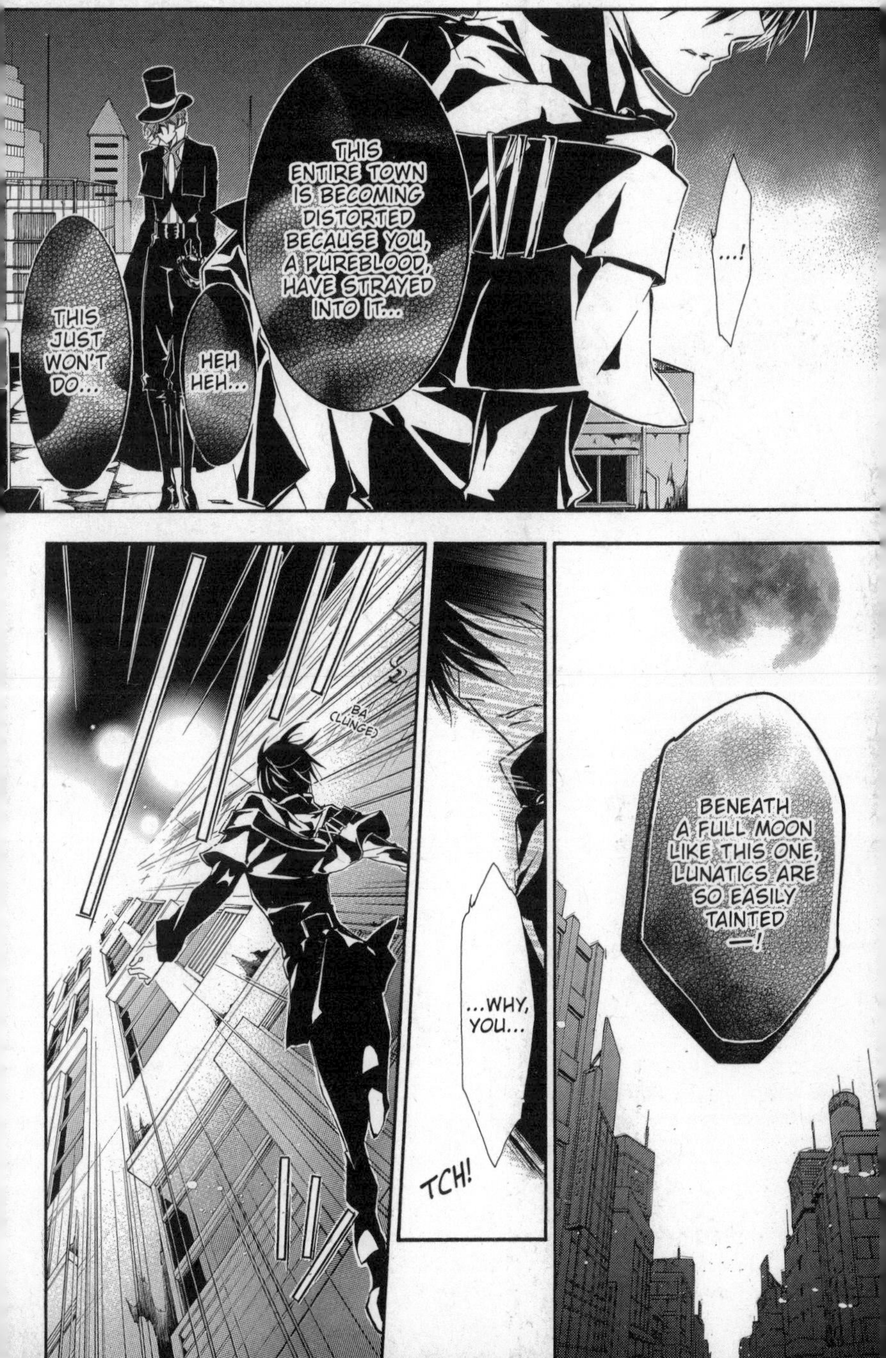
...!
THIS ENTIRE TOWN IS BECOMING DISTORTED BECAUSE YOU, A PUREBLOOD, HAVE STRAYED INTO IT...
HEH HEH...
THIS JUST WON'T DO...
BENEATH A FULL MOON LIKE THIS ONE, LUNATICS ARE SO EASILY TAINTED—!
...WHY, YOU...
TCH!
BA (LUNGE)

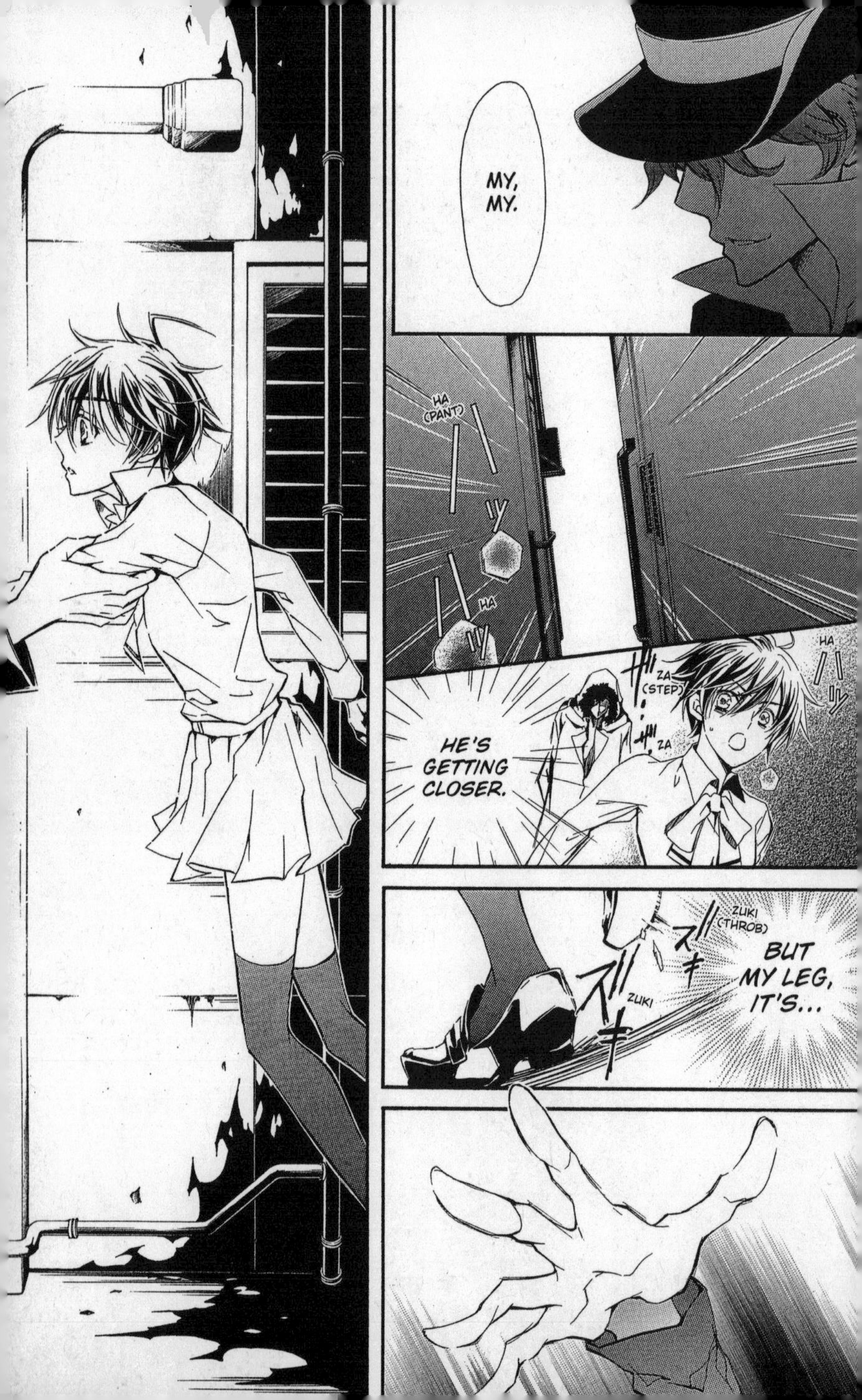

MY, MY.
HA (PANT)
HA
HA
ZA (STEP)
ZA
HE'S GETTING CLOSER.
ZUKI (THROB)
BUT MY LEG, IT'S...
ZUKI

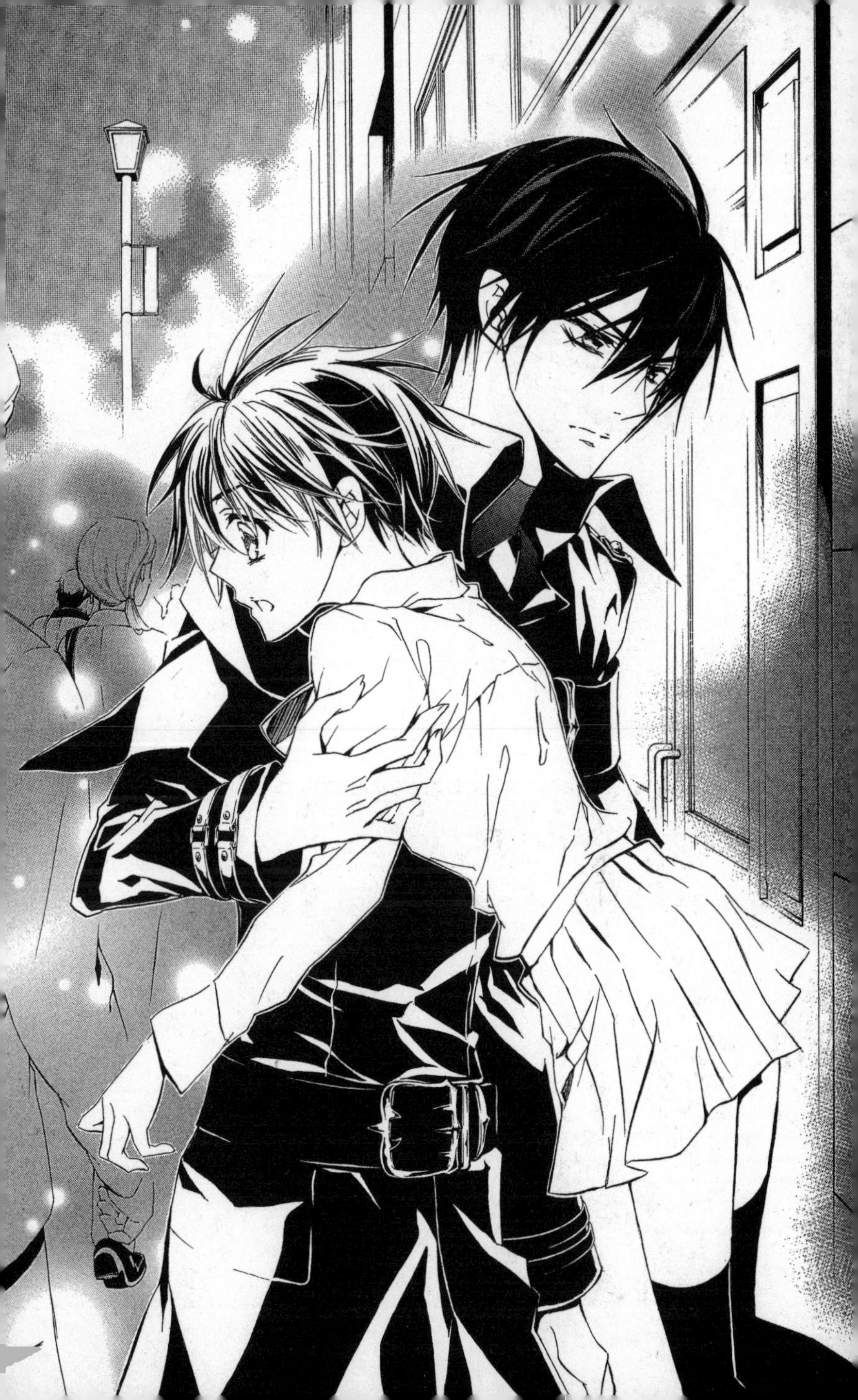

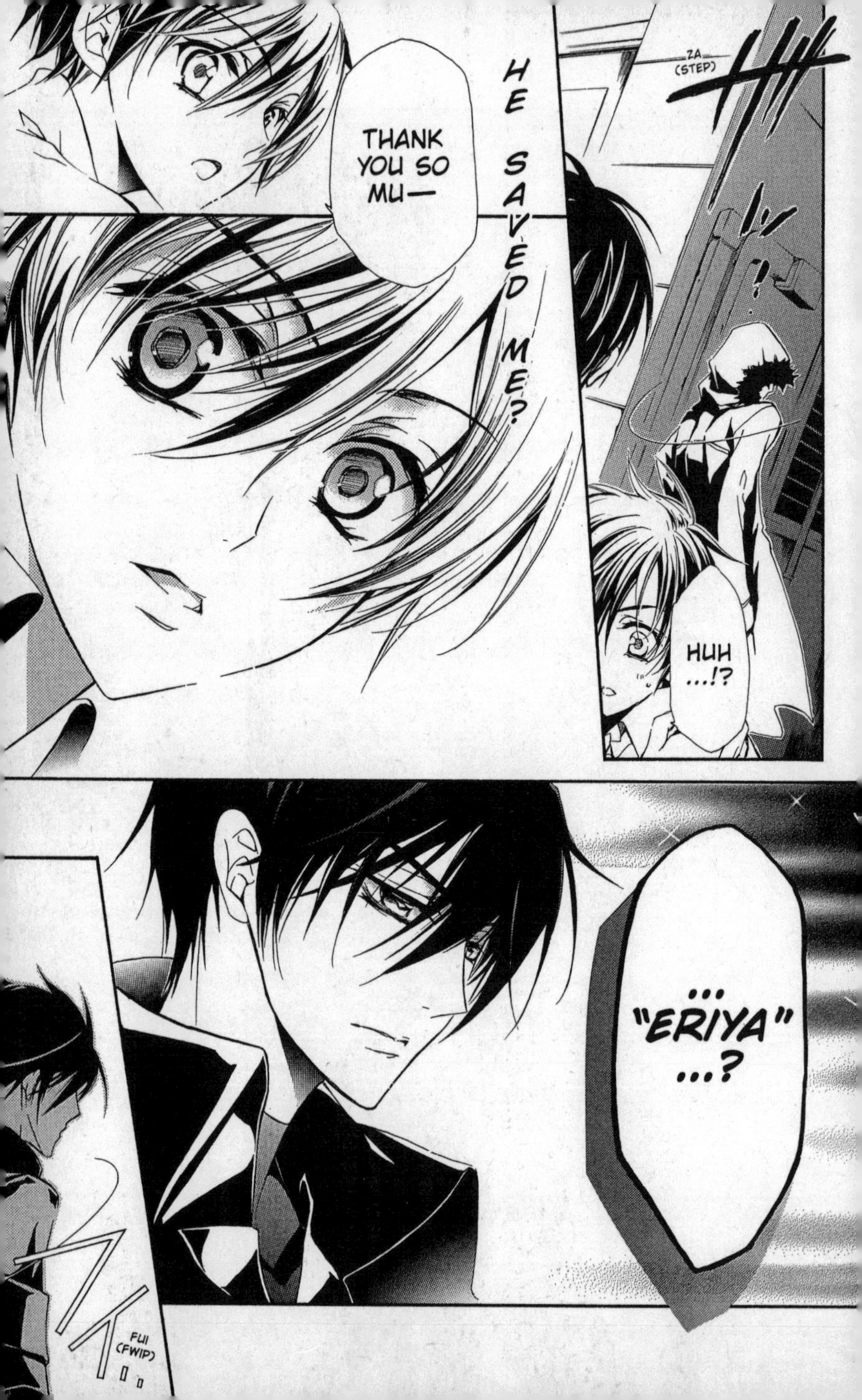
ZA (STEP)
HUH ...!?
THANK YOU SO MU—
HE SAVED ME?
... "ERIYA" ...?
FUI (FWIP)

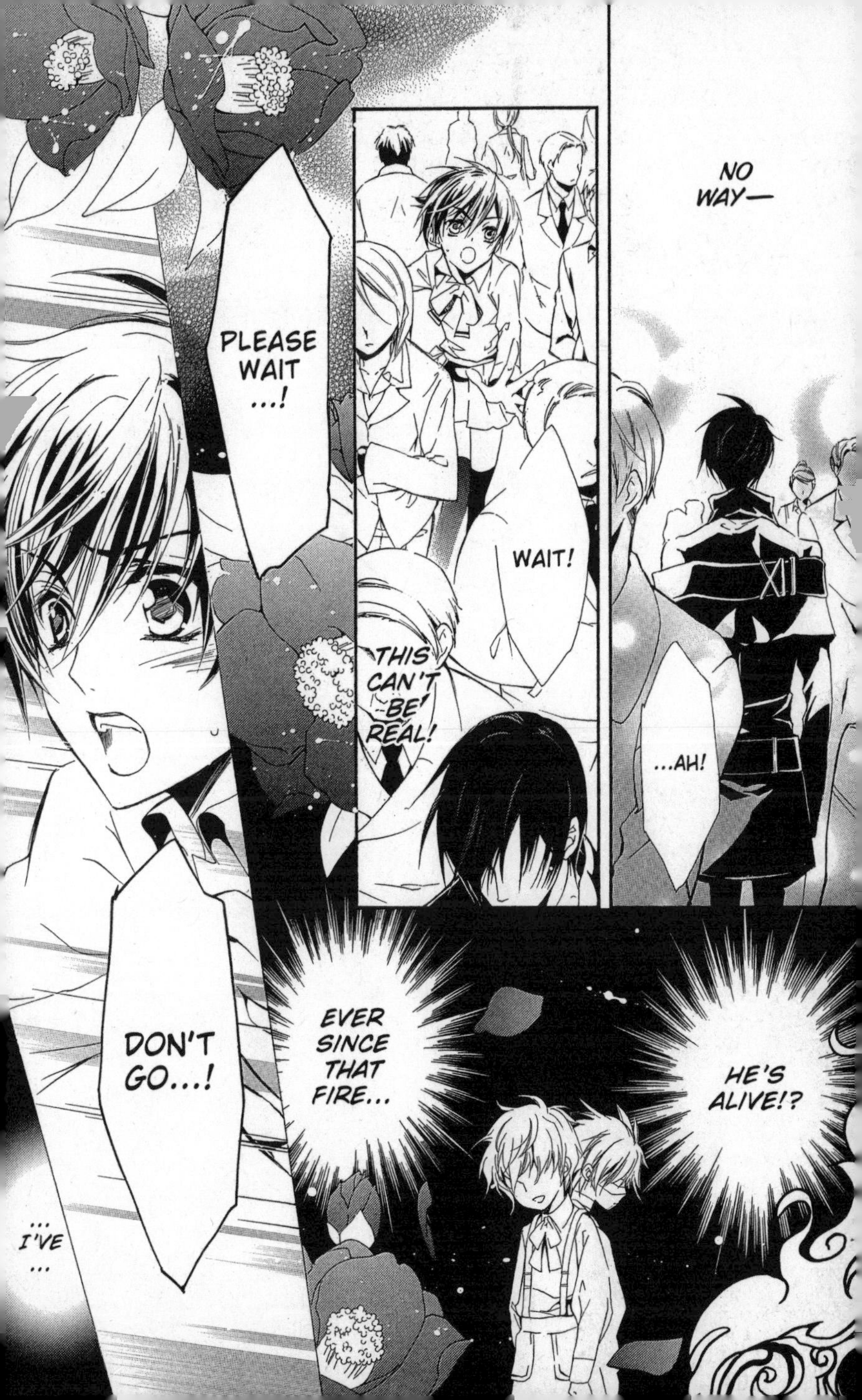
NO WAY—
...AH!
WAIT!
THIS CAN'T BE REAL!
HE'S ALIVE!?
EVER SINCE THAT FIRE...
PLEASE WAIT ...!
DON'T GO...!
... I'VE ...

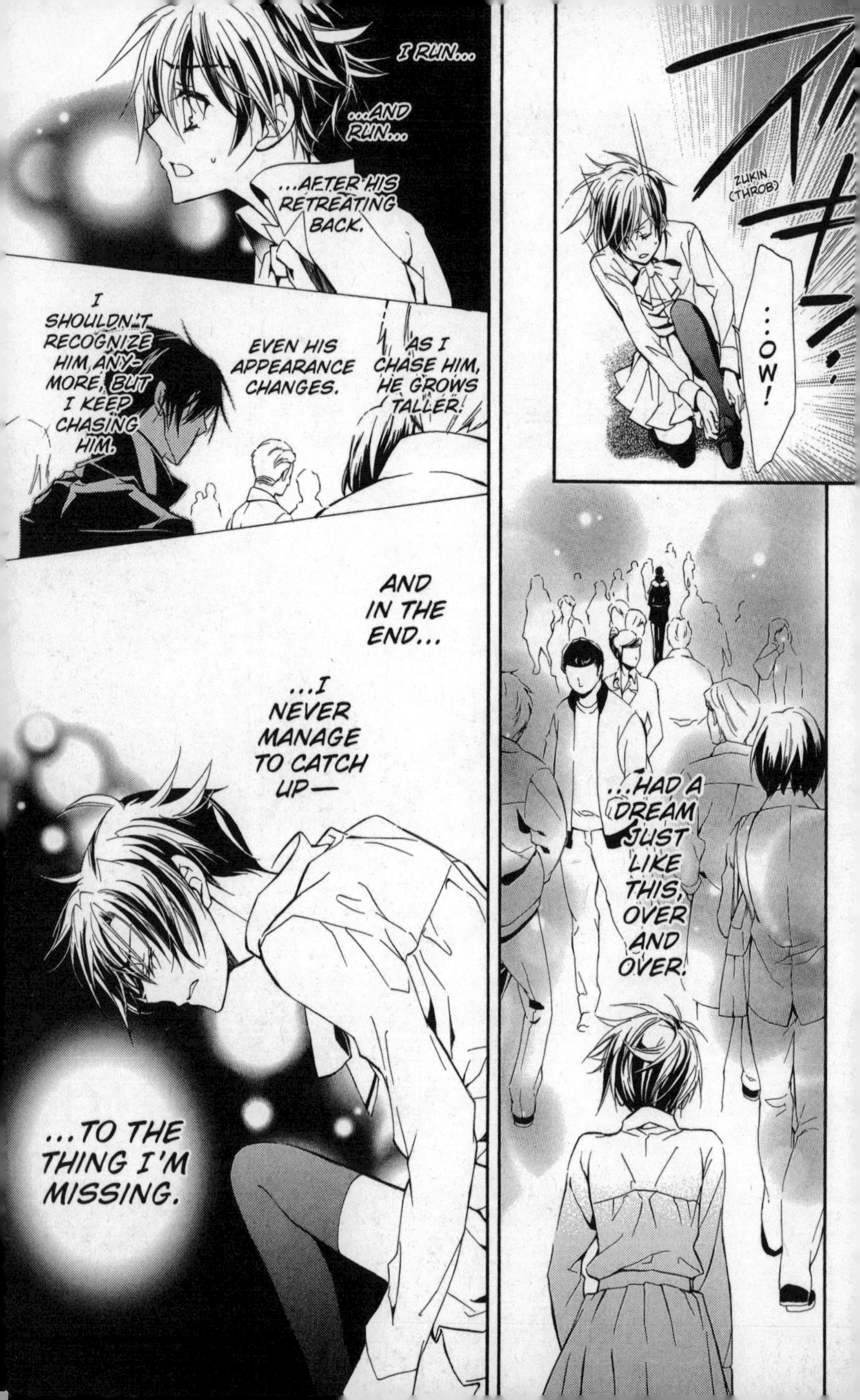
ZUKIN (THROB)
...OW!
...HAD A DREAM JUST LIKE THIS, OVER AND OVER.
I RUN...
...AND RUN...
...AFTER HIS RETREATING BACK.
AS I CHASE HIM, HE GROWS TALLER.
EVEN HIS APPEARANCE CHANGES.
I SHOULDN'T RECOGNIZE HIM ANYMORE, BUT I KEEP CHASING HIM.
AND IN THE END...
...I NEVER MANAGE TO CATCH UP—
...TO THE THING I'M MISSING.

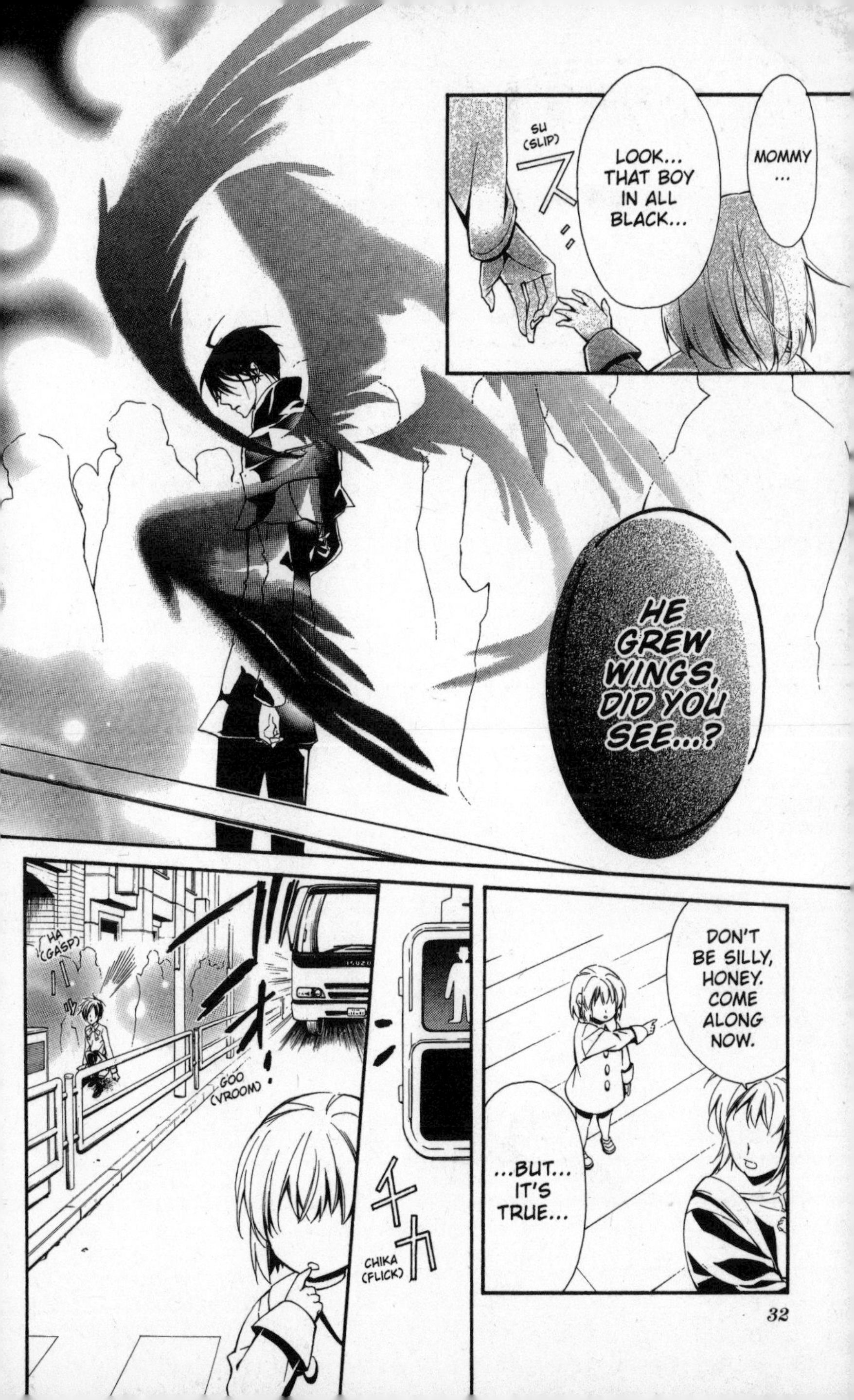
MOMMY...
LOOK... THAT BOY IN ALL BLACK...
SU (SLIP)
HE GREW WINGS, DID YOU SEE...?
DON'T BE SILLY, HONEY. COME ALONG NOW.
...BUT... IT'S TRUE...
HA (GASP)
GOO (VROOM)
CHIKA (FLICK)

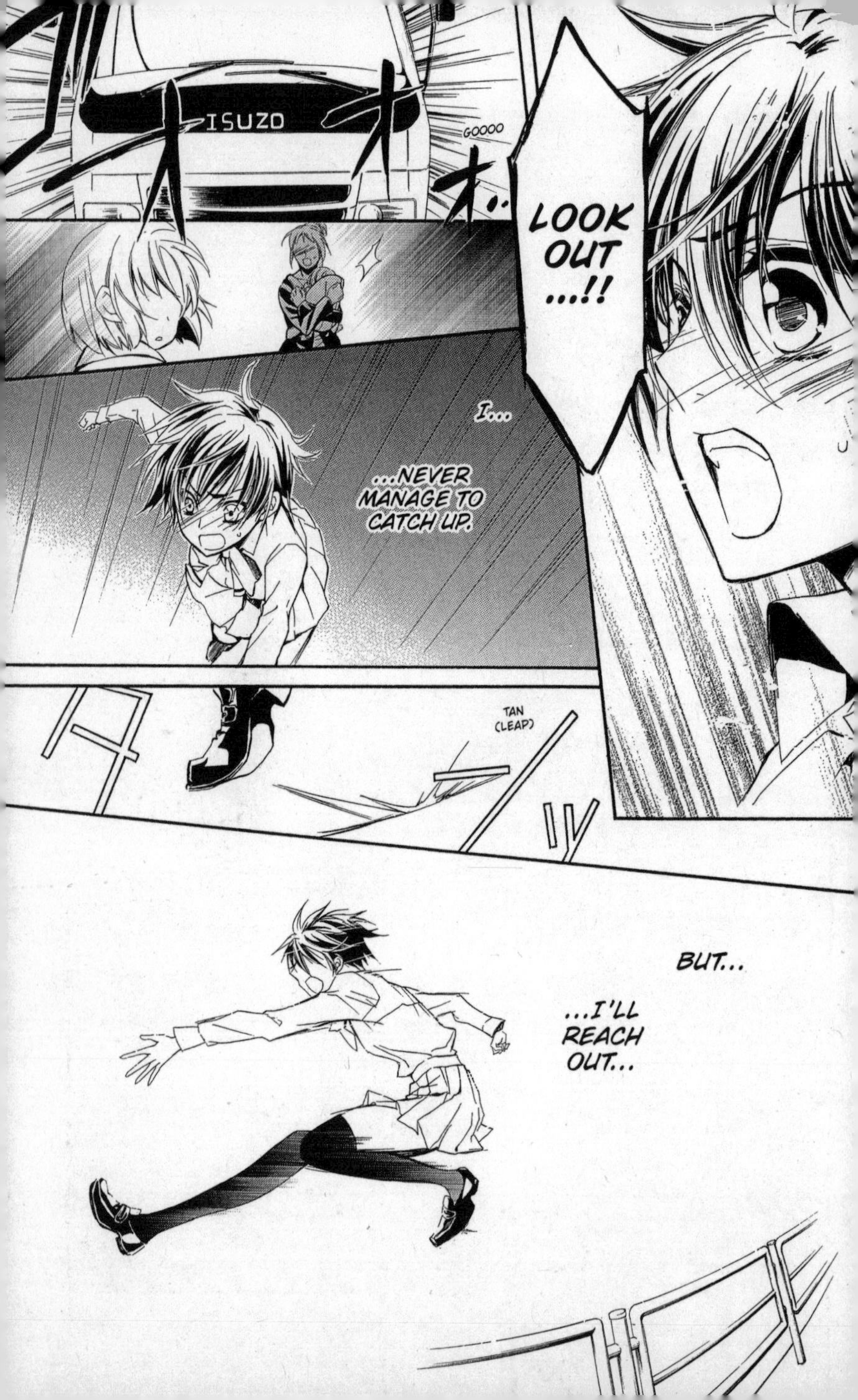
LOOK OUT ...!!
ISUZD
GOOOO
I...
...NEVER MANAGE TO CATCH UP.
TAN (LEAP)
BUT...
...I'LL REACH OUT...

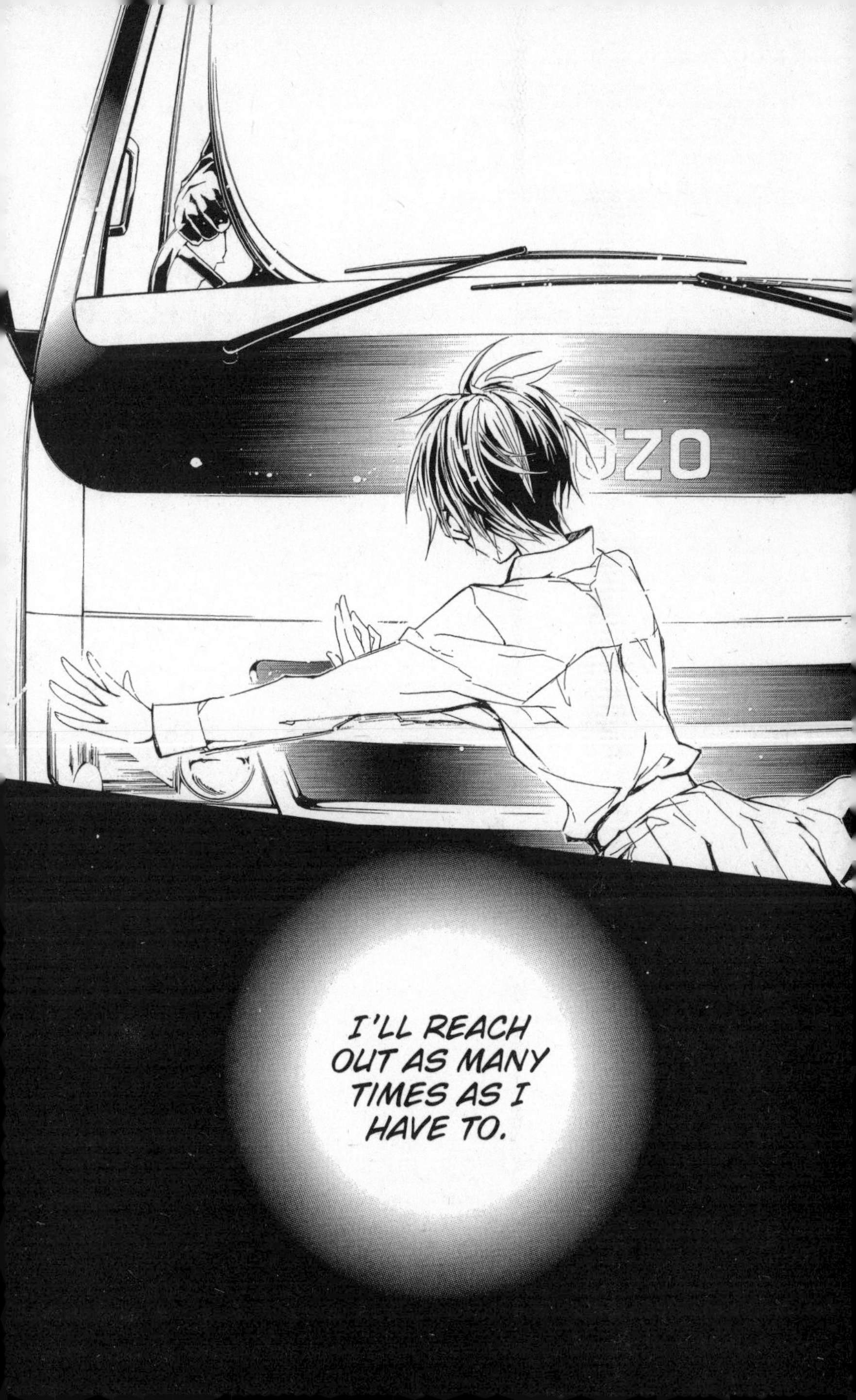
UZO
I'LL REACH OUT AS MANY TIMES AS I HAVE TO.

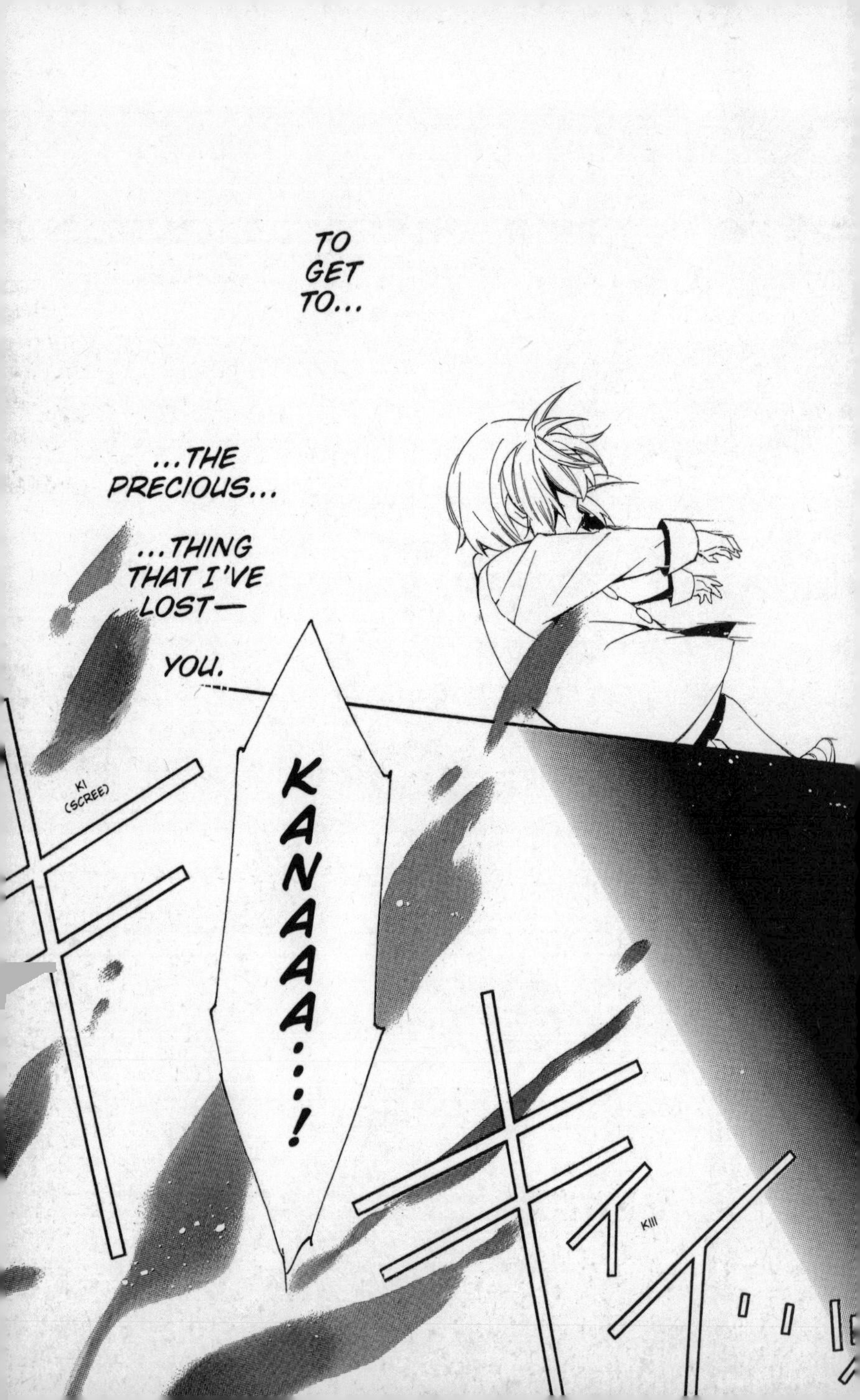
TO GET TO...
...THE PRECIOUS...
...THING THAT I'VE LOST—
YOU.
KANAAAA...!
KI (SCREE)
KIII

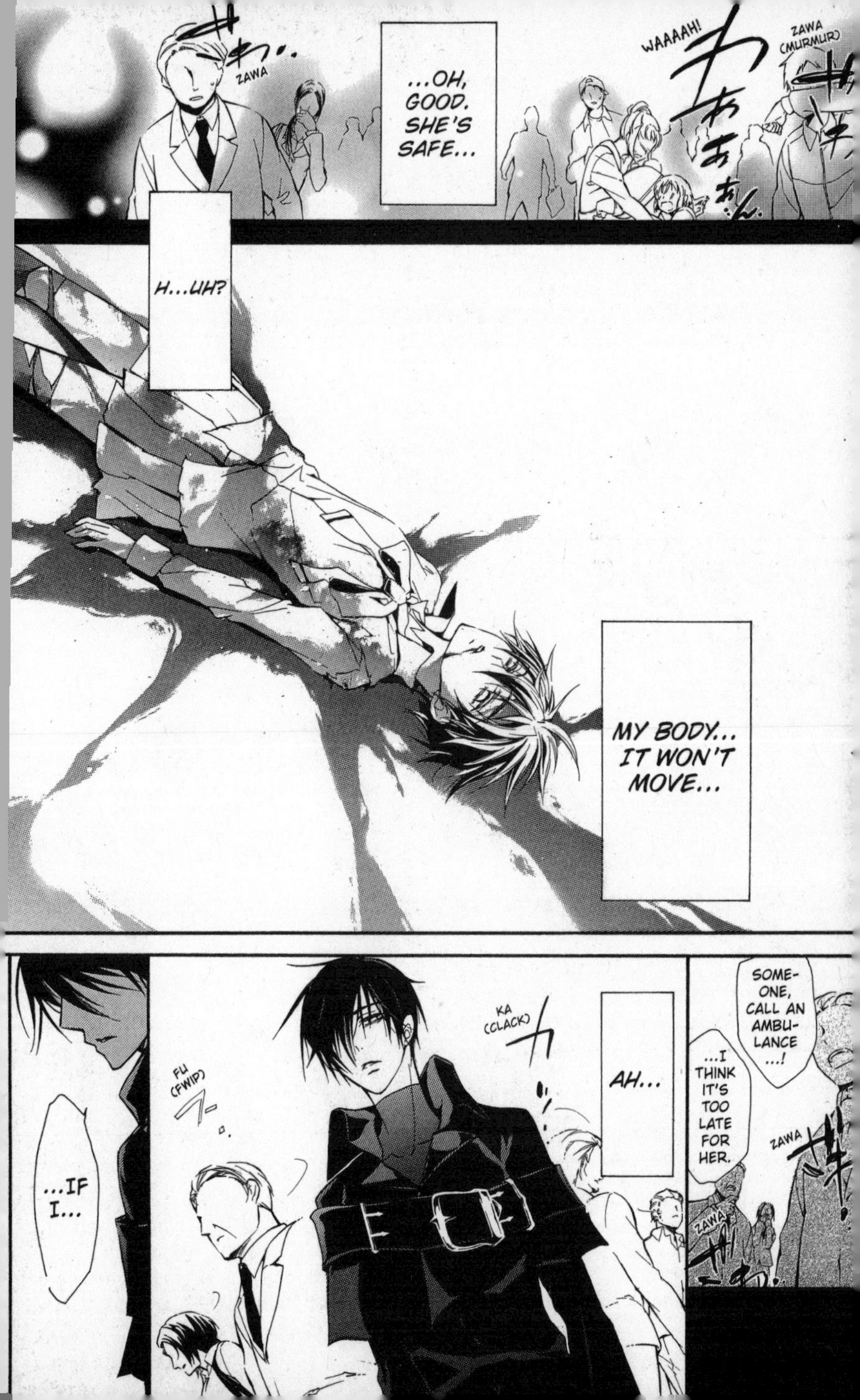
ZAWA (MURMUR)
WAAAAH!
...OH, GOOD. SHE'S SAFE...
ZAWA
H...UH?
MY BODY... IT WON'T MOVE...
SOME-ONE, CALL AN AMBU-LANCE ...!
...I THINK IT'S TOO LATE FOR HER.
ZAWA
ZAWA
AH...
KA (CLACK)
FU (FWIP)
...IF I...

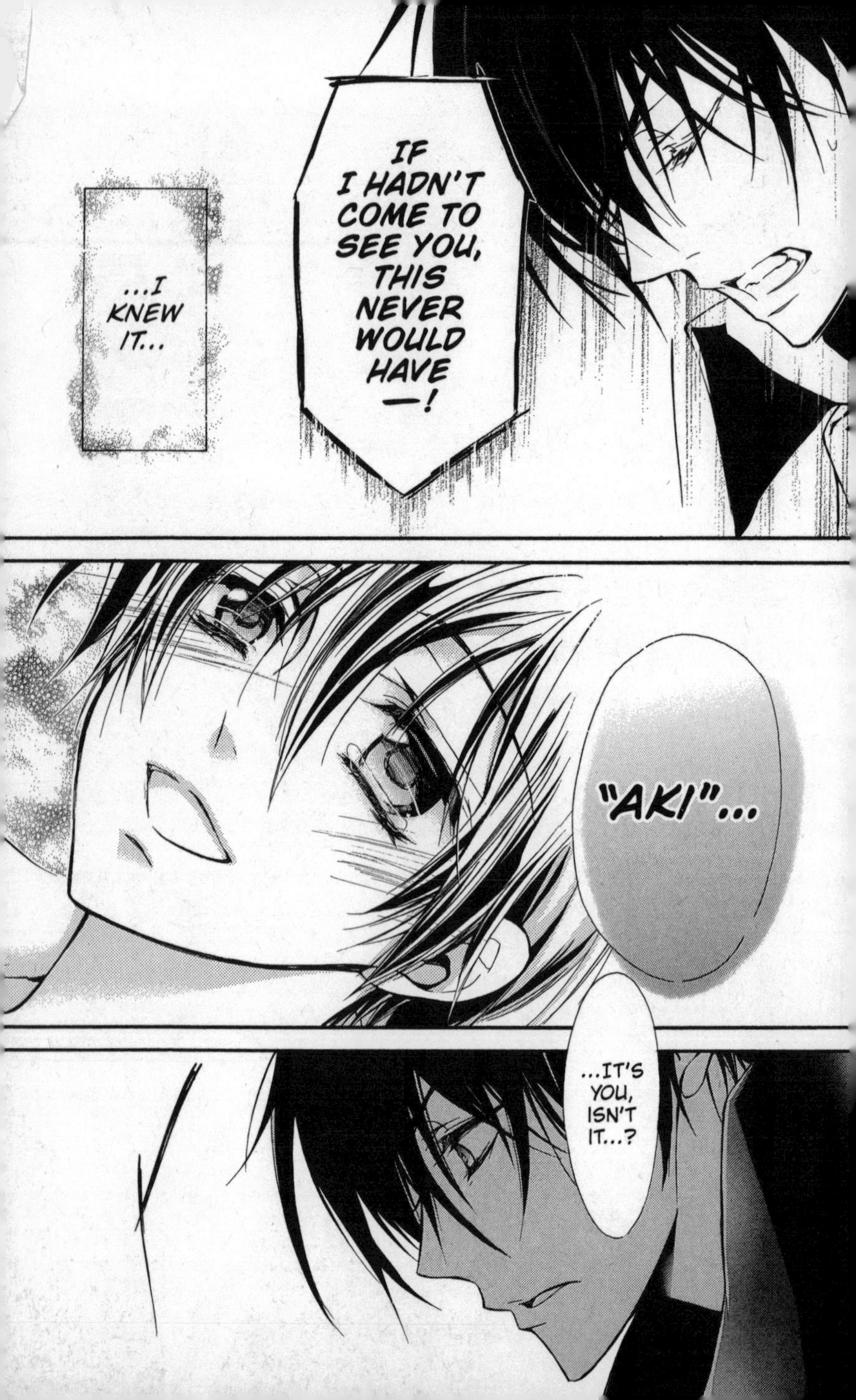
IF I HADN'T COME TO SEE YOU, THIS NEVER WOULD HAVE—!
...I KNEW IT...
"AKI"...
...IT'S YOU, ISN'T IT...?

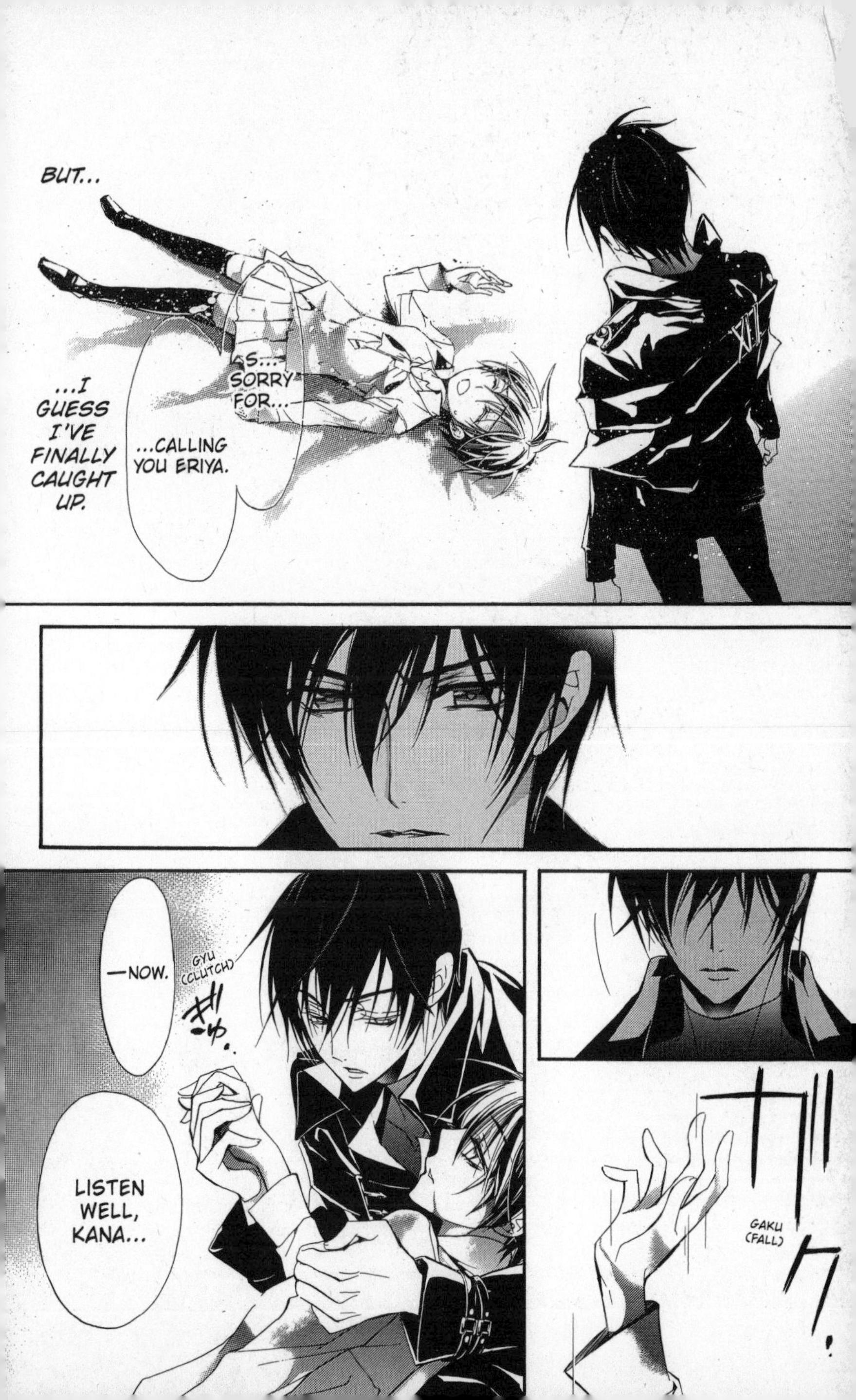
BUT...
S... SORRY FOR...
...CALLING YOU ERIYA.
...I GUESS I'VE FINALLY CAUGHT UP.
GAKU (FALL)
—NOW.
GYU (CLUTCH)
LISTEN WELL, KANA...

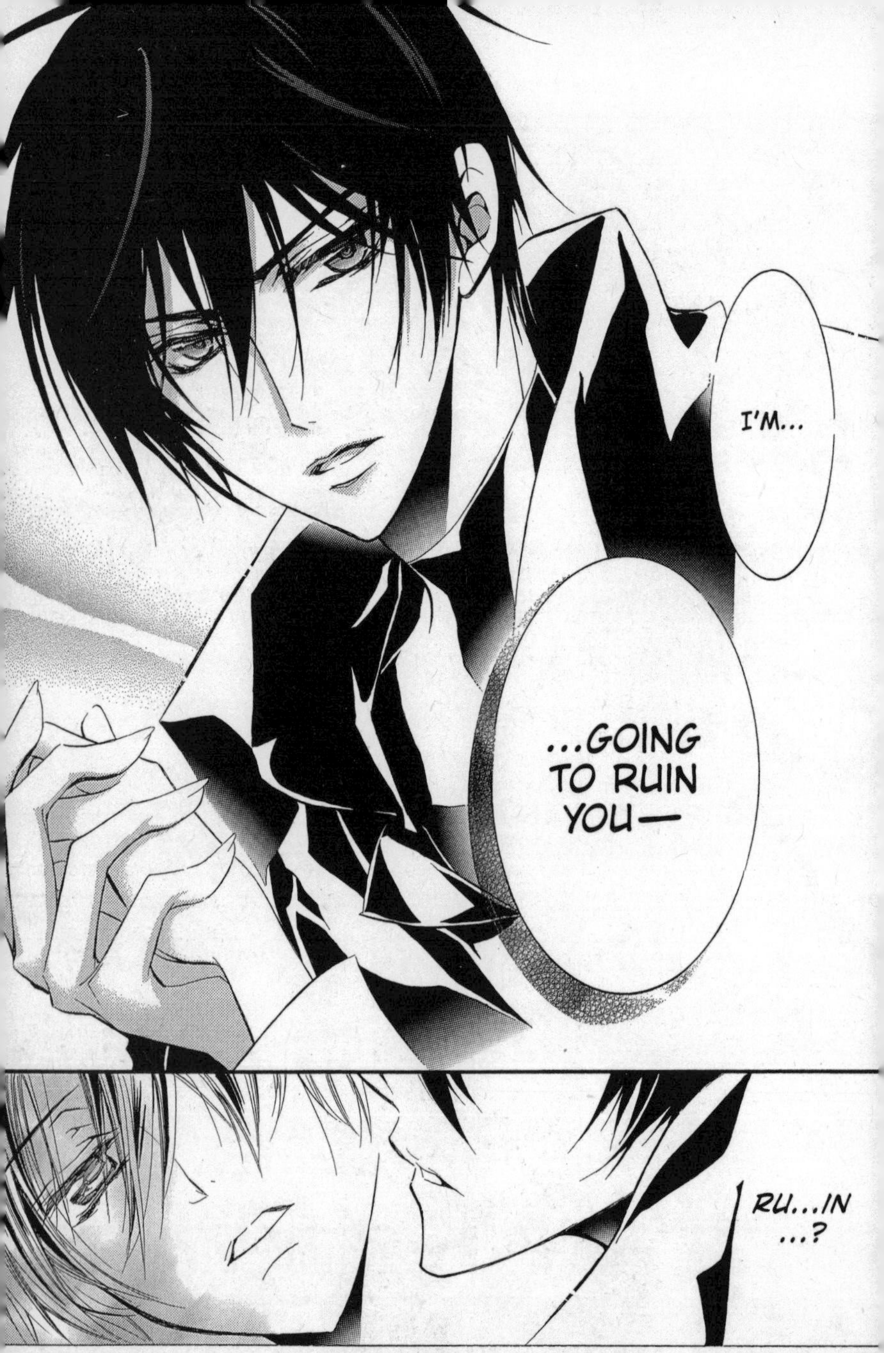
I'M...
...GOING TO RUIN YOU—
RU...IN ...?

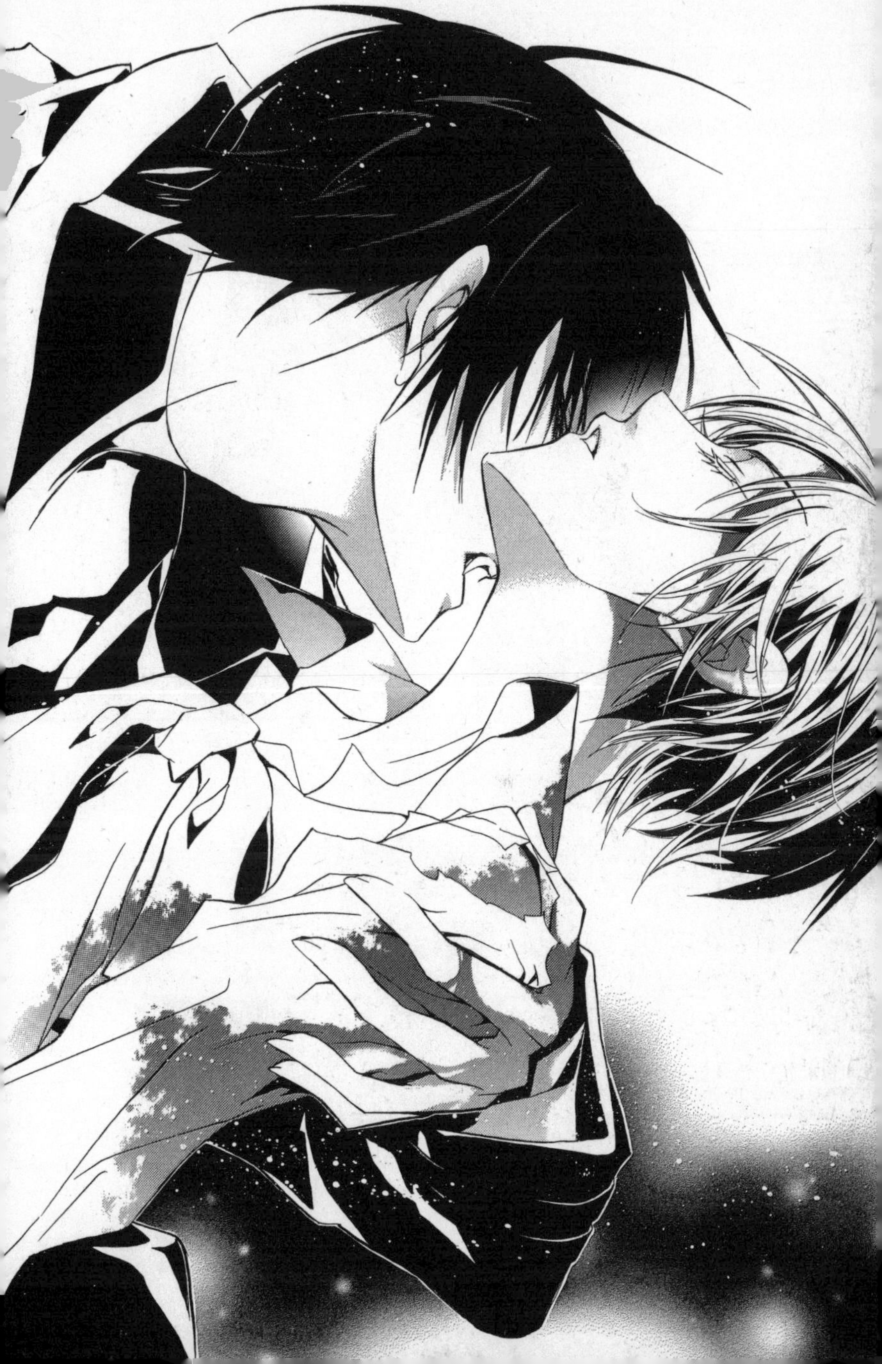

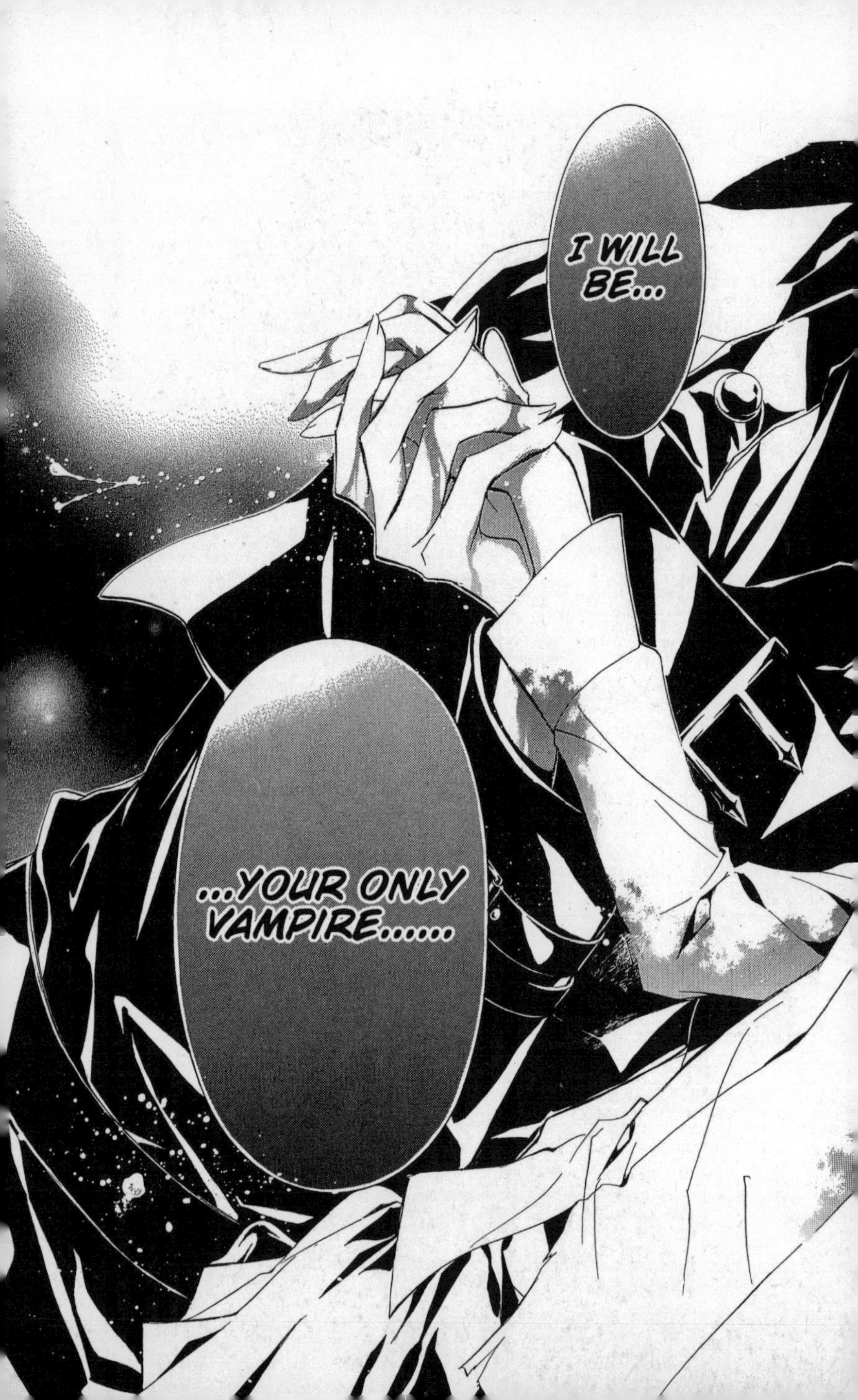
I WILL BE...
...YOUR ONLY VAMPIRE......

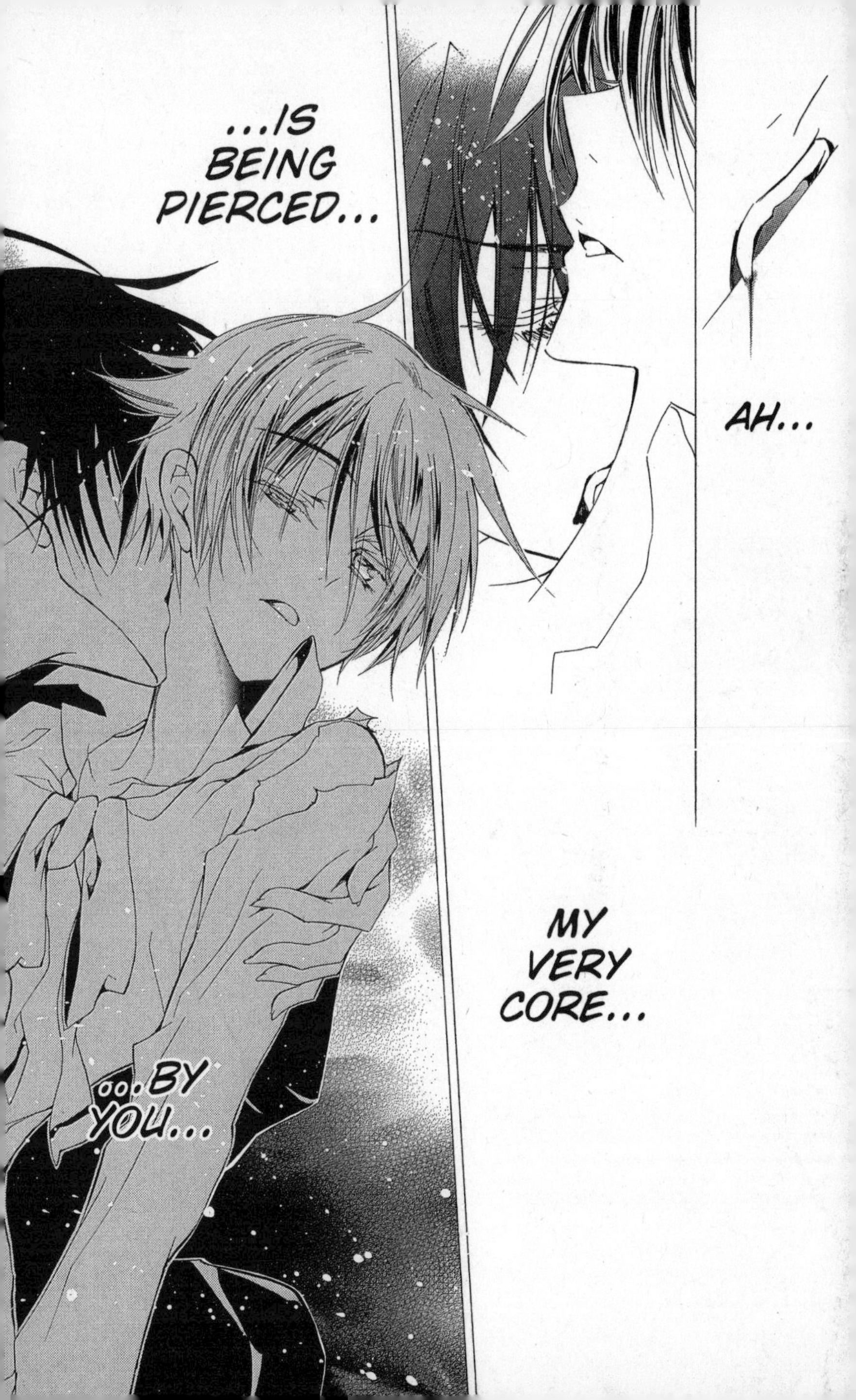
AH...
MY VERY CORE...
...IS BEING PIERCED...
...BY YOU...

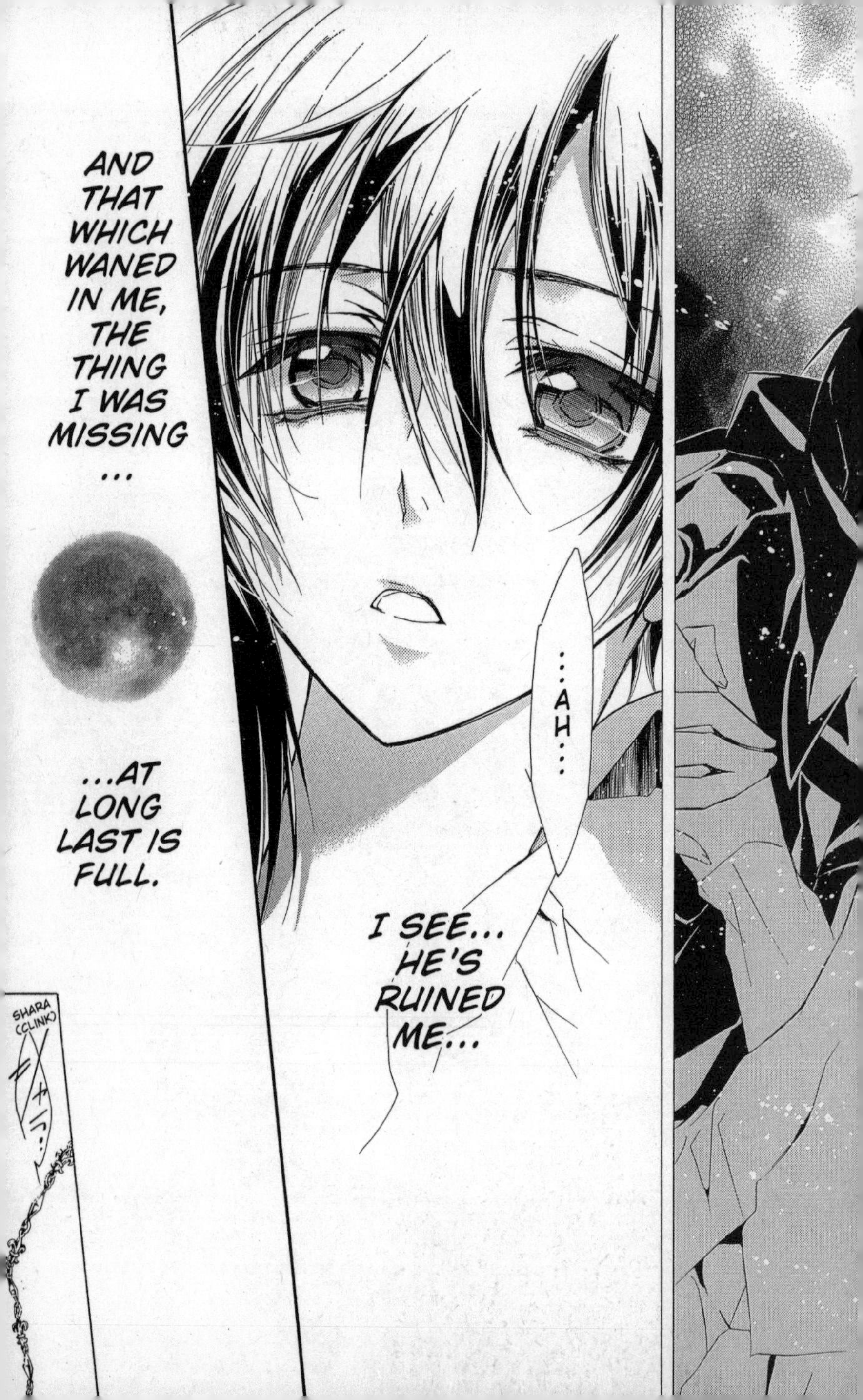
...AH...
I SEE... HE'S RUINED ME...
AND THAT WHICH WANED IN ME, THE THING I WAS MISSING...
...AT LONG LAST IS FULL.
SHARA (CLINK)

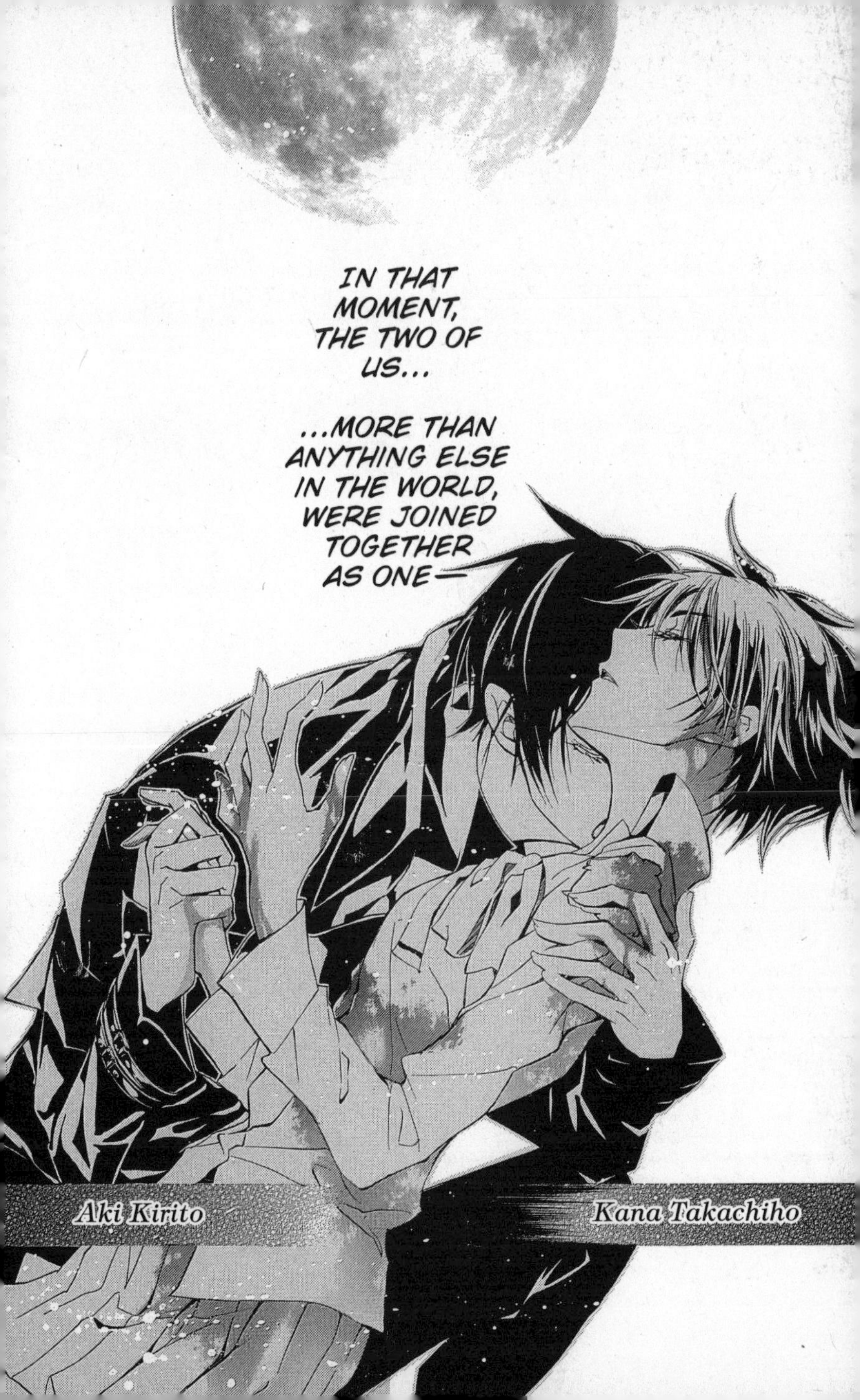
IN THAT MOMENT, THE TWO OF US...
...MORE THAN ANYTHING ELSE IN THE WORLD, WERE JOINED TOGETHER AS ONE—
Aki Kirito
Kana Takachiho

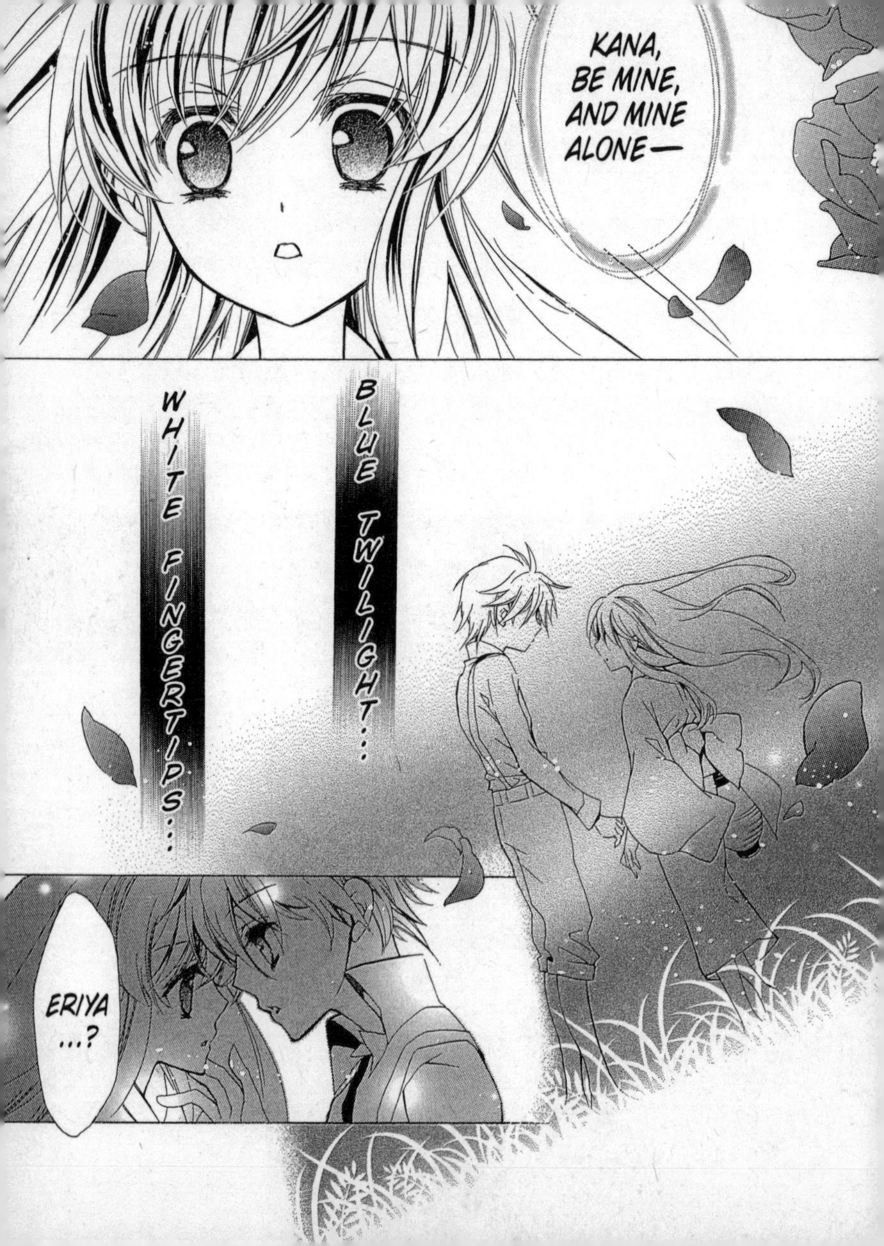
KANA, BE MINE, AND MINE ALONE—
BLUE TWILIGHT...
WHITE FINGERTIPS...
ERIYA ...?

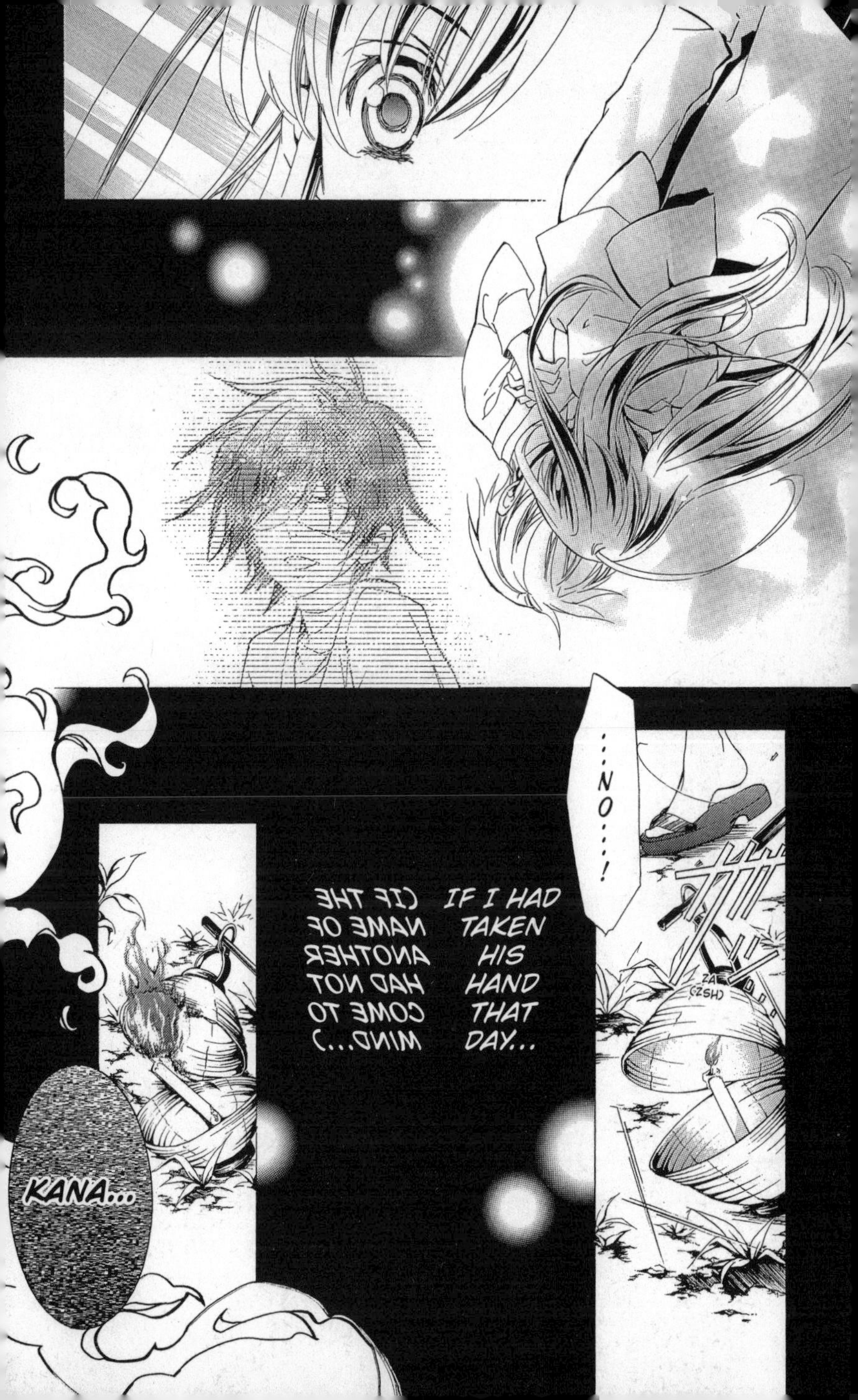
...NO...!
ZA (ZSH)
IF I HAD TAKEN HIS HAND THAT DAY...
(IF THE NAME OF ANOTHER HAD NOT COME TO MIND...)
KANA...

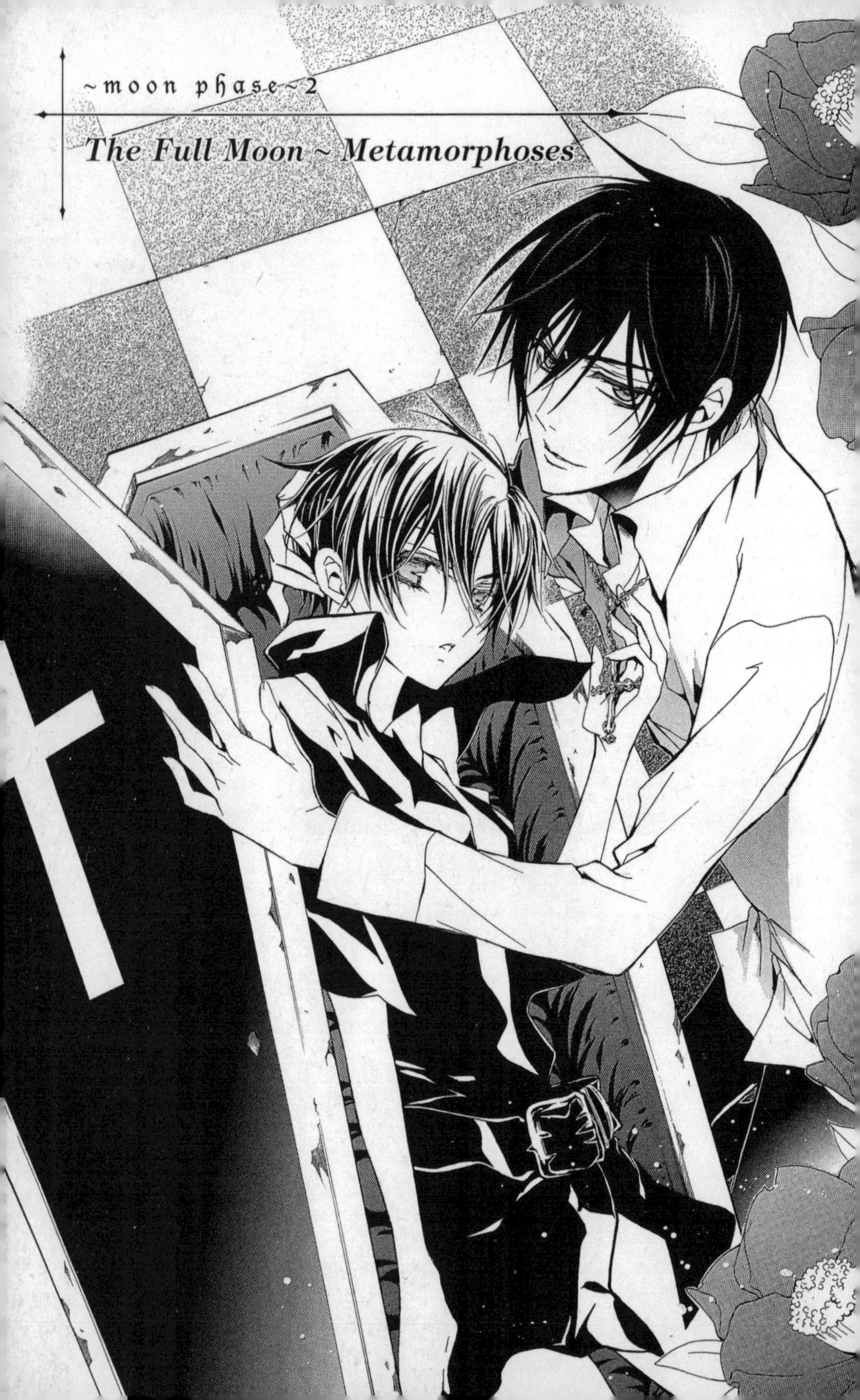
~moon phase~2
The Full Moon ~ Metamorphoses

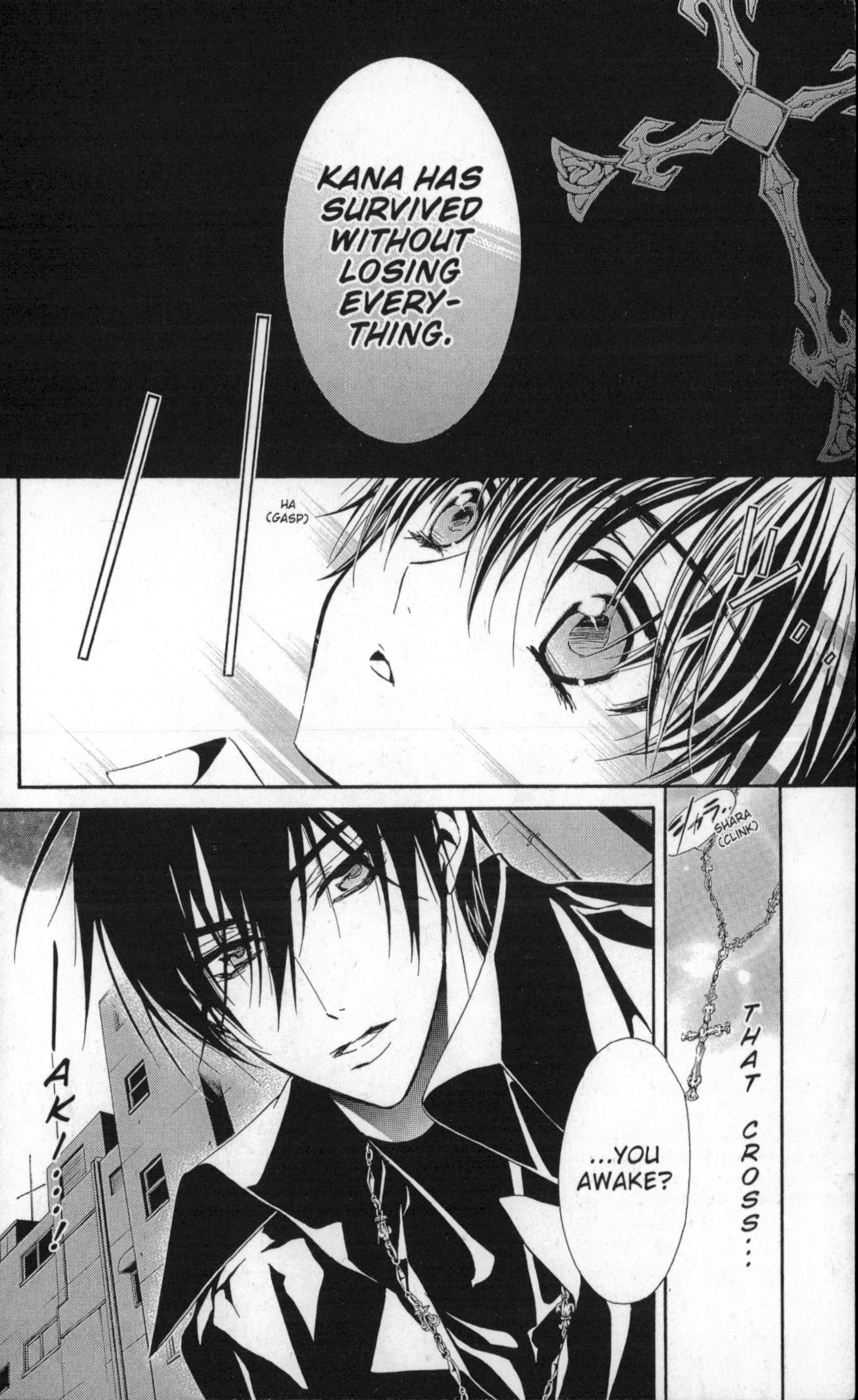
KANA HAS SURVIVED WITHOUT LOSING EVERY-THING.
HA (GASP)
シャラ SHARA (CLINK)
THAT CROSS...
...YOU AWAKE?
AKI......!

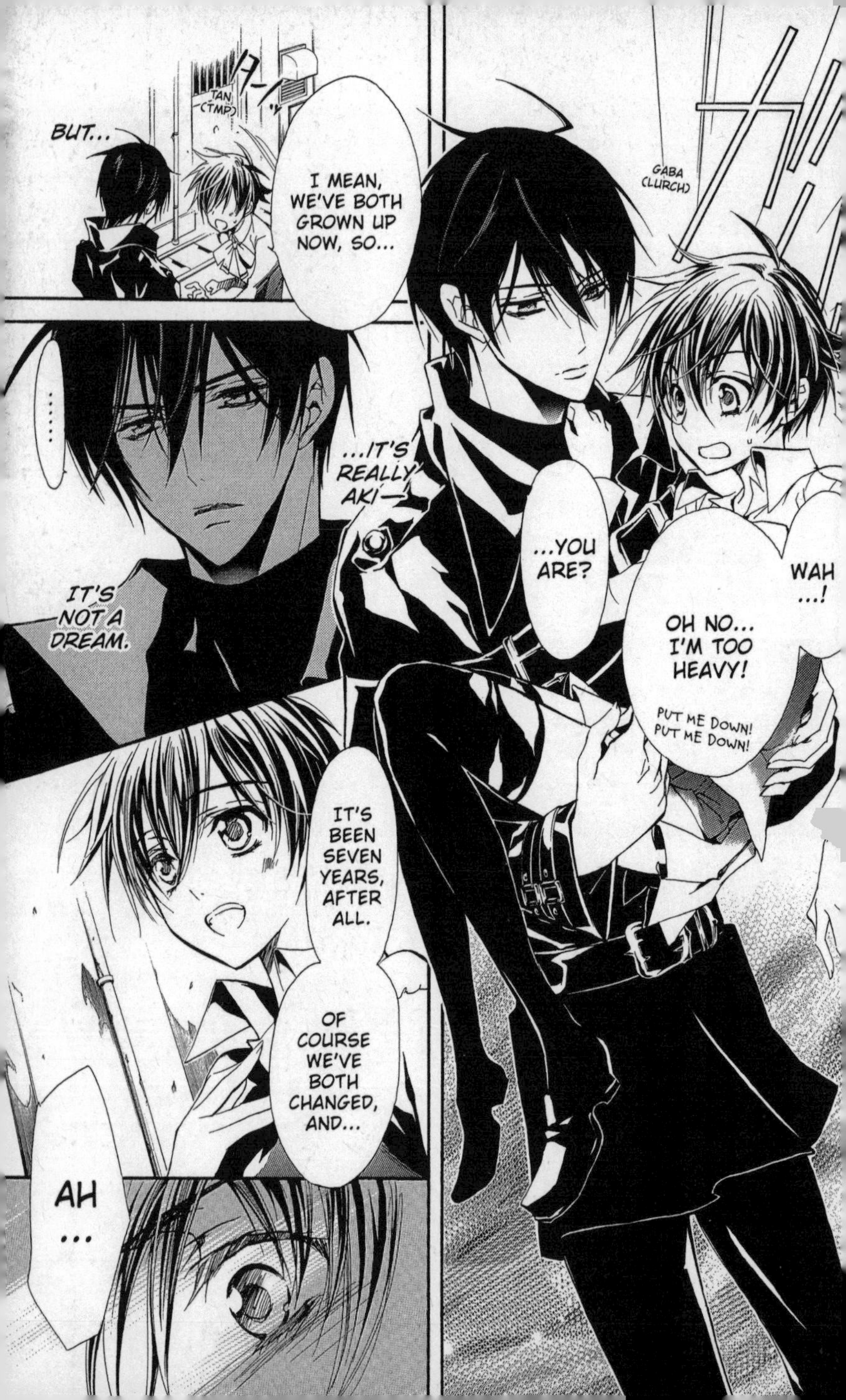
GABA (LURCH)
...YOU ARE?
WAH ...!
OH NO... I'M TOO HEAVY!
PUT ME DOWN! PUT ME DOWN!
TAN (TMP)
BUT...
I MEAN, WE'VE BOTH GROWN UP NOW, SO...
......
...IT'S REALLY AKI—
IT'S NOT A DREAM.
IT'S BEEN SEVEN YEARS, AFTER ALL.
OF COURSE WE'VE BOTH CHANGED, AND...
AH ...

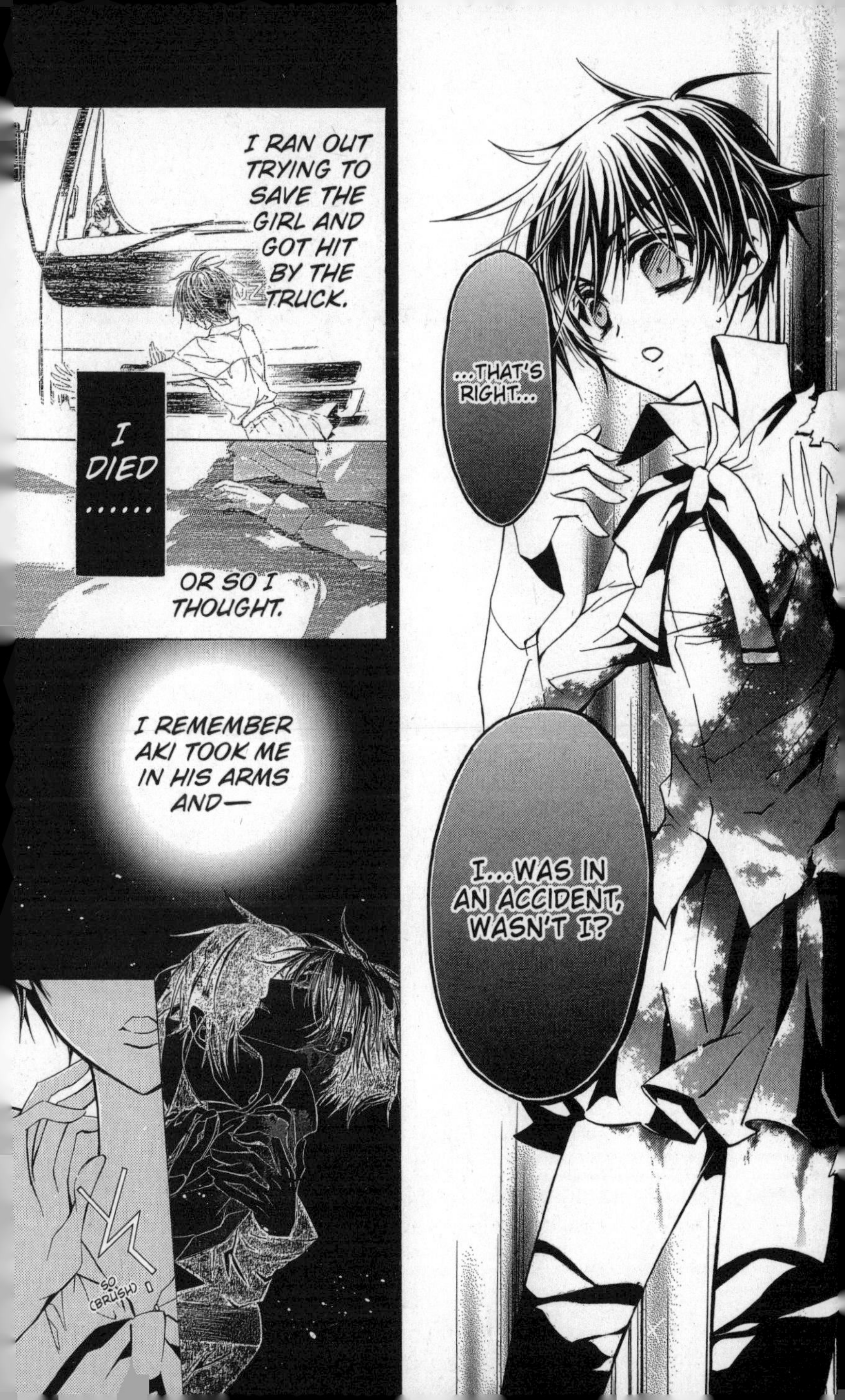
...THAT'S RIGHT...
I...WAS IN AN ACCIDENT, WASN'T I?
I RAN OUT TRYING TO SAVE THE GIRL AND GOT HIT BY THE TRUCK.
I DIED ......
OR SO I THOUGHT.
I REMEMBER AKI TOOK ME IN HIS ARMS AND—
SO (BRUSH)

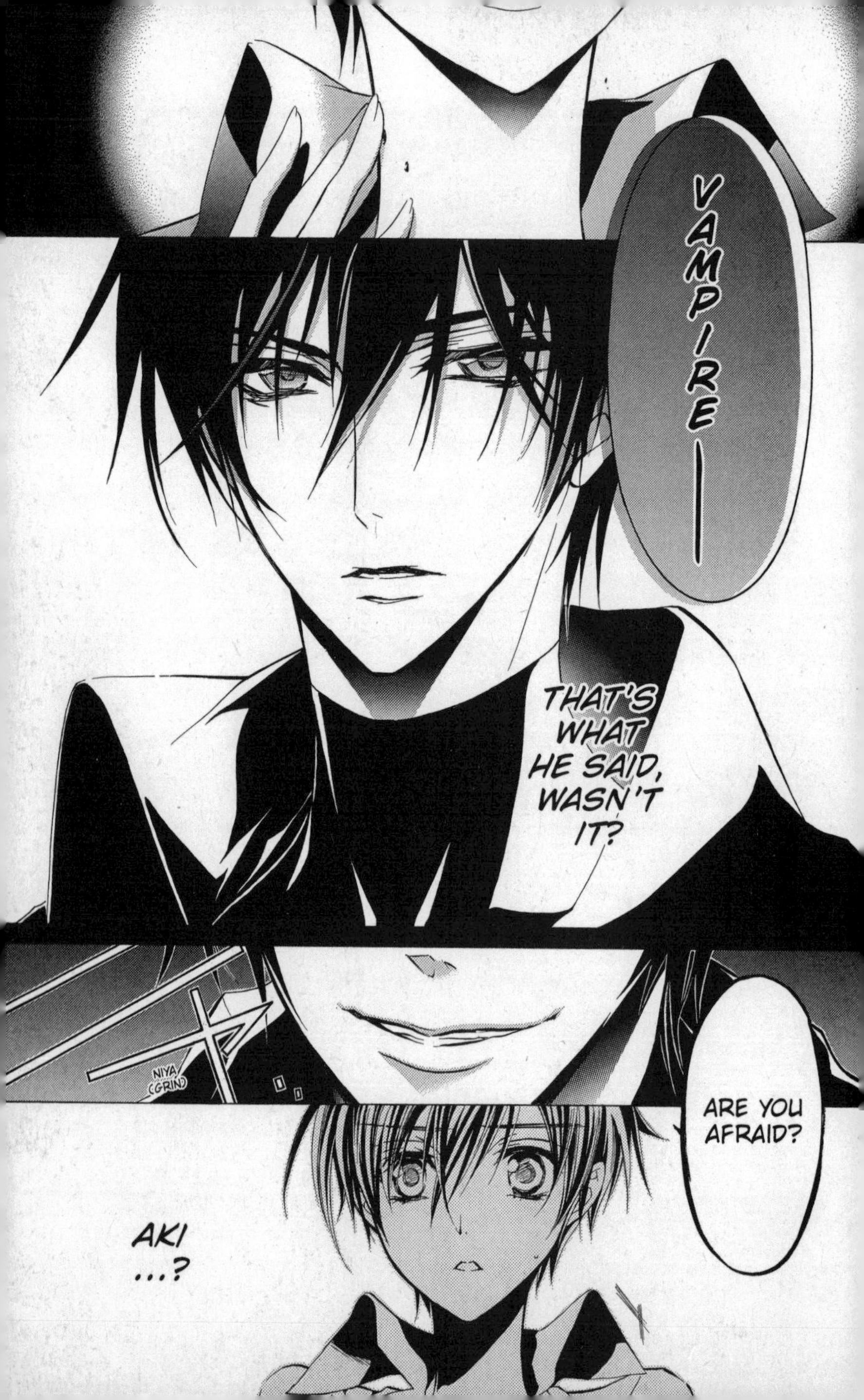
VAMPIRE—
THAT'S WHAT HE SAID, WASN'T IT?
NIYA (GRIN)
ARE YOU AFRAID?
AKI ...?

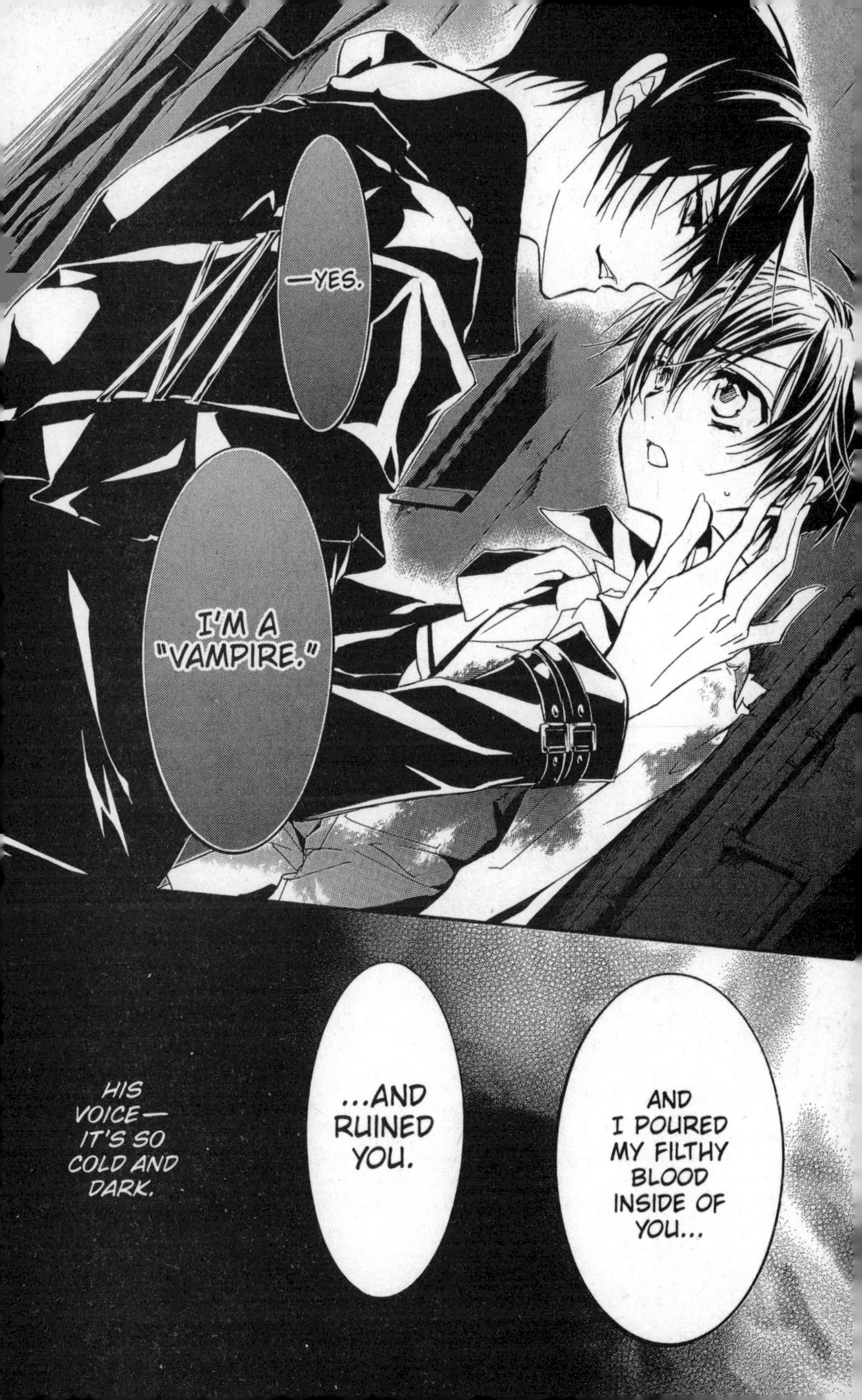
—YES.
I'M A "VAMPIRE."
AND I POURED MY FILTHY BLOOD INSIDE OF YOU...
...AND RUINED YOU.
HIS VOICE— IT'S SO COLD AND DARK.

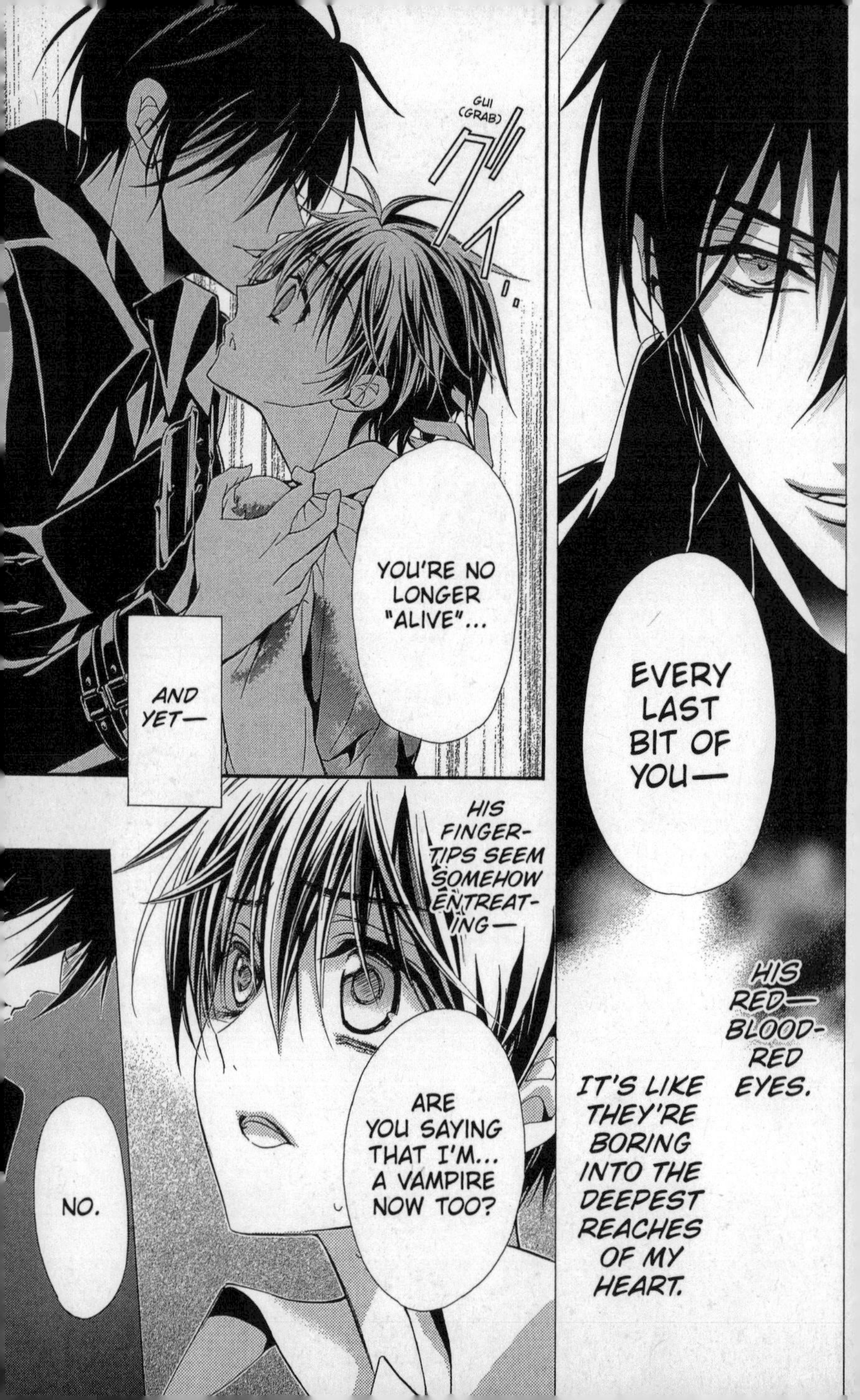
EVERY LAST BIT OF YOU—
HIS RED— BLOOD-RED EYES.
IT'S LIKE THEY'RE BORING INTO THE DEEPEST REACHES OF MY HEART.
GUI (GRAB)
YOU'RE NO LONGER "ALIVE"...
AND YET—
HIS FINGER-TIPS SEEM SOMEHOW ENTREAT-ING—
ARE YOU SAYING THAT I'M... A VAMPIRE NOW TOO?
NO.

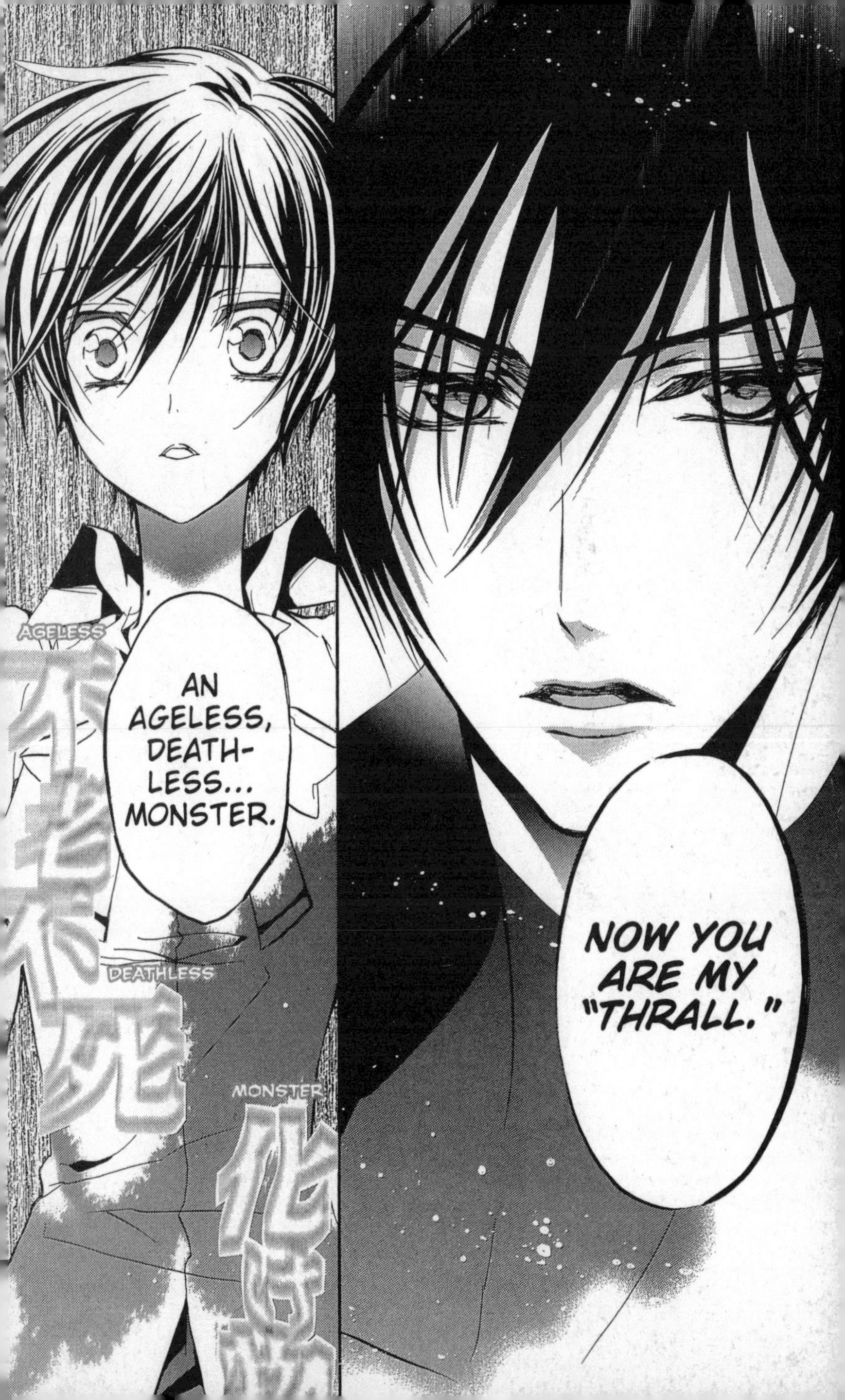
NOW YOU ARE MY "THRALL."
AN AGELESS, DEATH-LESS... MONSTER.
AGELESS
DEATHLESS
MONSTER

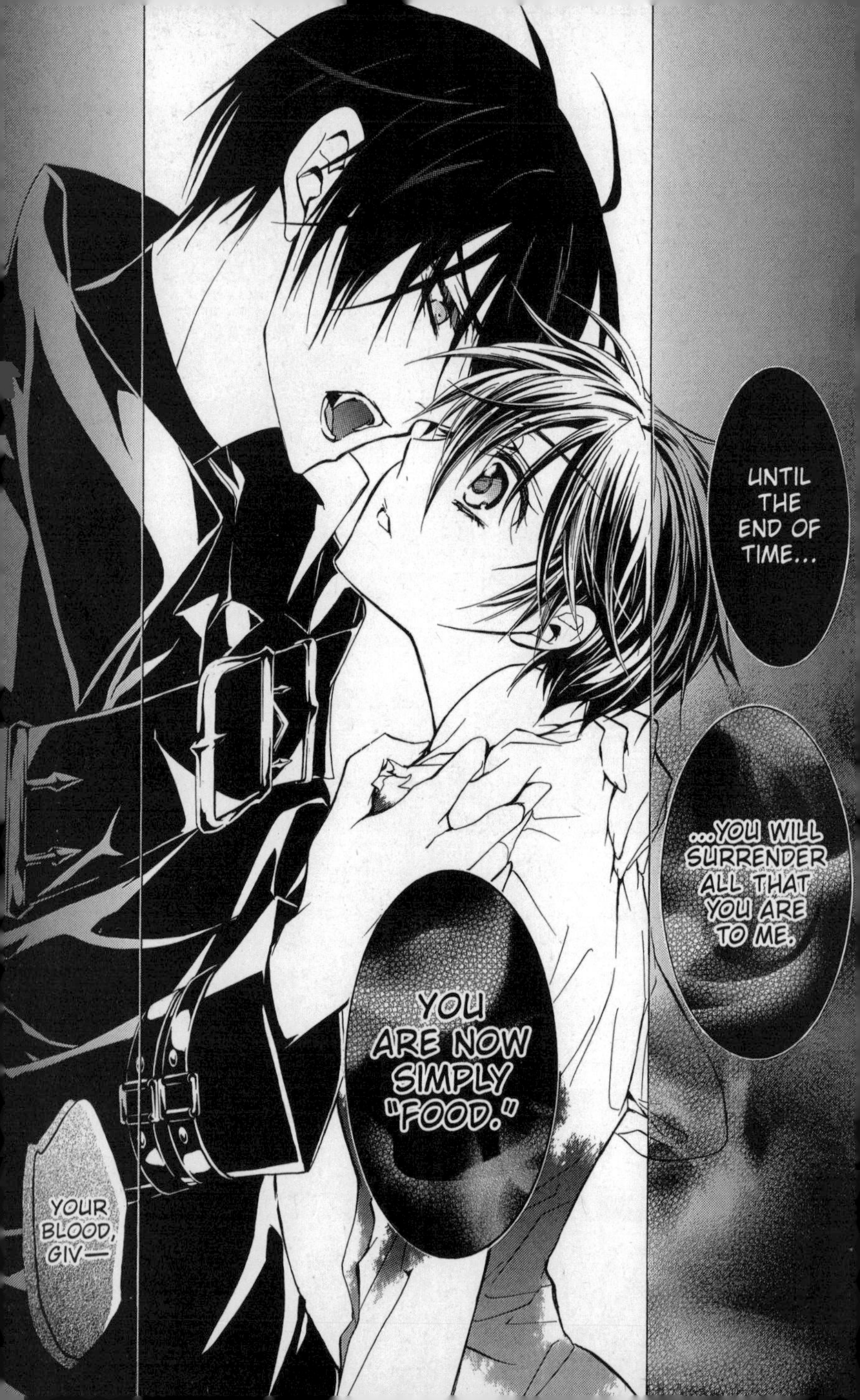
UNTIL THE END OF TIME...
...YOU WILL SURRENDER ALL THAT YOU ARE TO ME.
YOU ARE NOW SIMPLY "FOOD."
YOUR BLOOD, GIV—

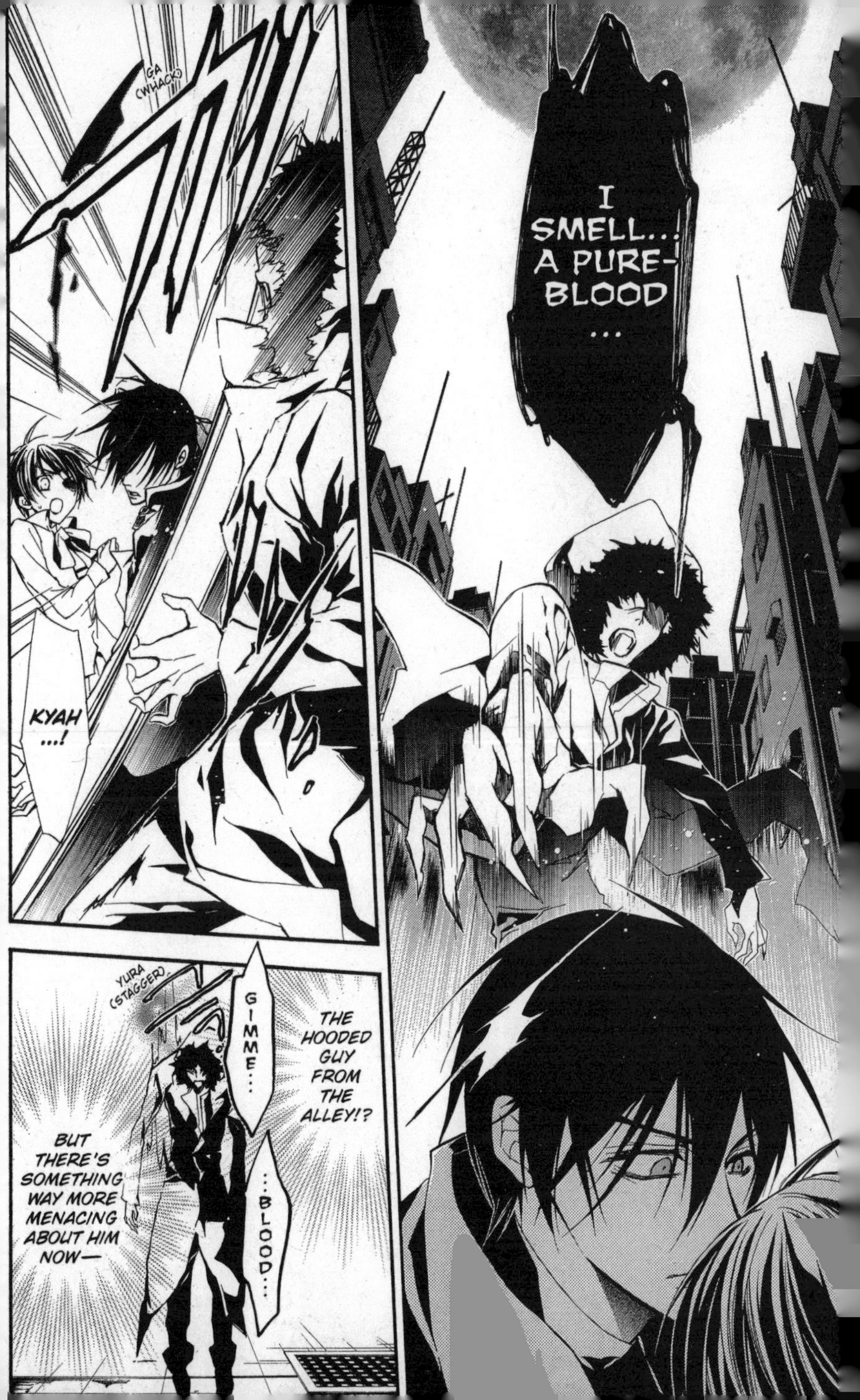
I SMELL... A PURE-BLOOD...
GA (WHACK)
KYAH ...!
YURA (STAGGER)
GIMME...
THE HOODED GUY FROM THE ALLEY!?
...BLOOD...
BUT THERE'S SOMETHING WAY MORE MENACING ABOUT HIM NOW—

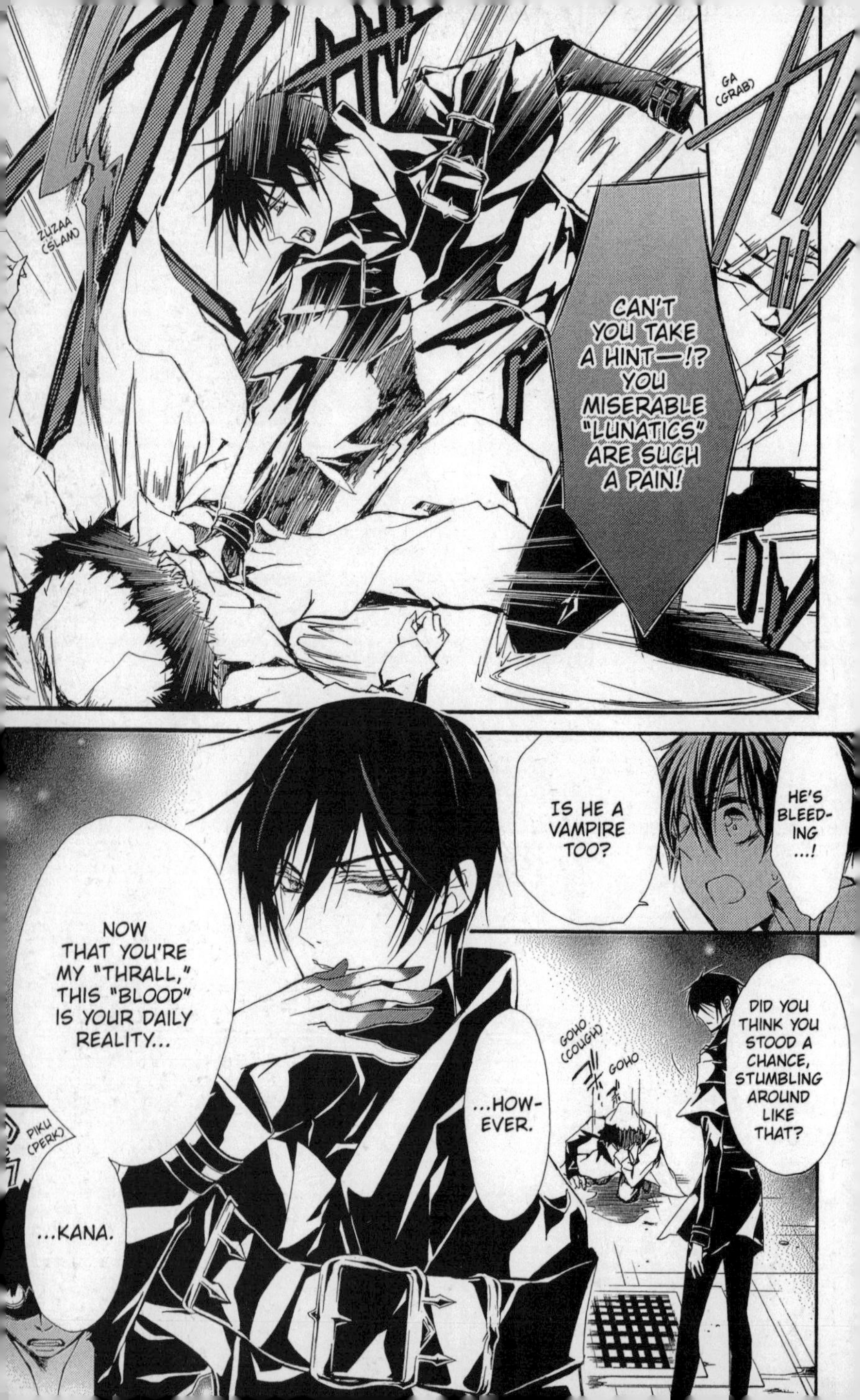
GA (GRAB)
CAN'T YOU TAKE A HINT—!? YOU MISERABLE "LUNATICS" ARE SUCH A PAIN!
ZUZAA (SLAM)
HE'S BLEED-ING ...!
IS HE A VAMPIRE TOO?
DID YOU THINK YOU STOOD A CHANCE, STUMBLING AROUND LIKE THAT?
GOHO (COUGH)
GOHO
...HOW-EVER.
NOW THAT YOU'RE MY "THRALL," THIS "BLOOD" IS YOUR DAILY REALITY...
PIKU (PERK)
...KANA.

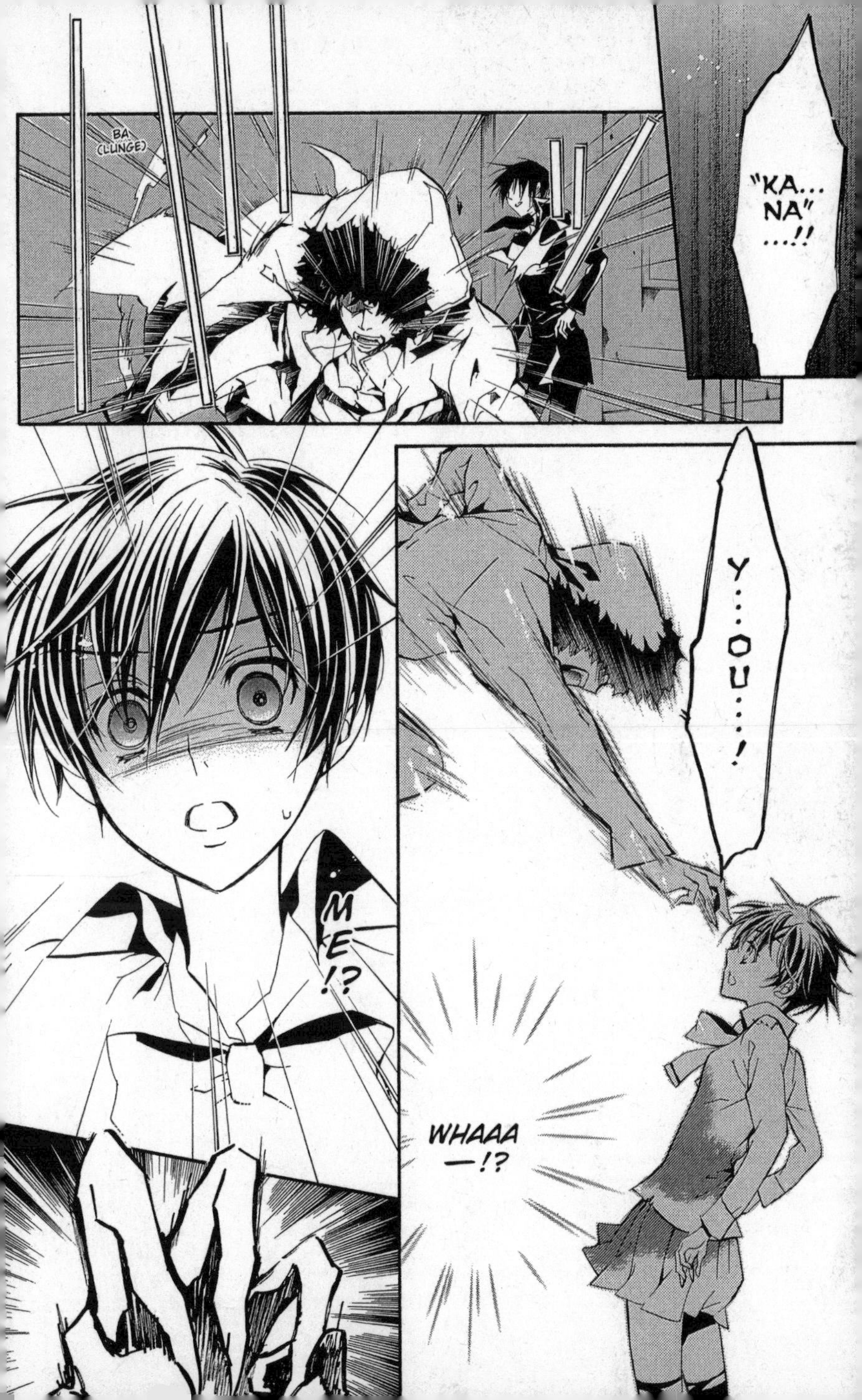
"KA... NA" ...!!
BA (LUNGE)
Y...OU...!
WHAAA—!?
ME!?

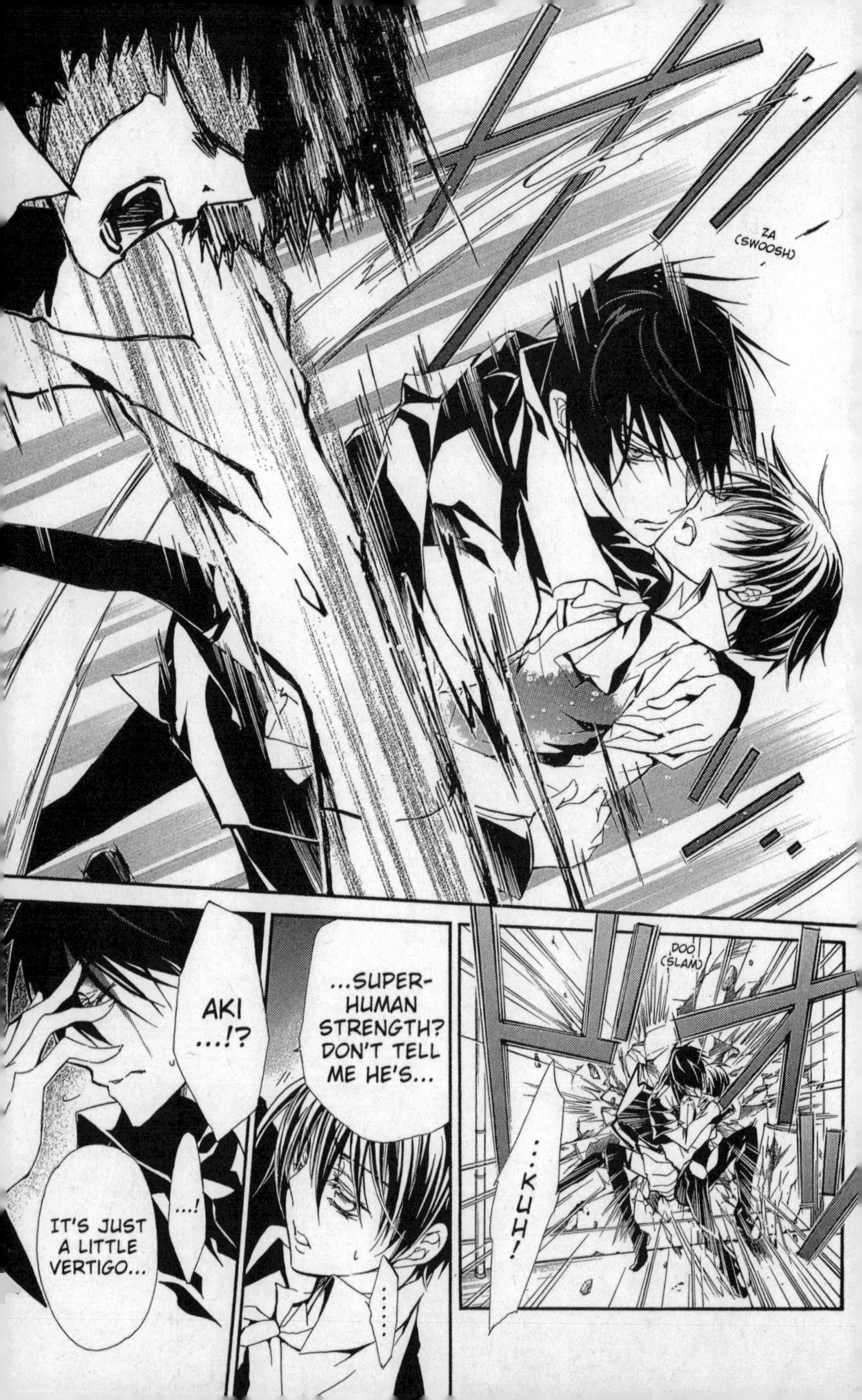
ZA (SWOOSH)
DOO (SLAM)
...KUH!
...SUPER-HUMAN STRENGTH? DON'T TELL ME HE'S...
AKI ...!?
...!
......
IT'S JUST A LITTLE VERTIGO...

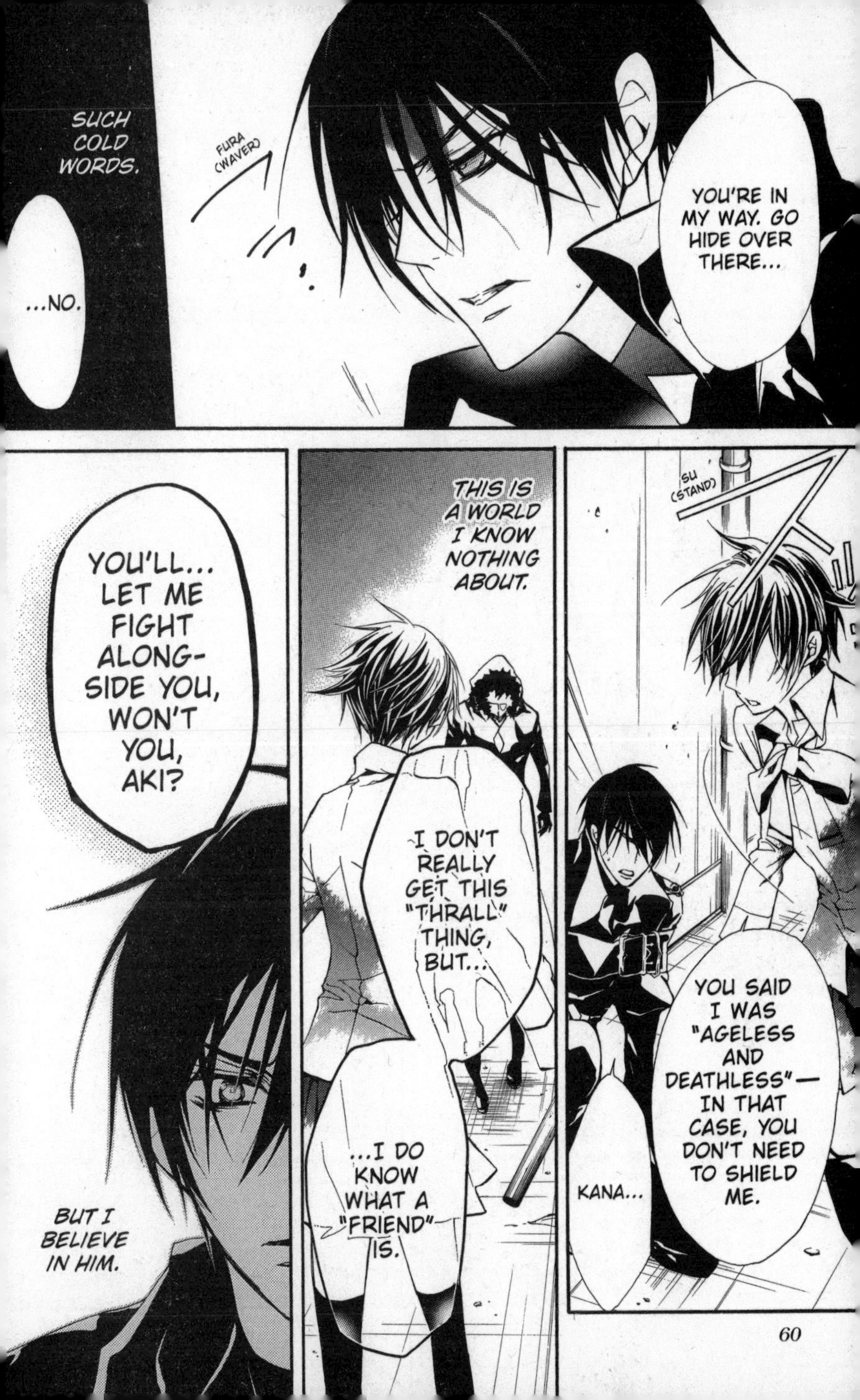
YOU'RE IN MY WAY. GO HIDE OVER THERE...
FURA (WAVER)
SUCH COLD WORDS.
...NO.
SU (STAND)
YOU SAID I WAS "AGELESS AND DEATHLESS"— IN THAT CASE, YOU DON'T NEED TO SHIELD ME.
KANA...
THIS IS A WORLD I KNOW NOTHING ABOUT.
I DON'T REALLY GET THIS "THRALL" THING, BUT...
...I DO KNOW WHAT A "FRIEND" IS.
YOU'LL... LET ME FIGHT ALONG-SIDE YOU, WON'T YOU, AKI?
BUT I BELIEVE IN HIM.

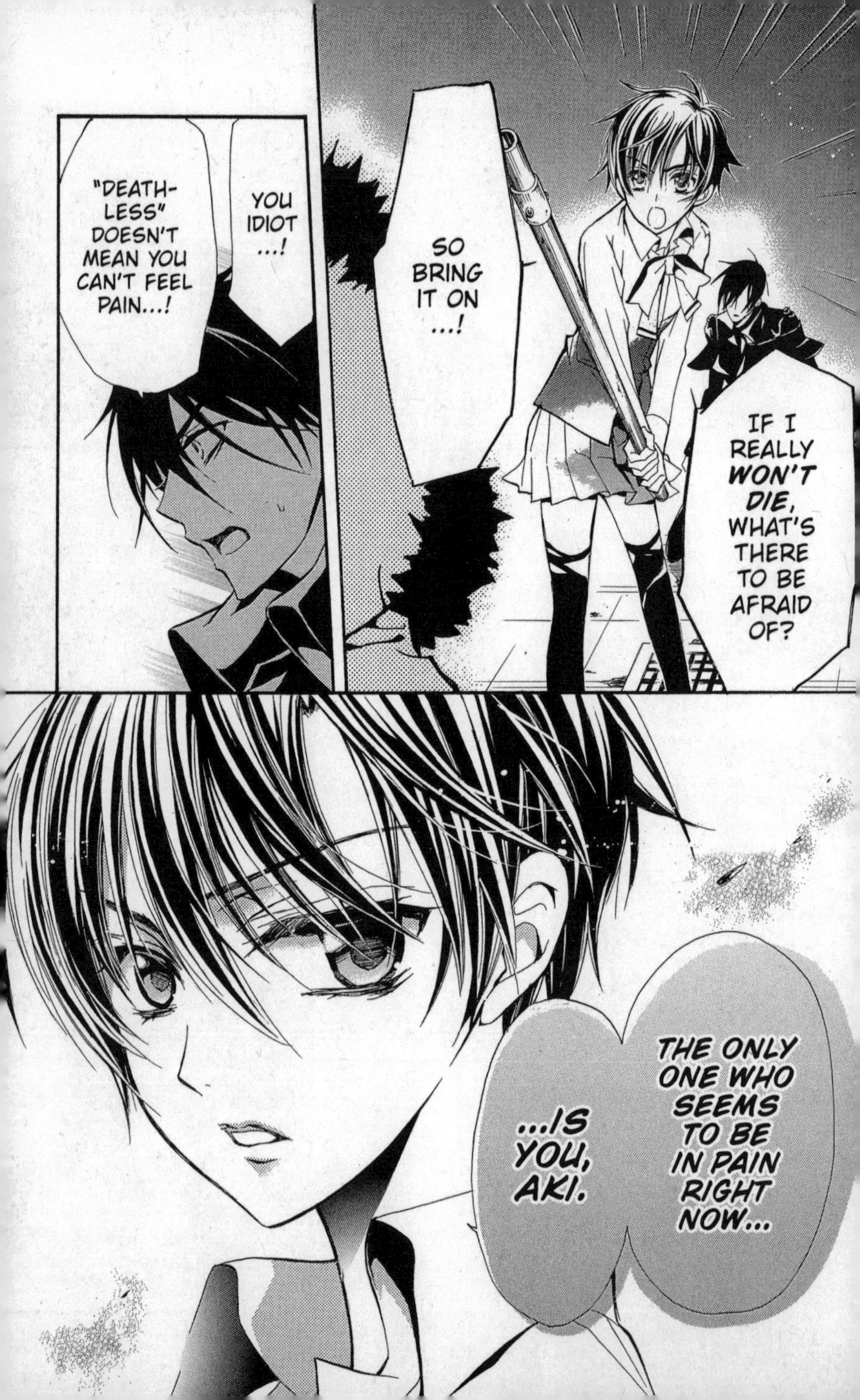
IF I REALLY *WON'T DIE*, WHAT'S THERE TO BE AFRAID OF?
SO BRING IT ON ...!
YOU IDIOT ...!
"DEATH-LESS" DOESN'T MEAN YOU CAN'T FEEL PAIN...!
THE ONLY ONE WHO SEEMS TO BE IN PAIN RIGHT NOW...
...IS YOU, AKI.

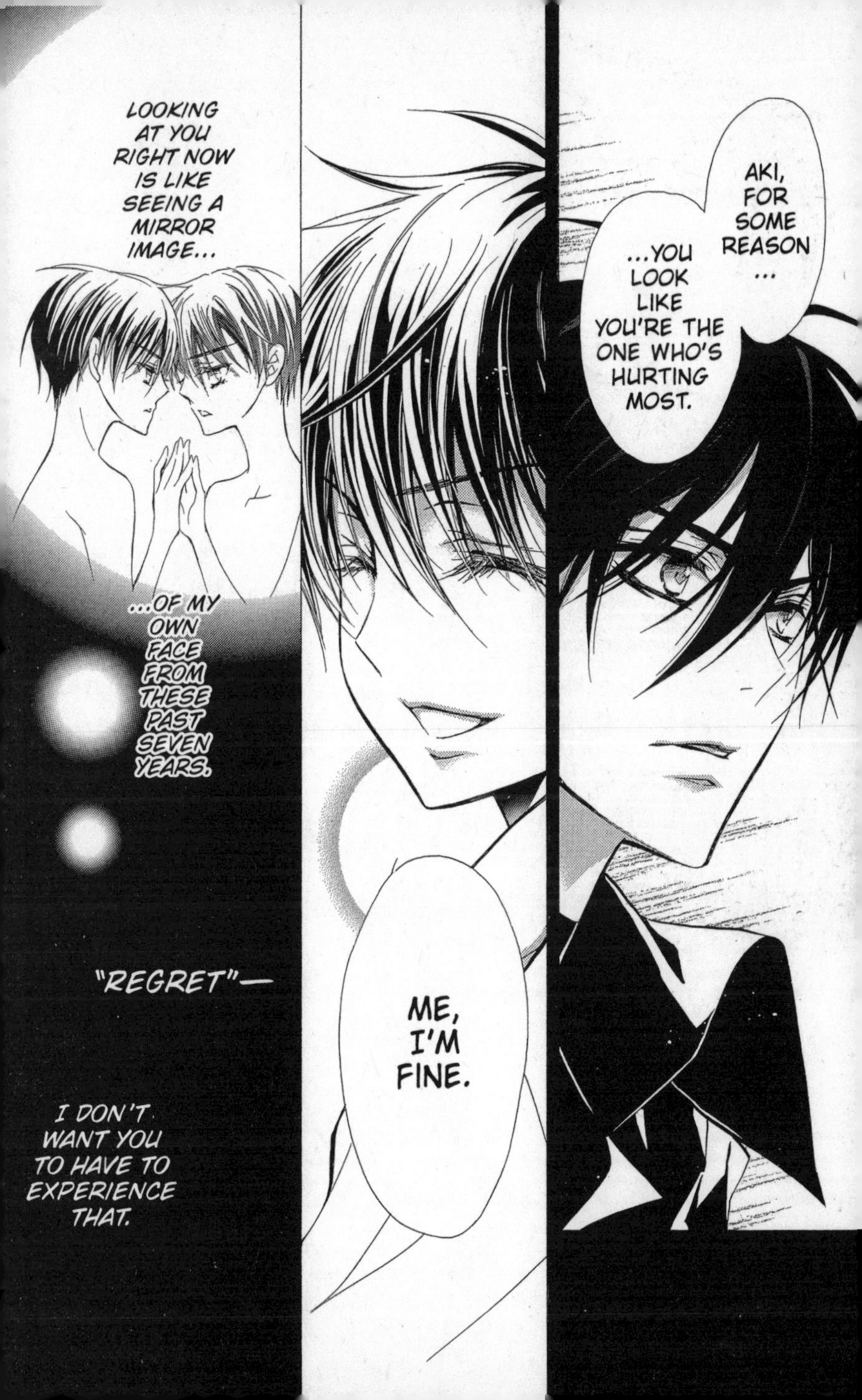
AKI, FOR SOME REASON ...
...YOU LOOK LIKE YOU'RE THE ONE WHO'S HURTING MOST.
ME, I'M FINE.
LOOKING AT YOU RIGHT NOW IS LIKE SEEING A MIRROR IMAGE...
...OF MY OWN FACE FROM THESE PAST SEVEN YEARS.
"REGRET"—
I DON'T WANT YOU TO HAVE TO EXPERIENCE THAT.

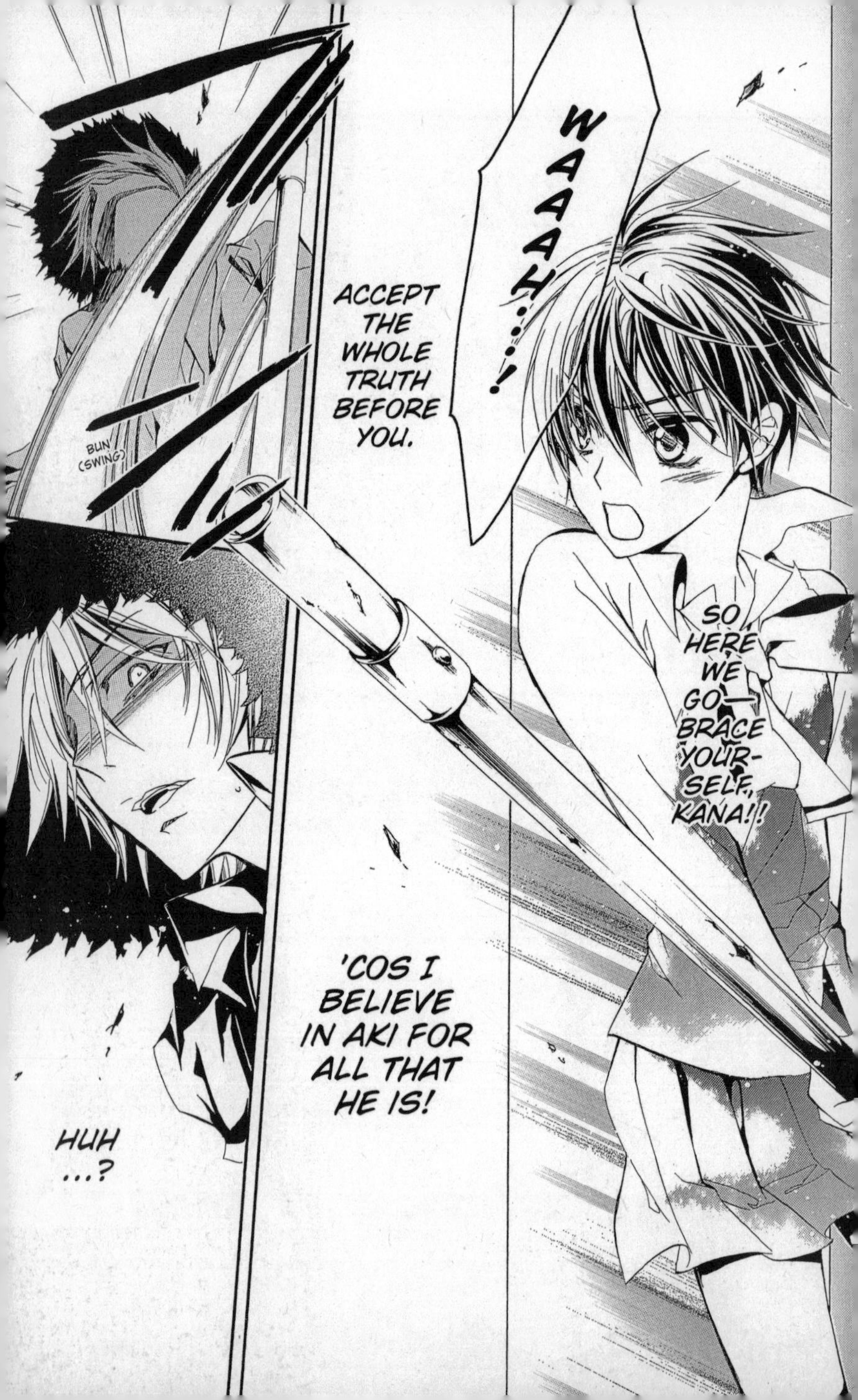
WAAAAH...!
SO HERE WE GO—BRACE YOURSELF, KANA!!
ACCEPT THE WHOLE TRUTH BEFORE YOU.
'COS I BELIEVE IN AKI FOR ALL THAT HE IS!
BUN (SWING)
HUH ...?

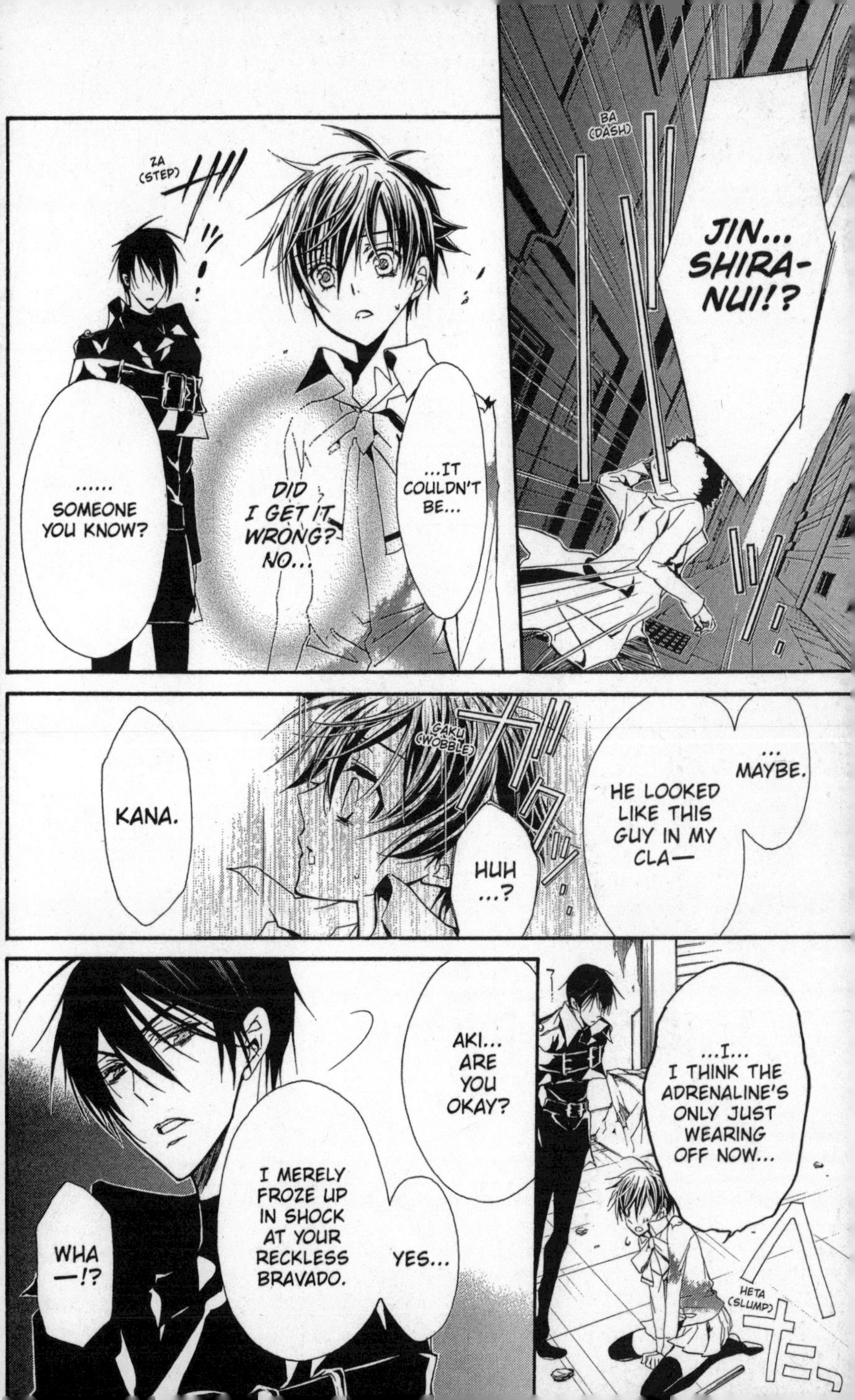
BA (DASH)
JIN... SHIRANUI!?
ZA (STEP)
...IT COULDN'T BE...
DID I GET IT WRONG? NO...
...... SOMEONE YOU KNOW?
... MAYBE.
HE LOOKED LIKE THIS GUY IN MY CLA—
GAKU (WOBBLE)
HUH ...?
KANA.
...I... I THINK THE ADRENALINE'S ONLY JUST WEARING OFF NOW...
HETA (SLUMP)
AKI... ARE YOU OKAY?
YES...
I MERELY FROZE UP IN SHOCK AT YOUR RECKLESS BRAVADO.
WHA—!?

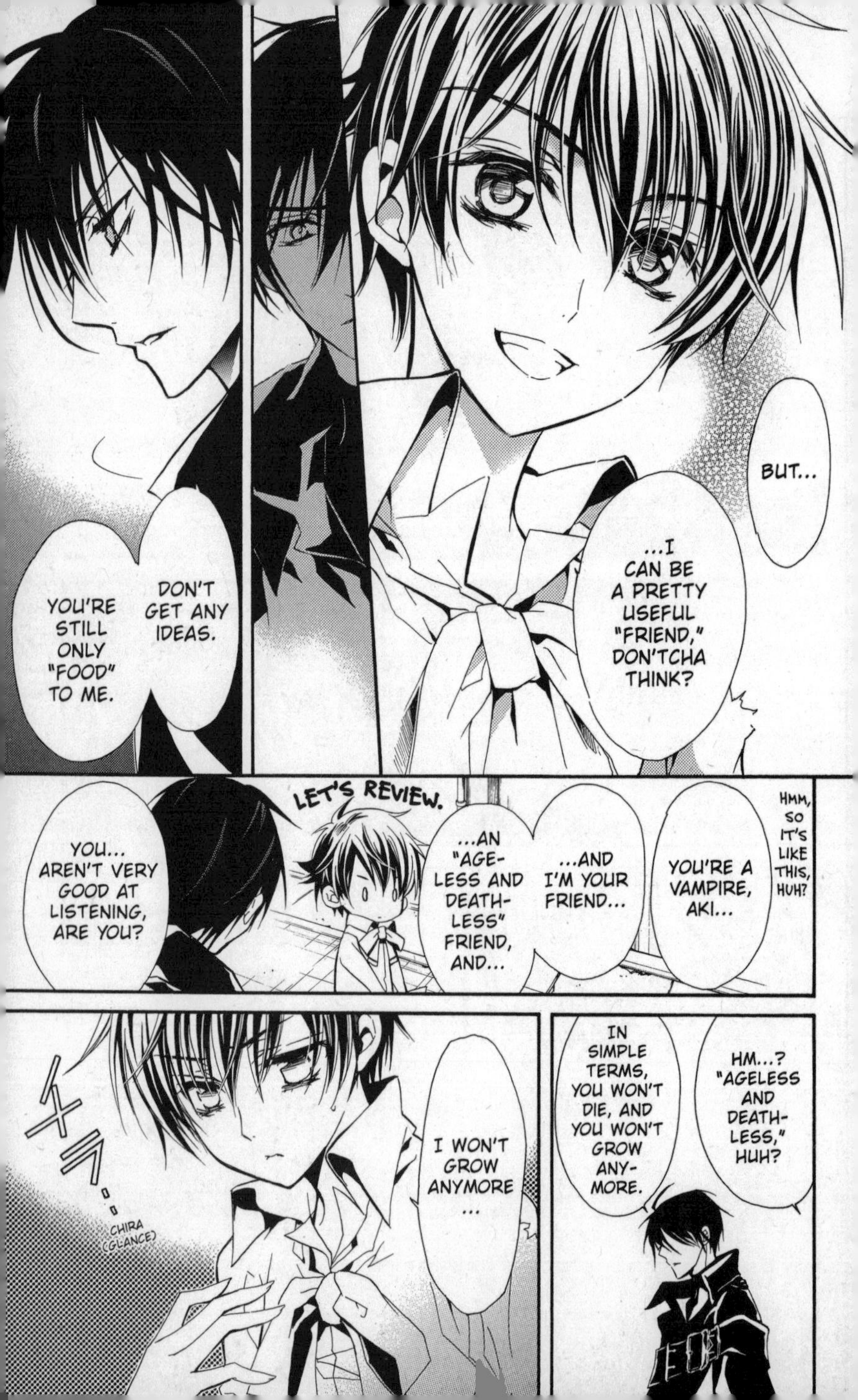
BUT...
...I CAN BE A PRETTY USEFUL "FRIEND," DON'TCHA THINK?
DON'T GET ANY IDEAS.
YOU'RE STILL ONLY "FOOD" TO ME.
HMM, SO IT'S LIKE THIS, HUH?
YOU'RE A VAMPIRE, AKI...
...AND I'M YOUR FRIEND...
...AN "AGE-LESS AND DEATH-LESS" FRIEND, AND...
LET'S REVIEW.
YOU... AREN'T VERY GOOD AT LISTENING, ARE YOU?
HM...? "AGELESS AND DEATH-LESS," HUH?
IN SIMPLE TERMS, YOU WON'T DIE, AND YOU WON'T GROW ANY-MORE.
I WON'T GROW ANYMORE...
CHIRA (GLANCE)

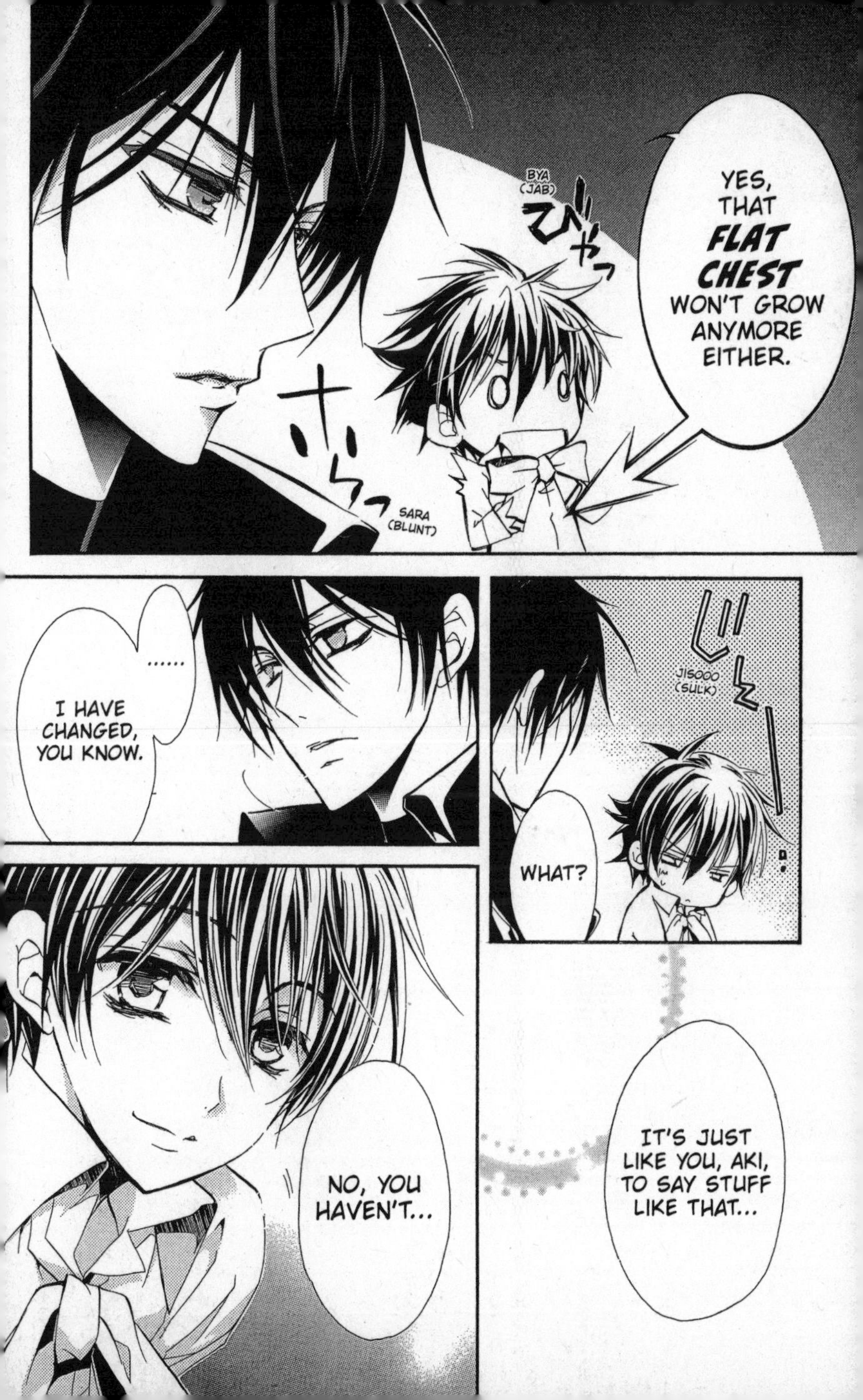
YES, THAT FLAT CHEST WON'T GROW ANYMORE EITHER.
BYA (JAB)
SARA (BLUNT)
JISOOO (SULK)
WHAT?
......
I HAVE CHANGED, YOU KNOW.
IT'S JUST LIKE YOU, AKI, TO SAY STUFF LIKE THAT...
NO, YOU HAVEN'T...

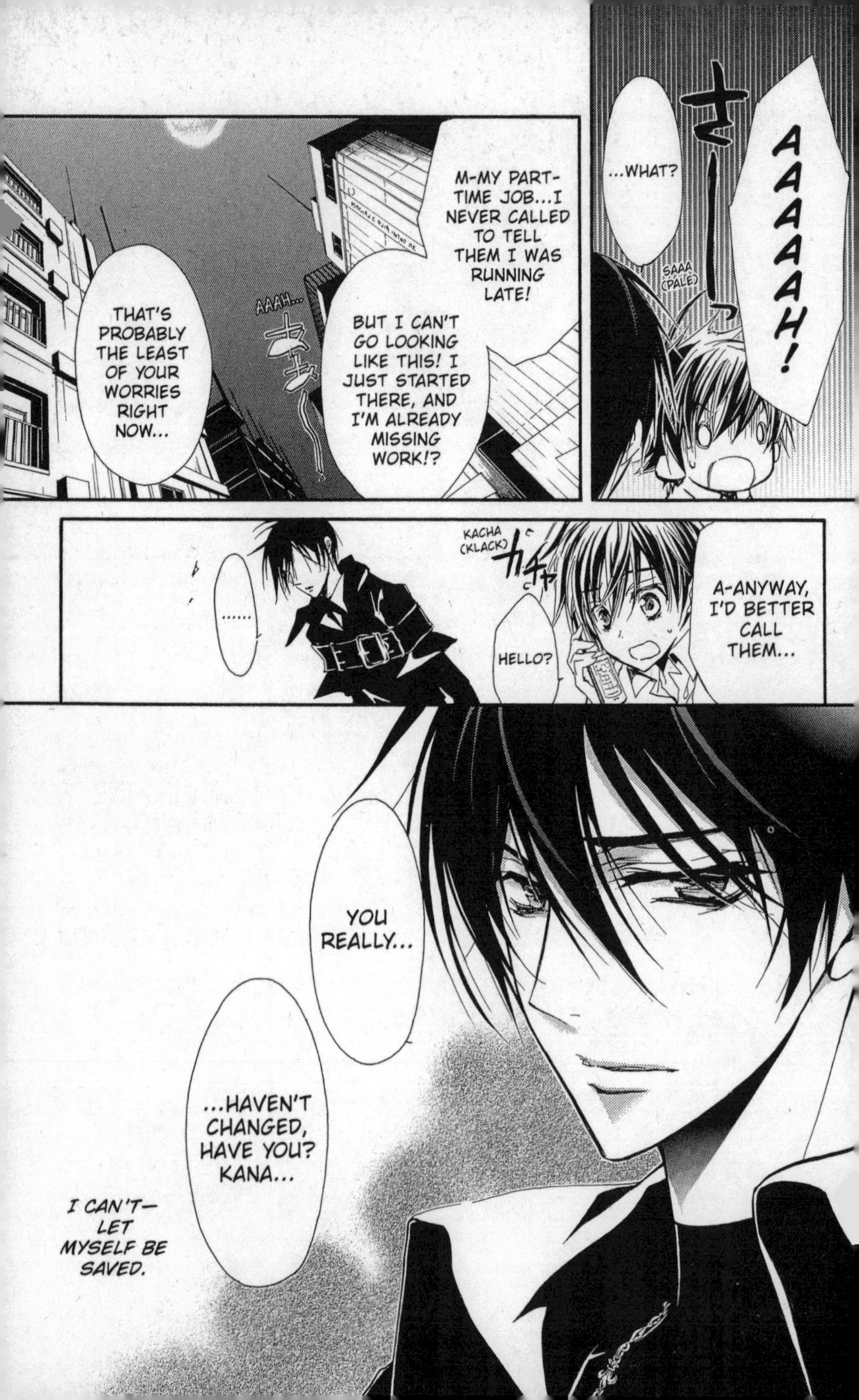
AAAAAH!
...WHAT?
SAAA (PALE)
M-MY PART-TIME JOB...I NEVER CALLED TO TELL THEM I WAS RUNNING LATE!
BUT I CAN'T GO LOOKING LIKE THIS! I JUST STARTED THERE, AND I'M ALREADY MISSING WORK!?
AAAH...
THAT'S PROBABLY THE LEAST OF YOUR WORRIES RIGHT NOW...
A-ANYWAY, I'D BETTER CALL THEM...
KACHA (KLACK)
HELLO?
......
YOU REALLY...
...HAVEN'T CHANGED, HAVE YOU? KANA...
I CAN'T— LET MYSELF BE SAVED.

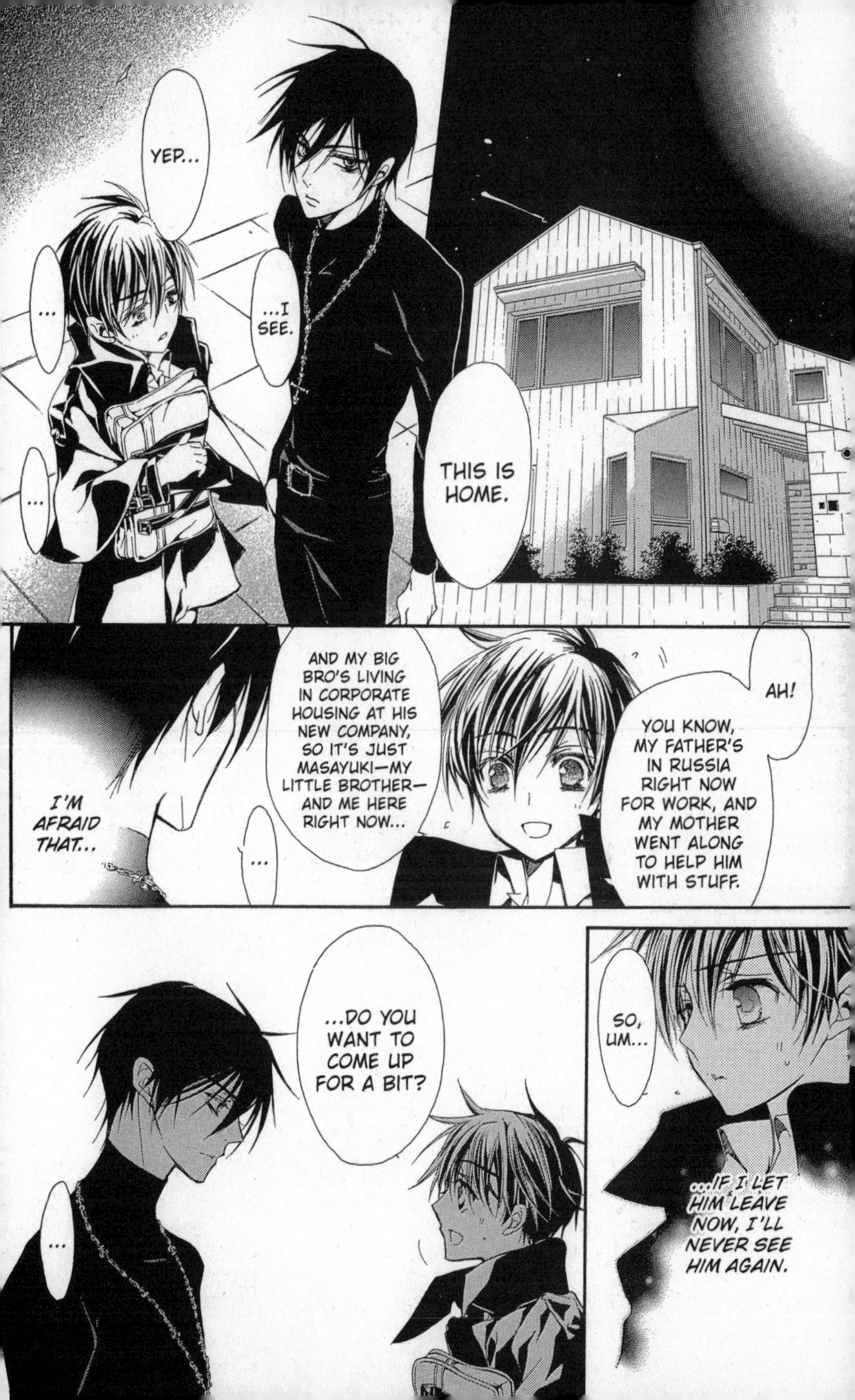
THIS IS HOME.
...I SEE.
YEP...
...
...
AH!
YOU KNOW, MY FATHER'S IN RUSSIA RIGHT NOW FOR WORK, AND MY MOTHER WENT ALONG TO HELP HIM WITH STUFF.
AND MY BIG BRO'S LIVING IN CORPORATE HOUSING AT HIS NEW COMPANY, SO IT'S JUST MASAYUKI—MY LITTLE BROTHER—AND ME HERE RIGHT NOW...
...
I'M AFRAID THAT...
SO, UM...
...IF I LET HIM LEAVE NOW, I'LL NEVER SEE HIM AGAIN.
...DO YOU WANT TO COME UP FOR A BIT?
...

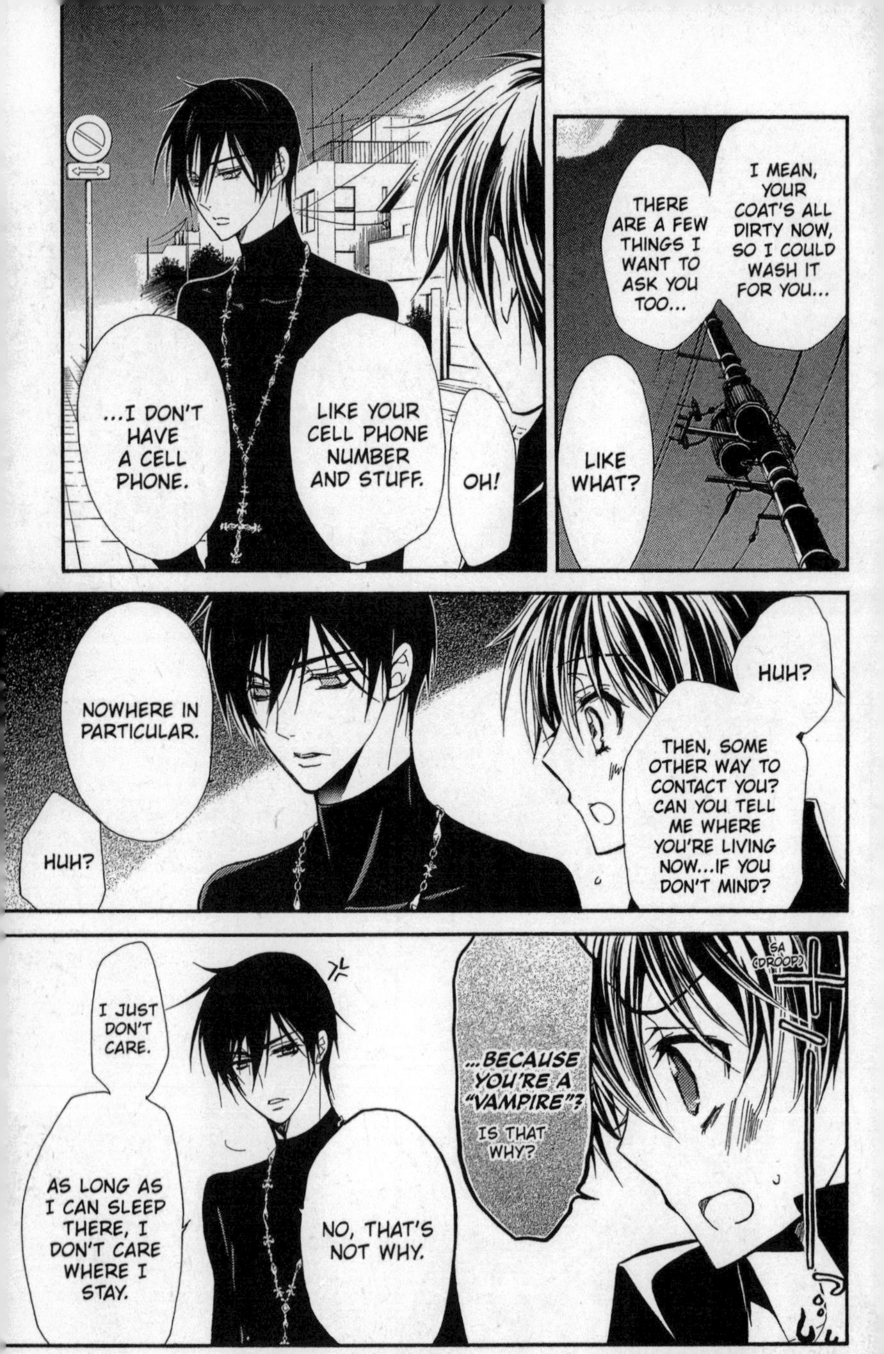
I MEAN, YOUR COAT'S ALL DIRTY NOW, SO I COULD WASH IT FOR YOU...
THERE ARE A FEW THINGS I WANT TO ASK YOU TOO...
LIKE WHAT?
OH!
LIKE YOUR CELL PHONE NUMBER AND STUFF.
...I DON'T HAVE A CELL PHONE.
HUH?
THEN, SOME OTHER WAY TO CONTACT YOU? CAN YOU TELL ME WHERE YOU'RE LIVING NOW...IF YOU DON'T MIND?
NOWHERE IN PARTICULAR.
HUH?
SA (DROOP)
...BECAUSE YOU'RE A "VAMPIRE"?
IS THAT WHY?
NO, THAT'S NOT WHY.
I JUST DON'T CARE.
AS LONG AS I CAN SLEEP THERE, I DON'T CARE WHERE I STAY.

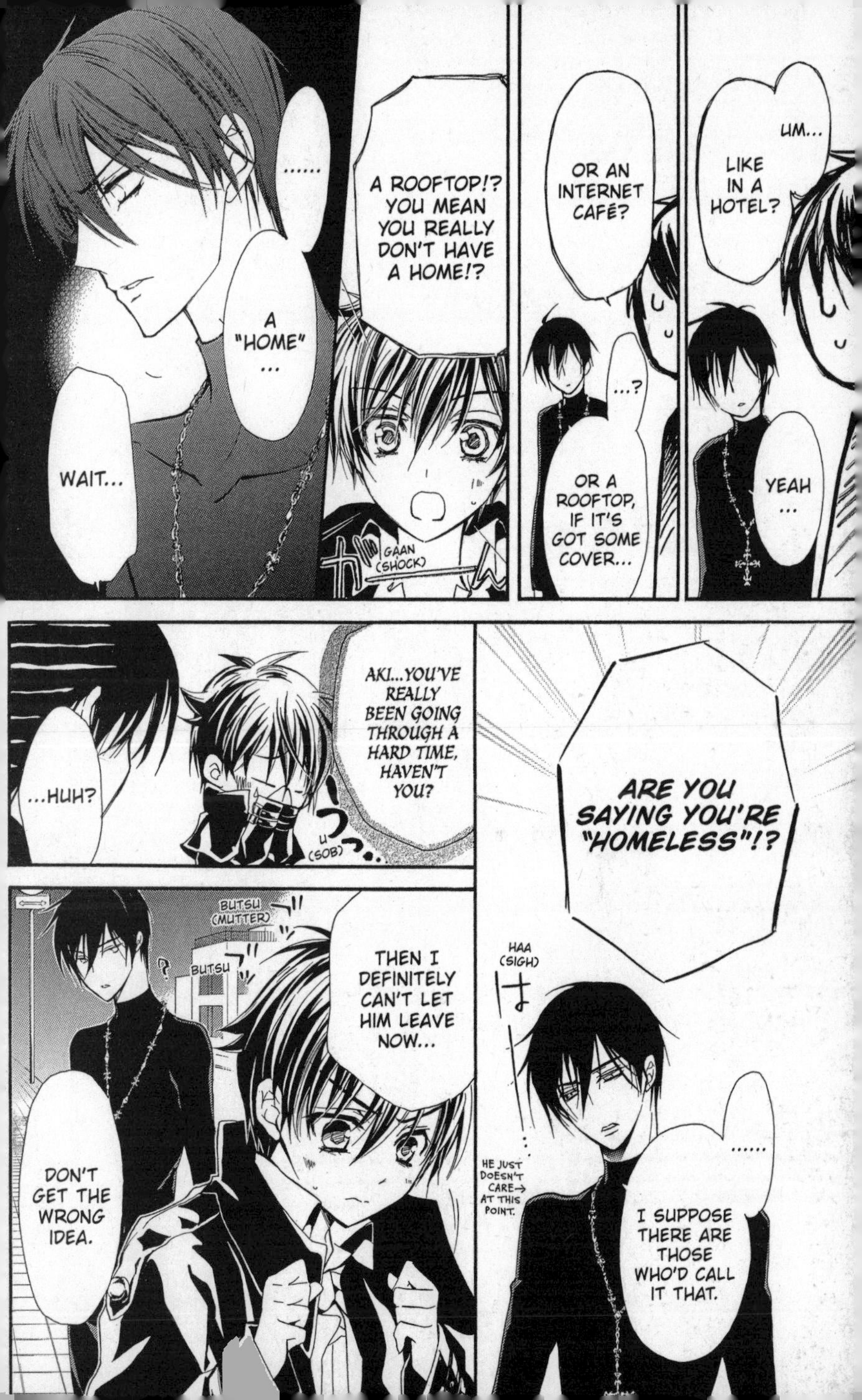
UM...
LIKE IN A HOTEL?
YEAH ...
OR AN INTERNET CAFÉ?
...?
OR A ROOFTOP, IF IT'S GOT SOME COVER...
A ROOFTOP!? YOU MEAN YOU REALLY DON'T HAVE A HOME!?
GAAN (SHOCK)
......
A "HOME" ...
WAIT...
ARE YOU SAYING YOU'RE "HOMELESS"!?
HAA (SIGH)
HE JUST DOESN'T CARE→ AT THIS POINT.
......
I SUPPOSE THERE ARE THOSE WHO'D CALL IT THAT.
AKI...YOU'VE REALLY BEEN GOING THROUGH A HARD TIME, HAVEN'T YOU?
U (SOB)
...HUH?
THEN I DEFINITELY CAN'T LET HIM LEAVE NOW...
BUTSU (MUTTER)
BUTSU
?
DON'T GET THE WRONG IDEA.

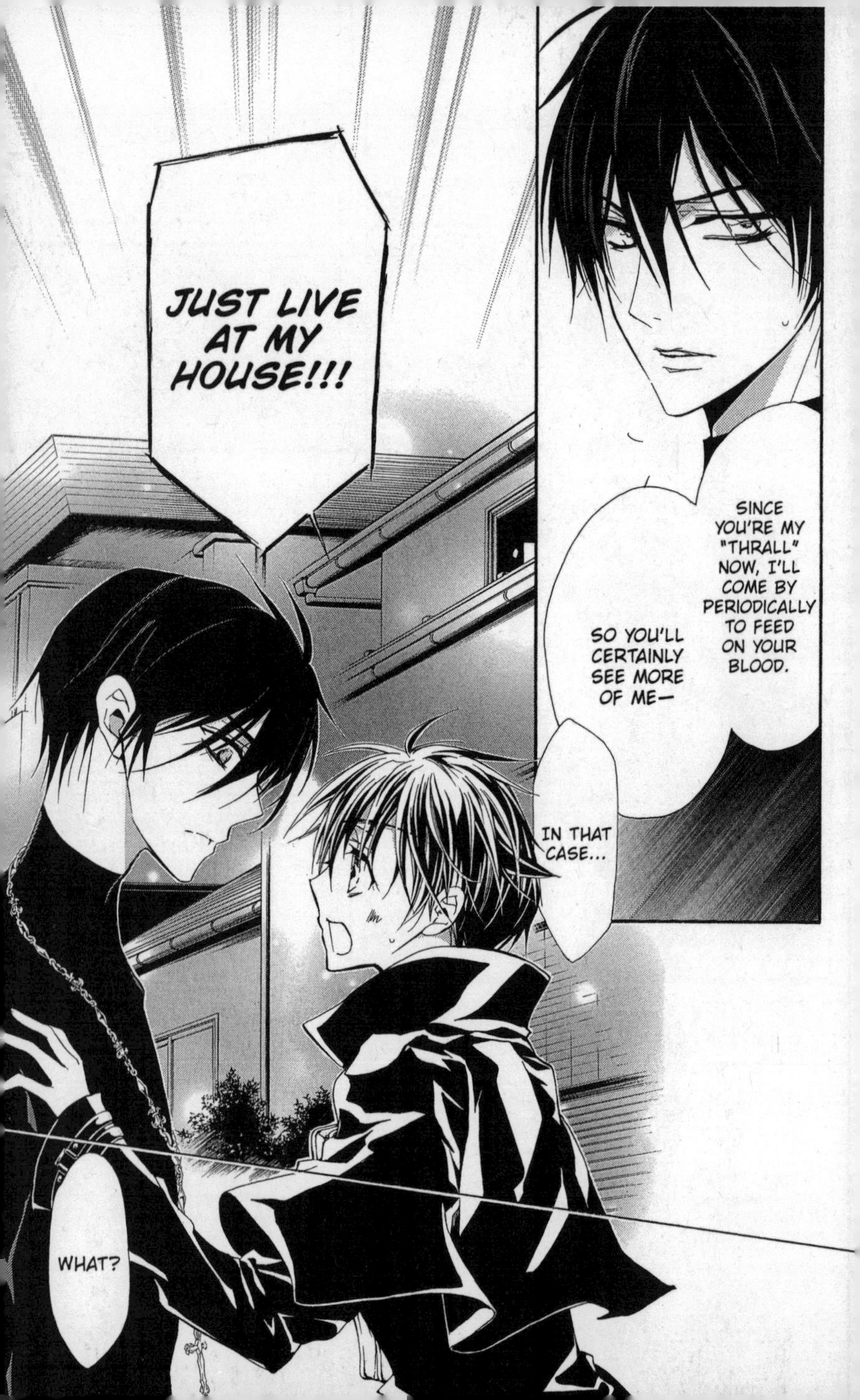
SINCE YOU'RE MY "THRALL" NOW, I'LL COME BY PERIODICALLY TO FEED ON YOUR BLOOD.
SO YOU'LL CERTAINLY SEE MORE OF ME—
IN THAT CASE...
JUST LIVE AT MY HOUSE!!!
WHAT?

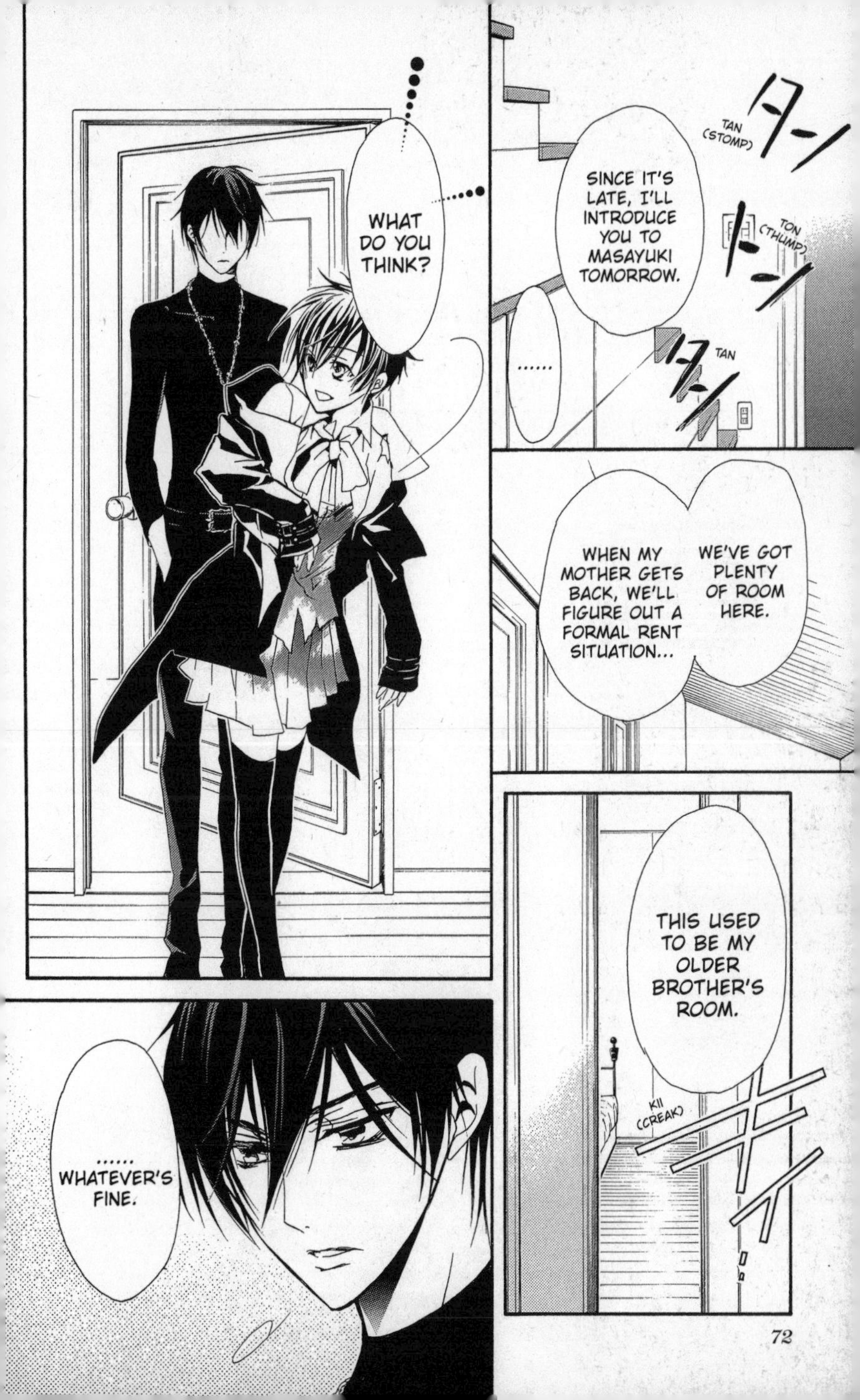
TAN (STOMP)
SINCE IT'S LATE, I'LL INTRODUCE YOU TO MASAYUKI TOMORROW.
TON (THUMP)
TAN
......
WE'VE GOT PLENTY OF ROOM HERE.
WHEN MY MOTHER GETS BACK, WE'LL FIGURE OUT A FORMAL RENT SITUATION...
THIS USED TO BE MY OLDER BROTHER'S ROOM.
KII (CREAK)
WHAT DO YOU THINK?
...... WHATEVER'S FINE.

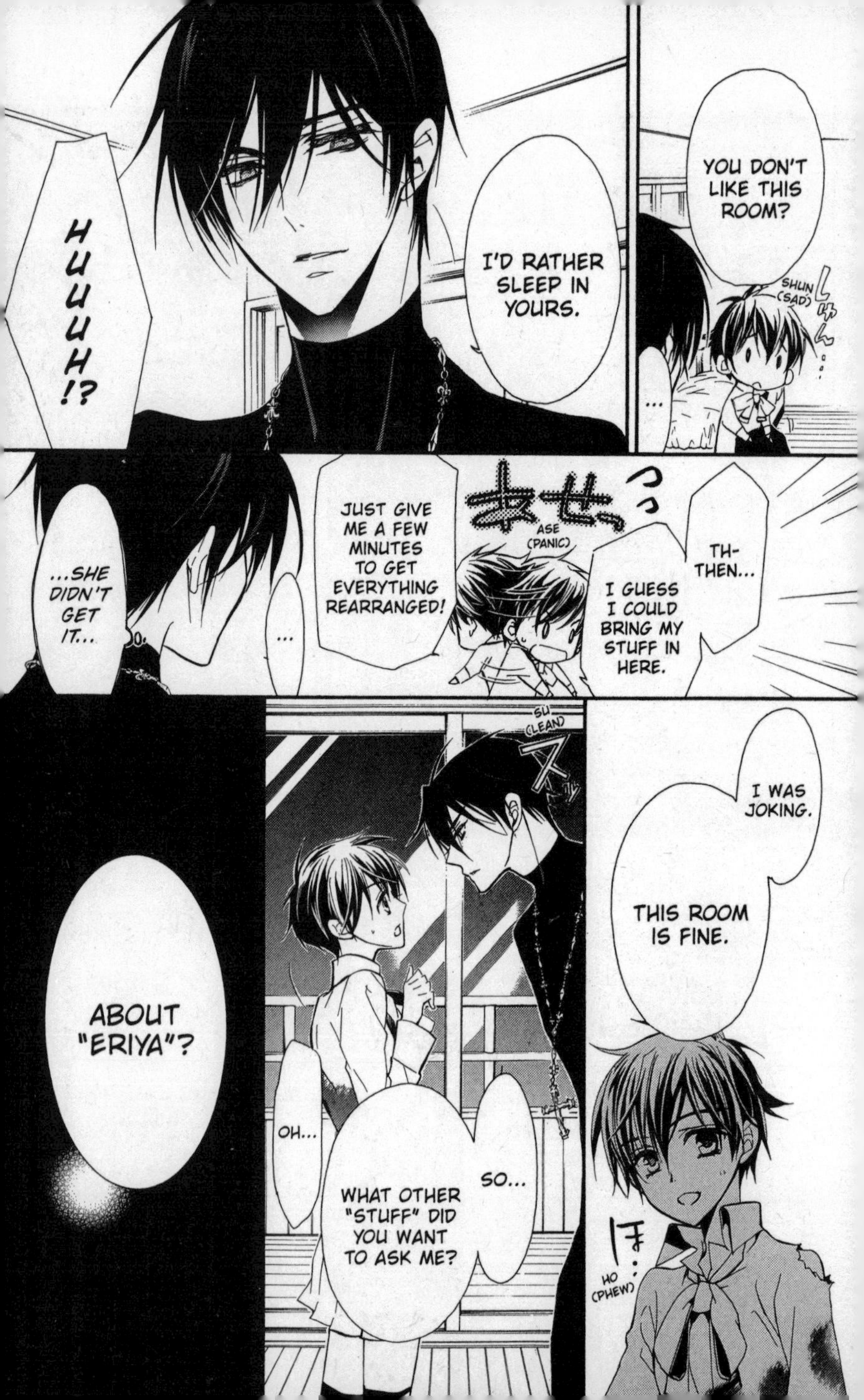
YOU DON'T LIKE THIS ROOM?
しゅん…
SHUN (SAD)
...
I'D RATHER SLEEP IN YOURS.
HUUUUH!?
TH- THEN...
I GUESS I COULD BRING MY STUFF IN HERE.
あせっ
ASE (PANIC)
JUST GIVE ME A FEW MINUTES TO GET EVERYTHING REARRANGED!
...
...SHE DIDN'T GET IT...
I WAS JOKING.
THIS ROOM IS FINE.
ほっ…
HO (PHEW)
スッ
SU (LEAN)
SO...
OH...
WHAT OTHER "STUFF" DID YOU WANT TO ASK ME?
ABOUT "ERIYA"?

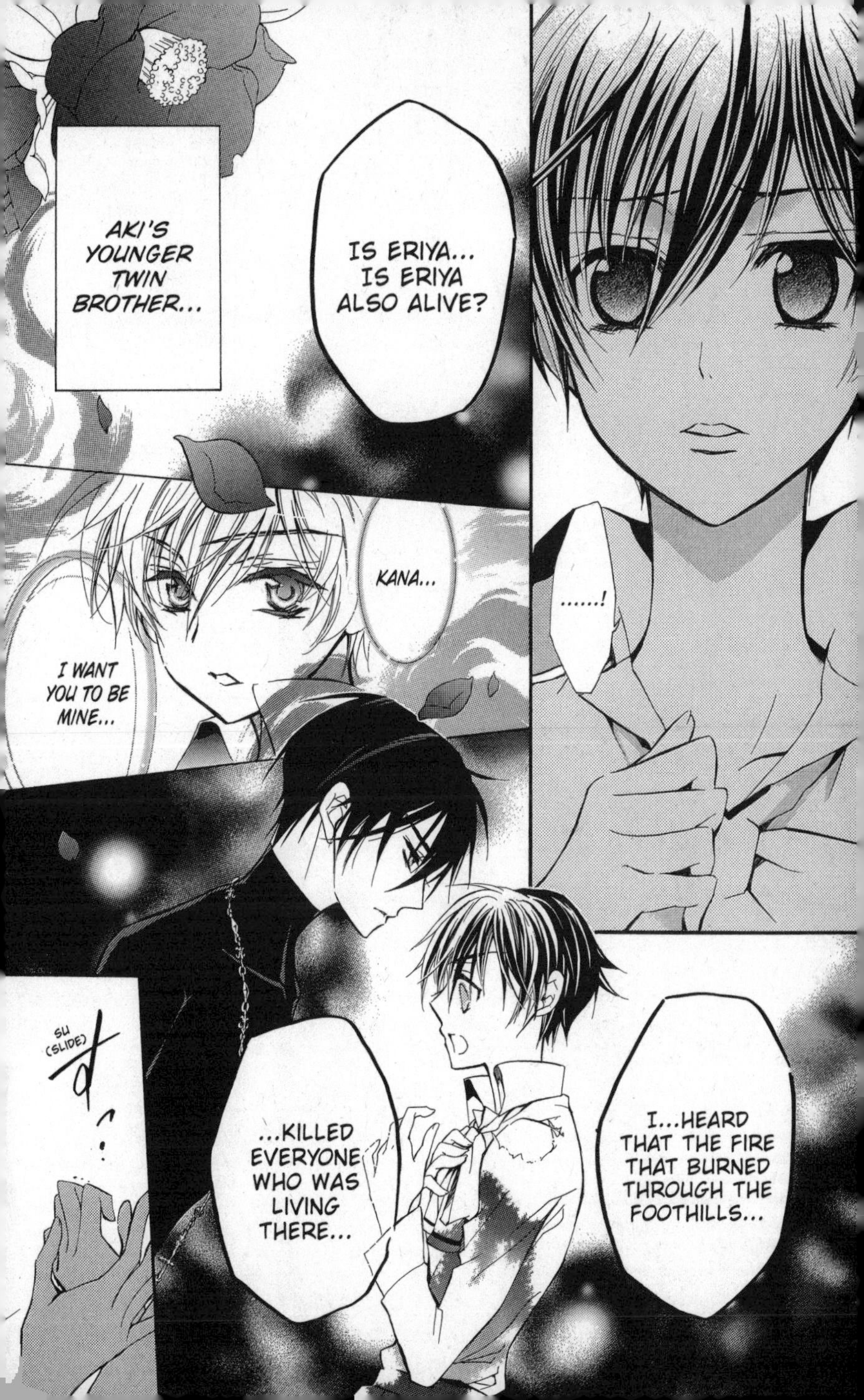
......!
IS ERIYA... IS ERIYA ALSO ALIVE?
AKI'S YOUNGER TWIN BROTHER...
KANA...
I WANT YOU TO BE MINE...
I...HEARD THAT THE FIRE THAT BURNED THROUGH THE FOOTHILLS...
...KILLED EVERYONE WHO WAS LIVING THERE...
SU (SLIDE)

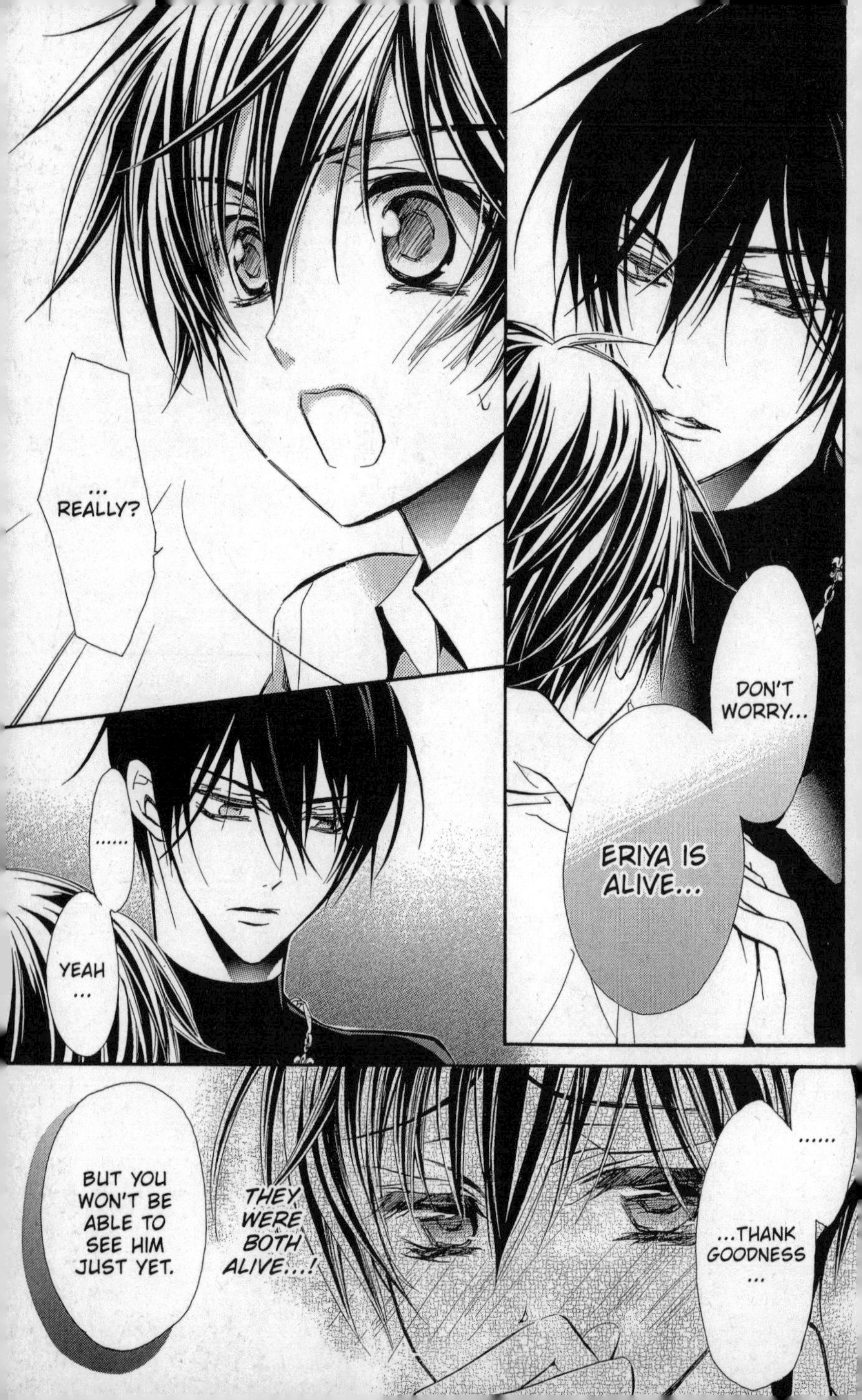
DON'T WORRY...
ERIYA IS ALIVE...
...REALLY?
......
YEAH...
......
...THANK GOODNESS...
THEY WERE BOTH ALIVE...!
BUT YOU WON'T BE ABLE TO SEE HIM JUST YET.

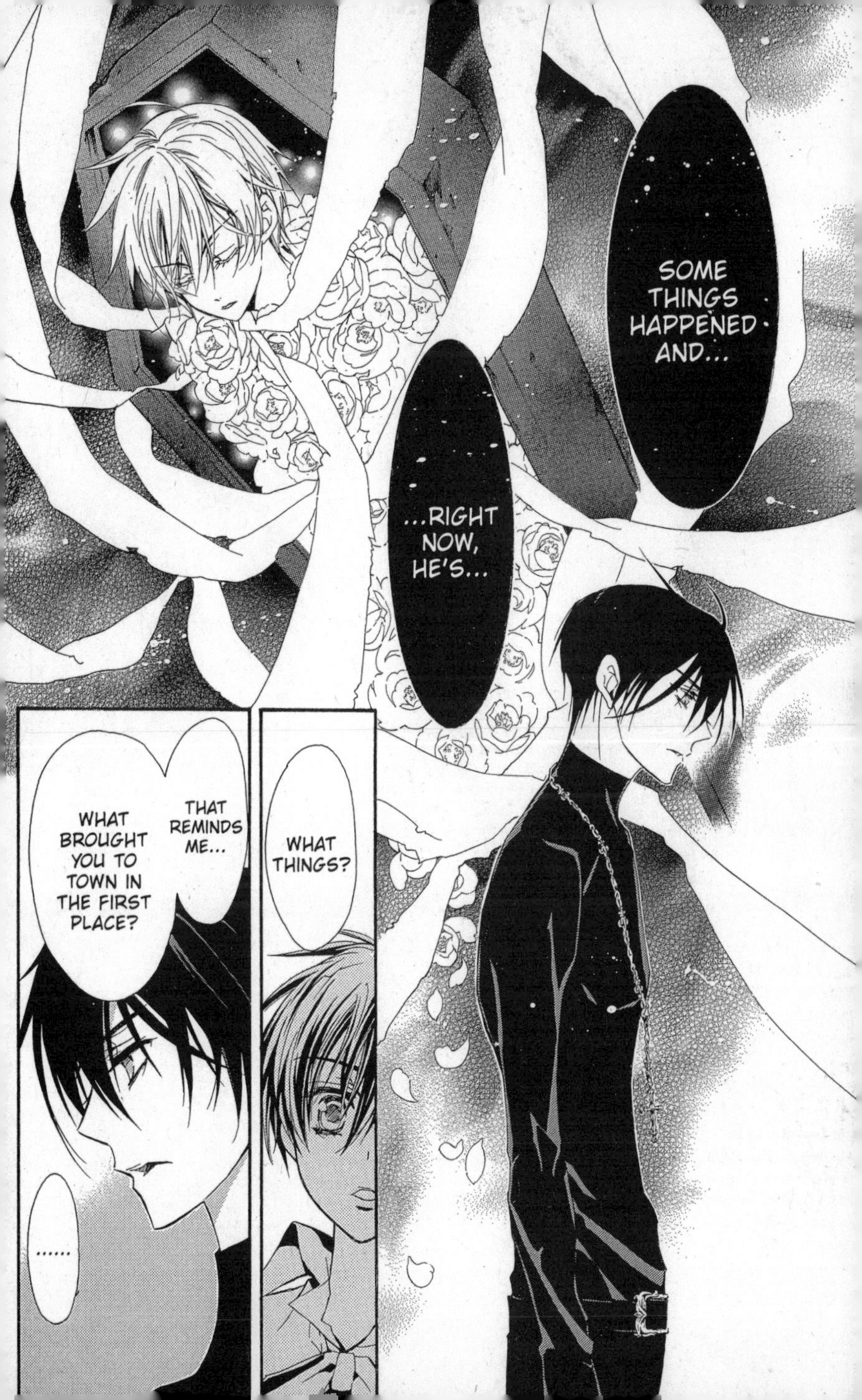
SOME THINGS HAPPENED AND...
...RIGHT NOW, HE'S...
WHAT THINGS?
THAT REMINDS ME...
WHAT BROUGHT YOU TO TOWN IN THE FIRST PLACE?
......

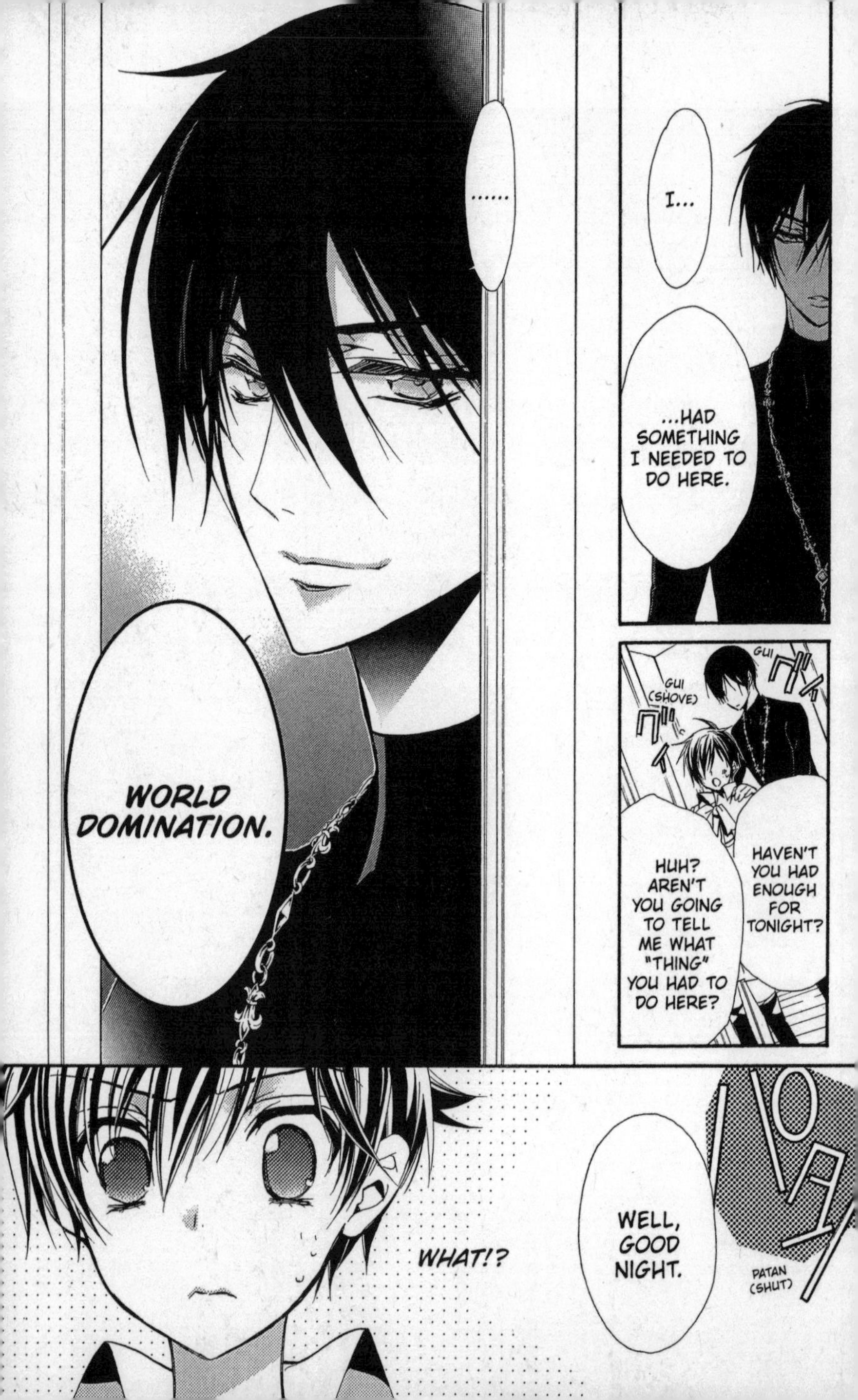
I...
...HAD SOMETHING I NEEDED TO DO HERE.
GUI
GUI (SHOVE)
HAVEN'T YOU HAD ENOUGH FOR TONIGHT?
HUH? AREN'T YOU GOING TO TELL ME WHAT "THING" YOU HAD TO DO HERE?
......
WORLD DOMINATION.
PATAN (SHUT)
WELL, GOOD NIGHT.
WHAT!?

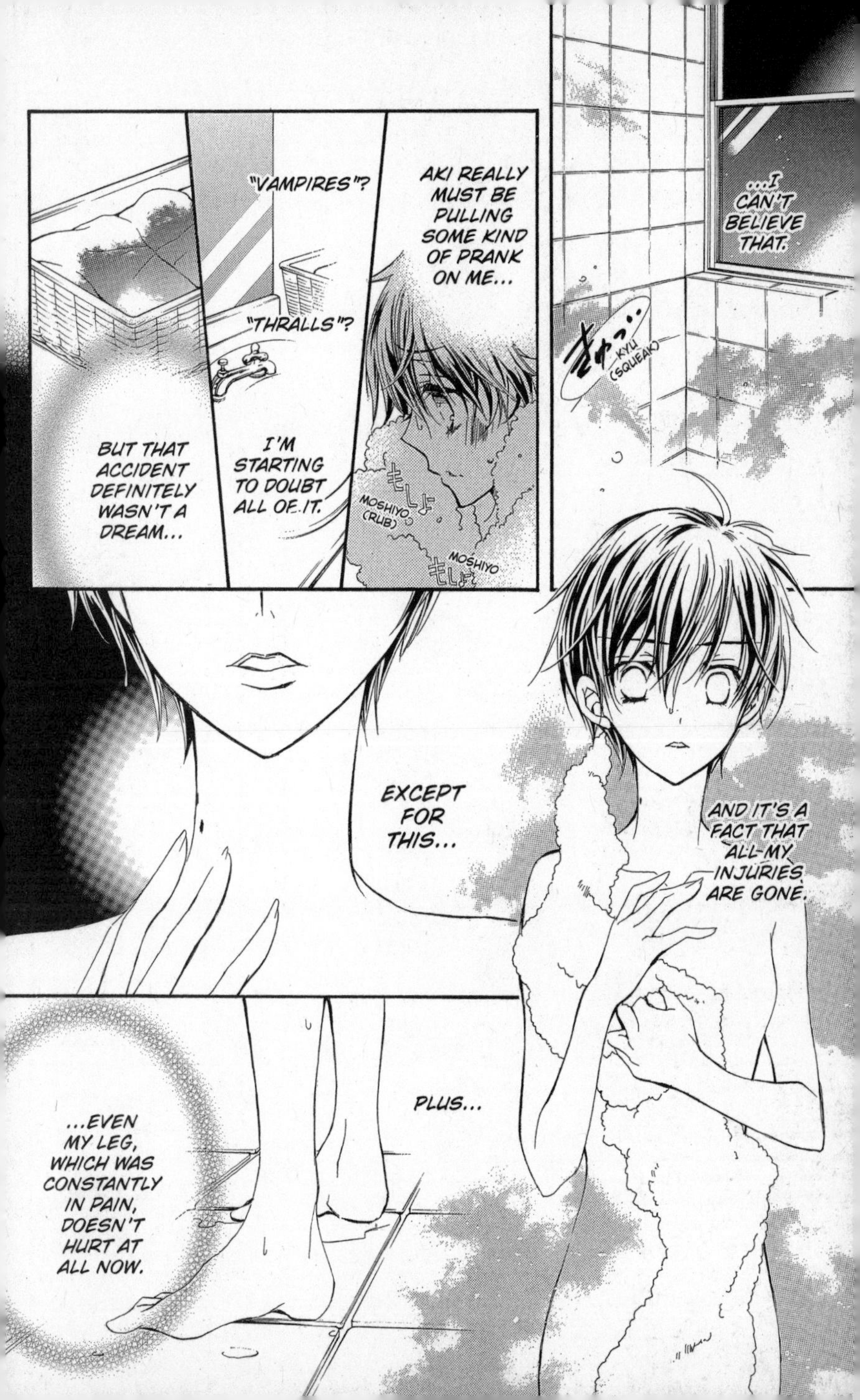
...I CAN'T BELIEVE THAT.
KYU (SQUEAK)
AKI REALLY MUST BE PULLING SOME KIND OF PRANK ON ME...
MOSHIYO (RUB)
MOSHIYO
"VAMPIRES"?
"THRALLS"?
I'M STARTING TO DOUBT ALL OF IT.
BUT THAT ACCIDENT DEFINITELY WASN'T A DREAM...
AND IT'S A FACT THAT ALL MY INJURIES ARE GONE.
EXCEPT FOR THIS...
PLUS...
...EVEN MY LEG, WHICH WAS CONSTANTLY IN PAIN, DOESN'T HURT AT ALL NOW.

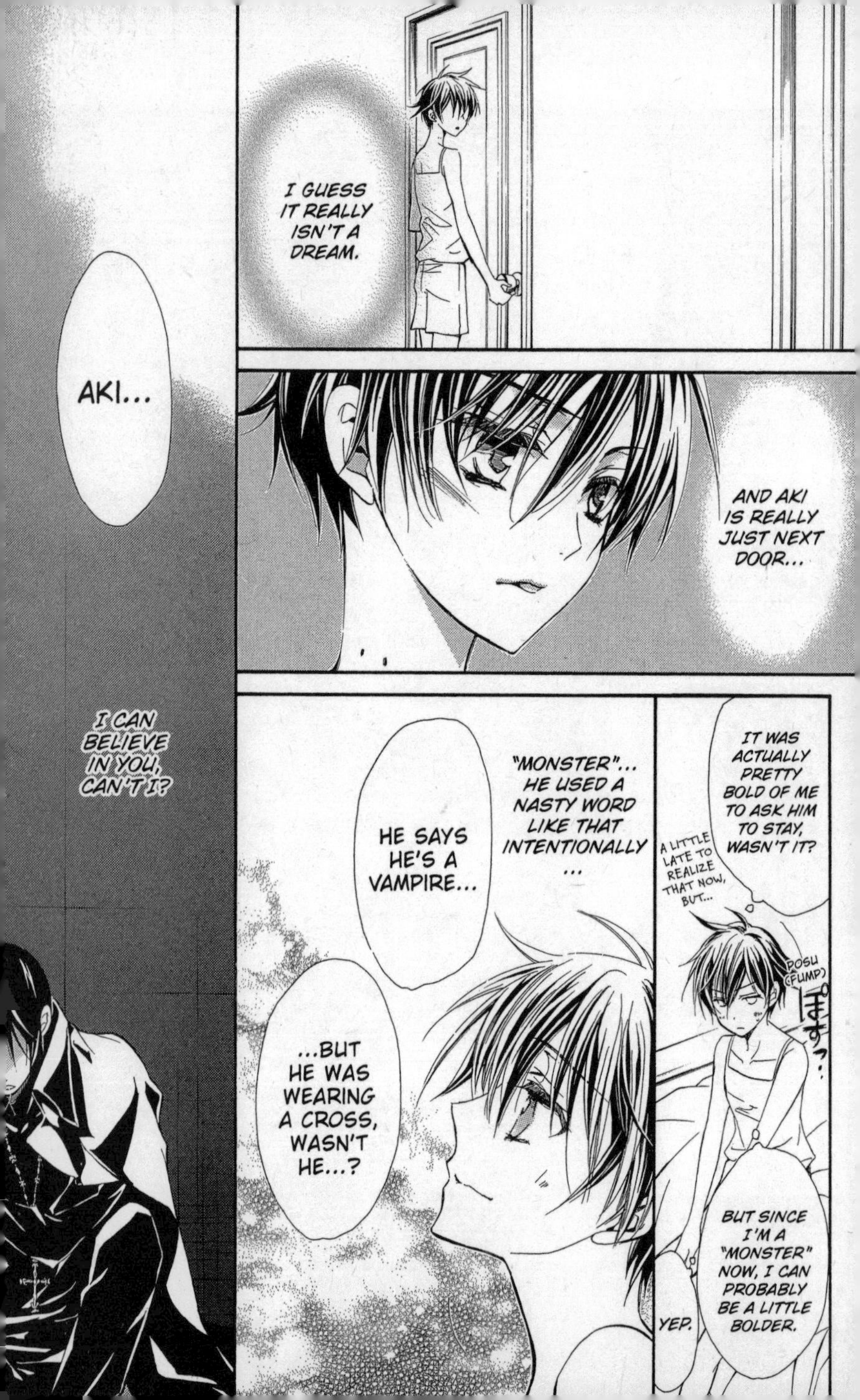
I GUESS IT REALLY ISN'T A DREAM.
AND AKI IS REALLY JUST NEXT DOOR...
IT WAS ACTUALLY PRETTY BOLD OF ME TO ASK HIM TO STAY, WASN'T IT?
A LITTLE LATE TO REALIZE THAT NOW, BUT...
POSU (FLUMP)
BUT SINCE I'M A "MONSTER" NOW, I CAN PROBABLY BE A LITTLE BOLDER.
YEP.
"MONSTER"... HE USED A NASTY WORD LIKE THAT INTENTIONALLY...
HE SAYS HE'S A VAMPIRE...
...BUT HE WAS WEARING A CROSS, WASN'T HE...?
AKI...
I CAN BELIEVE IN YOU, CAN'T I?

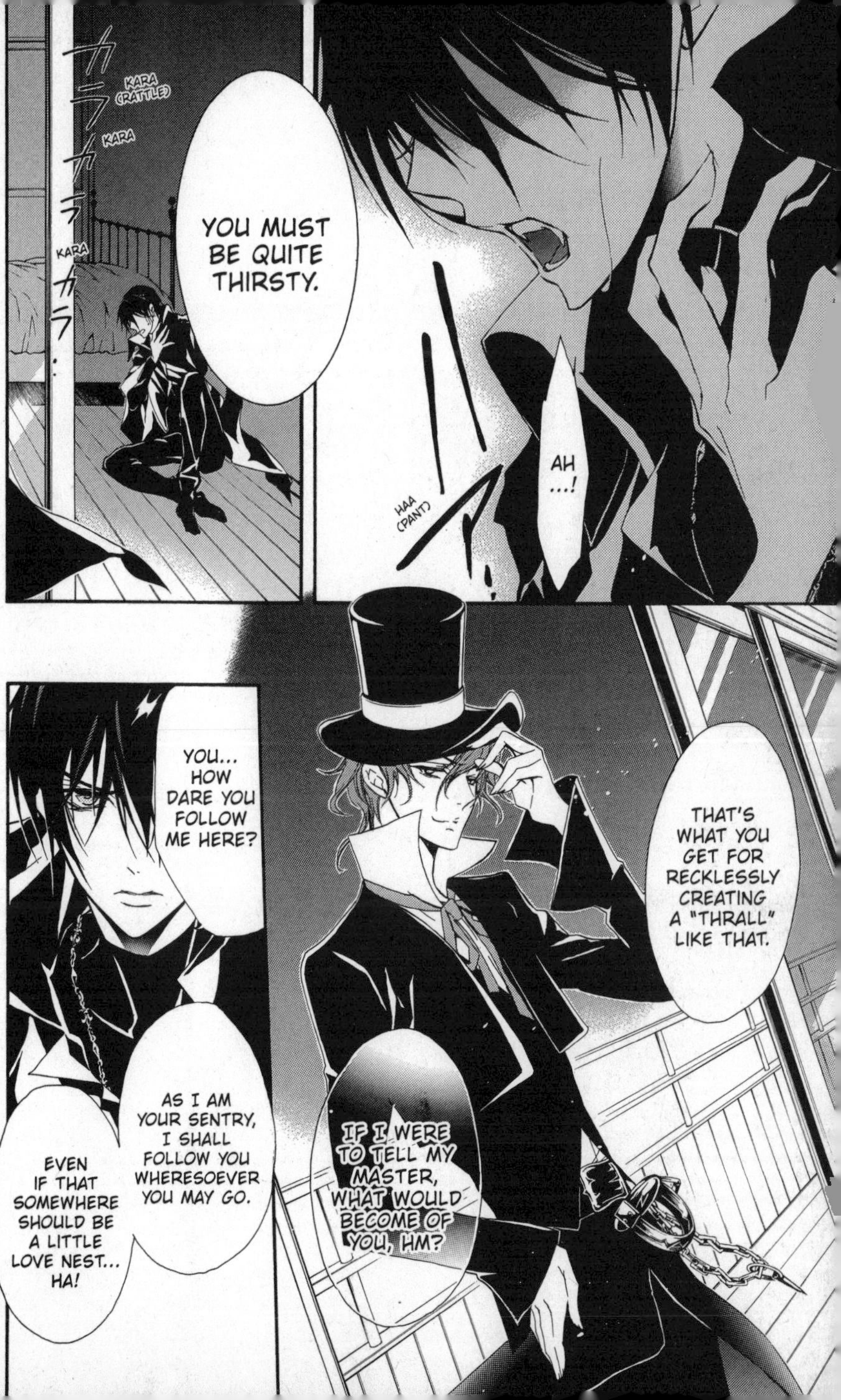
AH ...!
HAA (PANT)
KARA (RATTLE)
KARA
KARA
YOU MUST BE QUITE THIRSTY.
THAT'S WHAT YOU GET FOR RECKLESSLY CREATING A "THRALL" LIKE THAT.
IF I WERE TO TELL MY MASTER, WHAT WOULD BECOME OF YOU, HM?
YOU... HOW DARE YOU FOLLOW ME HERE?
AS I AM YOUR SENTRY, I SHALL FOLLOW YOU WHERESOEVER YOU MAY GO.
EVEN IF THAT SOMEWHERE SHOULD BE A LITTLE LOVE NEST... HA!

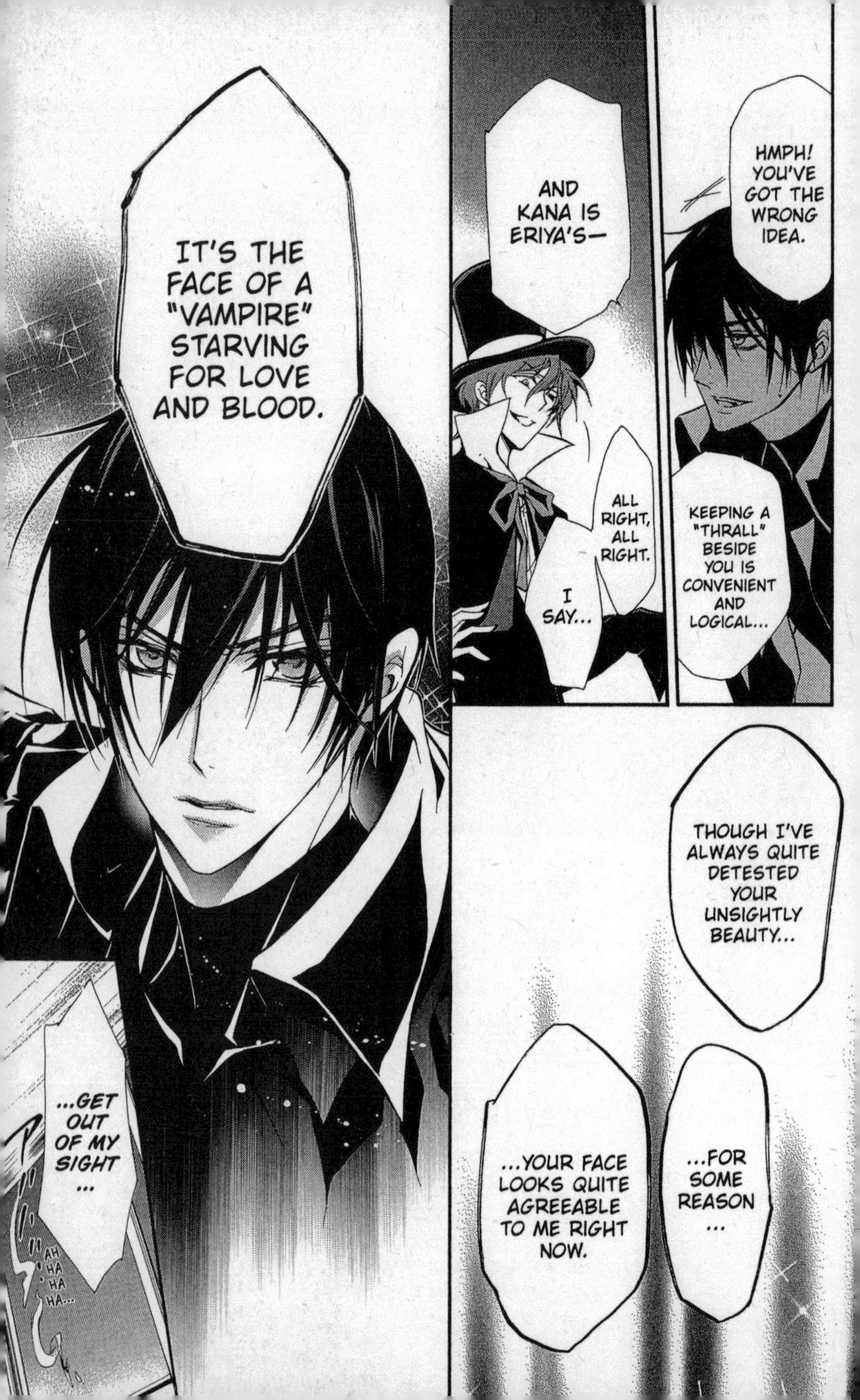
HMPH! YOU'VE GOT THE WRONG IDEA.
KEEPING A "THRALL" BESIDE YOU IS CONVENIENT AND LOGICAL...
AND KANA IS ERIYA'S—
ALL RIGHT, ALL RIGHT.
I SAY...
THOUGH I'VE ALWAYS QUITE DETESTED YOUR UNSIGHTLY BEAUTY...
...FOR SOME REASON...
...YOUR FACE LOOKS QUITE AGREEABLE TO ME RIGHT NOW.
IT'S THE FACE OF A "VAMPIRE" STARVING FOR LOVE AND BLOOD.
...GET OUT OF MY SIGHT...
AH HA HA HA...

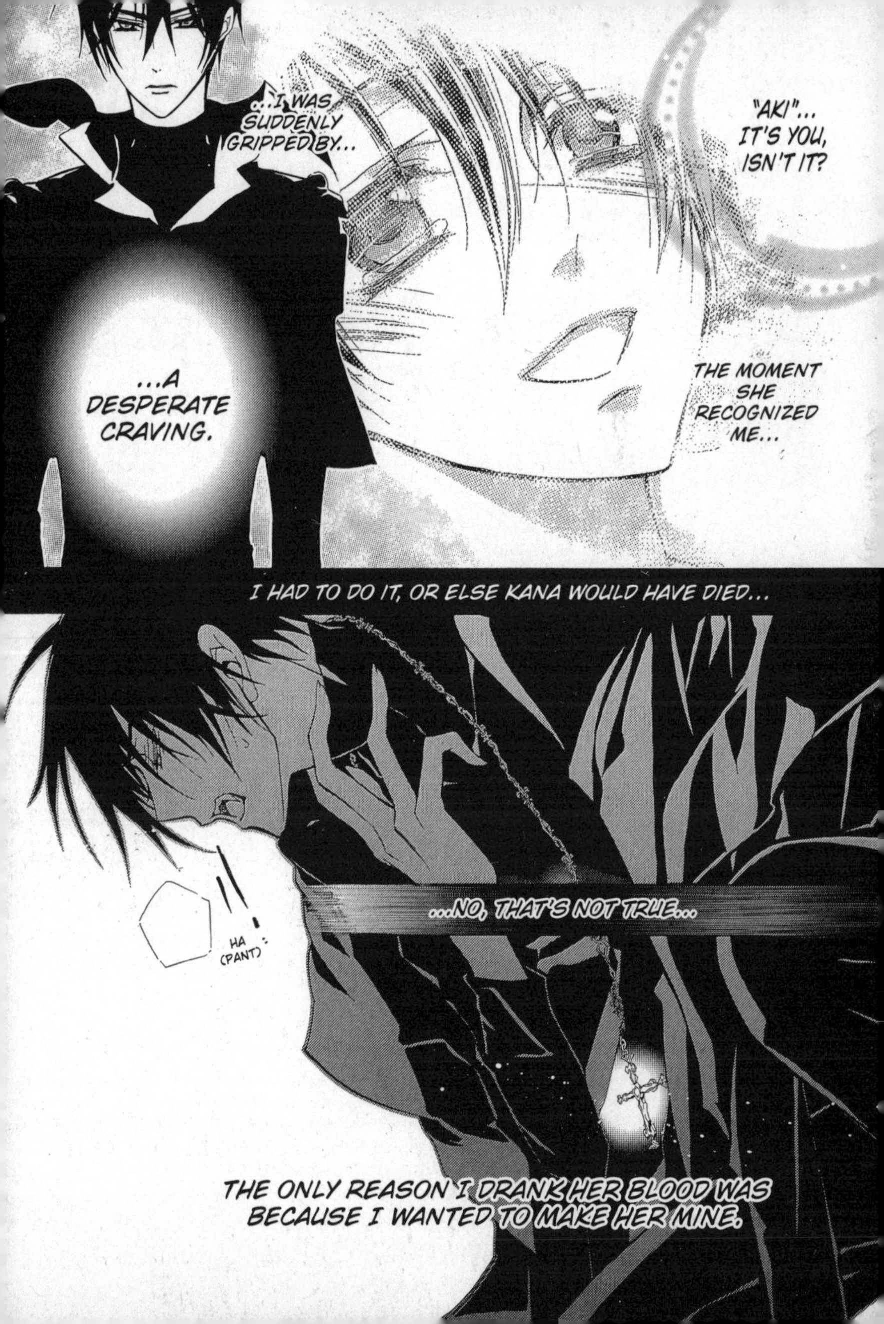
"AKI"... IT'S YOU, ISN'T IT?
THE MOMENT SHE RECOGNIZED ME...
...I WAS SUDDENLY GRIPPED BY...
...A DESPERATE CRAVING.
I HAD TO DO IT, OR ELSE KANA WOULD HAVE DIED...
HA (PANT)
...NO, THAT'S NOT TRUE...
THE ONLY REASON I DRANK HER BLOOD WAS BECAUSE I WANTED TO MAKE HER MINE.

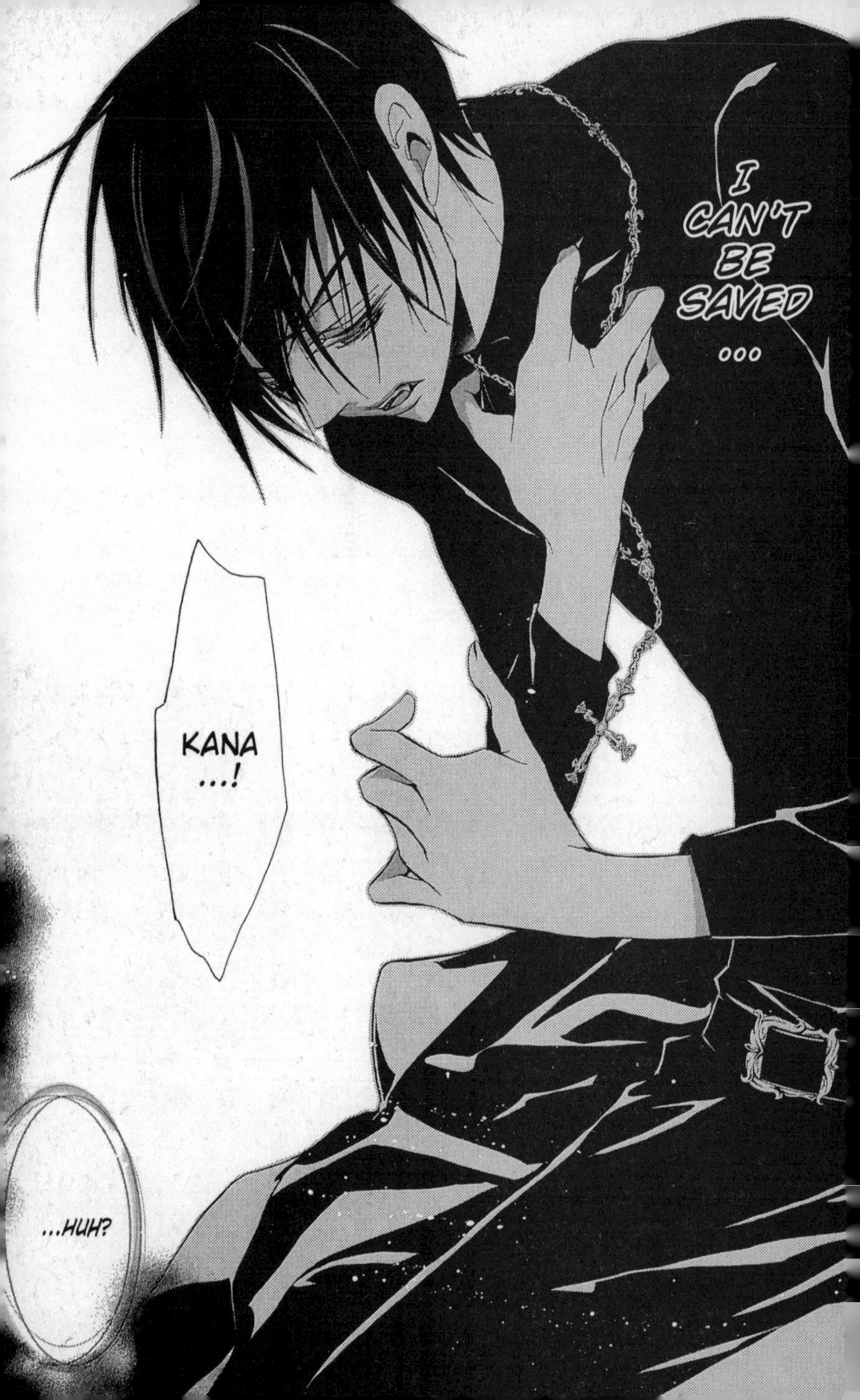
I CAN'T BE SAVED...
KANA...!
...HUH?

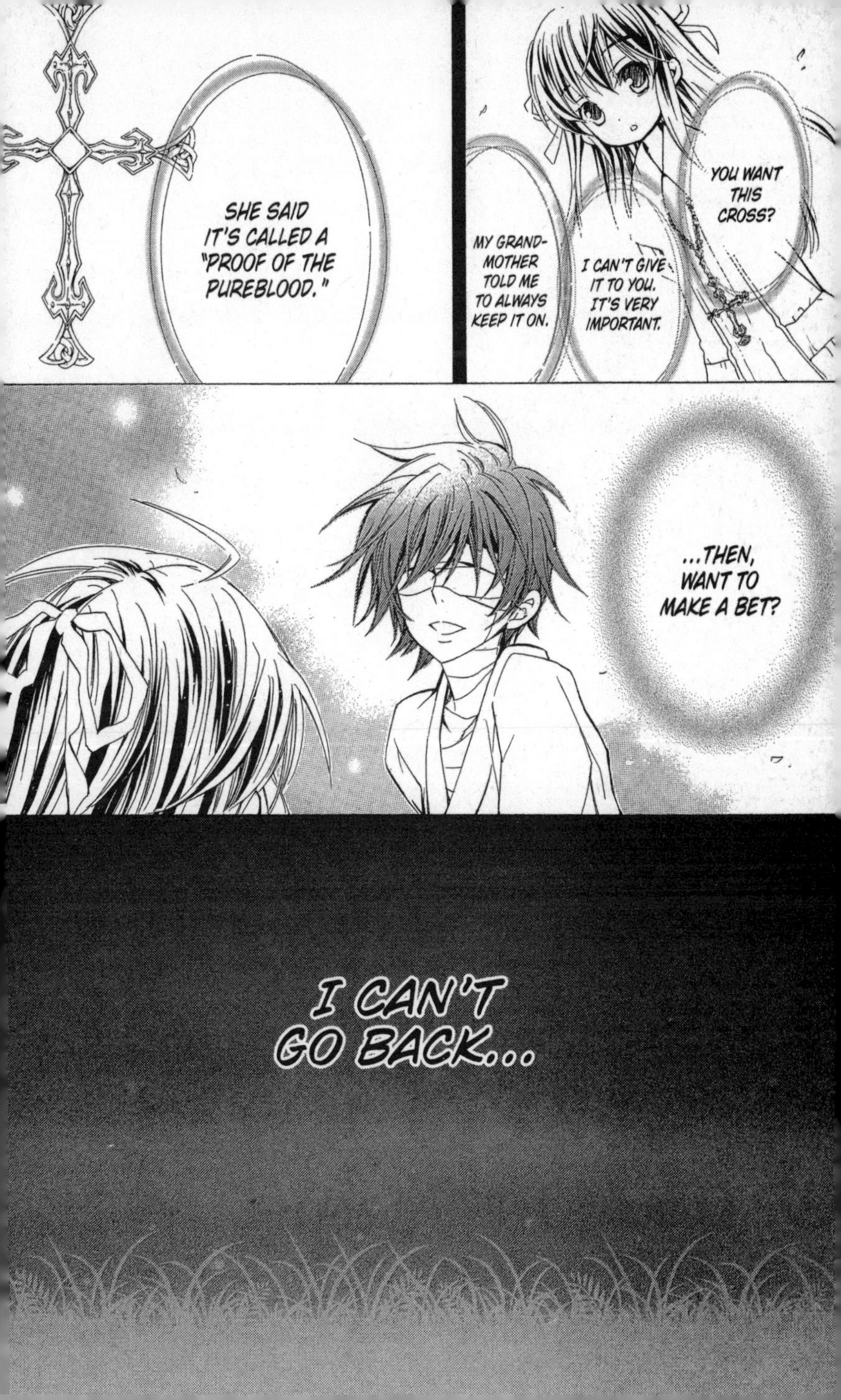
YOU WANT THIS CROSS?
I CAN'T GIVE IT TO YOU. IT'S VERY IMPORTANT.
MY GRAND-MOTHER TOLD ME TO ALWAYS KEEP IT ON.
SHE SAID IT'S CALLED A "PROOF OF THE PUREBLOOD."
...THEN, WANT TO MAKE A BET?
I CAN'T GO BACK...

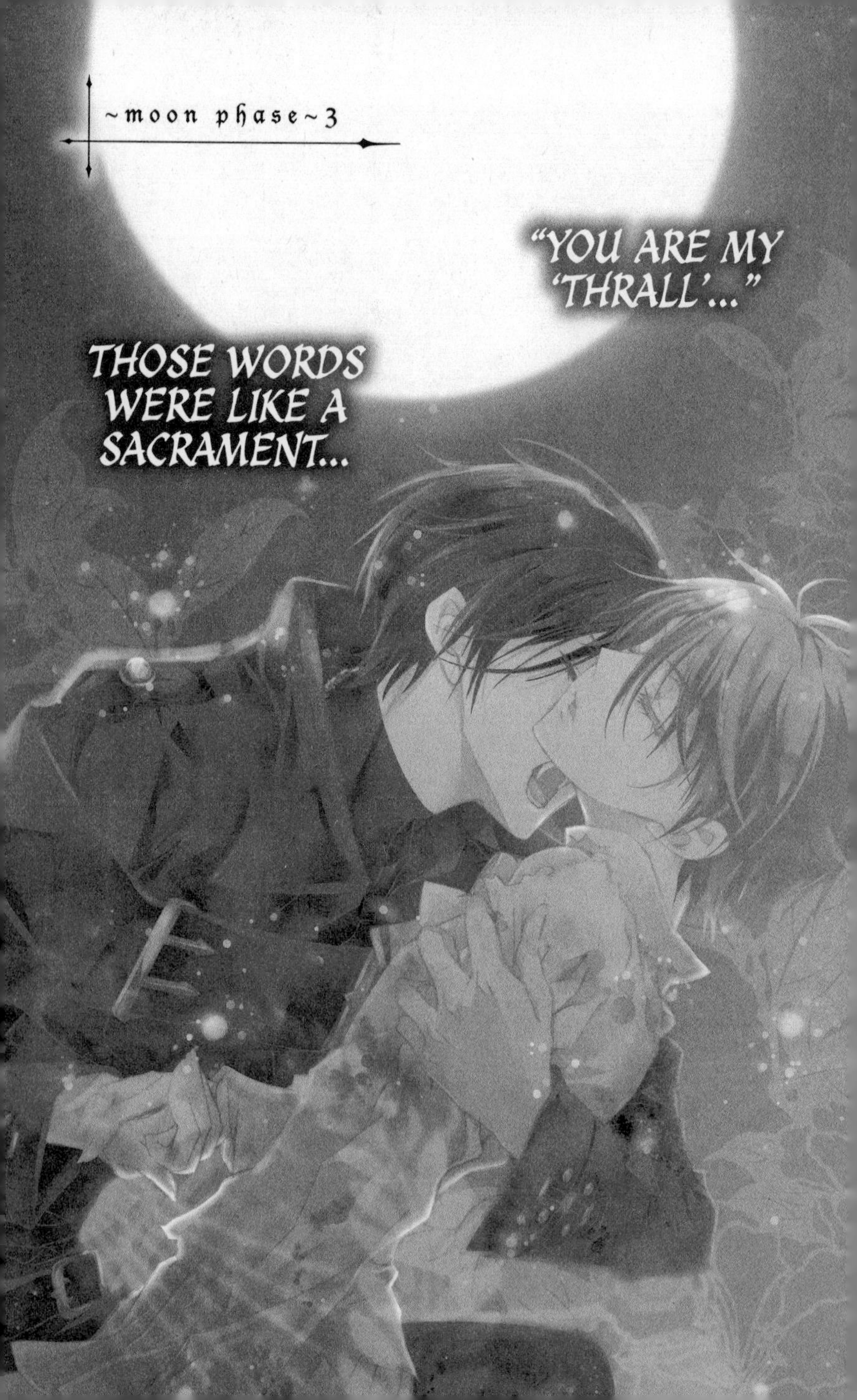
~moon phase~3
"YOU ARE MY 'THRALL'..."
THOSE WORDS WERE LIKE A SACRAMENT...

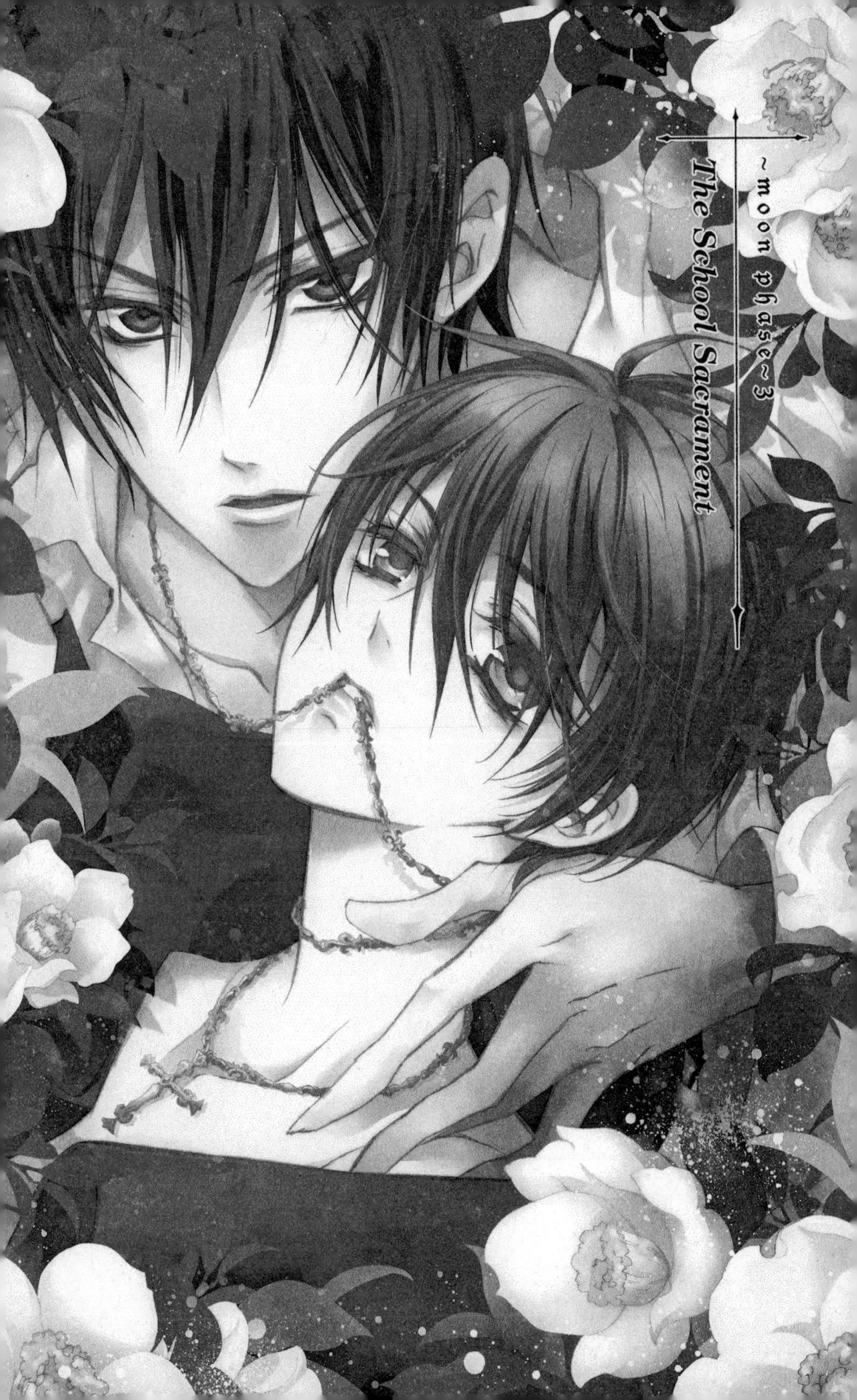
~moon phase~3
The School Sacrament

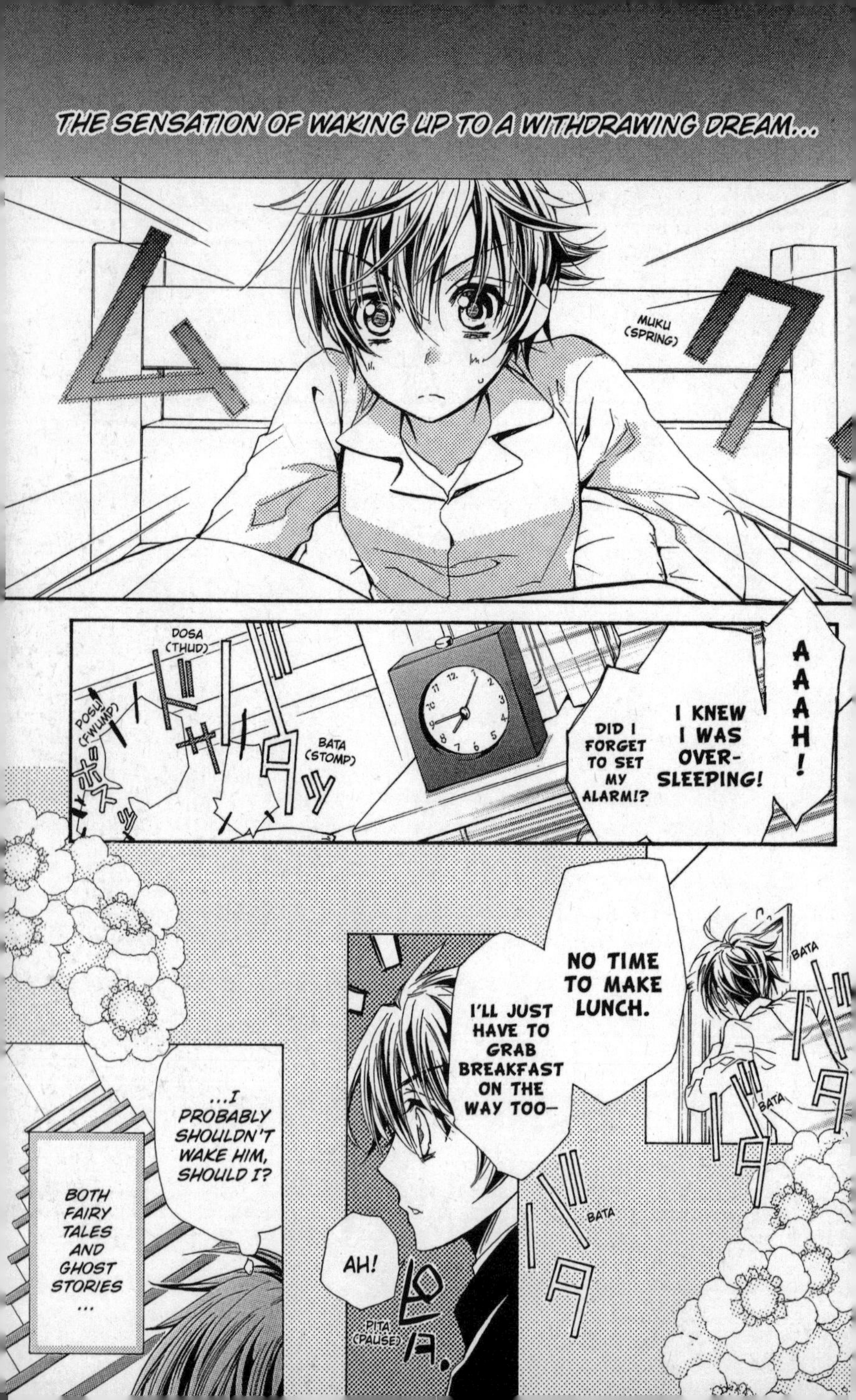
THE SENSATION OF WAKING UP TO A WITHDRAWING DREAM...
MUKU (SPRING)
AAAH!
I KNEW I WAS OVER-SLEEPING!
DID I FORGET TO SET MY ALARM!?
BATA (STOMP)
DOSA (THUD)
POSU (FWUMP)
BATA
BATA
NO TIME TO MAKE LUNCH.
I'LL JUST HAVE TO GRAB BREAKFAST ON THE WAY TOO—
BATA
AH!
PITA (PAUSE)
...I PROBABLY SHOULDN'T WAKE HIM, SHOULD I?
BOTH FAIRY TALES AND GHOST STORIES ...

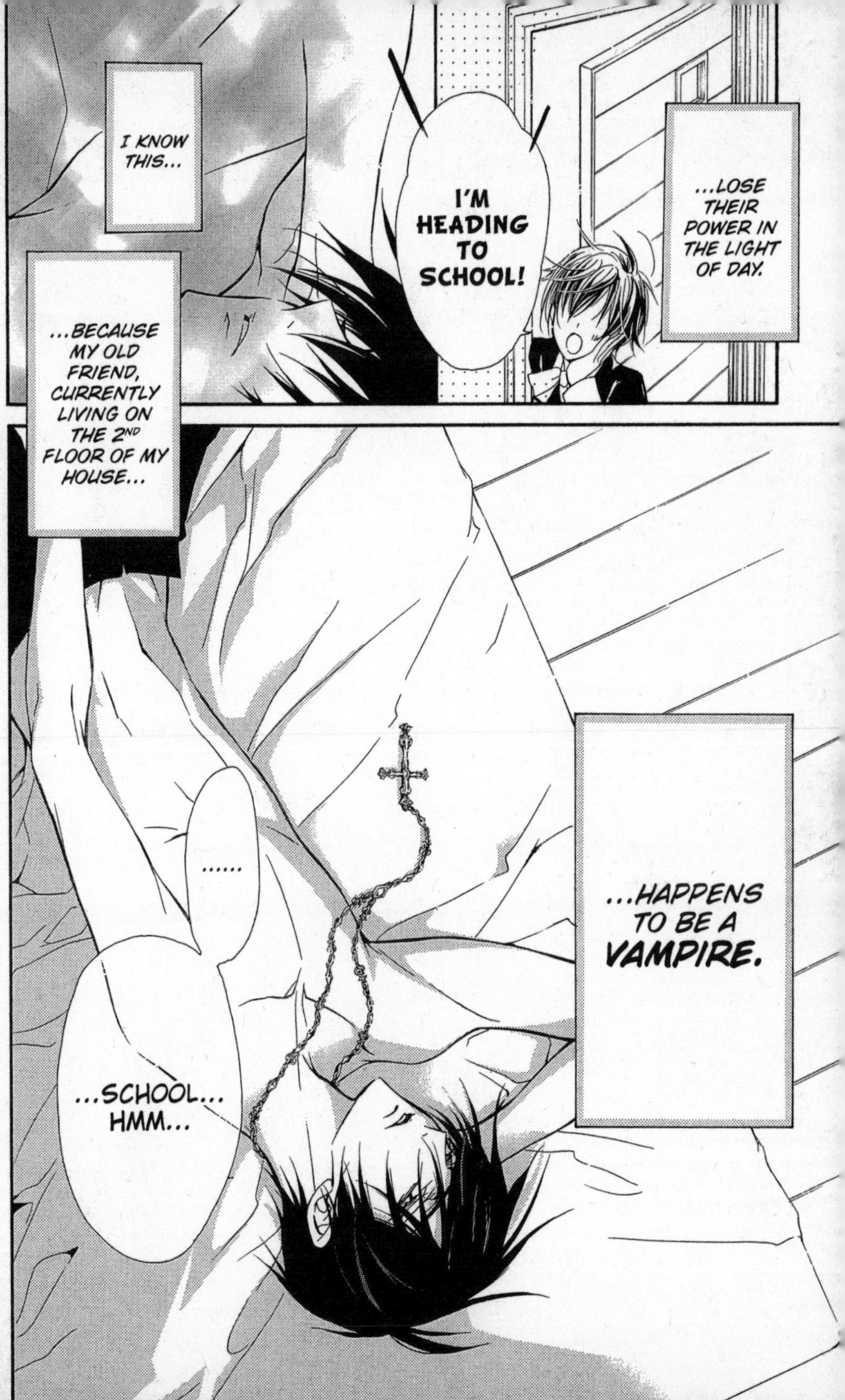
...LOSE THEIR POWER IN THE LIGHT OF DAY.
I'M HEADING TO SCHOOL!
I KNOW THIS...
...BECAUSE MY OLD FRIEND, CURRENTLY LIVING ON THE 2ND FLOOR OF MY HOUSE...
...HAPPENS TO BE A VAMPIRE.
......
...SCHOOL... HMM...

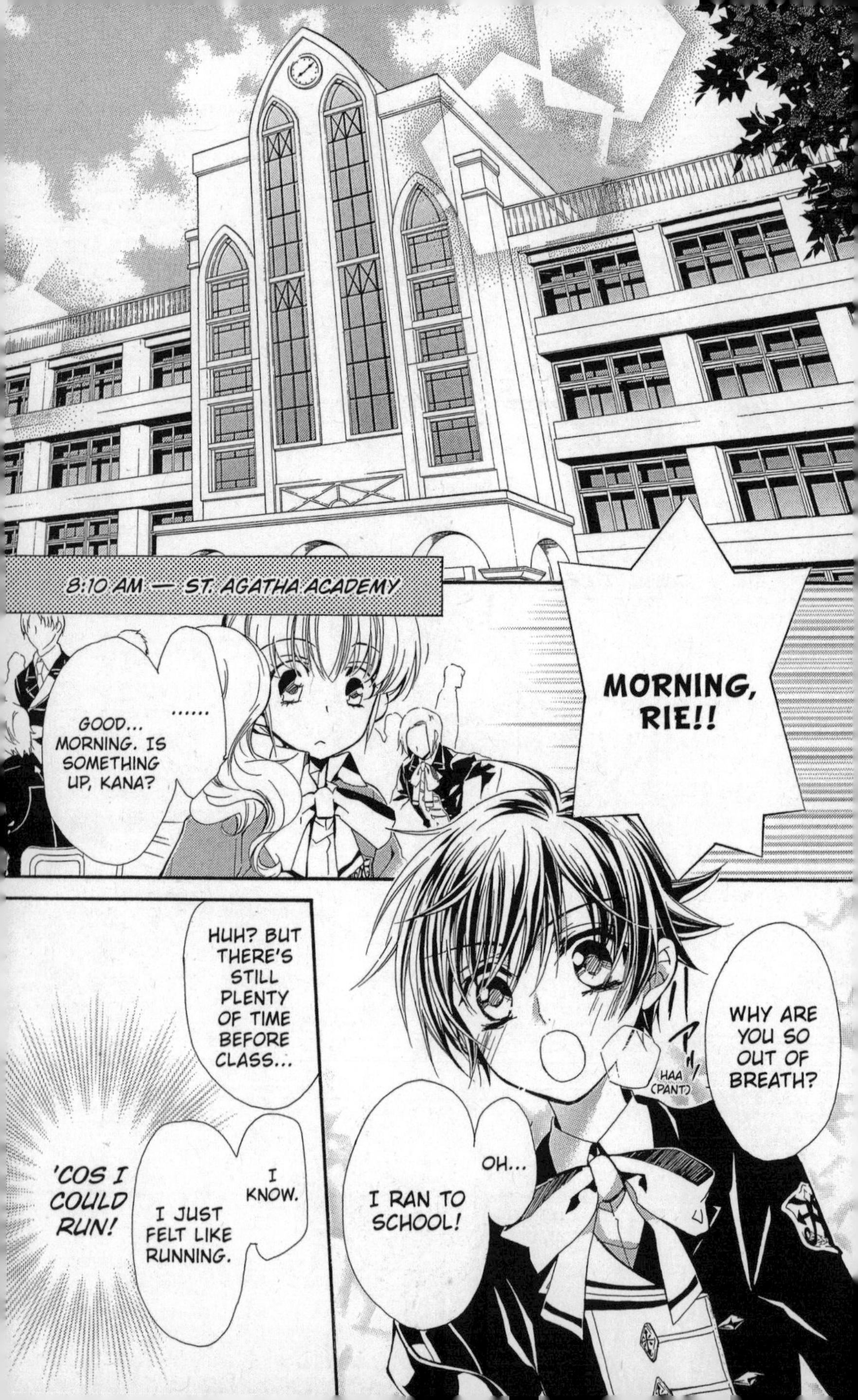
8:10 AM — ST. AGATHA ACADEMY
MORNING, RIE!!
......
GOOD... MORNING. IS SOMETHING UP, KANA?
WHY ARE YOU SO OUT OF BREATH?
HAA (PANT)
OH...
I RAN TO SCHOOL!
HUH? BUT THERE'S STILL PLENTY OF TIME BEFORE CLASS...
I KNOW.
I JUST FELT LIKE RUNNING.
'COS I COULD RUN!

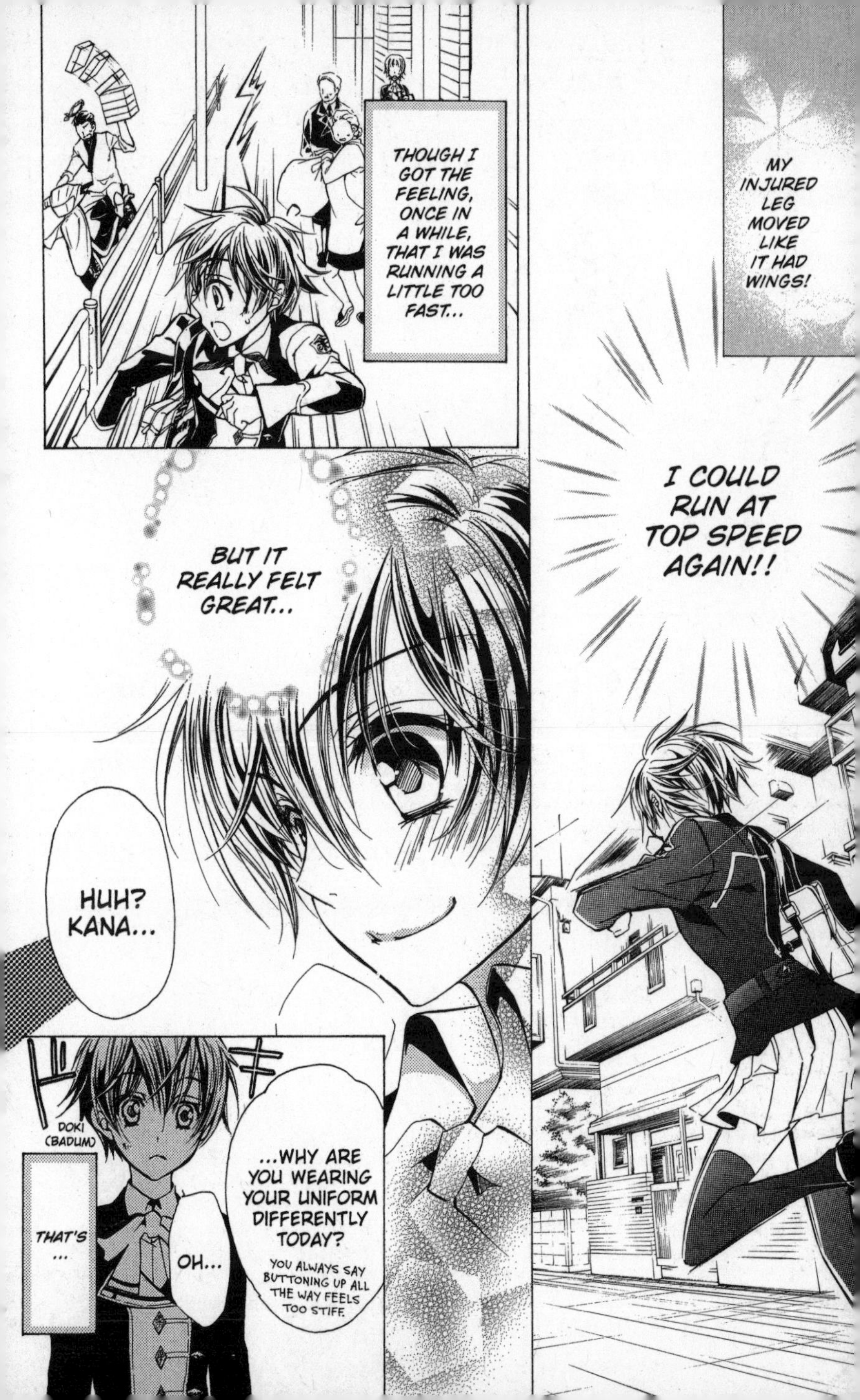
MY INJURED LEG MOVED LIKE IT HAD WINGS!
I COULD RUN AT TOP SPEED AGAIN!!
THOUGH I GOT THE FEELING, ONCE IN A WHILE, THAT I WAS RUNNING A LITTLE TOO FAST...
BUT IT REALLY FELT GREAT...
HUH? KANA...
...WHY ARE YOU WEARING YOUR UNIFORM DIFFERENTLY TODAY?
YOU ALWAYS SAY BUTTONING UP ALL THE WAY FEELS TOO STIFF.
DOKI (BADUM)
OH...
THAT'S ...

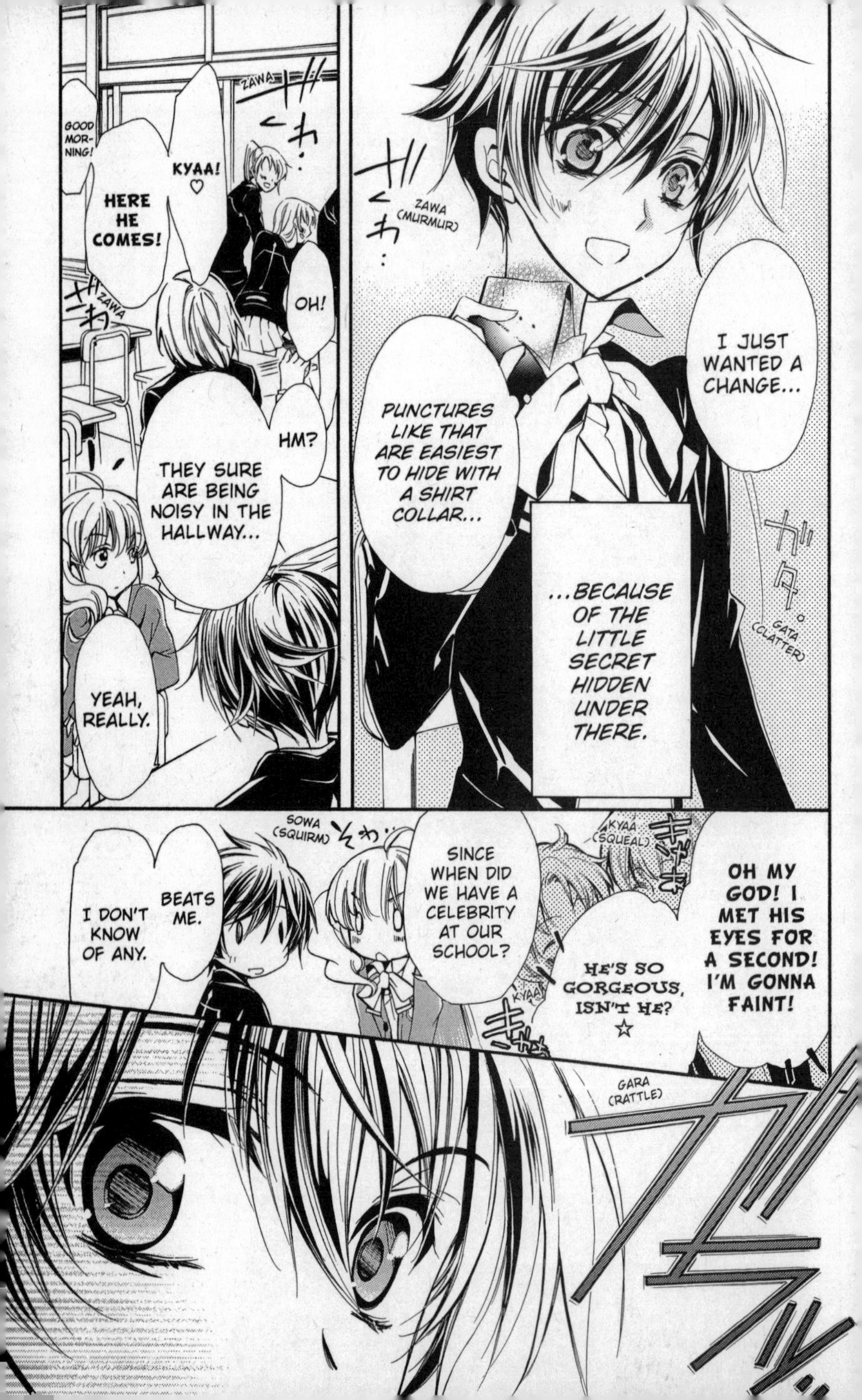
ZAWA (MURMUR)
I JUST WANTED A CHANGE...
PUNCTURES LIKE THAT ARE EASIEST TO HIDE WITH A SHIRT COLLAR...
...BECAUSE OF THE LITTLE SECRET HIDDEN UNDER THERE.
GATA (CLATTER)
ZAWA
GOOD MORNING!
KYAA! ♡
HERE HE COMES!
ZAWA
OH!
HM?
THEY SURE ARE BEING NOISY IN THE HALLWAY...
YEAH, REALLY.
KYAA (SQUEAL)
OH MY GOD! I MET HIS EYES FOR A SECOND! I'M GONNA FAINT!
HE'S SO GORGEOUS, ISN'T HE? ☆
KYAA
SINCE WHEN DID WE HAVE A CELEBRITY AT OUR SCHOOL?
SOWA (SQUIRM)
BEATS ME.
I DON'T KNOW OF ANY.
GARA (RATTLE)

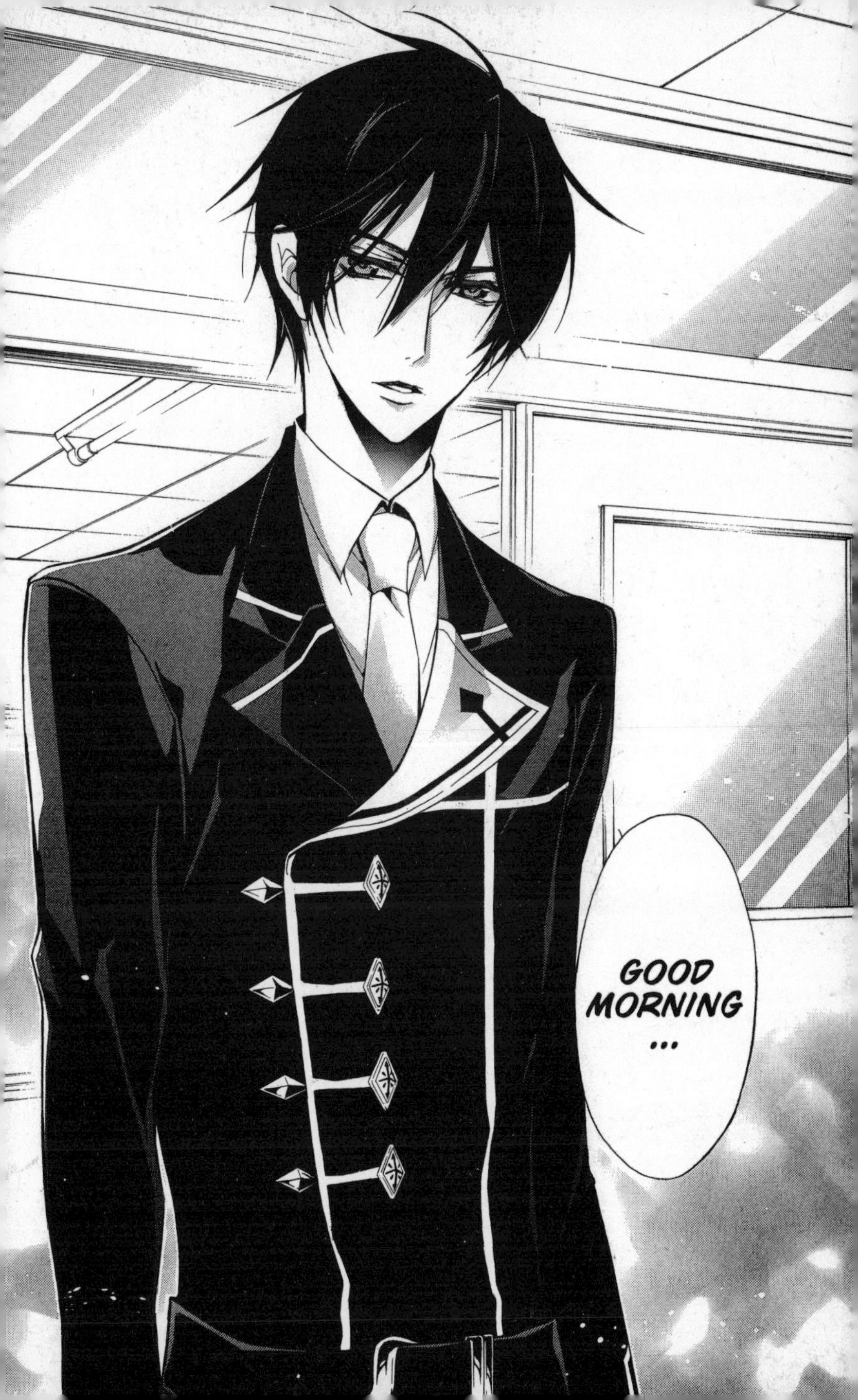
GOOD MORNING ...

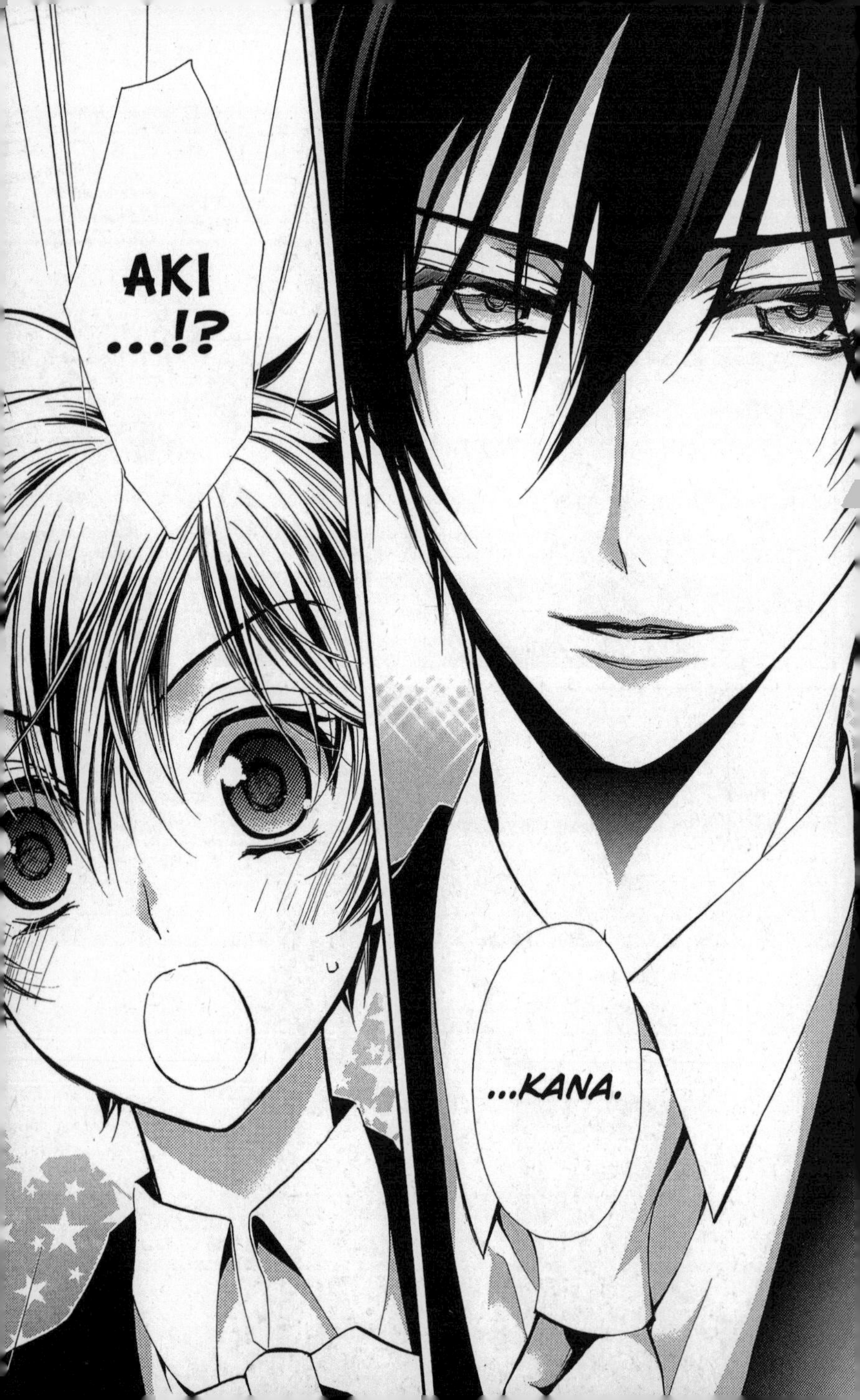
...KANA.
AKI ...!?

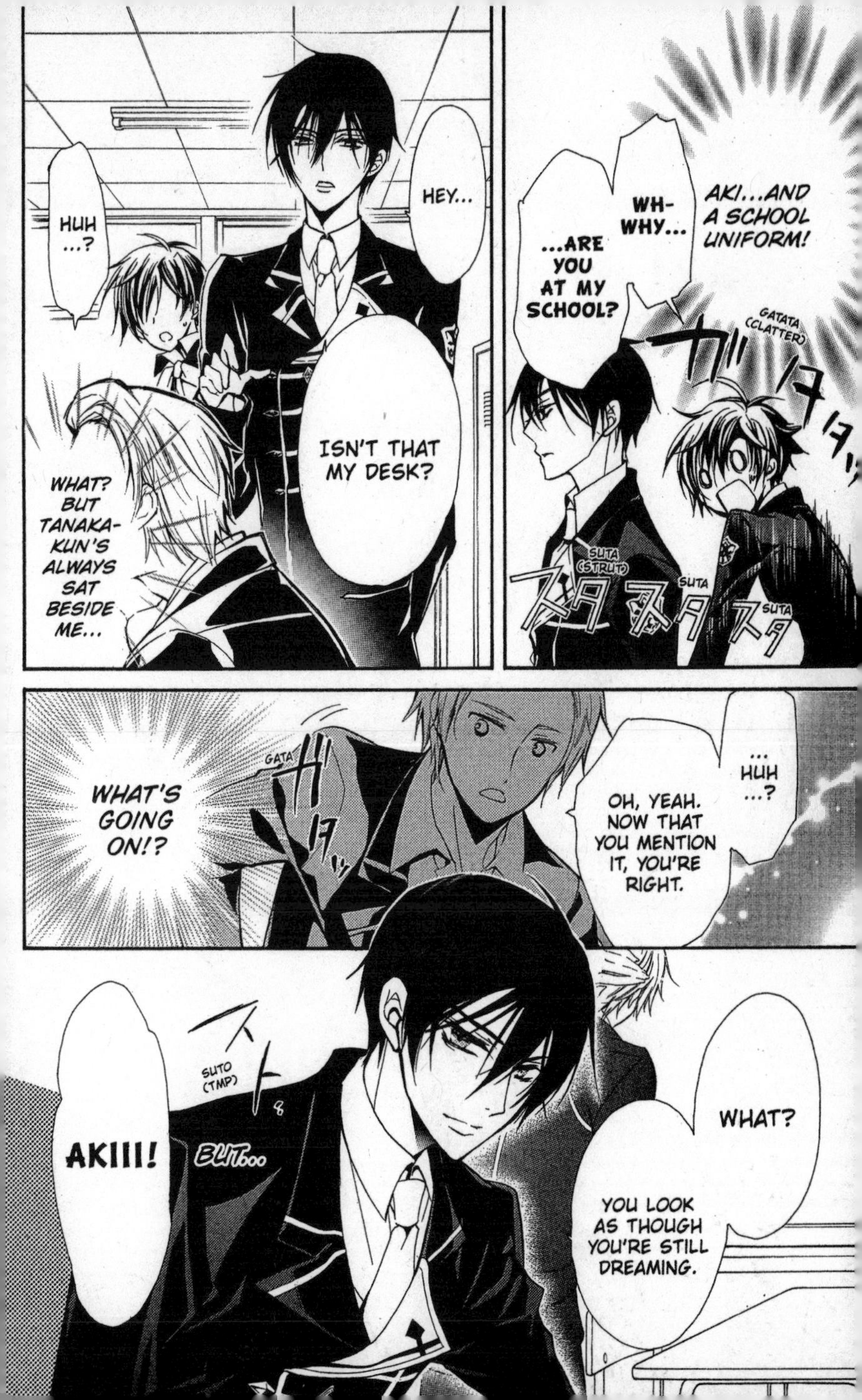
AKI...AND A SCHOOL UNIFORM!
WH-WHY...
...ARE YOU AT MY SCHOOL?
GATATA (CLATTER)
SUTA (STRUT)
SUTA
SUTA
HEY...
ISN'T THAT MY DESK?
HUH ...?
WHAT? BUT TANAKA-KUN'S ALWAYS SAT BESIDE ME...
... HUH ...?
OH, YEAH. NOW THAT YOU MENTION IT, YOU'RE RIGHT.
GATA
WHAT'S GOING ON!?
WHAT?
YOU LOOK AS THOUGH YOU'RE STILL DREAMING.
SUTO (TMP)
BUT...
AKIII!

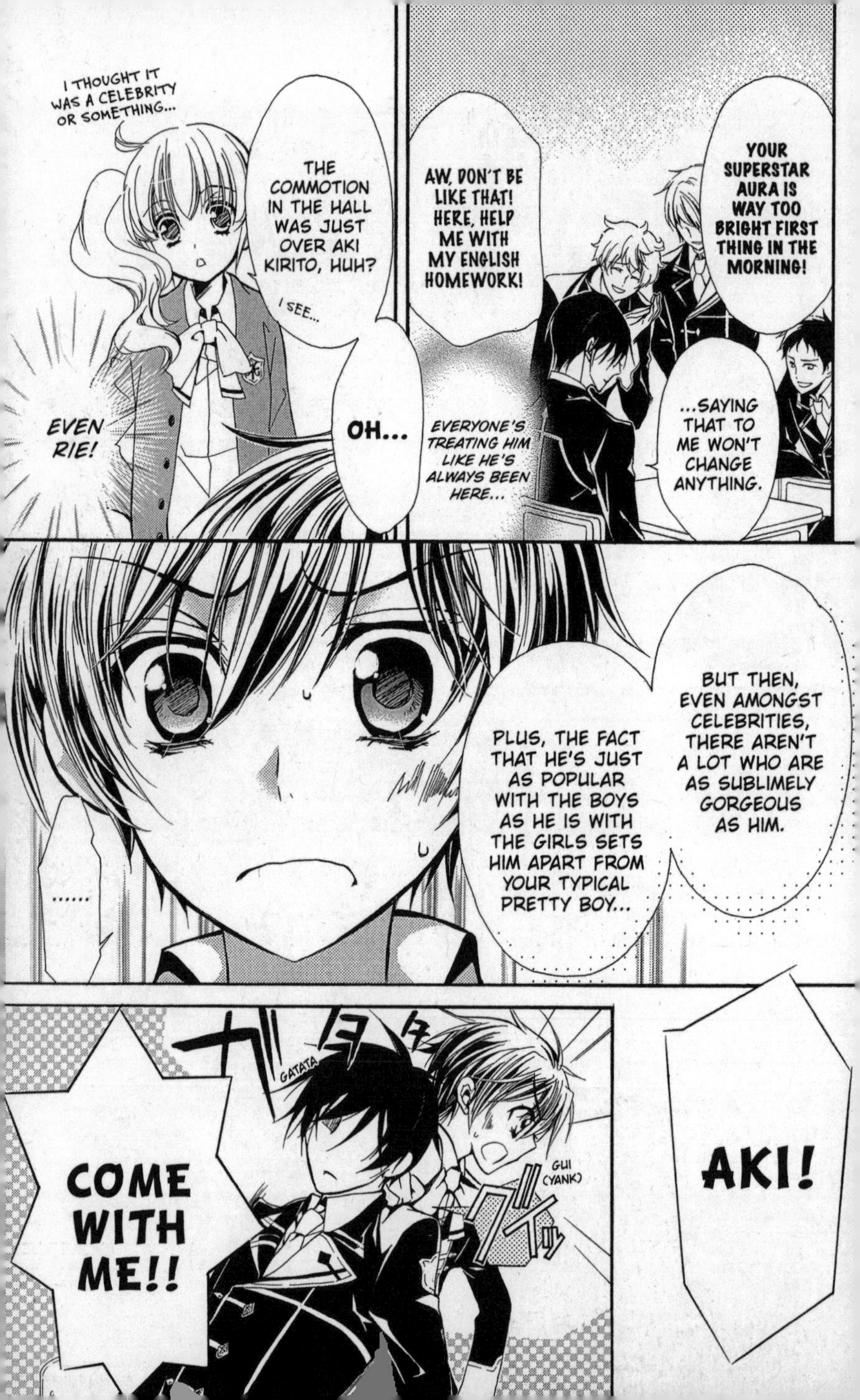
YOUR SUPERSTAR AURA IS WAY TOO BRIGHT FIRST THING IN THE MORNING!
AW, DON'T BE LIKE THAT! HERE, HELP ME WITH MY ENGLISH HOMEWORK!
...SAYING THAT TO ME WON'T CHANGE ANYTHING.
EVERYONE'S TREATING HIM LIKE HE'S ALWAYS BEEN HERE...
I THOUGHT IT WAS A CELEBRITY OR SOMETHING...
THE COMMOTION IN THE HALL WAS JUST OVER AKI KIRITO, HUH?
I SEE...
OH...
EVEN RIE!
BUT THEN, EVEN AMONGST CELEBRITIES, THERE AREN'T A LOT WHO ARE AS SUBLIMELY GORGEOUS AS HIM.
PLUS, THE FACT THAT HE'S JUST AS POPULAR WITH THE BOYS AS HE IS WITH THE GIRLS SETS HIM APART FROM YOUR TYPICAL PRETTY BOY...
......
AKI!
GATATA
GUI (YANK)
COME WITH ME!!

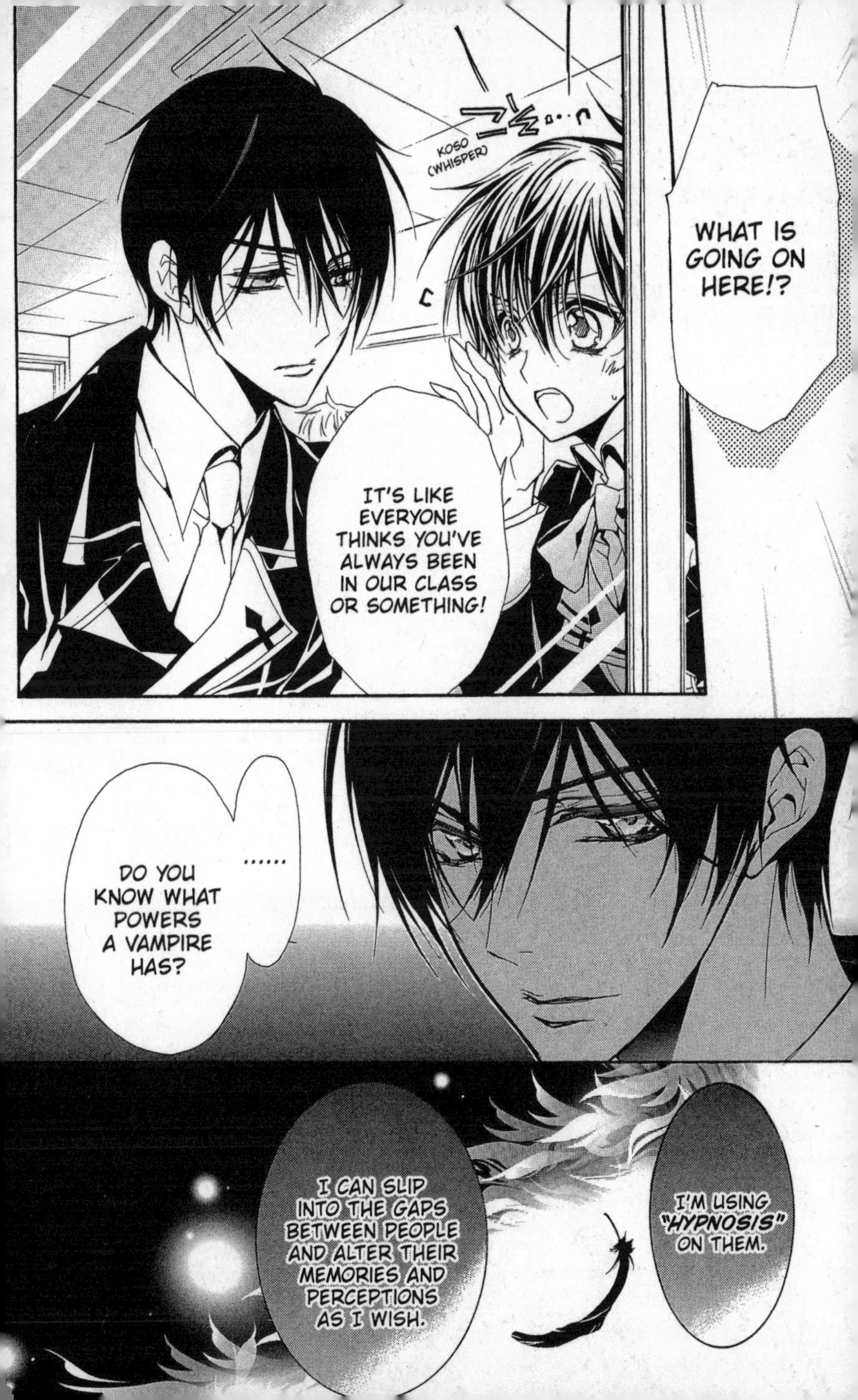
WHAT IS GOING ON HERE!?
KOSO (WHISPER)
IT'S LIKE EVERYONE THINKS YOU'VE ALWAYS BEEN IN OUR CLASS OR SOMETHING!
......
DO YOU KNOW WHAT POWERS A VAMPIRE HAS?
I'M USING "HYPNOSIS" ON THEM.
I CAN SLIP INTO THE GAPS BETWEEN PEOPLE AND ALTER THEIR MEMORIES AND PERCEPTIONS AS I WISH.

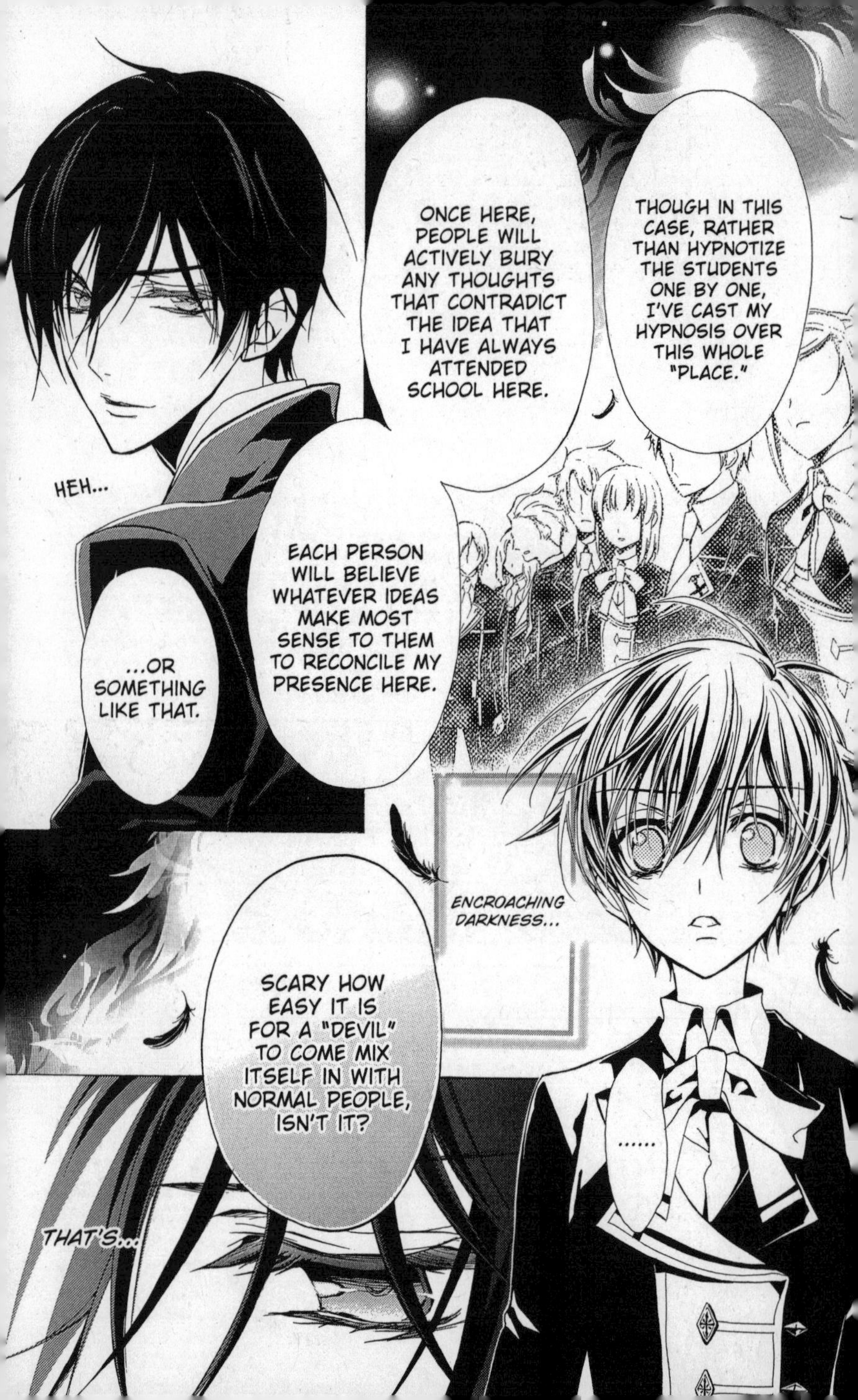
THOUGH IN THIS CASE, RATHER THAN HYPNOTIZE THE STUDENTS ONE BY ONE, I'VE CAST MY HYPNOSIS OVER THIS WHOLE "PLACE."
ONCE HERE, PEOPLE WILL ACTIVELY BURY ANY THOUGHTS THAT CONTRADICT THE IDEA THAT I HAVE ALWAYS ATTENDED SCHOOL HERE.
EACH PERSON WILL BELIEVE WHATEVER IDEAS MAKE MOST SENSE TO THEM TO RECONCILE MY PRESENCE HERE.
HEH...
...OR SOMETHING LIKE THAT.
ENCROACHING DARKNESS...
......
SCARY HOW EASY IT IS FOR A "DEVIL" TO COME MIX ITSELF IN WITH NORMAL PEOPLE, ISN'T IT?
THAT'S...

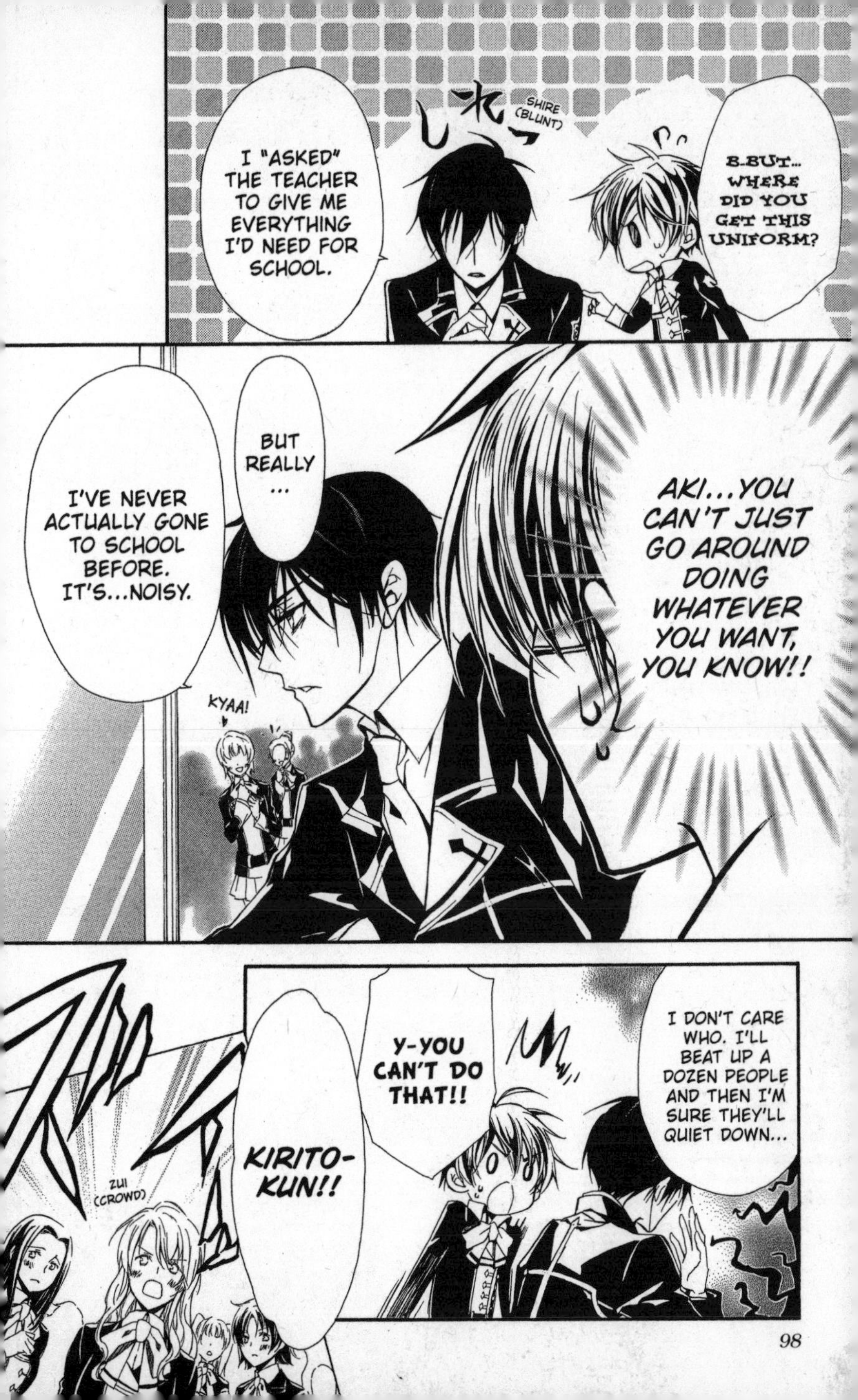

B-BUT... WHERE DID YOU GET THIS UNIFORM?
SHIRE (BLUNT)
I "ASKED" THE TEACHER TO GIVE ME EVERYTHING I'D NEED FOR SCHOOL.
AKI...YOU CAN'T JUST GO AROUND DOING WHATEVER YOU WANT, YOU KNOW!!
BUT REALLY ...
I'VE NEVER ACTUALLY GONE TO SCHOOL BEFORE. IT'S...NOISY.
KYAA!
I DON'T CARE WHO. I'LL BEAT UP A DOZEN PEOPLE AND THEN I'M SURE THEY'LL QUIET DOWN...
Y-YOU CAN'T DO THAT!!
KIRITO-KUN!!
ZUI (CROWD)

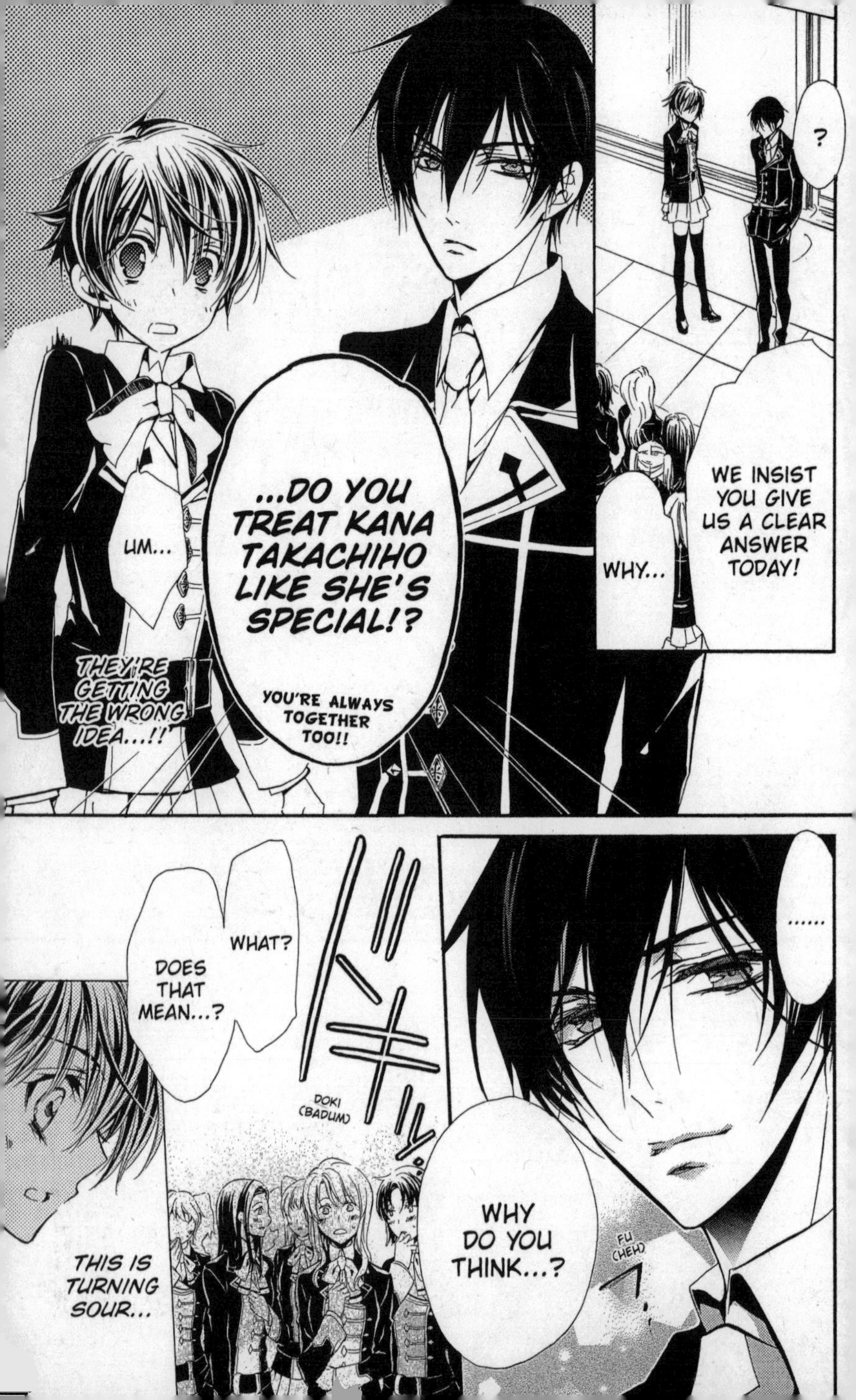
?
WE INSIST YOU GIVE US A CLEAR ANSWER TODAY!
WHY...
...DO YOU TREAT KANA TAKACHIHO LIKE SHE'S SPECIAL!?
YOU'RE ALWAYS TOGETHER TOO!!
UM...
THEY'RE GETTING THE WRONG IDEA...!!
......
WHY DO YOU THINK...?
FU (HEH)
DOKI (BADUM)
WHAT?
DOES THAT MEAN...?
THIS IS TURNING SOUR...

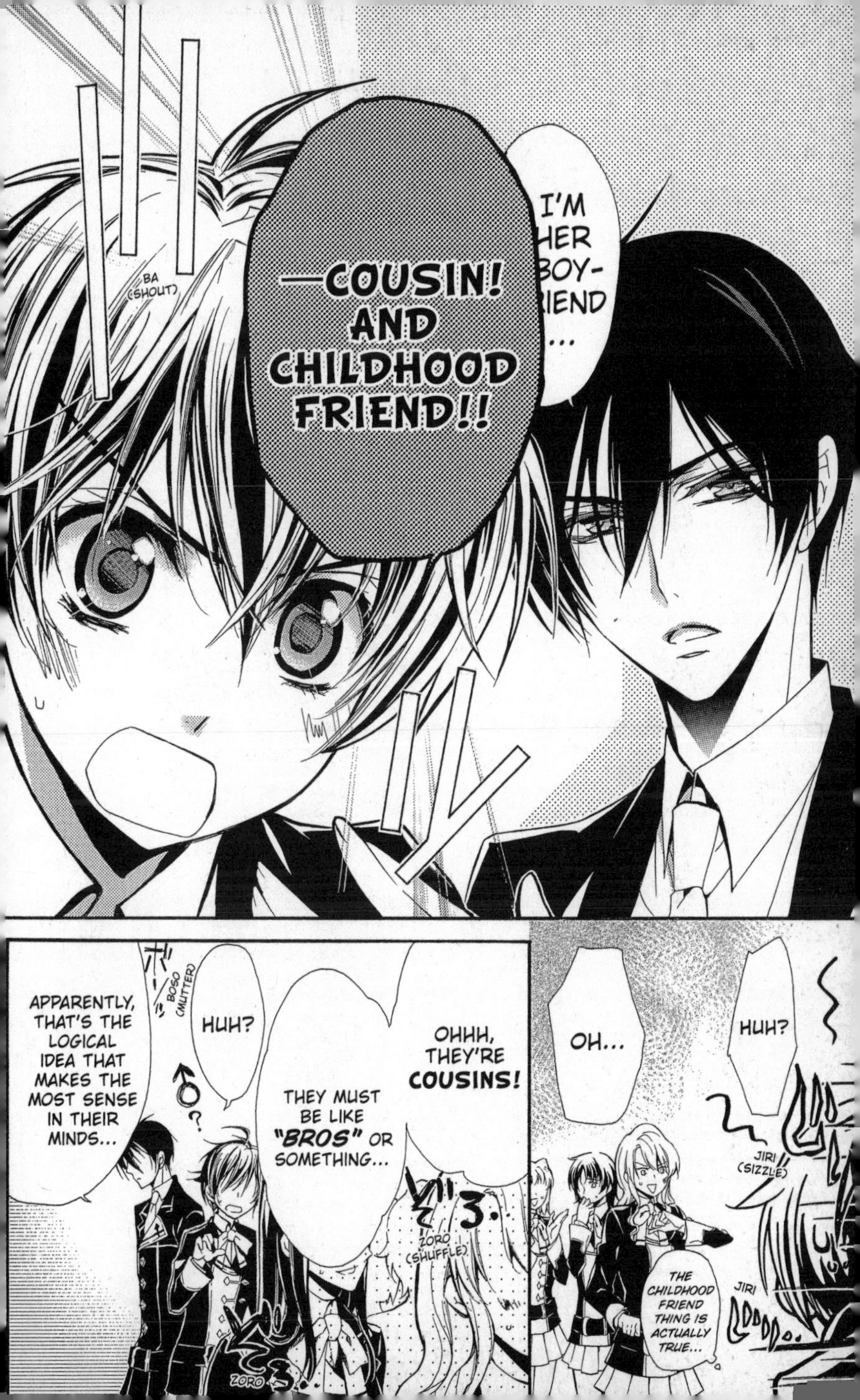
I'M HER BOY-FRIEND...
—COUSIN! AND CHILDHOOD FRIEND!!
BA (SHOUT)
HUH?
OH...
JIRI (SIZZLE)
THE CHILDHOOD FRIEND THING IS ACTUALLY TRUE...
JIRI
OHHH, THEY'RE COUSINS!
THEY MUST BE LIKE "BROS" OR SOMETHING...
ZORO (SHUFFLE)
HUH?
BOSO (MUTTER)
APPARENTLY, THAT'S THE LOGICAL IDEA THAT MAKES THE MOST SENSE IN THEIR MINDS...
ZORO

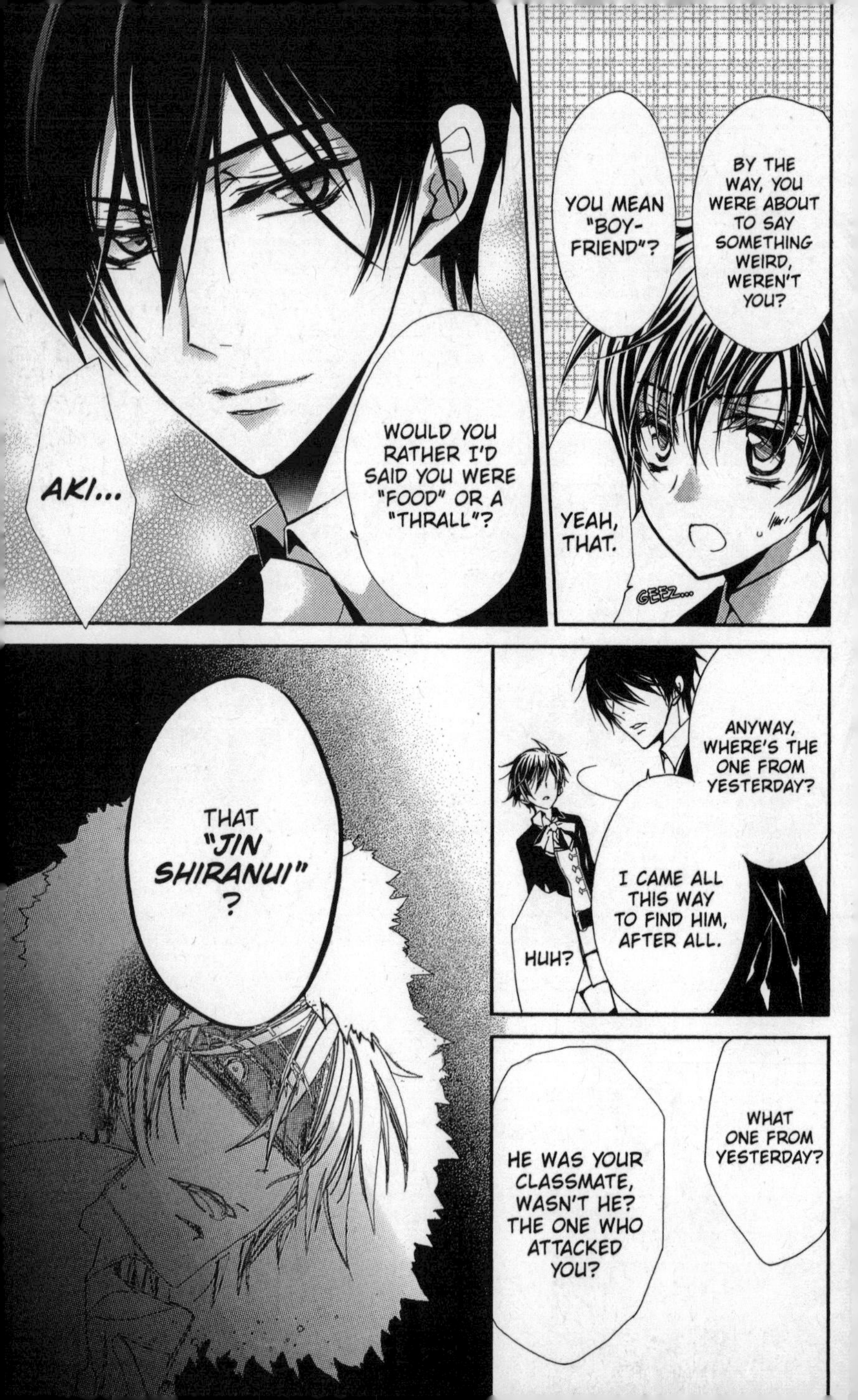
BY THE WAY, YOU WERE ABOUT TO SAY SOMETHING WEIRD, WEREN'T YOU?
YOU MEAN "BOY-FRIEND"?
YEAH, THAT.
GEEZ...
WOULD YOU RATHER I'D SAID YOU WERE "FOOD" OR A "THRALL"?
AKI...
ANYWAY, WHERE'S THE ONE FROM YESTERDAY?
I CAME ALL THIS WAY TO FIND HIM, AFTER ALL.
HUH?
WHAT ONE FROM YESTERDAY?
HE WAS YOUR CLASSMATE, WASN'T HE? THE ONE WHO ATTACKED YOU?
THAT "JIN SHIRANUI"?

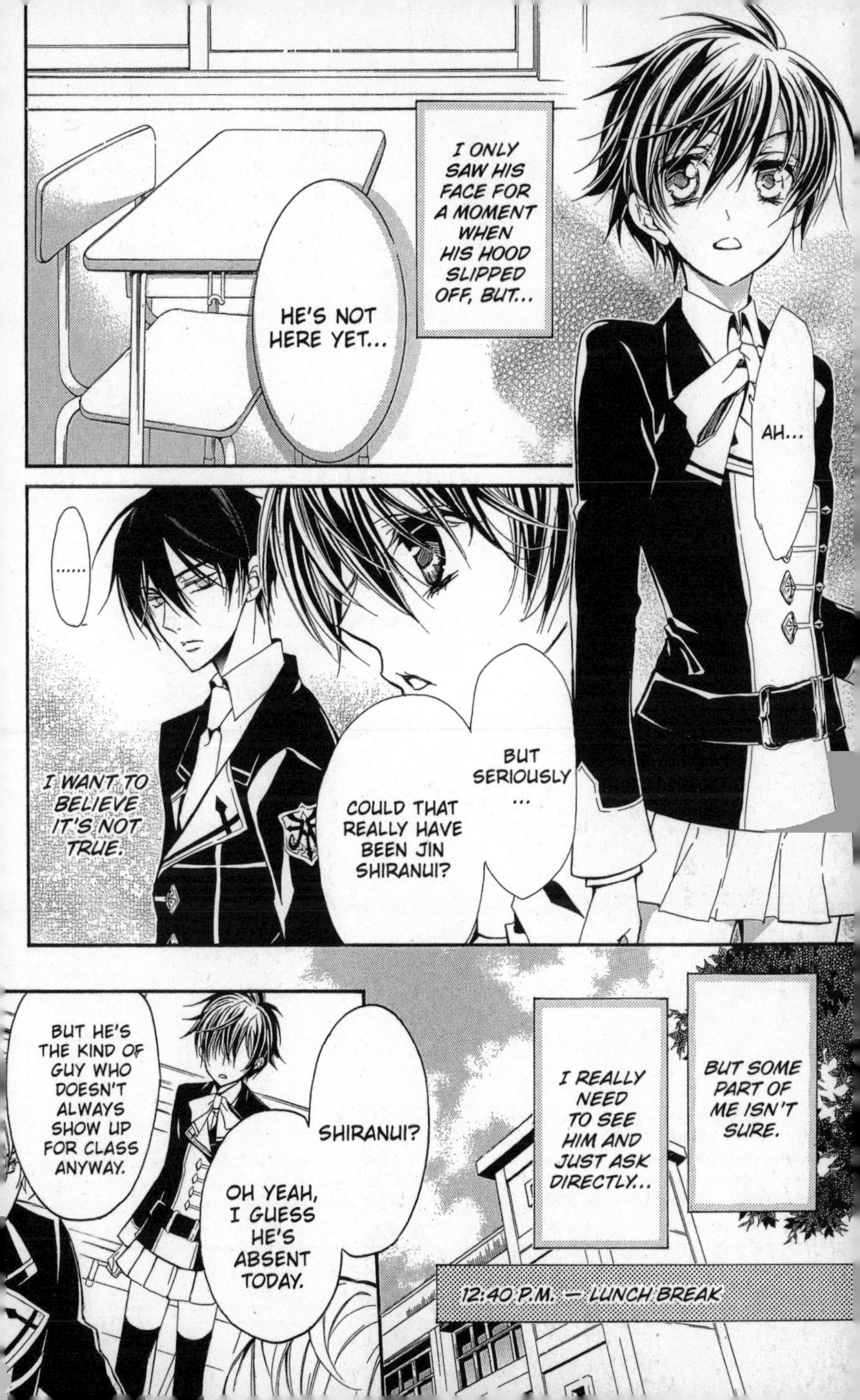
AH...
I ONLY SAW HIS FACE FOR A MOMENT WHEN HIS HOOD SLIPPED OFF, BUT...
HE'S NOT HERE YET...
BUT SERIOUSLY...
COULD THAT REALLY HAVE BEEN JIN SHIRANUI?
......
I WANT TO BELIEVE IT'S NOT TRUE.
BUT SOME PART OF ME ISN'T SURE.
I REALLY NEED TO SEE HIM AND JUST ASK DIRECTLY...
12:40 P.M. — LUNCH BREAK
SHIRANUI?
OH YEAH, I GUESS HE'S ABSENT TODAY.
BUT HE'S THE KIND OF GUY WHO DOESN'T ALWAYS SHOW UP FOR CLASS ANYWAY.

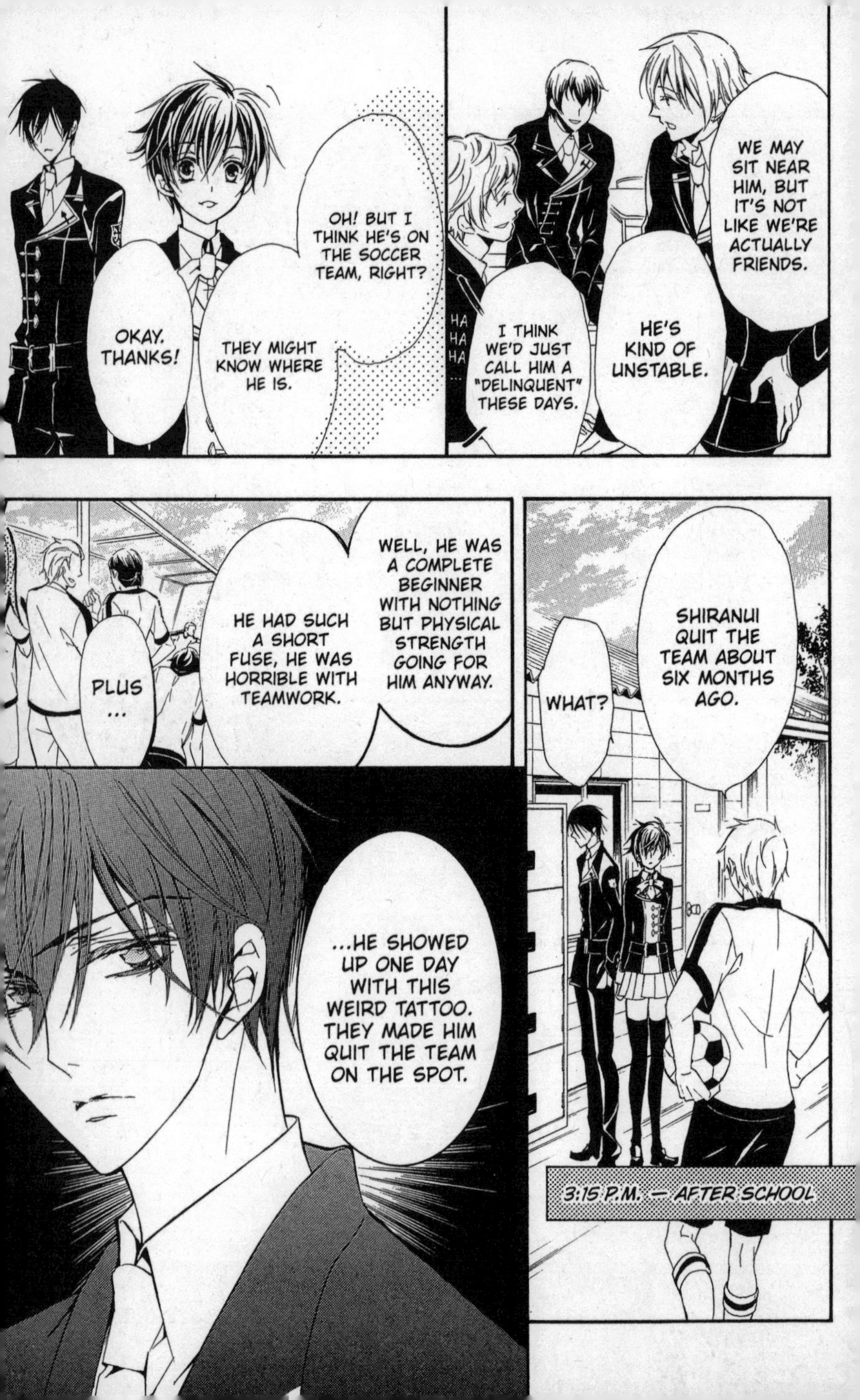
WE MAY SIT NEAR HIM, BUT IT'S NOT LIKE WE'RE ACTUALLY FRIENDS.
HE'S KIND OF UNSTABLE.
I THINK WE'D JUST CALL HIM A "DELINQUENT" THESE DAYS.
HA HA HA ...
OH! BUT I THINK HE'S ON THE SOCCER TEAM, RIGHT?
THEY MIGHT KNOW WHERE HE IS.
OKAY. THANKS!
SHIRANUI QUIT THE TEAM ABOUT SIX MONTHS AGO.
WHAT?
3:15 P.M. — AFTER SCHOOL
WELL, HE WAS A COMPLETE BEGINNER WITH NOTHING BUT PHYSICAL STRENGTH GOING FOR HIM ANYWAY.
HE HAD SUCH A SHORT FUSE, HE WAS HORRIBLE WITH TEAMWORK.
PLUS ...
...HE SHOWED UP ONE DAY WITH THIS WEIRD TATTOO. THEY MADE HIM QUIT THE TEAM ON THE SPOT.

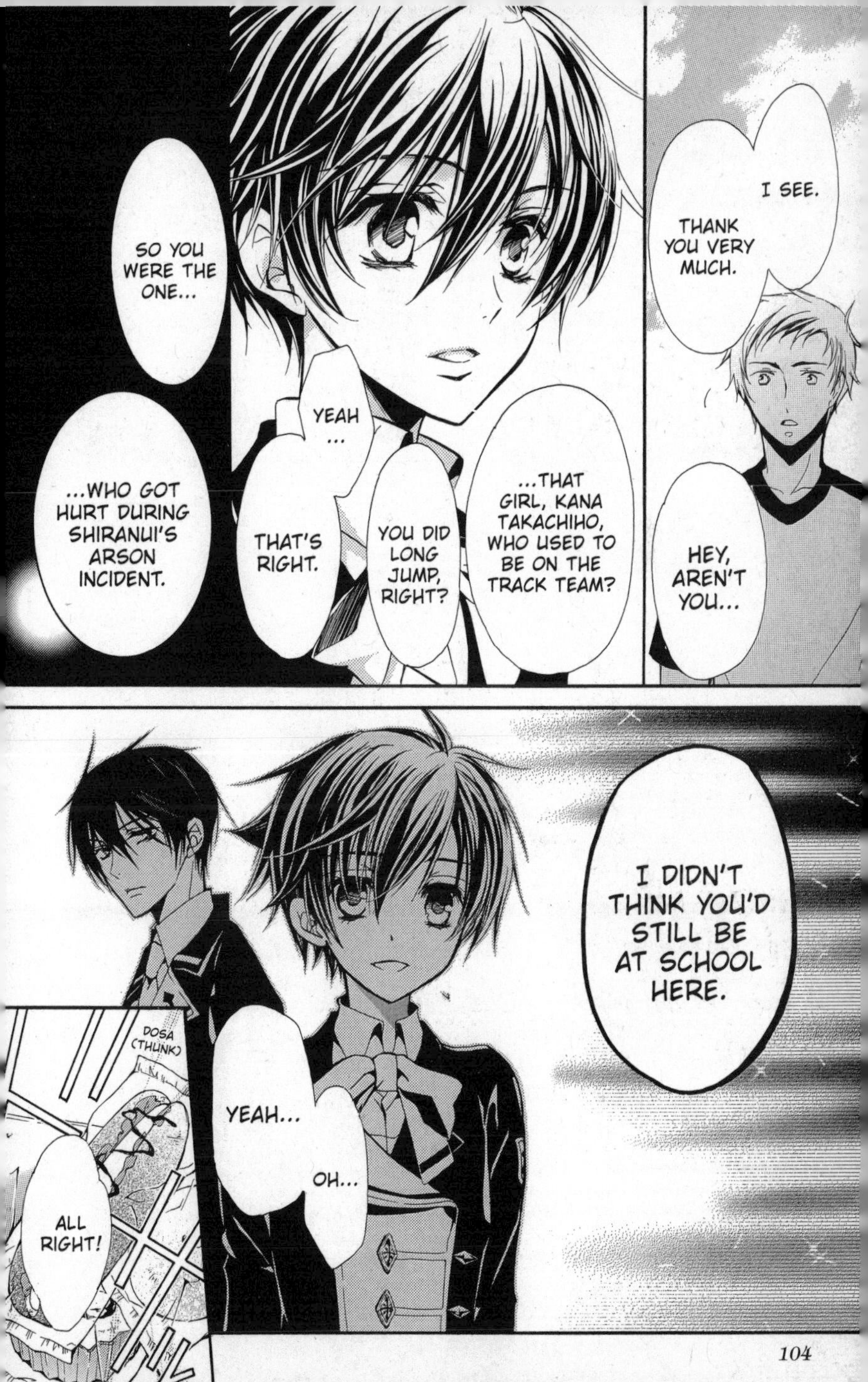
I SEE.
THANK YOU VERY MUCH.
HEY, AREN'T YOU...
...THAT GIRL, KANA TAKACHIHO, WHO USED TO BE ON THE TRACK TEAM?
YOU DID LONG JUMP, RIGHT?
YEAH...
THAT'S RIGHT.
SO YOU WERE THE ONE...
...WHO GOT HURT DURING SHIRANUI'S ARSON INCIDENT.
I DIDN'T THINK YOU'D STILL BE AT SCHOOL HERE.
YEAH...
OH...
DOSA (THUNK)
ALL RIGHT!

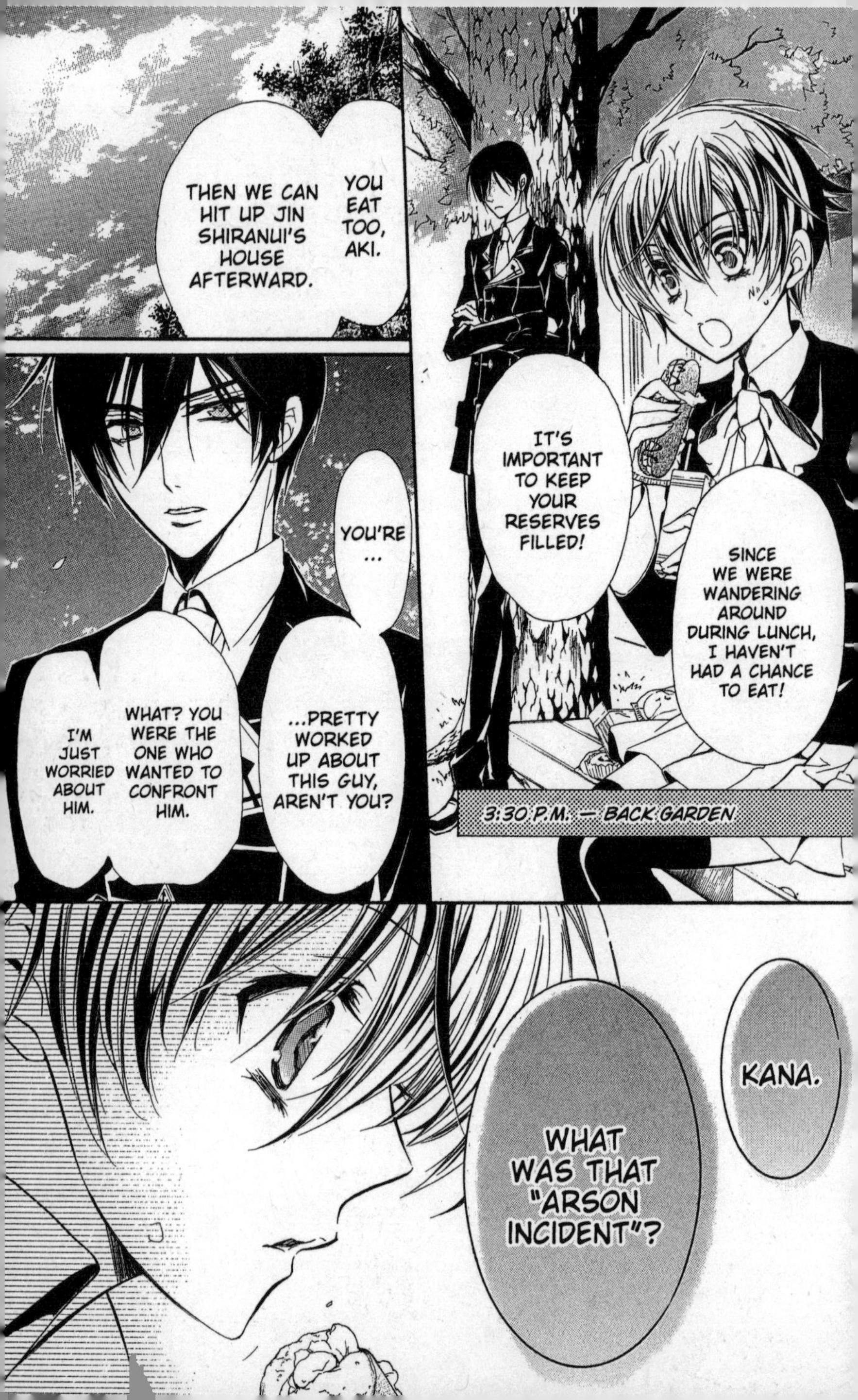

SINCE WE WERE WANDERING AROUND DURING LUNCH, I HAVEN'T HAD A CHANCE TO EAT!
IT'S IMPORTANT TO KEEP YOUR RESERVES FILLED!
3:30 P.M. — BACK GARDEN
YOU EAT TOO, AKI.
THEN WE CAN HIT UP JIN SHIRANUI'S HOUSE AFTERWARD.
YOU'RE ...
...PRETTY WORKED UP ABOUT THIS GUY, AREN'T YOU?
WHAT? YOU WERE THE ONE WHO WANTED TO CONFRONT HIM.
I'M JUST WORRIED ABOUT HIM.
KANA.
WHAT WAS THAT "ARSON INCIDENT"?

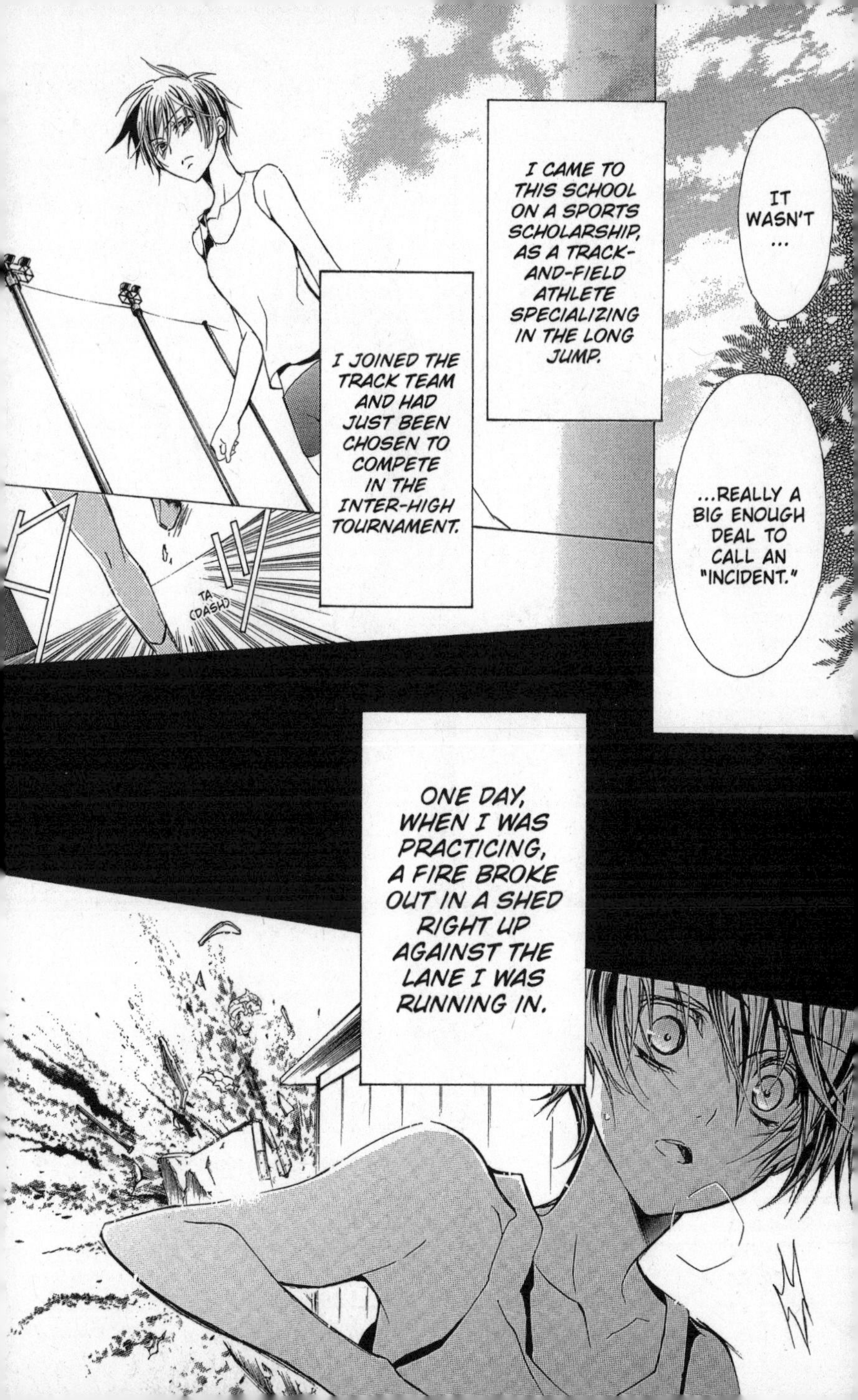
IT WASN'T ...
...REALLY A BIG ENOUGH DEAL TO CALL AN "INCIDENT."
I CAME TO THIS SCHOOL ON A SPORTS SCHOLARSHIP, AS A TRACK-AND-FIELD ATHLETE SPECIALIZING IN THE LONG JUMP.
I JOINED THE TRACK TEAM AND HAD JUST BEEN CHOSEN TO COMPETE IN THE INTER-HIGH TOURNAMENT.
TA (DASH)
ONE DAY, WHEN I WAS PRACTICING, A FIRE BROKE OUT IN A SHED RIGHT UP AGAINST THE LANE I WAS RUNNING IN.

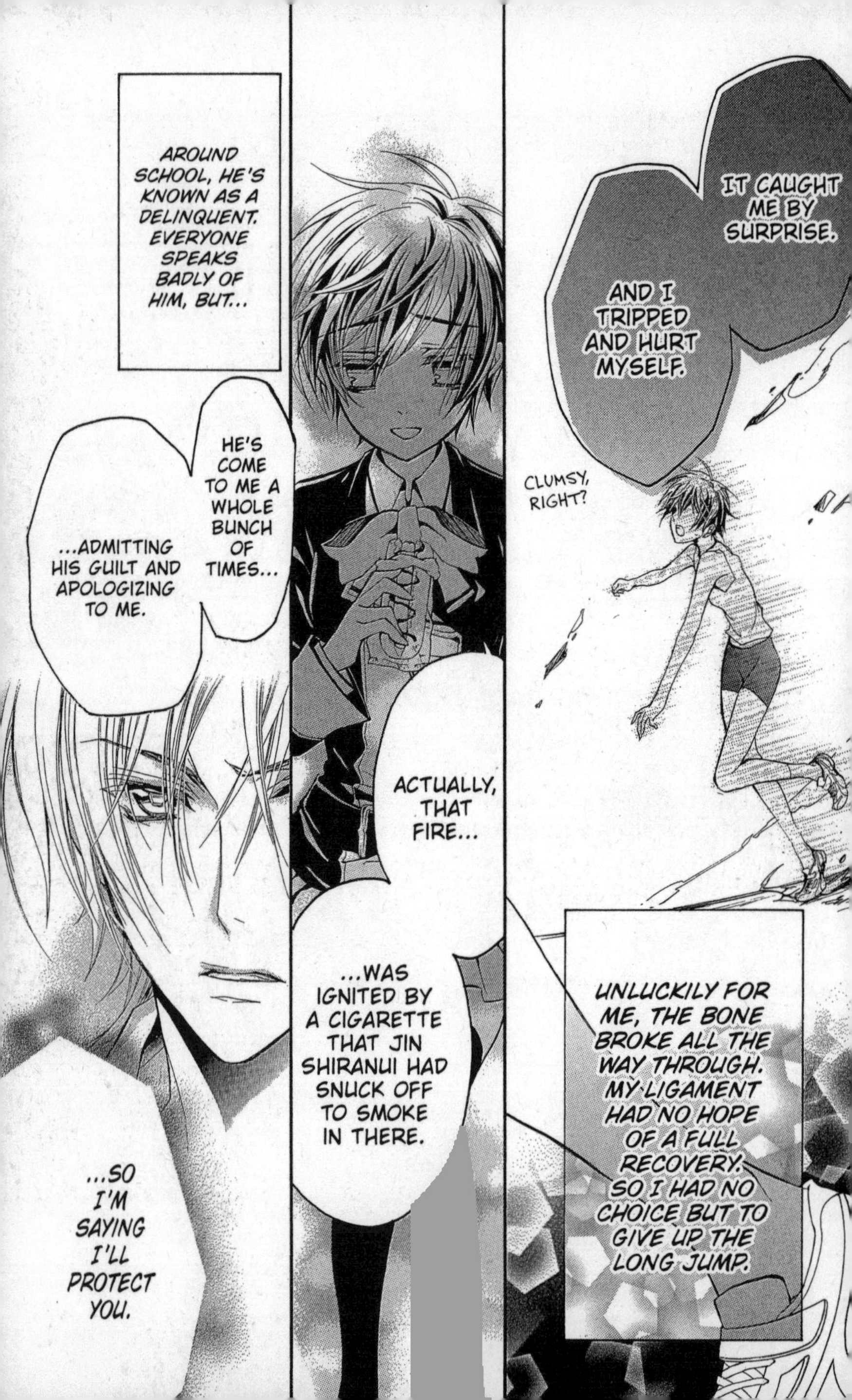
IT CAUGHT ME BY SURPRISE.
AND I TRIPPED AND HURT MYSELF.
CLUMSY, RIGHT?
UNLUCKILY FOR ME, THE BONE BROKE ALL THE WAY THROUGH. MY LIGAMENT HAD NO HOPE OF A FULL RECOVERY. SO I HAD NO CHOICE BUT TO GIVE UP THE LONG JUMP.
ACTUALLY, THAT FIRE...
...WAS IGNITED BY A CIGARETTE THAT JIN SHIRANUI HAD SNUCK OFF TO SMOKE IN THERE.
AROUND SCHOOL, HE'S KNOWN AS A DELINQUENT. EVERYONE SPEAKS BADLY OF HIM, BUT...
HE'S COME TO ME A WHOLE BUNCH OF TIMES...
...ADMITTING HIS GUILT AND APOLOGIZING TO ME.
...SO I'M SAYING I'LL PROTECT YOU.

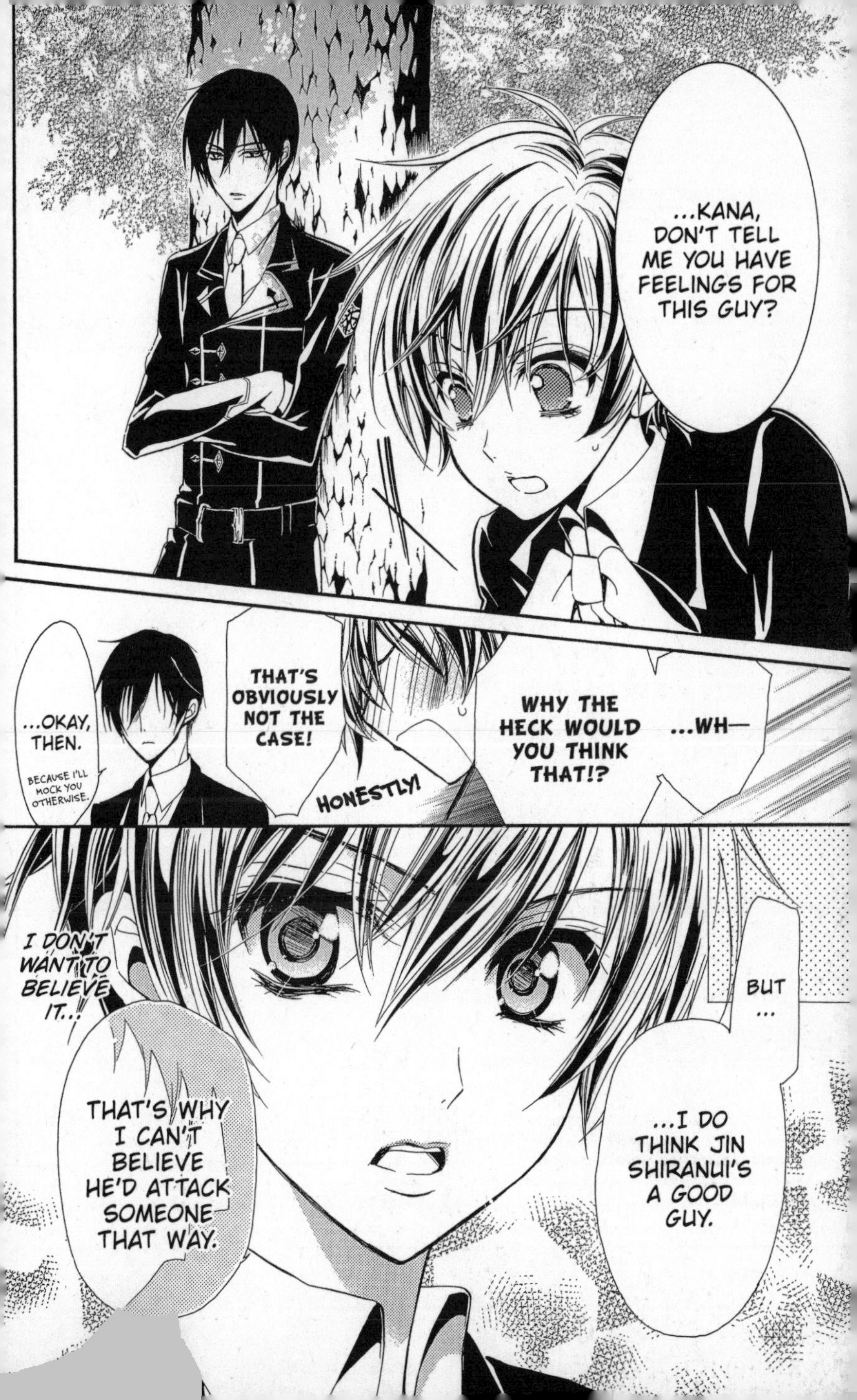
...KANA, DON'T TELL ME YOU HAVE FEELINGS FOR THIS GUY?
...WH—
WHY THE HECK WOULD YOU THINK THAT!?
THAT'S OBVIOUSLY NOT THE CASE!
HONESTLY!
...OKAY, THEN.
BECAUSE I'LL MOCK YOU OTHERWISE.
BUT ...
...I DO THINK JIN SHIRANUI'S A GOOD GUY.
I DON'T WANT TO BELIEVE IT...
THAT'S WHY I CAN'T BELIEVE HE'D ATTACK SOMEONE THAT WAY.

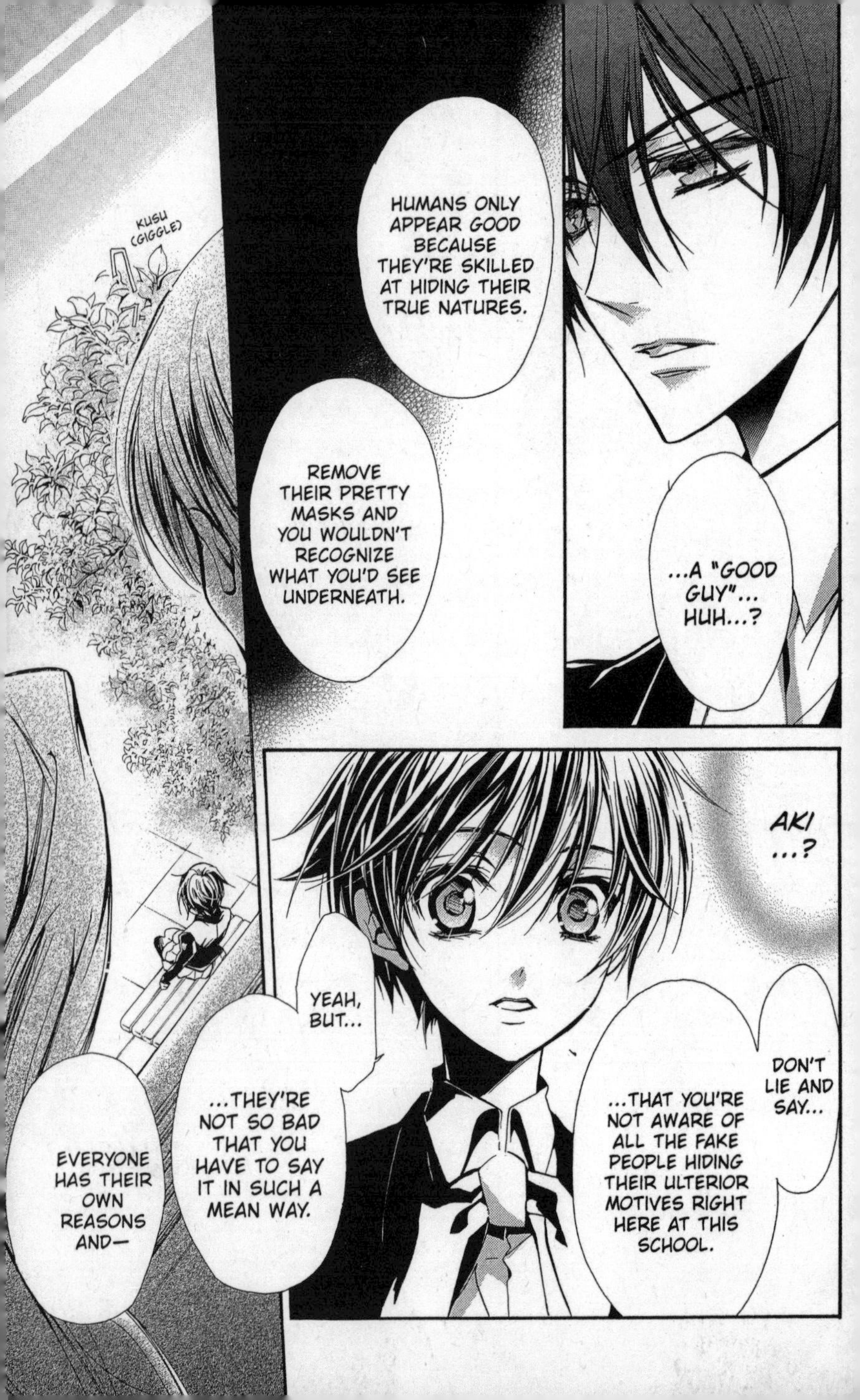
...A "GOOD GUY"... HUH...?
HUMANS ONLY APPEAR GOOD BECAUSE THEY'RE SKILLED AT HIDING THEIR TRUE NATURES.
REMOVE THEIR PRETTY MASKS AND YOU WOULDN'T RECOGNIZE WHAT YOU'D SEE UNDERNEATH.
AKI ...?
DON'T LIE AND SAY...
...THAT YOU'RE NOT AWARE OF ALL THE FAKE PEOPLE HIDING THEIR ULTERIOR MOTIVES RIGHT HERE AT THIS SCHOOL.
YEAH, BUT...
...THEY'RE NOT SO BAD THAT YOU HAVE TO SAY IT IN SUCH A MEAN WAY.
KUSU (GIGGLE)
EVERYONE HAS THEIR OWN REASONS AND—

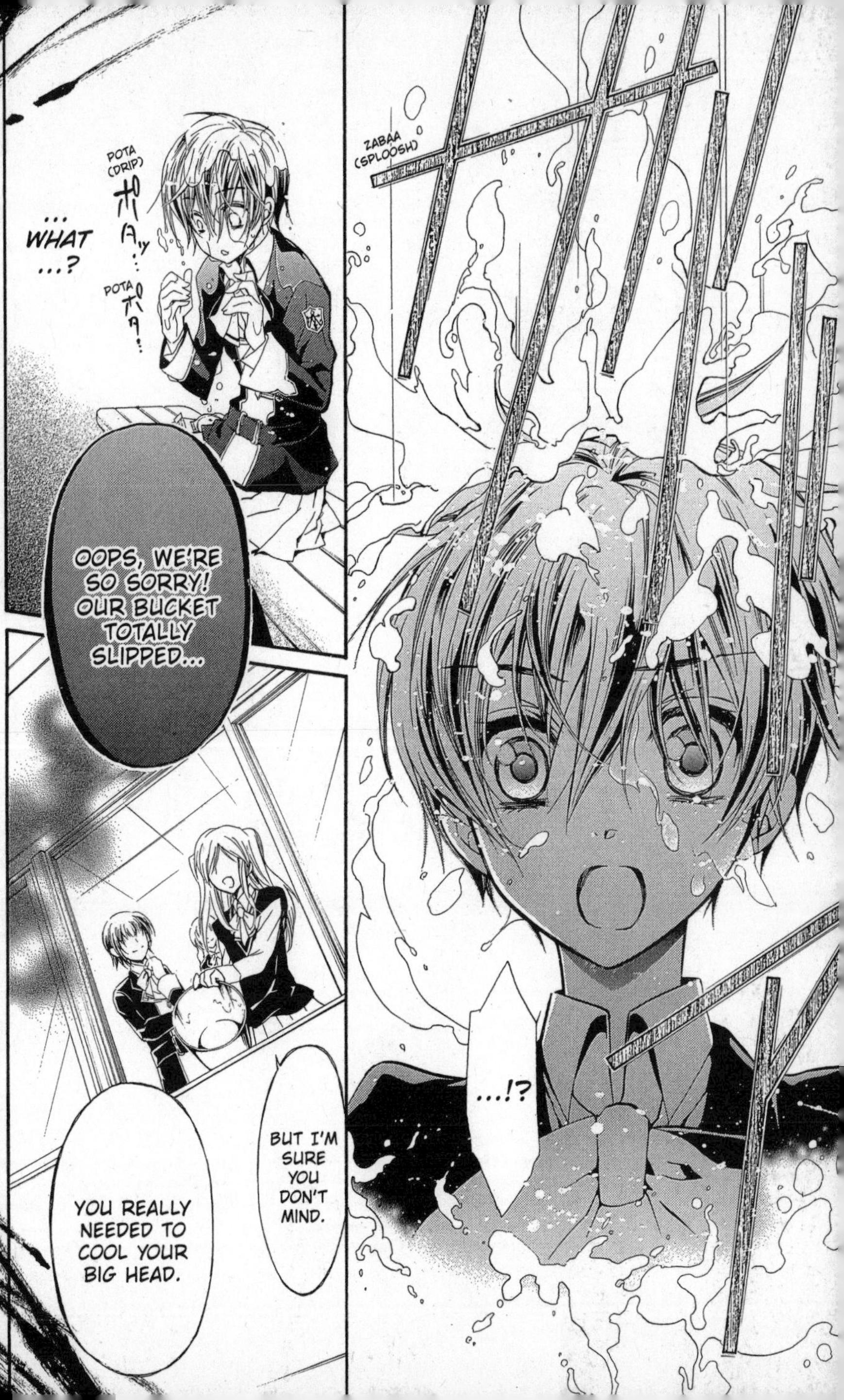
ZABAA (SPLOOSH)
...!?
POTA (DRIP)
ポタッ…
POTA
ポタ…
...WHAT...?
OOPS, WE'RE SO SORRY! OUR BUCKET TOTALLY SLIPPED...
BUT I'M SURE YOU DON'T MIND.
YOU REALLY NEEDED TO COOL YOUR BIG HEAD.

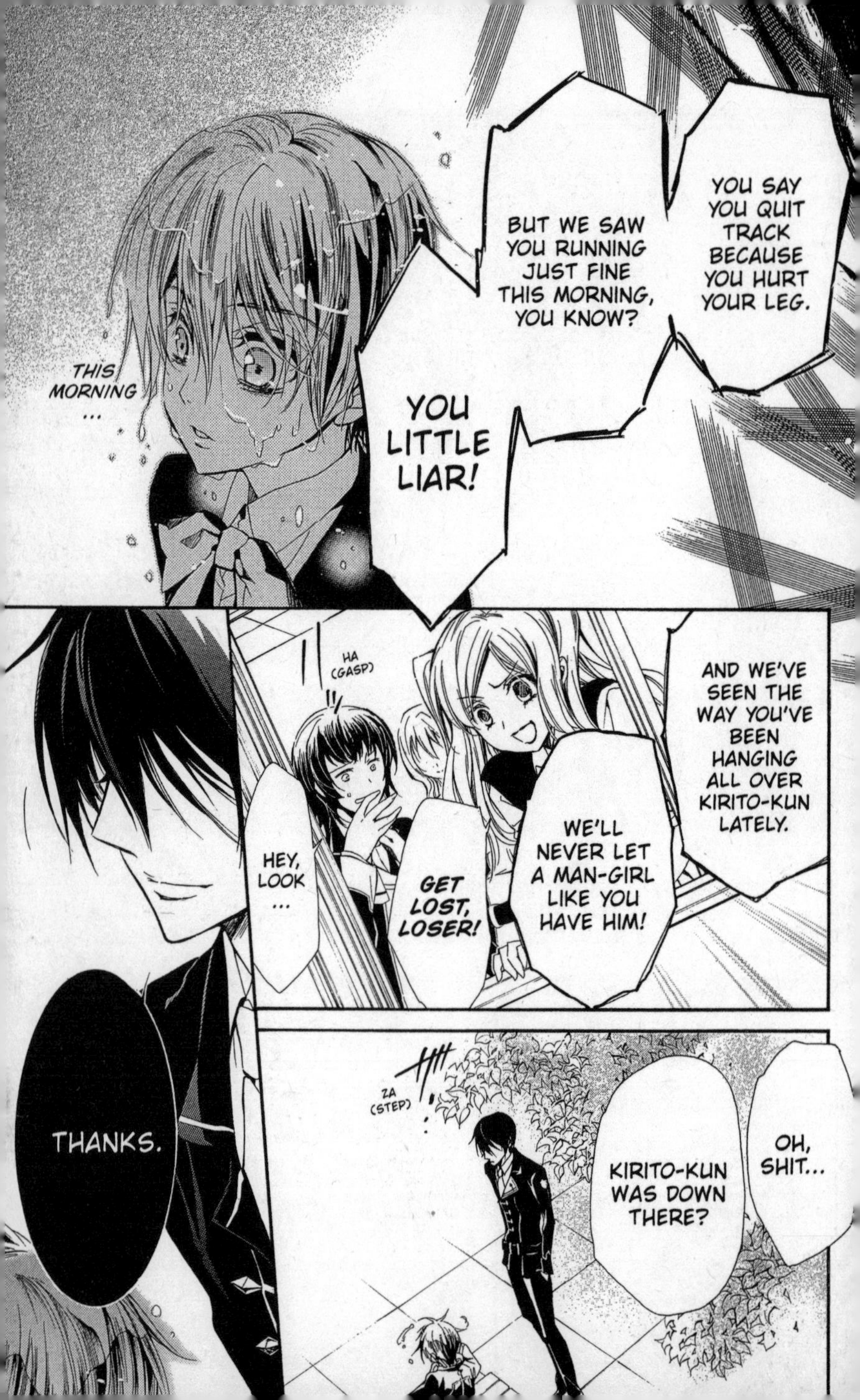
YOU SAY YOU QUIT TRACK BECAUSE YOU HURT YOUR LEG.
BUT WE SAW YOU RUNNING JUST FINE THIS MORNING, YOU KNOW?
YOU LITTLE LIAR!
THIS MORNING...
AND WE'VE SEEN THE WAY YOU'VE BEEN HANGING ALL OVER KIRITO-KUN LATELY.
WE'LL NEVER LET A MAN-GIRL LIKE YOU HAVE HIM!
GET LOST, LOSER!
HA (GASP)
HEY, LOOK...
OH, SHIT...
KIRITO-KUN WAS DOWN THERE?
ZA (STEP)
THANKS.

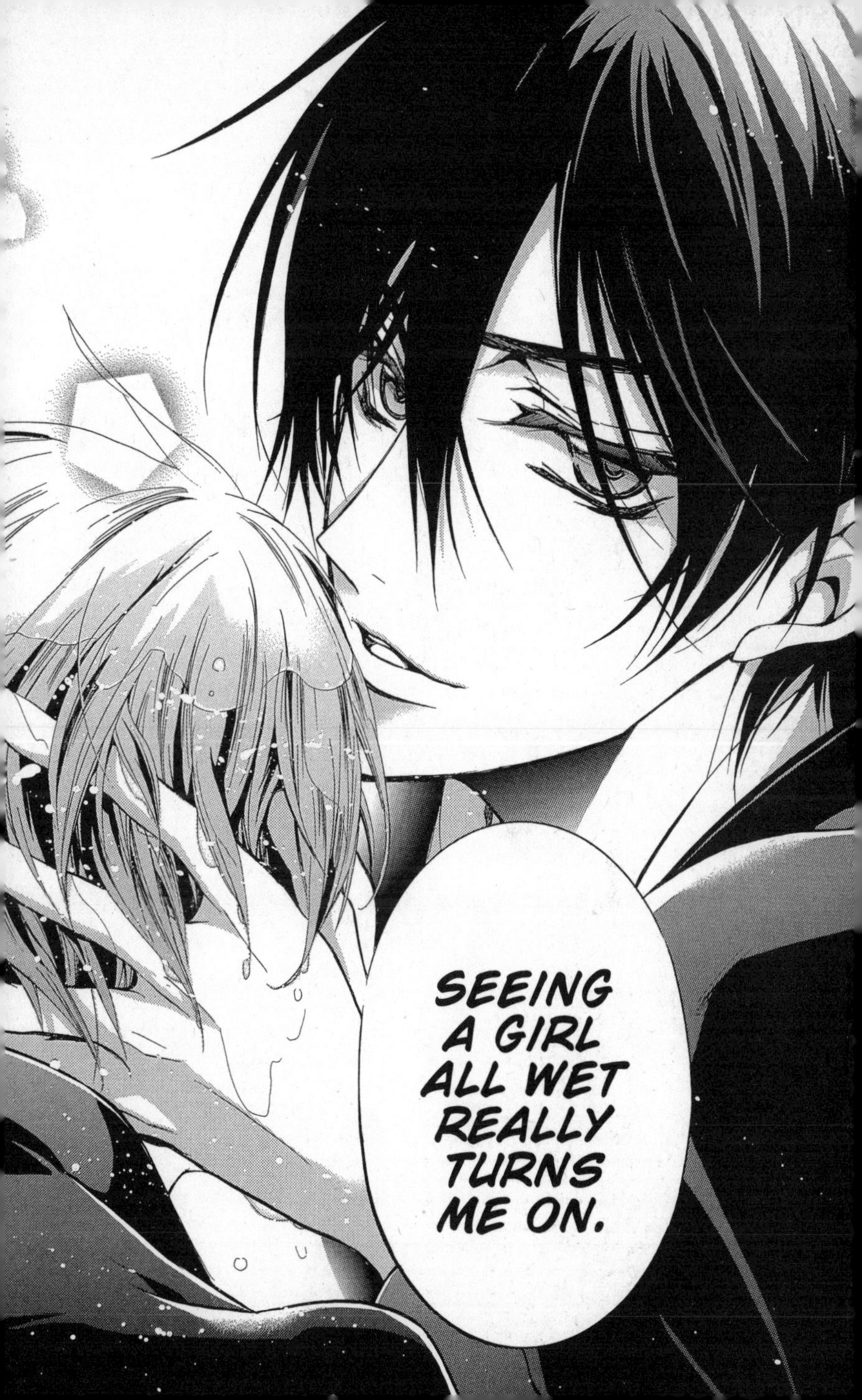
SEEING A GIRL ALL WET REALLY TURNS ME ON.

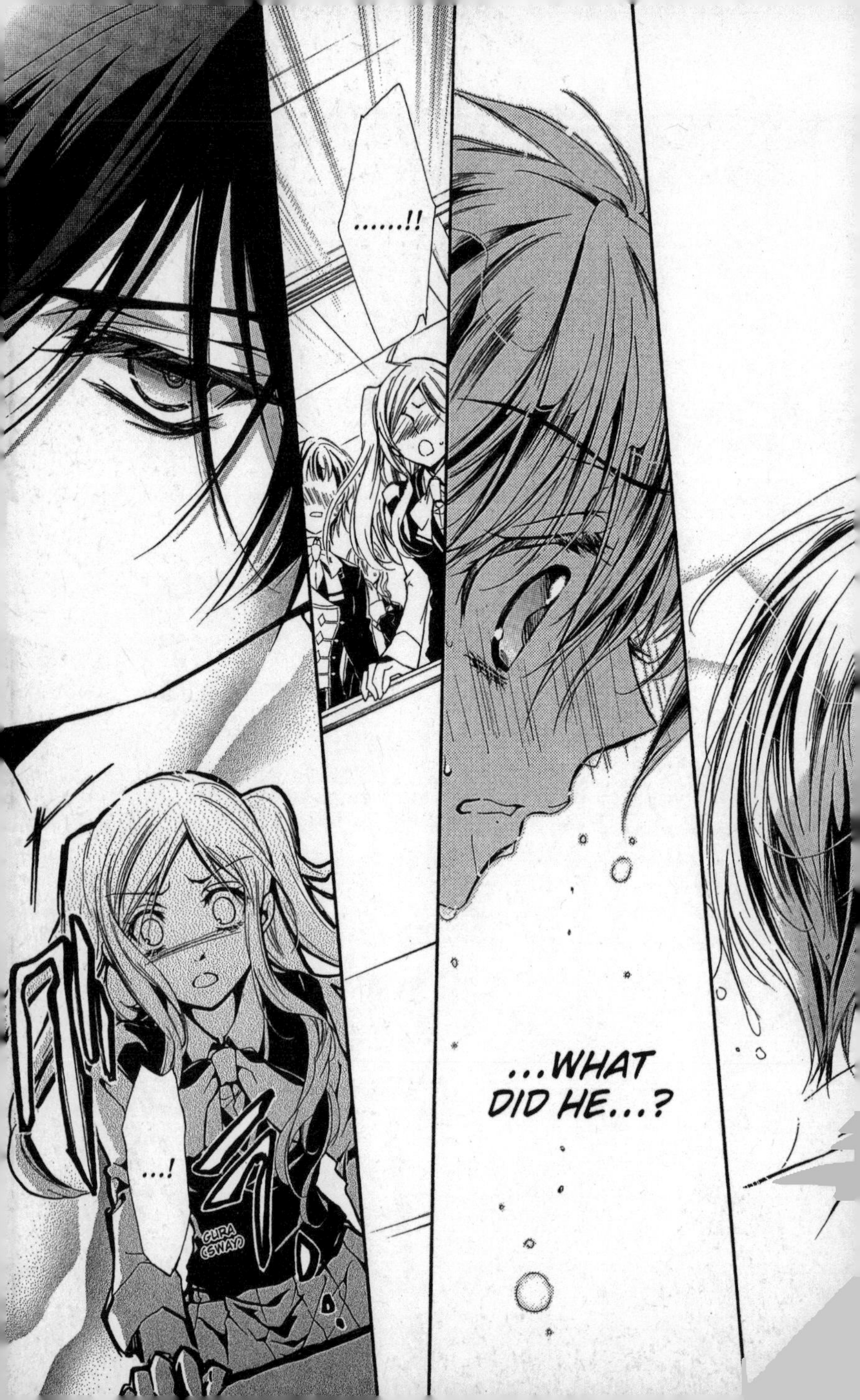
...WHAT DID HE...?
......!!
...!
GURA (SWAY)

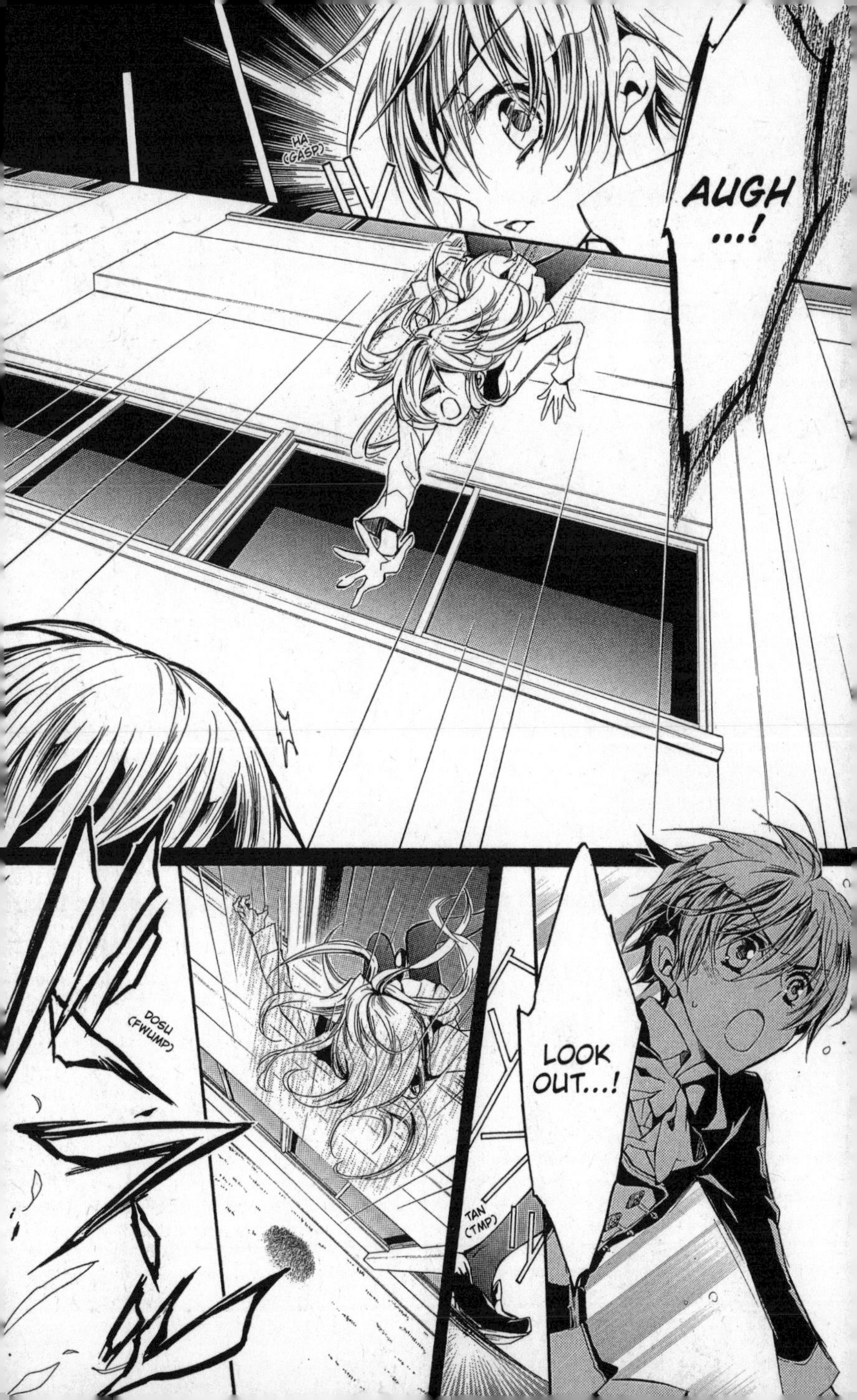
AUGH ...!
HA (GASP)
LOOK OUT...!
TAN (TMP)
DOSU (FWUMP)

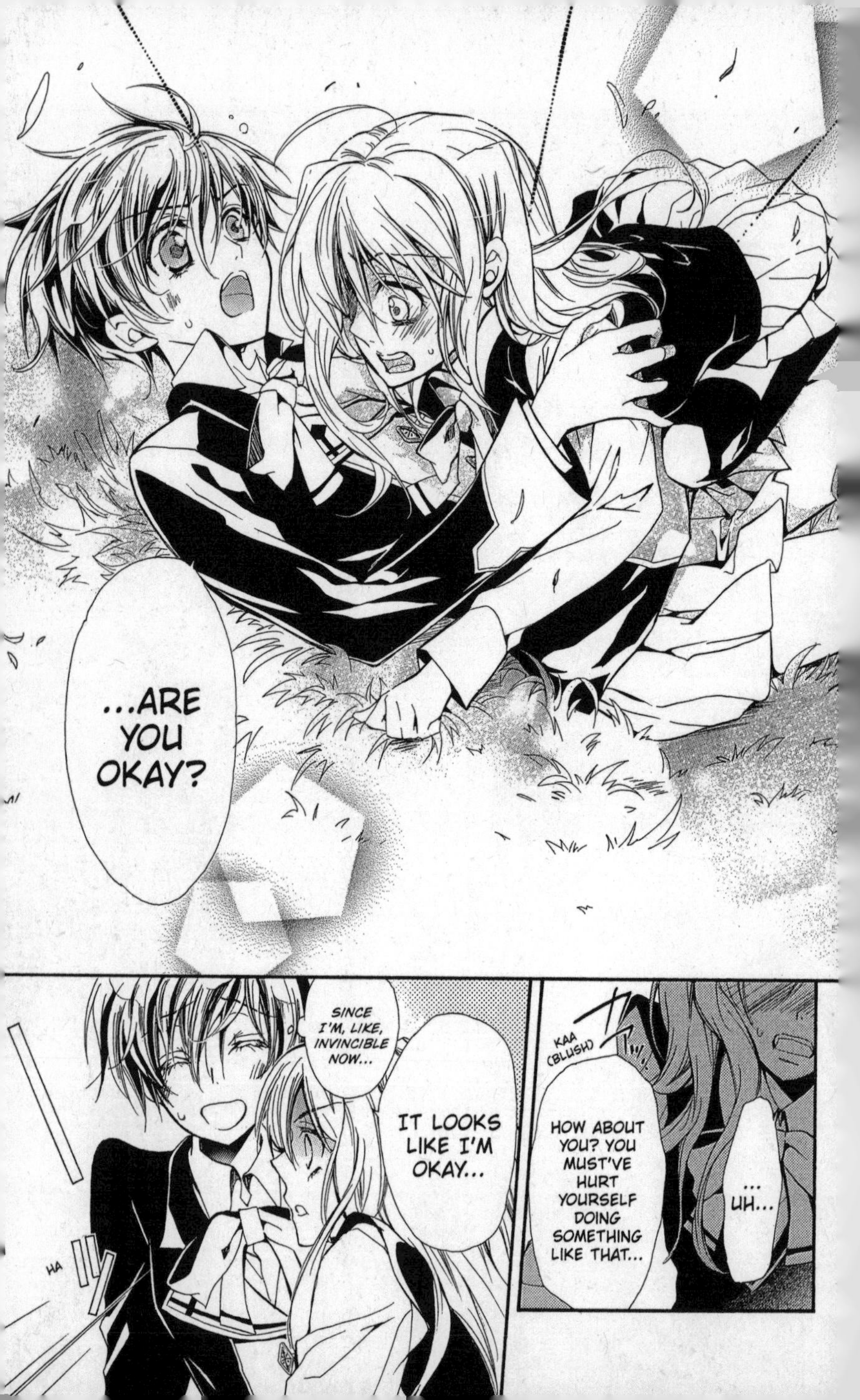
...ARE YOU OKAY?
SINCE I'M, LIKE, INVINCIBLE NOW...
IT LOOKS LIKE I'M OKAY...
HA
KAA (BLUSH)
... UH...
HOW ABOUT YOU? YOU MUST'VE HURT YOURSELF DOING SOMETHING LIKE THAT...

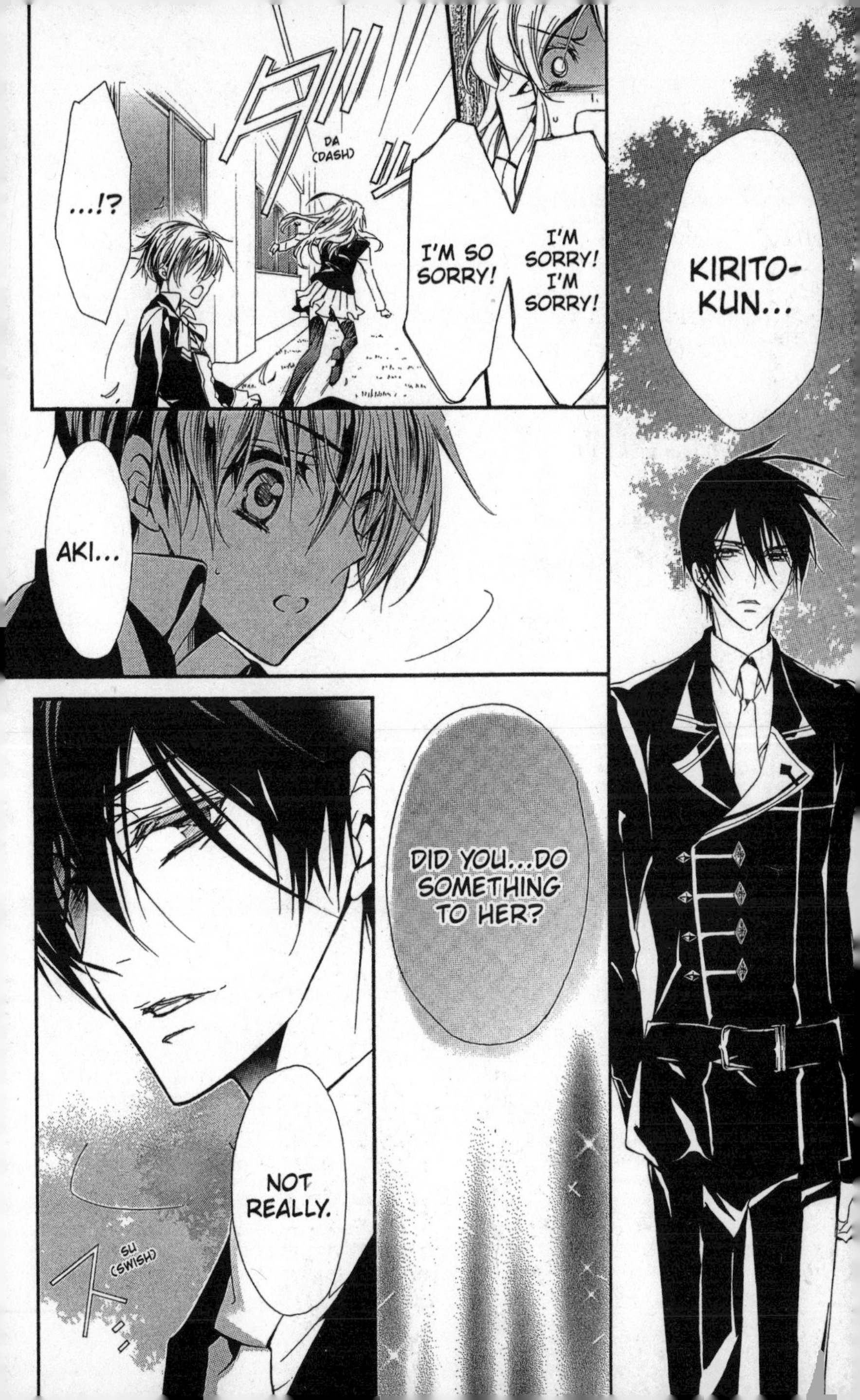
KIRITO-KUN...
I'M SORRY! I'M SORRY!
I'M SO SORRY!
DA (DASH)
...!?
AKI...
DID YOU...DO SOMETHING TO HER?
NOT REALLY.
SU (SWISH)

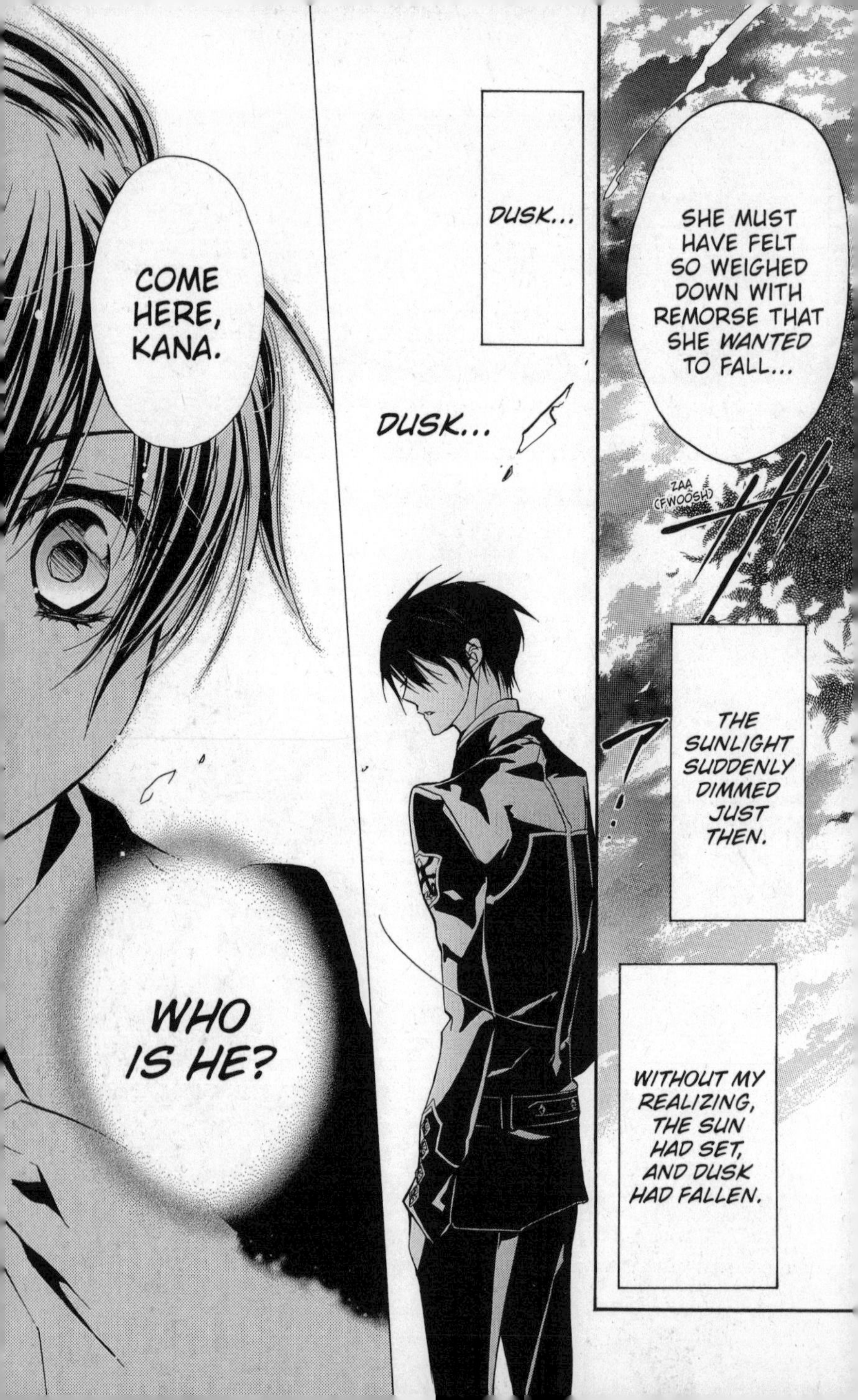
SHE MUST HAVE FELT SO WEIGHED DOWN WITH REMORSE THAT SHE WANTED TO FALL...
ZAA (FWOOSH)
THE SUNLIGHT SUDDENLY DIMMED JUST THEN.
WITHOUT MY REALIZING, THE SUN HAD SET, AND DUSK HAD FALLEN.
DUSK...
DUSK...
COME HERE, KANA.
WHO IS HE?

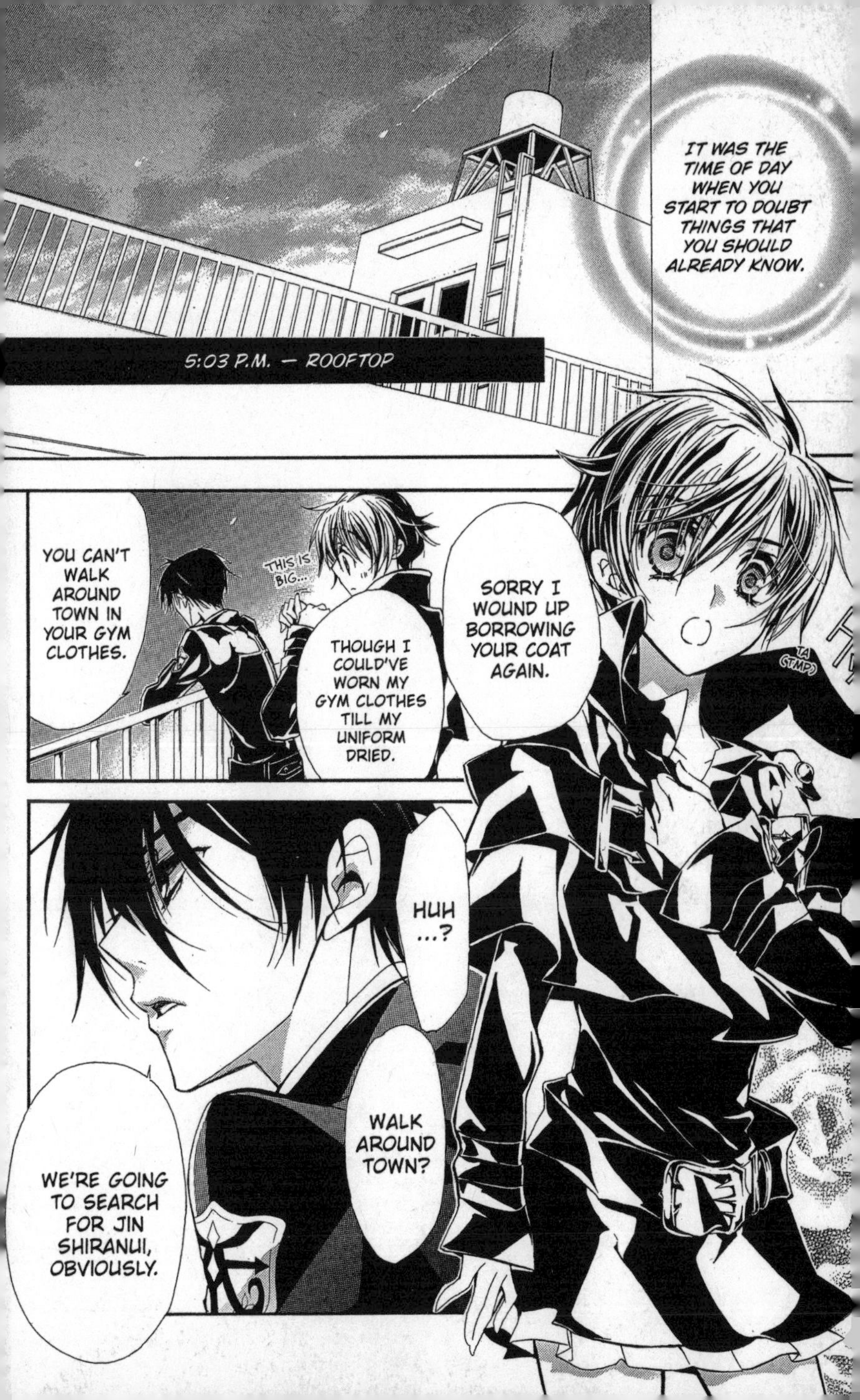
IT WAS THE TIME OF DAY WHEN YOU START TO DOUBT THINGS THAT YOU SHOULD ALREADY KNOW.
5:03 P.M. — ROOFTOP
TA (TMP)
SORRY I WOUND UP BORROWING YOUR COAT AGAIN.
THOUGH I COULD'VE WORN MY GYM CLOTHES TILL MY UNIFORM DRIED.
THIS IS BIG...
YOU CAN'T WALK AROUND TOWN IN YOUR GYM CLOTHES.
HUH ...?
WALK AROUND TOWN?
WE'RE GOING TO SEARCH FOR JIN SHIRANUI, OBVIOUSLY.

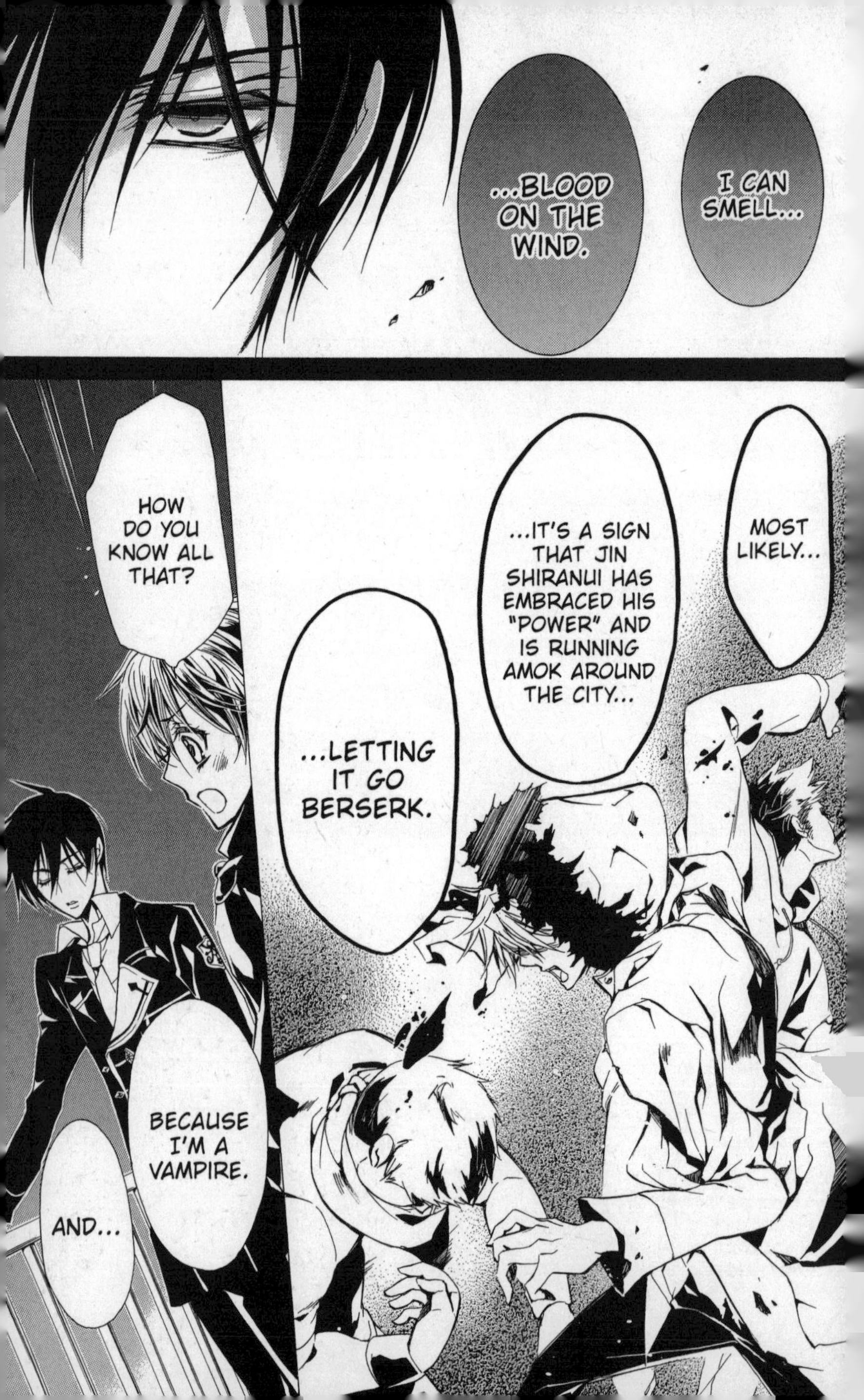
I CAN SMELL...
...BLOOD ON THE WIND.
MOST LIKELY...
...IT'S A SIGN THAT JIN SHIRANUI HAS EMBRACED HIS "POWER" AND IS RUNNING AMOK AROUND THE CITY...
...LETTING IT GO BERSERK.
HOW DO YOU KNOW ALL THAT?
BECAUSE I'M A VAMPIRE.
AND...

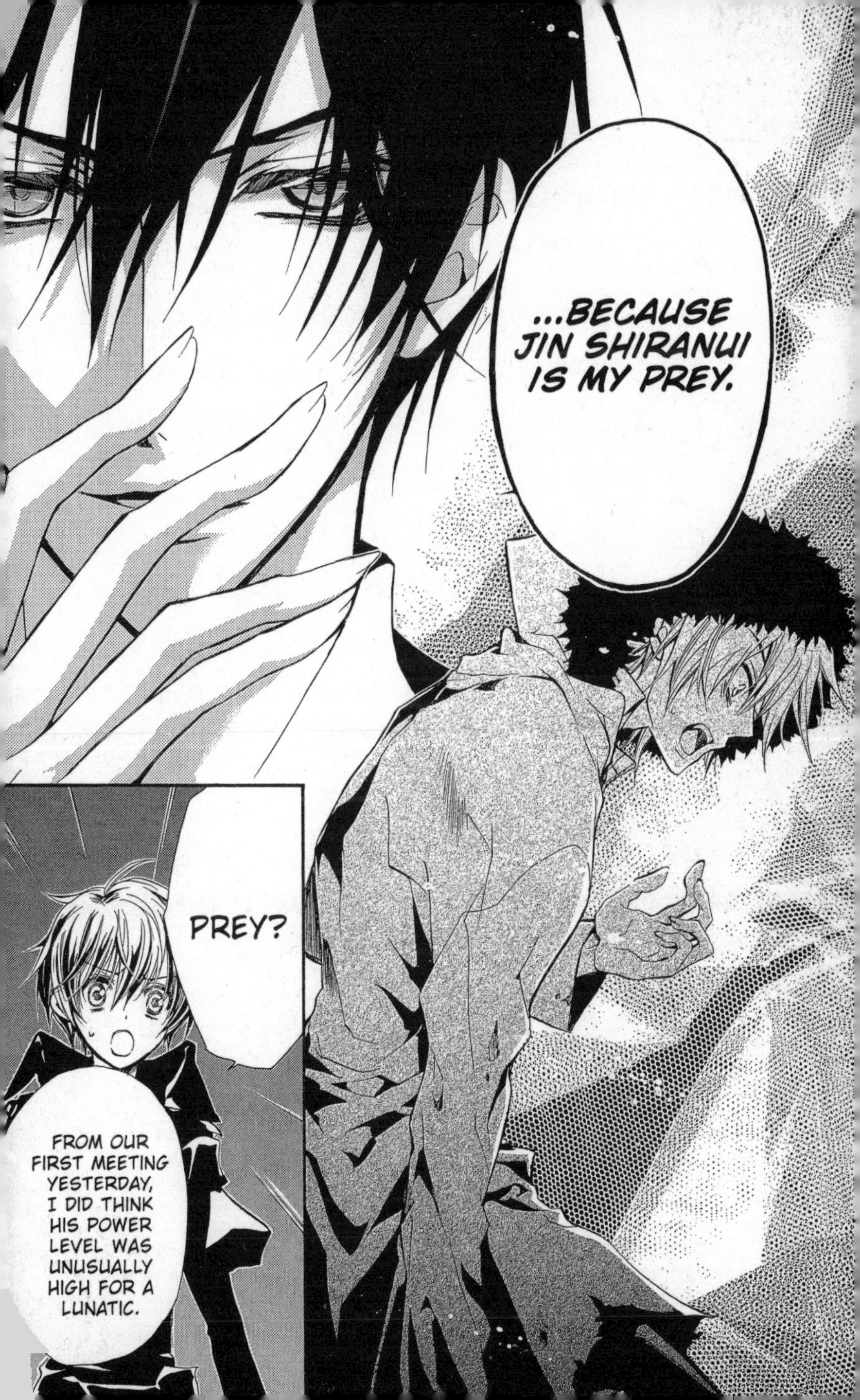
...BECAUSE JIN SHIRANUI IS MY PREY.
PREY?
FROM OUR FIRST MEETING YESTERDAY, I DID THINK HIS POWER LEVEL WAS UNUSUALLY HIGH FOR A LUNATIC.

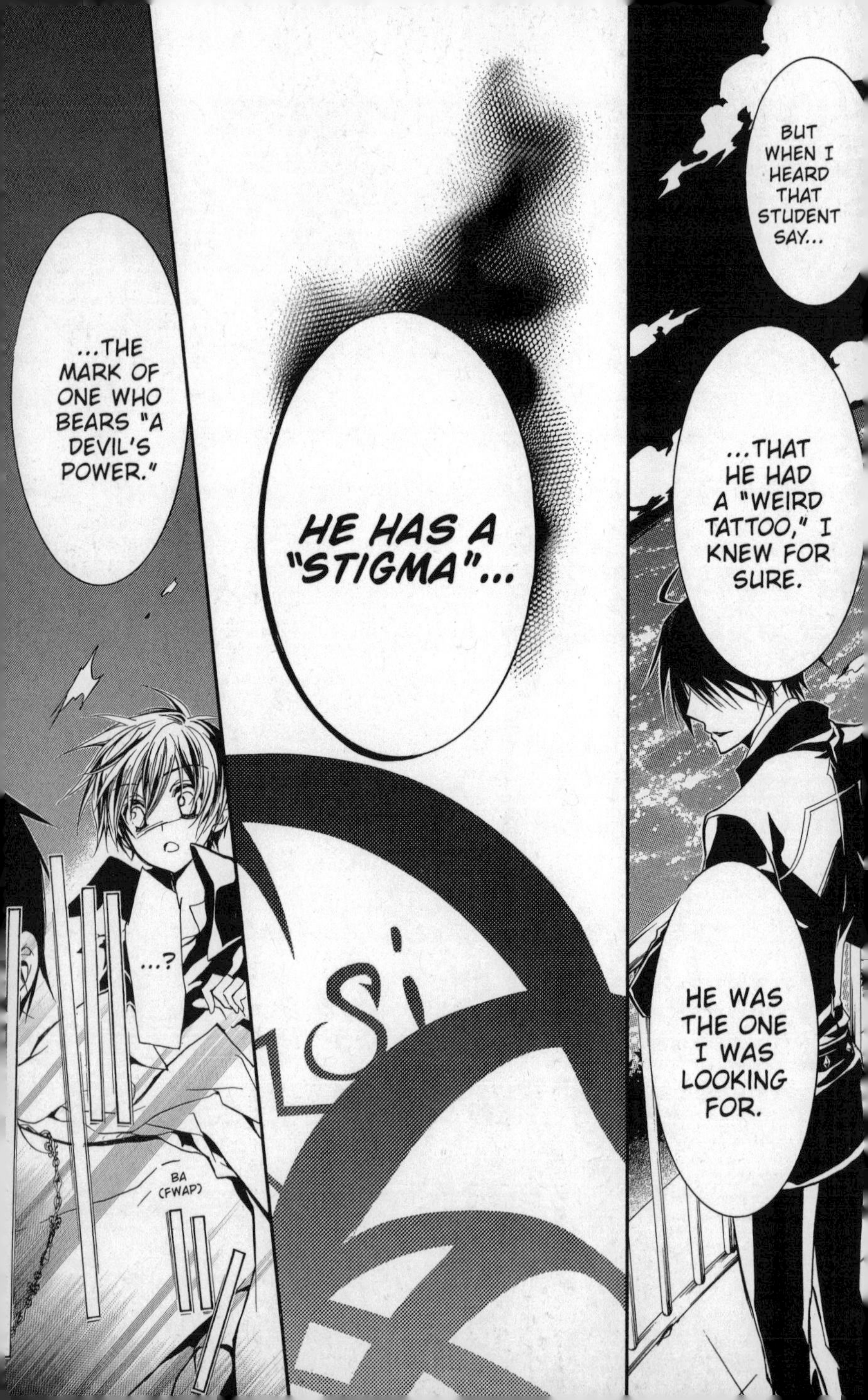
BUT WHEN I HEARD THAT STUDENT SAY...
...THAT HE HAD A "WEIRD TATTOO," I KNEW FOR SURE.
HE WAS THE ONE I WAS LOOKING FOR.
HE HAS A "STIGMA"...
...THE MARK OF ONE WHO BEARS "A DEVIL'S POWER."
...?
BA (FWAP)

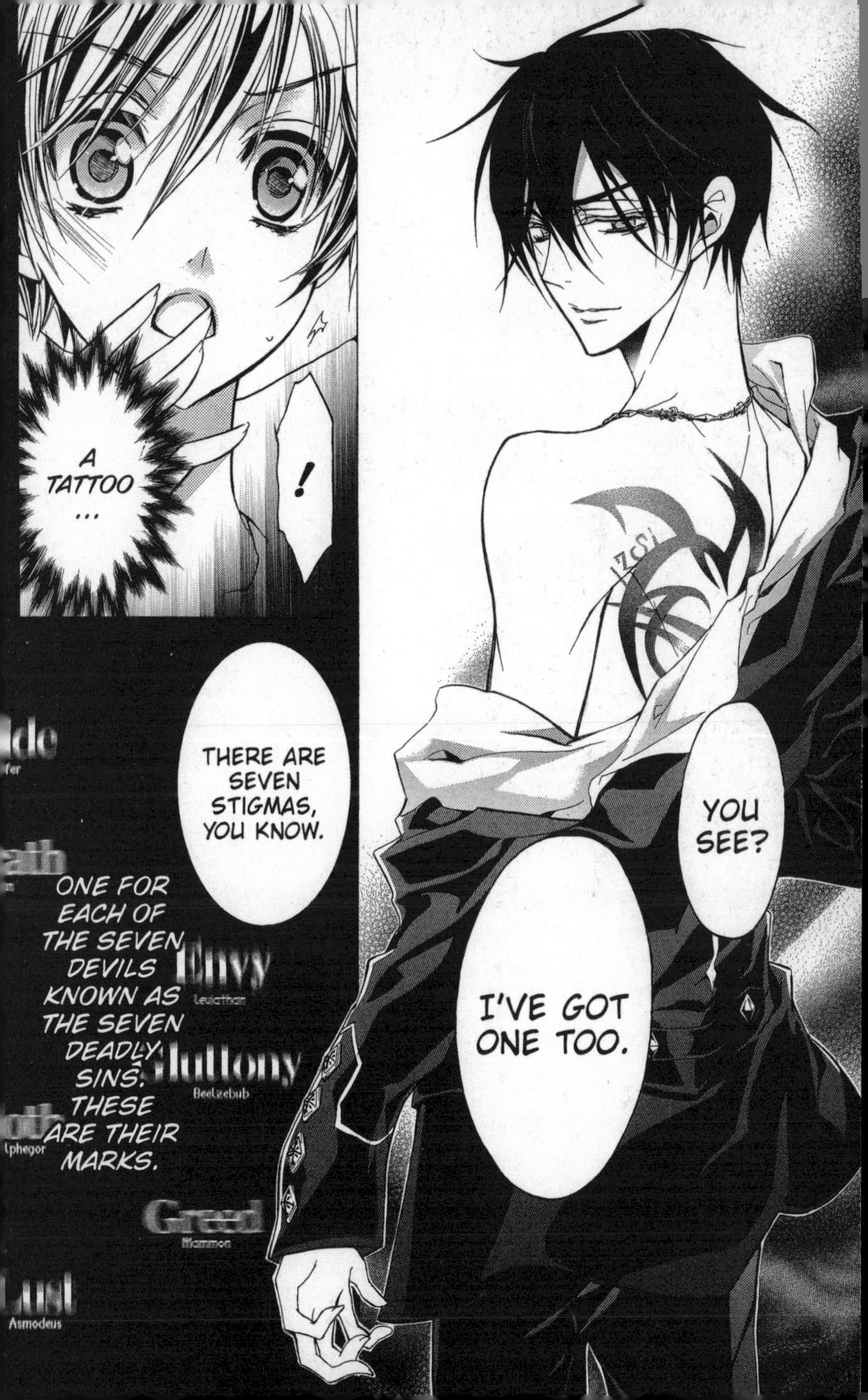
YOU SEE?
I'VE GOT ONE TOO.
!
A TATTOO...
THERE ARE SEVEN STIGMAS, YOU KNOW.
ONE FOR EACH OF THE SEVEN DEVILS KNOWN AS THE SEVEN DEADLY SINS. THESE ARE THEIR MARKS.
Envy
Leviathan
Beelzebub
Greed
Mammon
Lust
Asmodeus

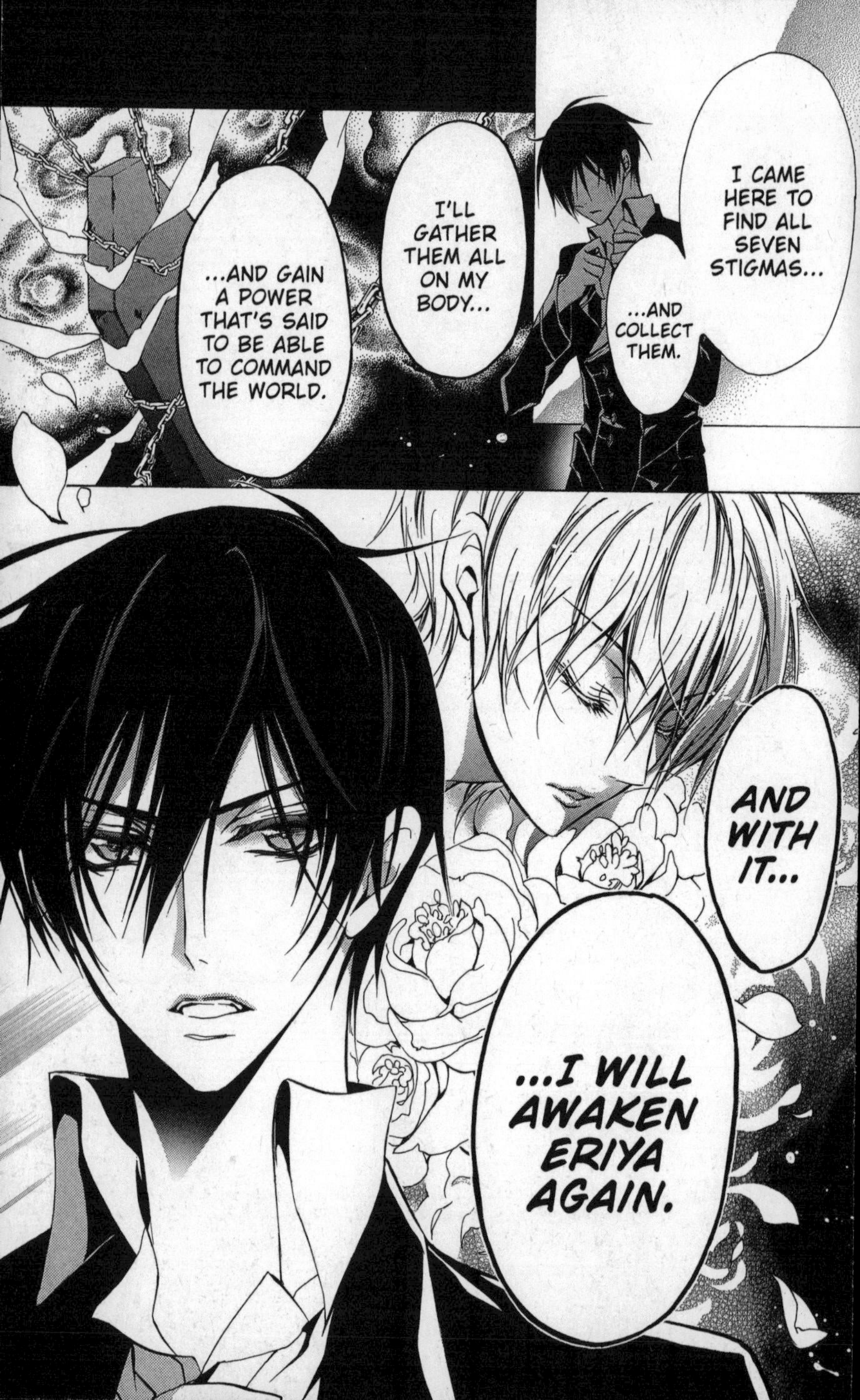
I CAME HERE TO FIND ALL SEVEN STIGMAS...
...AND COLLECT THEM.
I'LL GATHER THEM ALL ON MY BODY...
...AND GAIN A POWER THAT'S SAID TO BE ABLE TO COMMAND THE WORLD.
AND WITH IT...
...I WILL AWAKEN ERIYA AGAIN.

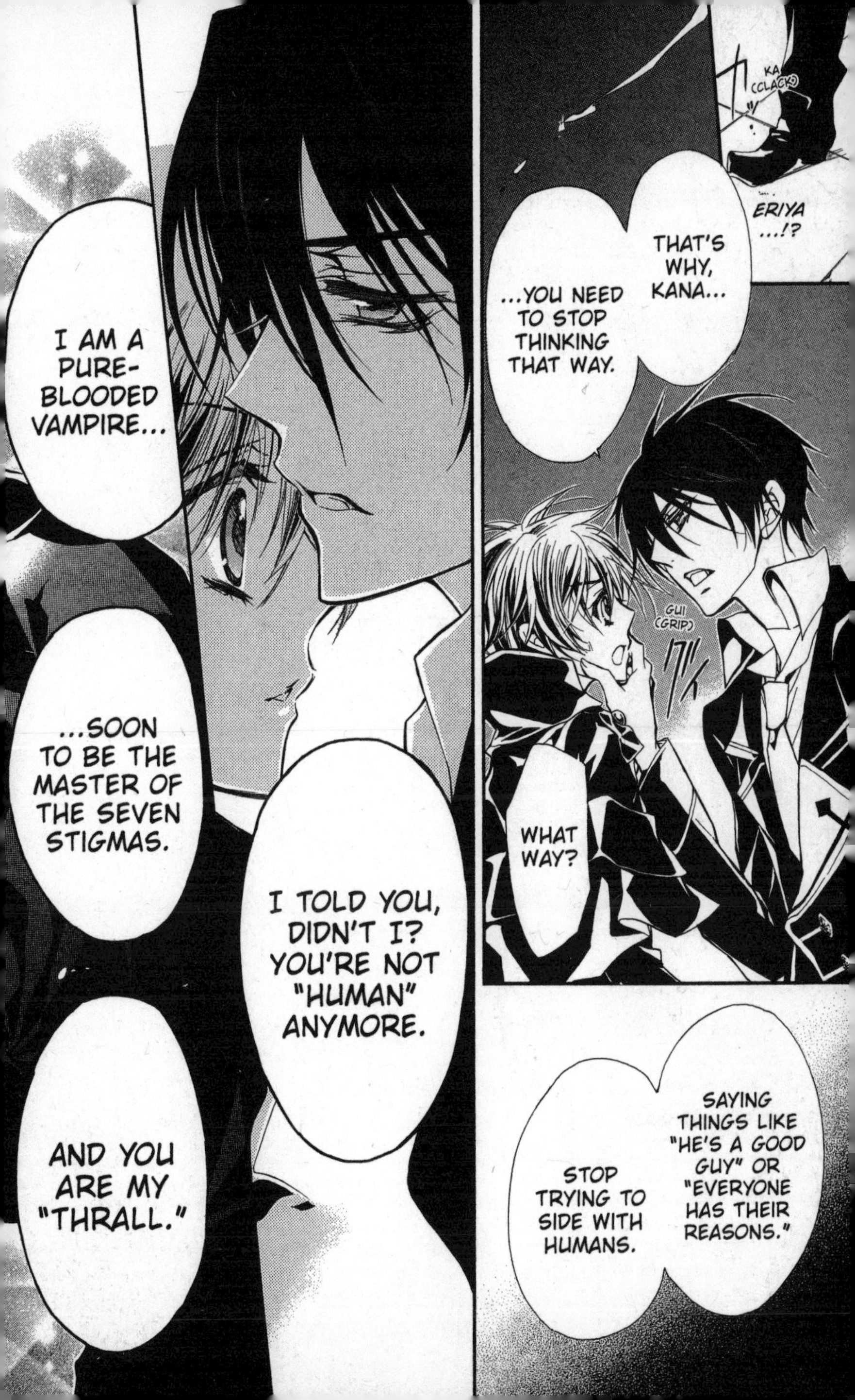
KA (CLACK)
ERIYA ...!?
THAT'S WHY, KANA...
...YOU NEED TO STOP THINKING THAT WAY.
GUI (GRIP)
WHAT WAY?
SAYING THINGS LIKE "HE'S A GOOD GUY" OR "EVERYONE HAS THEIR REASONS."
STOP TRYING TO SIDE WITH HUMANS.
I TOLD YOU, DIDN'T I? YOU'RE NOT "HUMAN" ANYMORE.
I AM A PURE-BLOODED VAMPIRE...
...SOON TO BE THE MASTER OF THE SEVEN STIGMAS.
AND YOU ARE MY "THRALL."

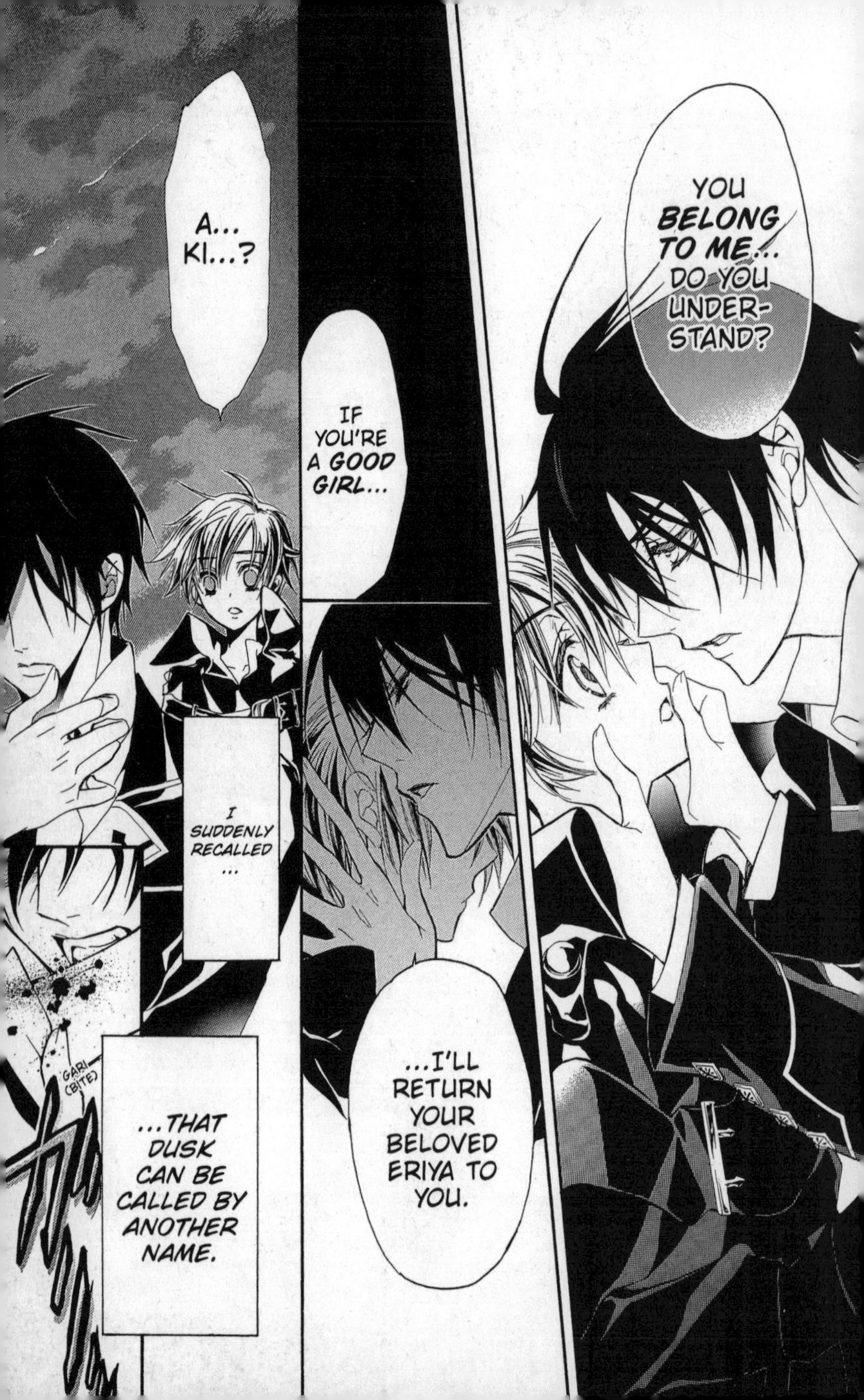
YOU BELONG TO ME... DO YOU UNDERSTAND?
IF YOU'RE A GOOD GIRL...
...I'LL RETURN YOUR BELOVED ERIYA TO YOU.
A... KI...?
I SUDDENLY RECALLED...
GARI (BITE)
...THAT DUSK CAN BE CALLED BY ANOTHER NAME.

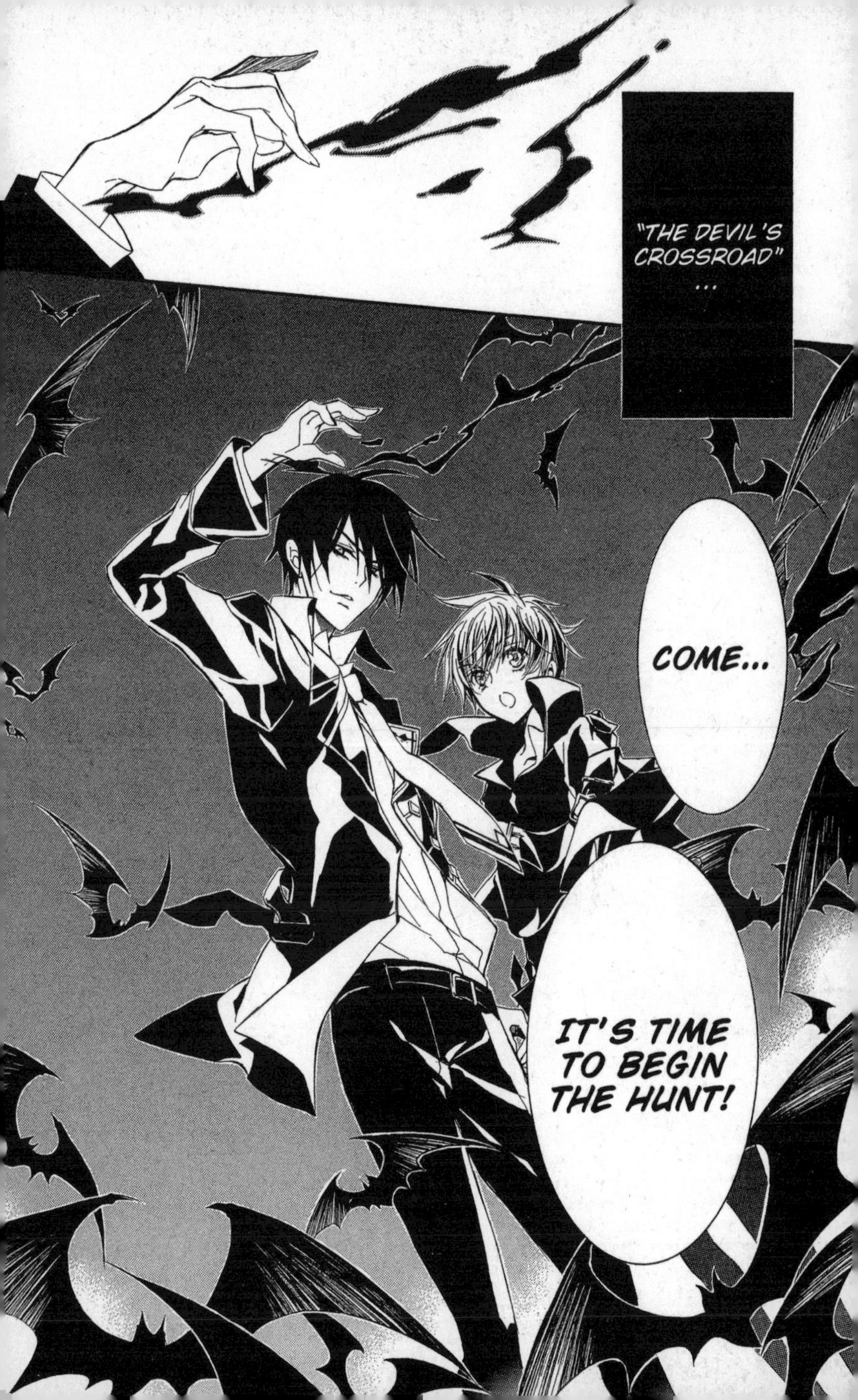
"THE DEVIL'S CROSSROAD" ...
COME...
IT'S TIME TO BEGIN THE HUNT!

~moon phase~4

The Hunter's Triangle

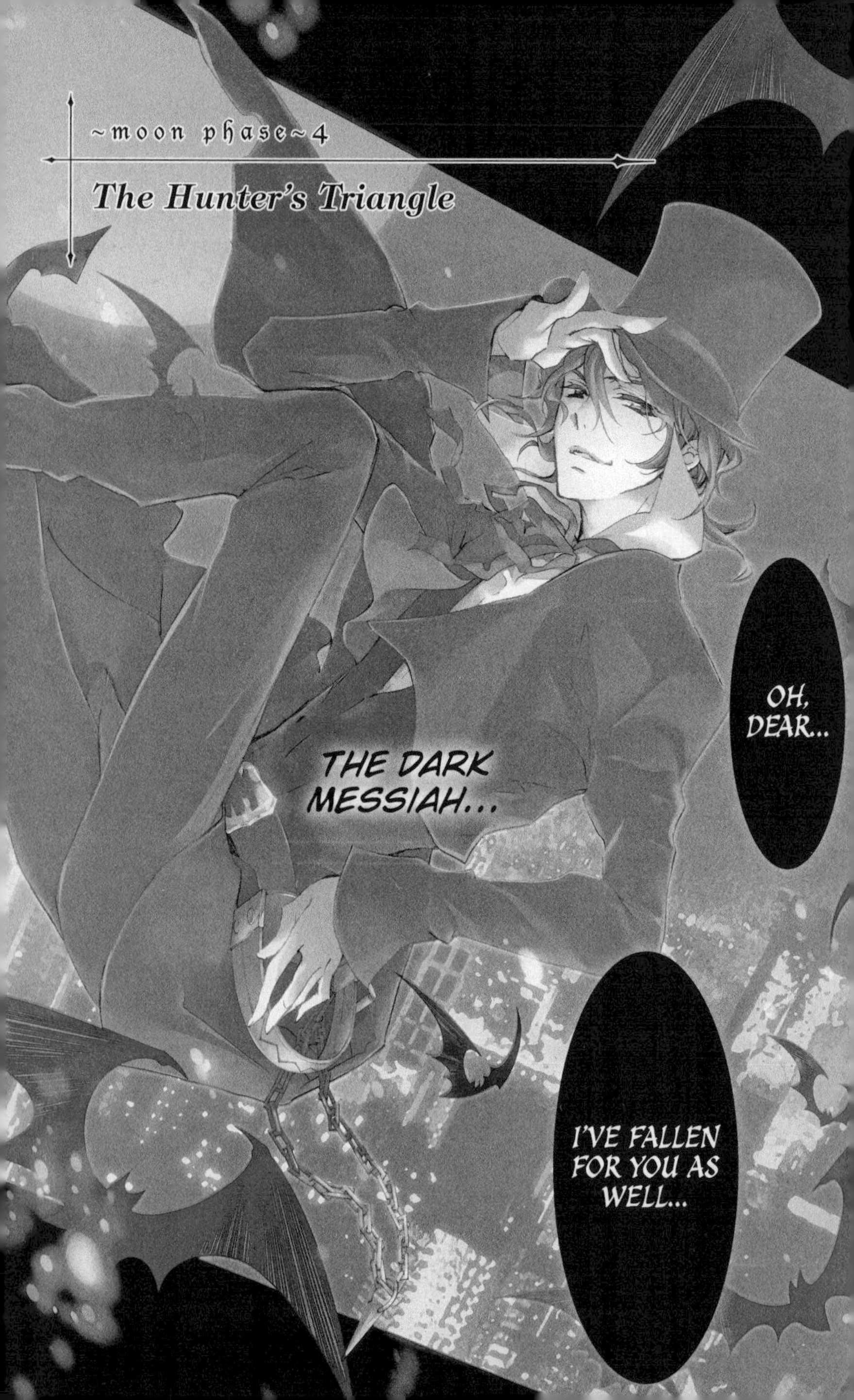
OH, DEAR...
THE DARK MESSIAH...
I'VE FALLEN FOR YOU AS WELL...

He's my only vampire
Aya Shouoto

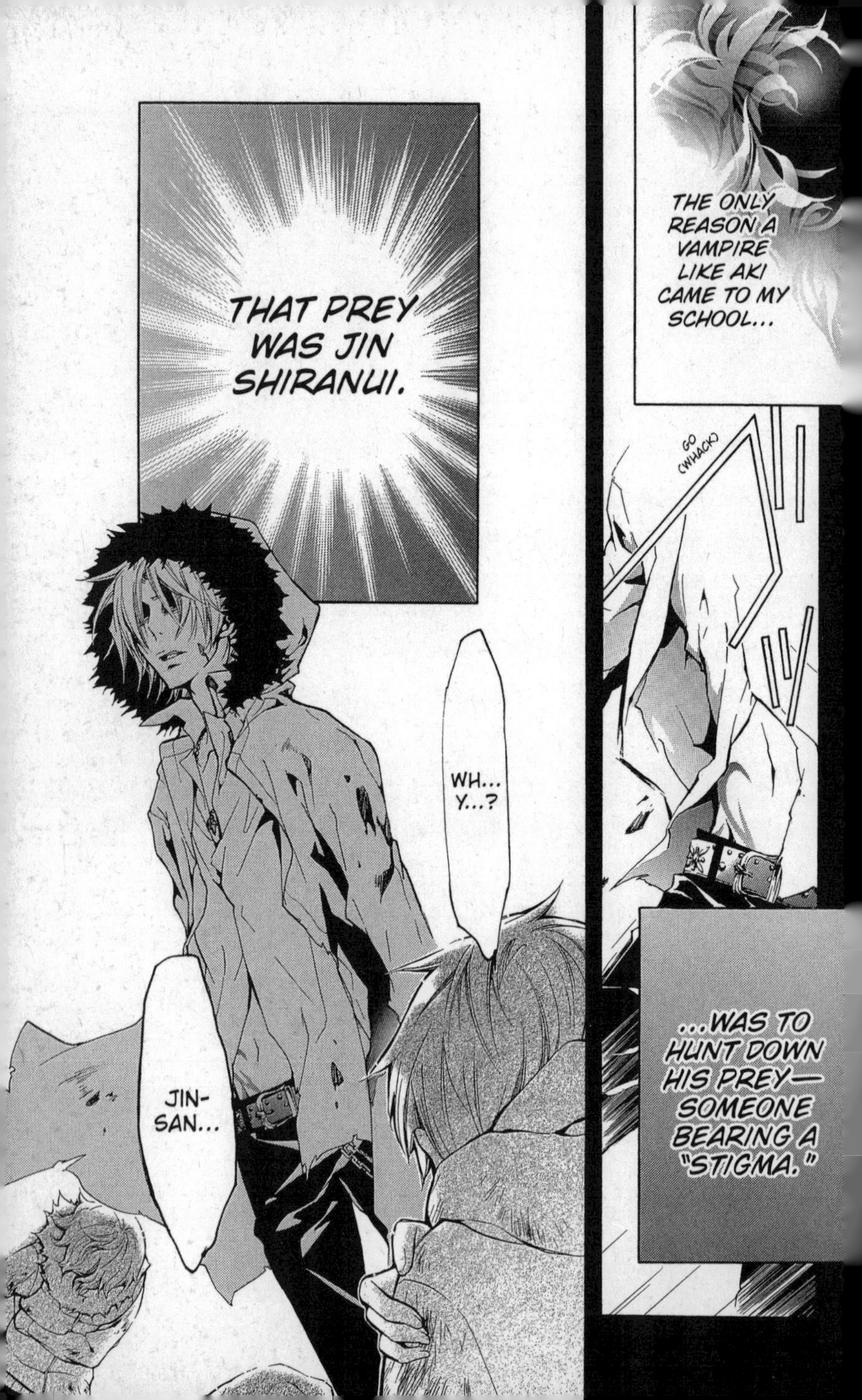
THE ONLY REASON A VAMPIRE LIKE AKI CAME TO MY SCHOOL...
GO (WHACK)
...WAS TO HUNT DOWN HIS PREY—SOMEONE BEARING A "STIGMA."
THAT PREY WAS JIN SHIRANUI.
WH... Y...?
JIN-SAN...

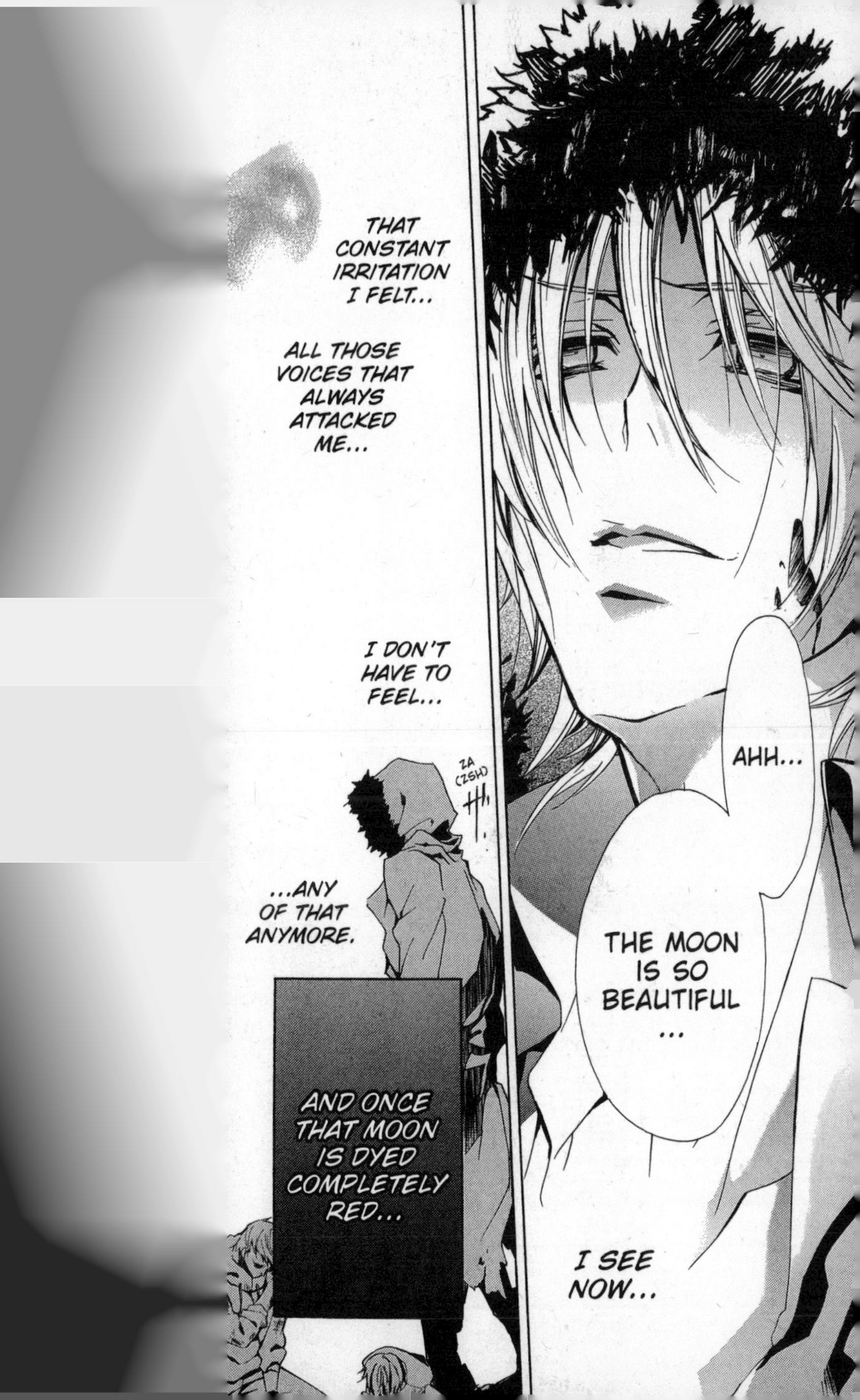
AHH...
THE MOON IS SO BEAUTIFUL ...
I SEE NOW...
THAT CONSTANT IRRITATION I FELT...
ALL THOSE VOICES THAT ALWAYS ATTACKED ME...
I DON'T HAVE TO FEEL...
ZA (ZSH)
...ANY OF THAT ANYMORE.
AND ONCE THAT MOON IS DYED COMPLETELY RED...

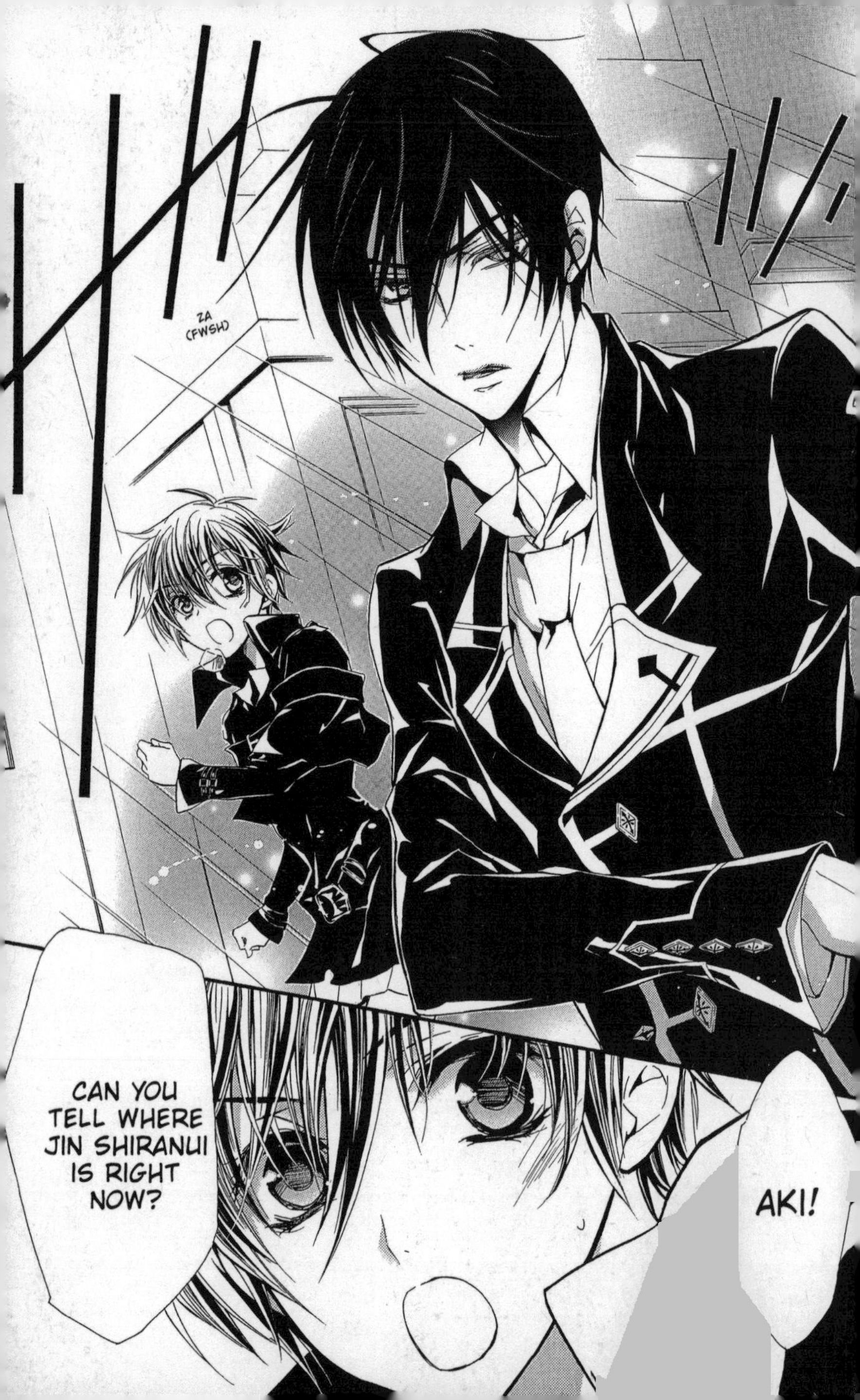
ZA (FWSH)
AKI!
CAN YOU TELL WHERE JIN SHIRANUI IS RIGHT NOW?

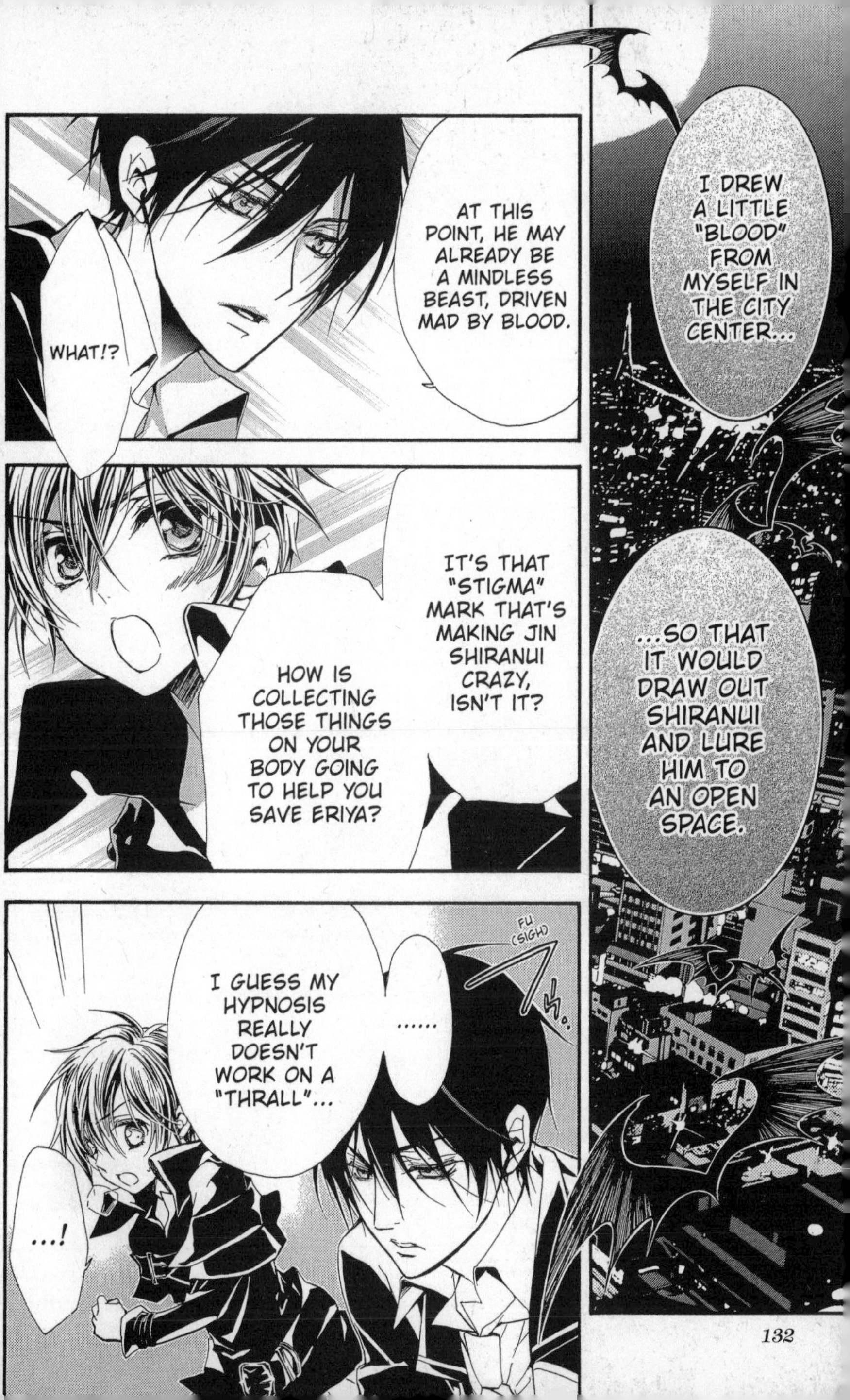
I DREW A LITTLE "BLOOD" FROM MYSELF IN THE CITY CENTER...
...SO THAT IT WOULD DRAW OUT SHIRANUI AND LURE HIM TO AN OPEN SPACE.
AT THIS POINT, HE MAY ALREADY BE A MINDLESS BEAST, DRIVEN MAD BY BLOOD.
WHAT!?
IT'S THAT "STIGMA" MARK THAT'S MAKING JIN SHIRANUI CRAZY, ISN'T IT?
HOW IS COLLECTING THOSE THINGS ON YOUR BODY GOING TO HELP YOU SAVE ERIYA?
FU (SIGH)
......
I GUESS MY HYPNOSIS REALLY DOESN'T WORK ON A "THRALL"...
...!

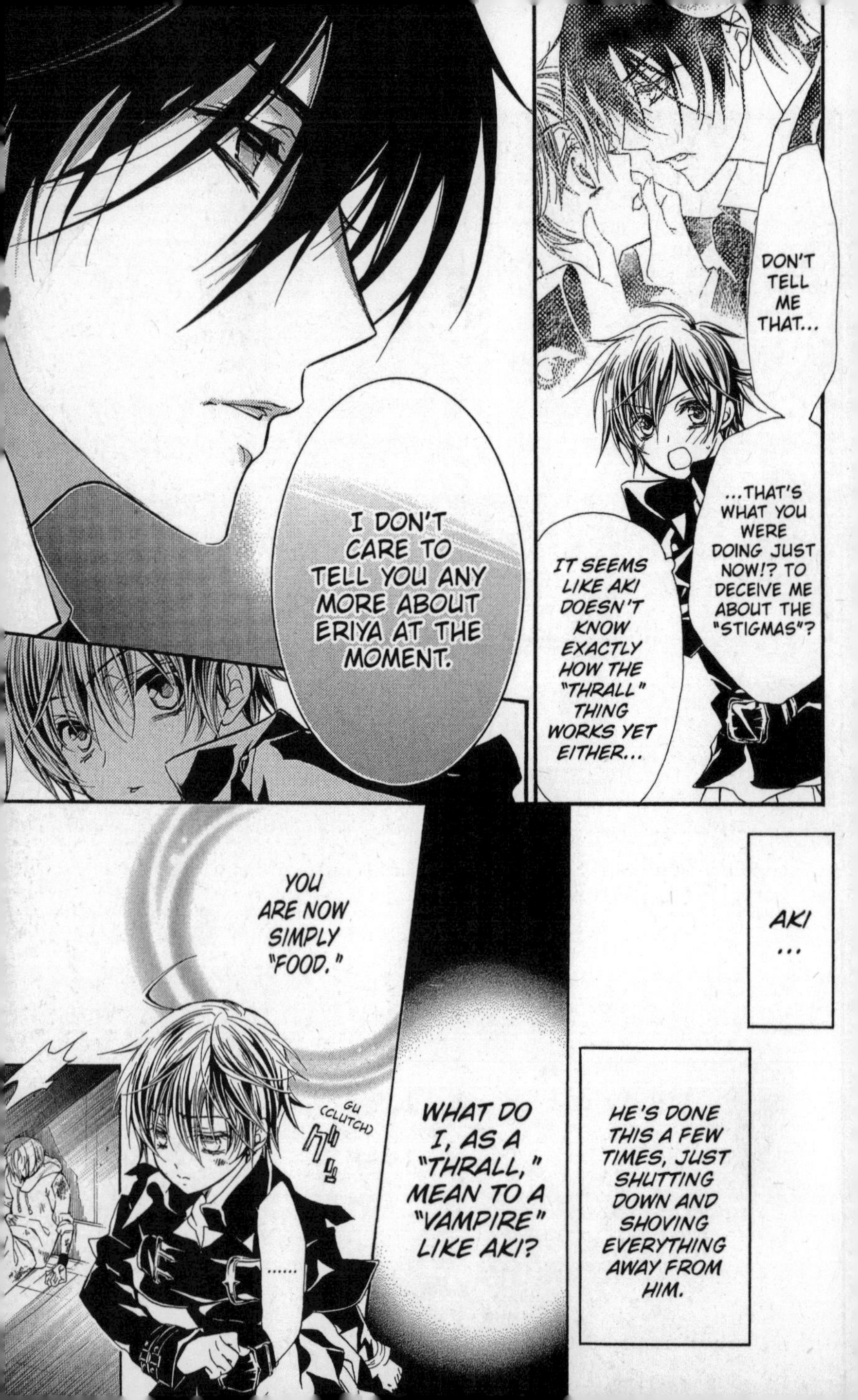
DON'T TELL ME THAT...
...THAT'S WHAT YOU WERE DOING JUST NOW!? TO DECEIVE ME ABOUT THE "STIGMAS"?
IT SEEMS LIKE AKI DOESN'T KNOW EXACTLY HOW THE "THRALL" THING WORKS YET EITHER...
I DON'T CARE TO TELL YOU ANY MORE ABOUT ERIYA AT THE MOMENT.
AKI ...
HE'S DONE THIS A FEW TIMES, JUST SHUTTING DOWN AND SHOVING EVERYTHING AWAY FROM HIM.
WHAT DO I, AS A "THRALL," MEAN TO A "VAMPIRE" LIKE AKI?
YOU ARE NOW SIMPLY "FOOD."
GU (CLUTCH)
......

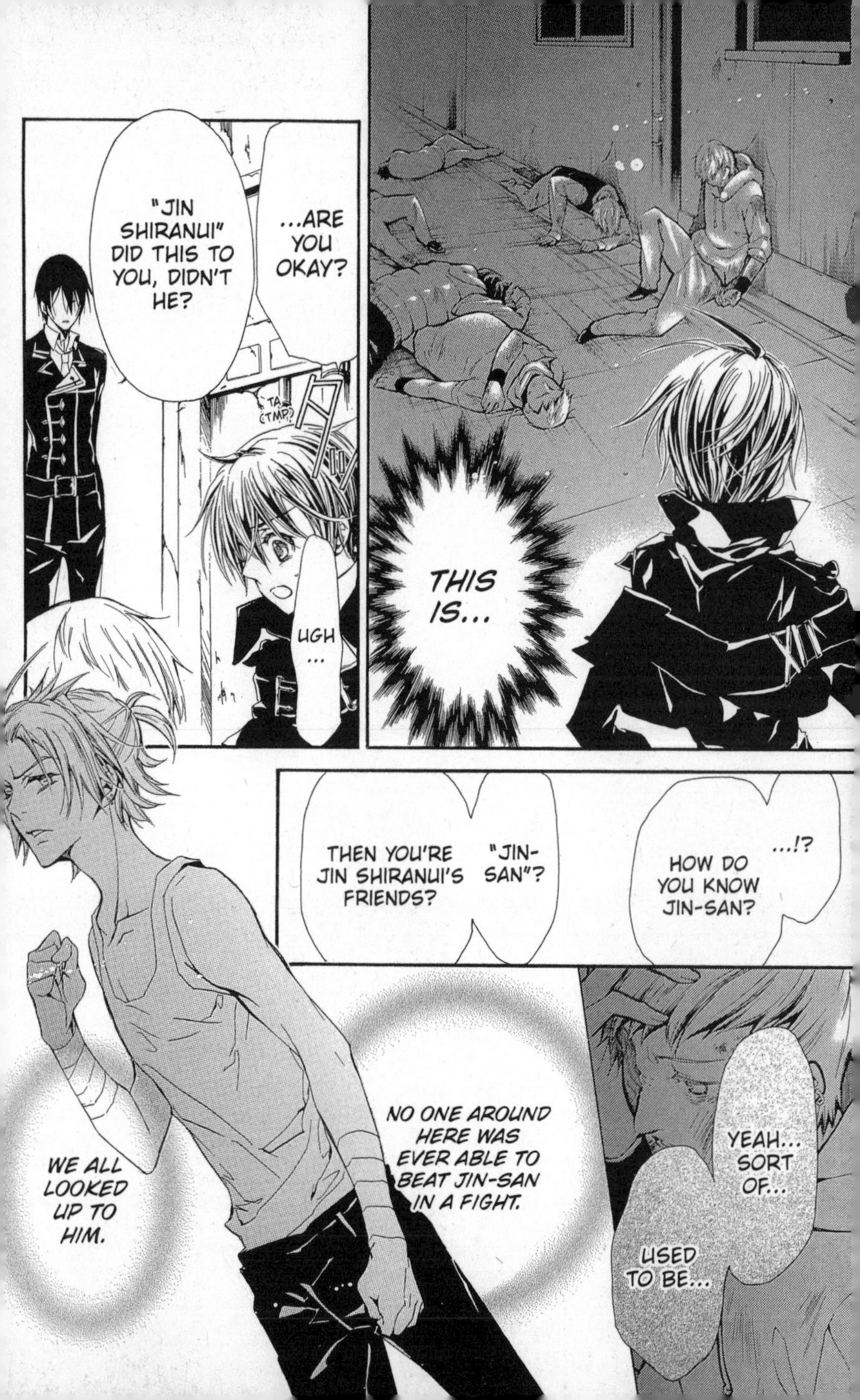
THIS IS...
...ARE YOU OKAY?
"JIN SHIRANUI" DID THIS TO YOU, DIDN'T HE?
TA TMP
UGH...
...!?
HOW DO YOU KNOW JIN-SAN?
"JIN-SAN"?
THEN YOU'RE JIN SHIRANUI'S FRIENDS?
YEAH... SORT OF...
USED TO BE...
NO ONE AROUND HERE WAS EVER ABLE TO BEAT JIN-SAN IN A FIGHT.
WE ALL LOOKED UP TO HIM.

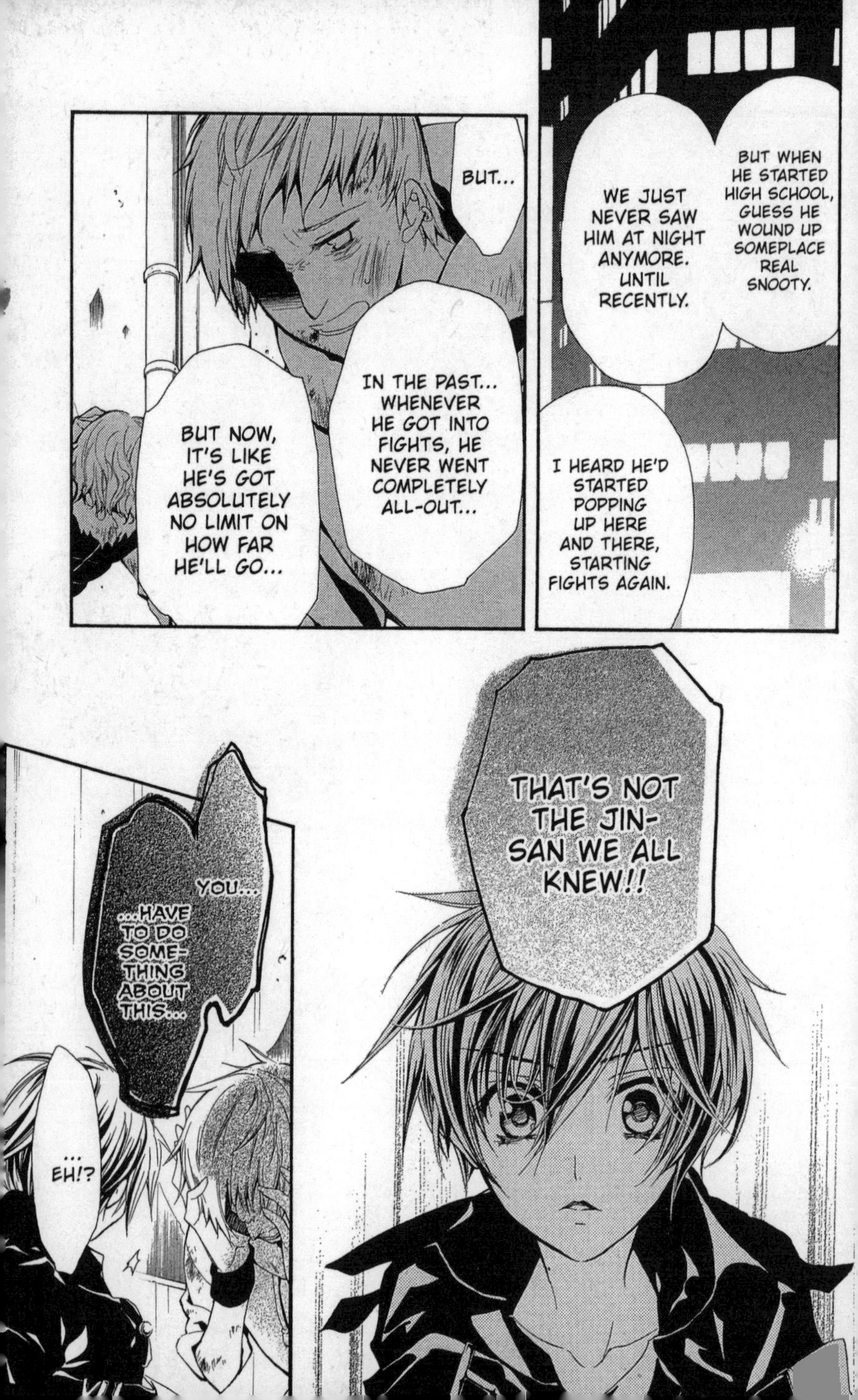
BUT WHEN HE STARTED HIGH SCHOOL, GUESS HE WOUND UP SOMEPLACE REAL SNOOTY.
WE JUST NEVER SAW HIM AT NIGHT ANYMORE. UNTIL RECENTLY.
I HEARD HE'D STARTED POPPING UP HERE AND THERE, STARTING FIGHTS AGAIN.
BUT...
IN THE PAST... WHENEVER HE GOT INTO FIGHTS, HE NEVER WENT COMPLETELY ALL-OUT...
BUT NOW, IT'S LIKE HE'S GOT ABSOLUTELY NO LIMIT ON HOW FAR HE'LL GO...
THAT'S NOT THE JIN-SAN WE ALL KNEW!!
YOU...
...HAVE TO DO SOME-THING ABOUT THIS...
...EH!?

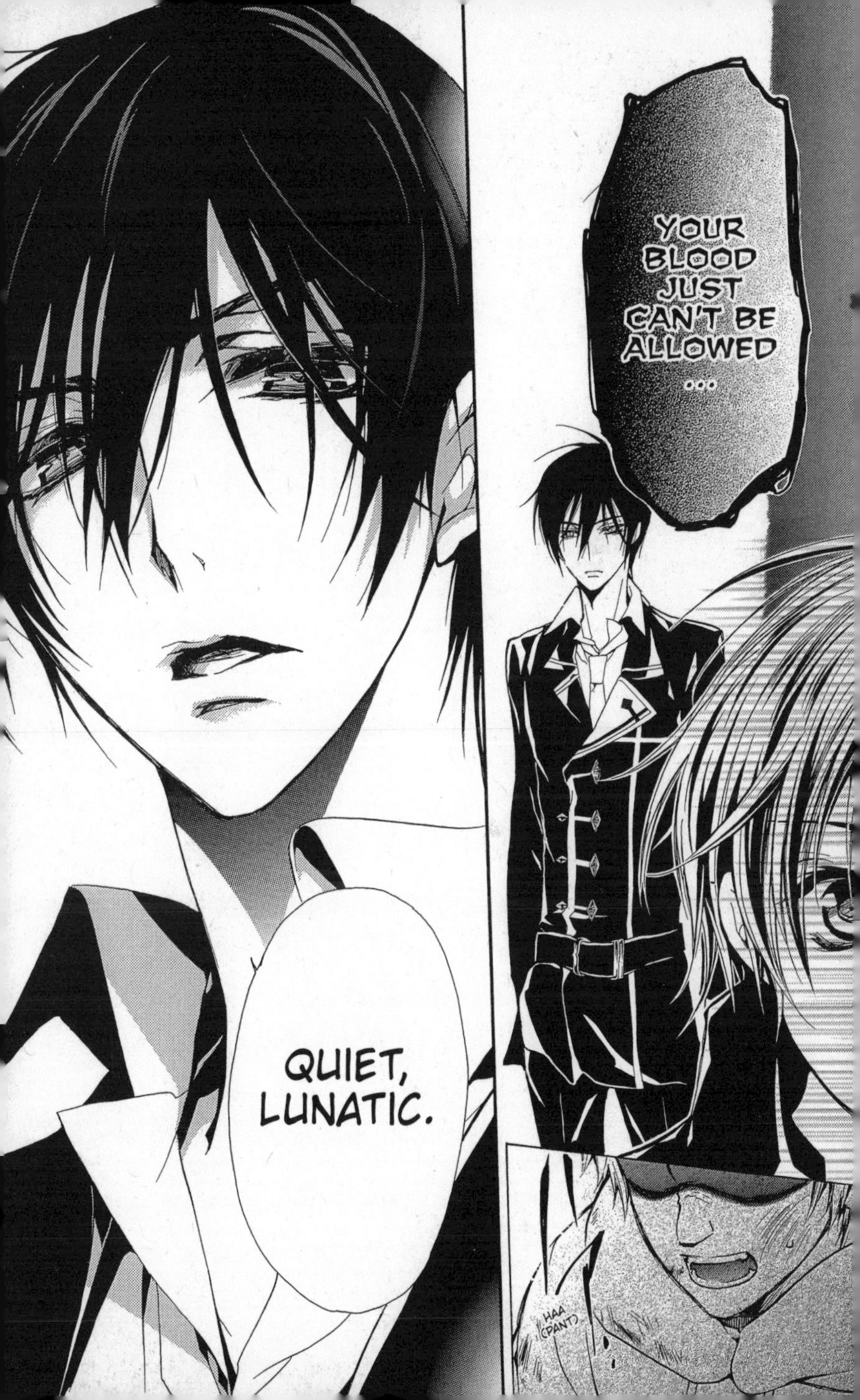
YOUR BLOOD JUST CAN'T BE ALLOWED...
HAA (PANT)
QUIET, LUNATIC.

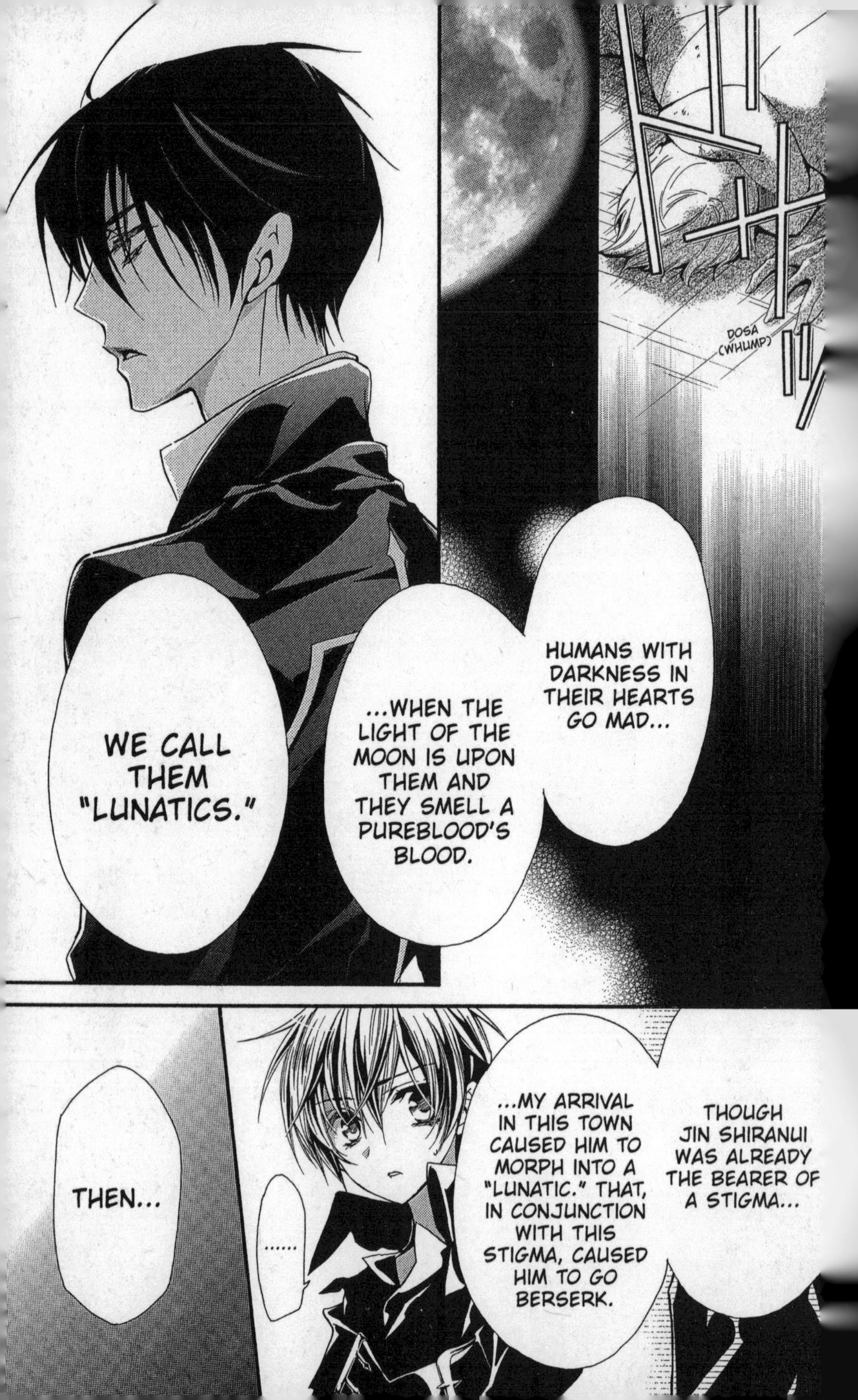
DOSA (WHUMP)
HUMANS WITH DARKNESS IN THEIR HEARTS GO MAD...
...WHEN THE LIGHT OF THE MOON IS UPON THEM AND THEY SMELL A PUREBLOOD'S BLOOD.
WE CALL THEM "LUNATICS."
THOUGH JIN SHIRANUI WAS ALREADY THE BEARER OF A STIGMA...
...MY ARRIVAL IN THIS TOWN CAUSED HIM TO MORPH INTO A "LUNATIC." THAT, IN CONJUNCTION WITH THIS STIGMA, CAUSED HIM TO GO BERSERK.
......
THEN...

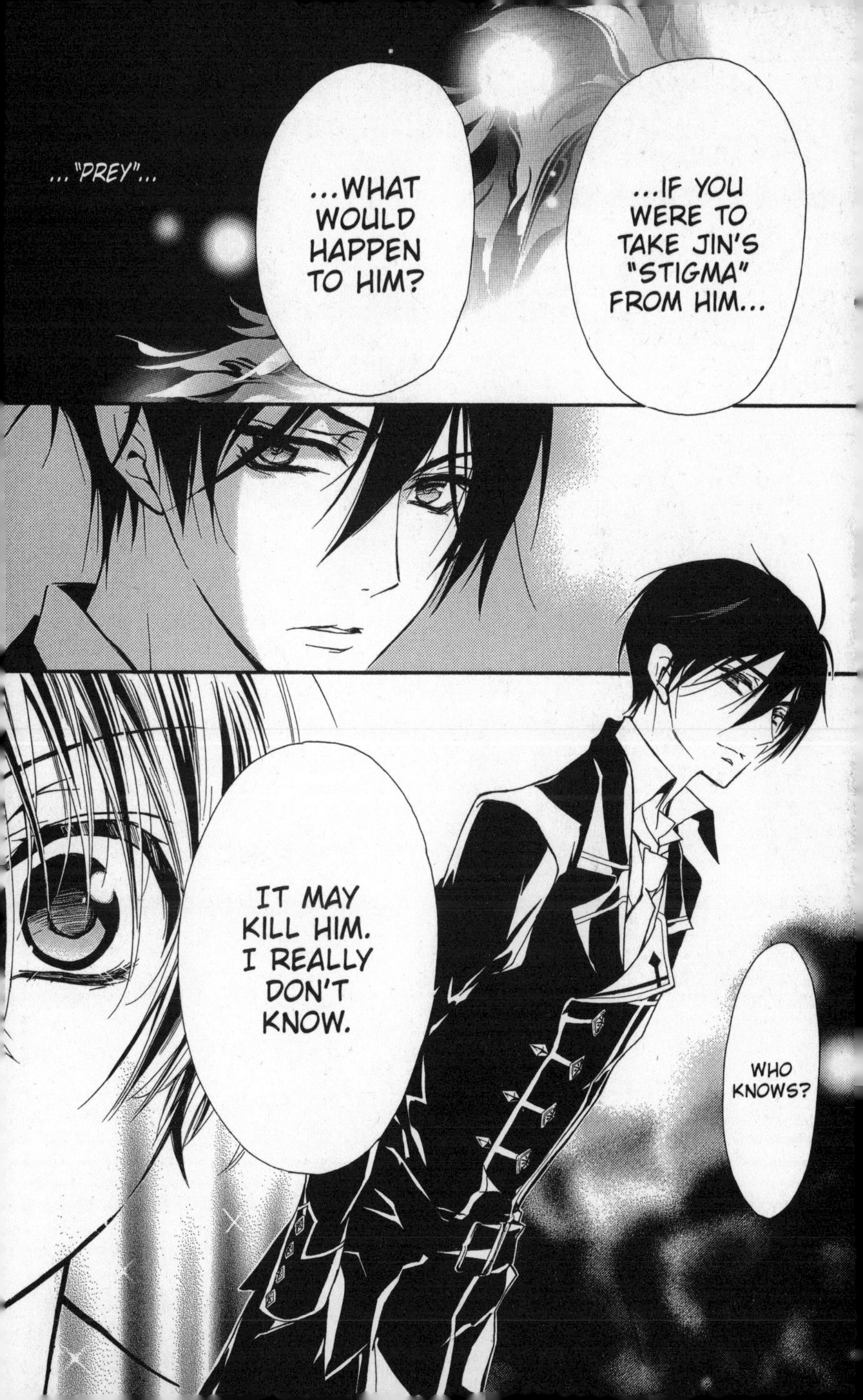
...IF YOU WERE TO TAKE JIN'S "STIGMA" FROM HIM...
...WHAT WOULD HAPPEN TO HIM?
..."PREY"...
WHO KNOWS?
IT MAY KILL HIM. I REALLY DON'T KNOW.

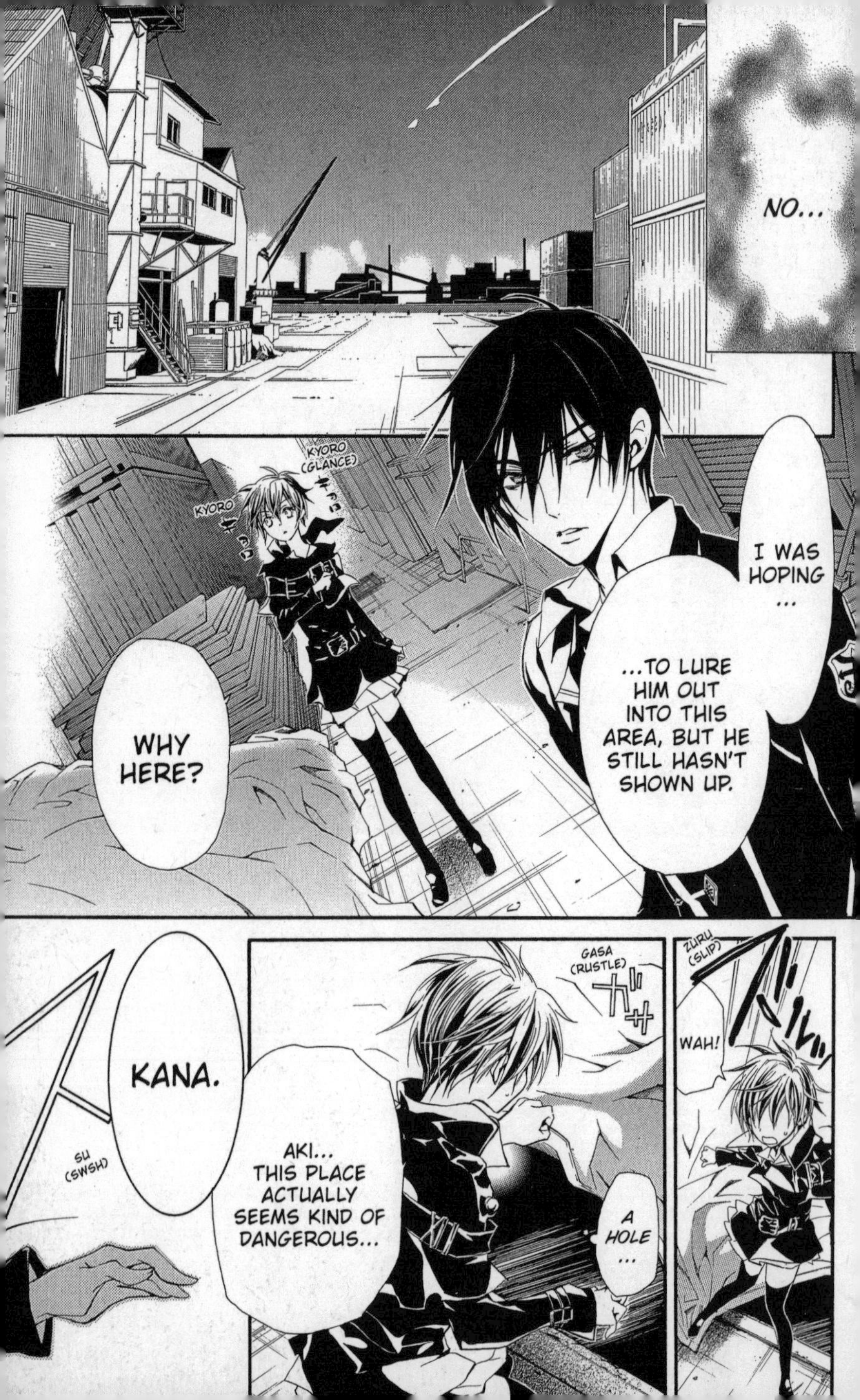
NO...
I WAS HOPING...
...TO LURE HIM OUT INTO THIS AREA, BUT HE STILL HASN'T SHOWN UP.
KYORO (GLANCE)
KYORO
WHY HERE?
ZURU (SLIP)
WAH!
GASA (RUSTLE)
A HOLE...
AKI... THIS PLACE ACTUALLY SEEMS KIND OF DANGEROUS...
KANA.
SU (SWSH)

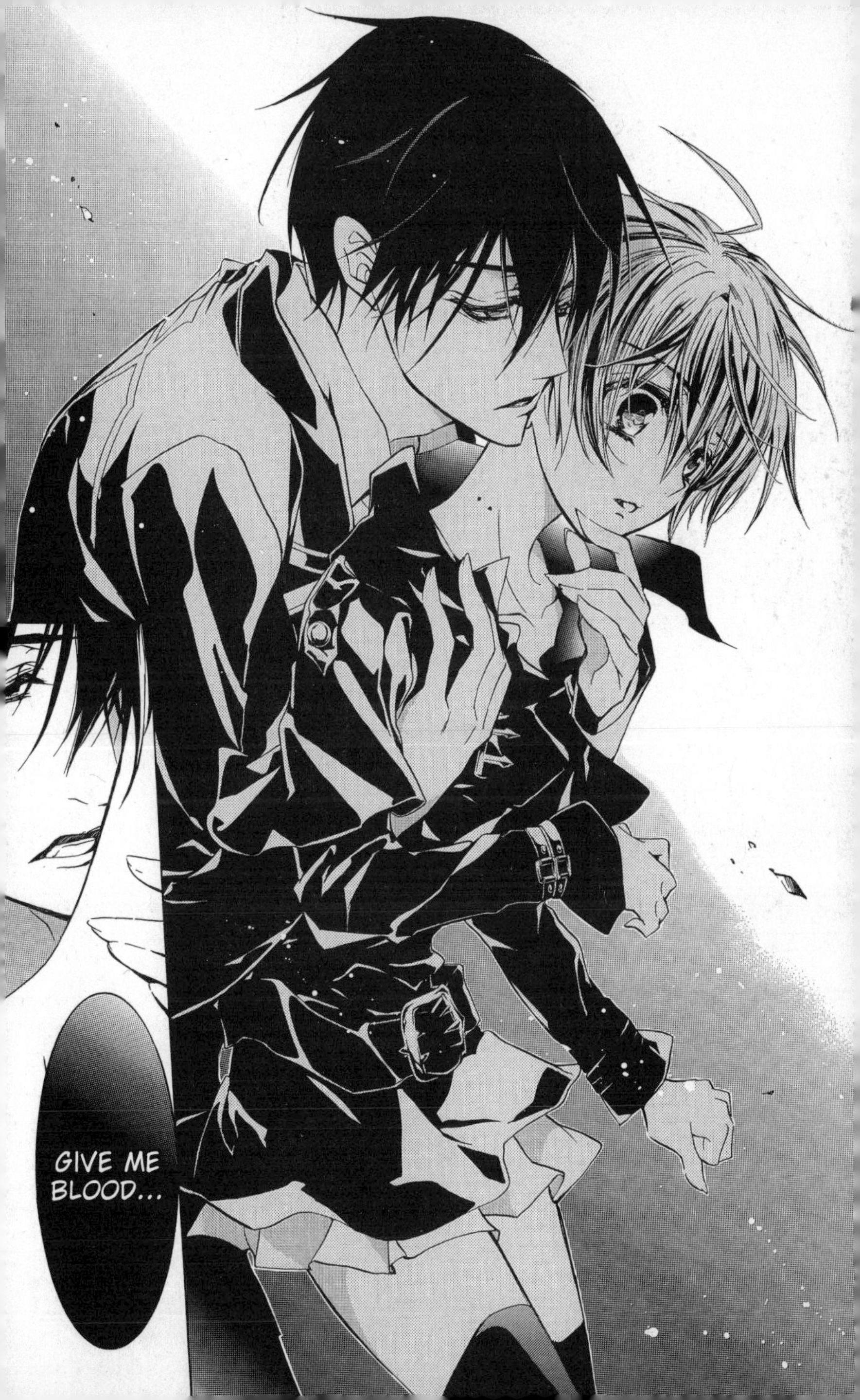
GIVE ME BLOOD...

GUI (SQUEEZE)
...!
HERE...!? NOW...!?
OF COURSE ...
PON (POP)
WEREN'T YOU SAYING IT'S IMPORTANT TO KEEP YOUR RESERVES FILLED?
!
THAT WAS JUST ...
A LIE?
...DON'T RUN FROM ME.
THAT WAS UNFAIR ...

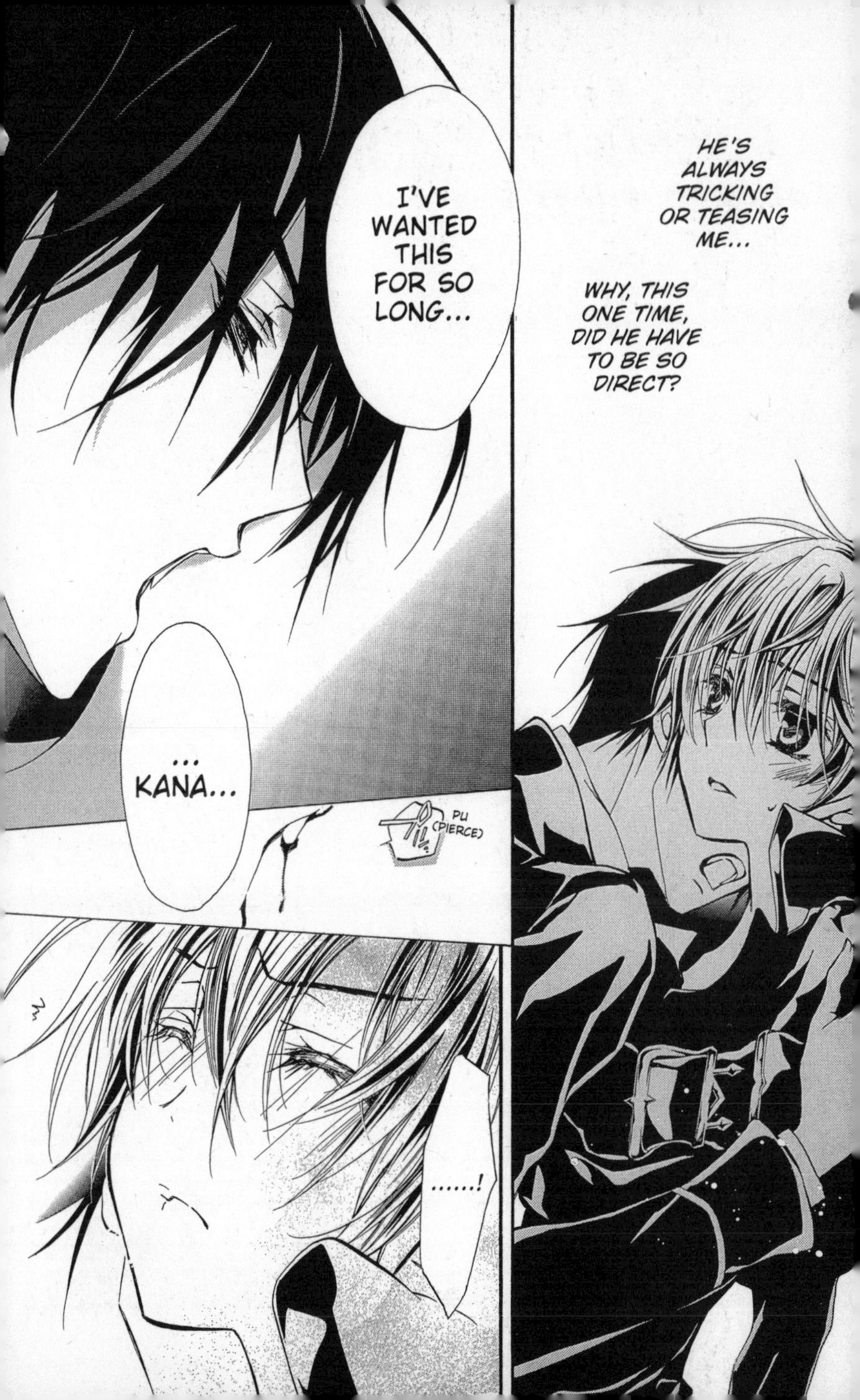
HE'S ALWAYS TRICKING OR TEASING ME...
WHY, THIS ONE TIME, DID HE HAVE TO BE SO DIRECT?
I'VE WANTED THIS FOR SO LONG...
... KANA...
PU (PIERCE)
......!

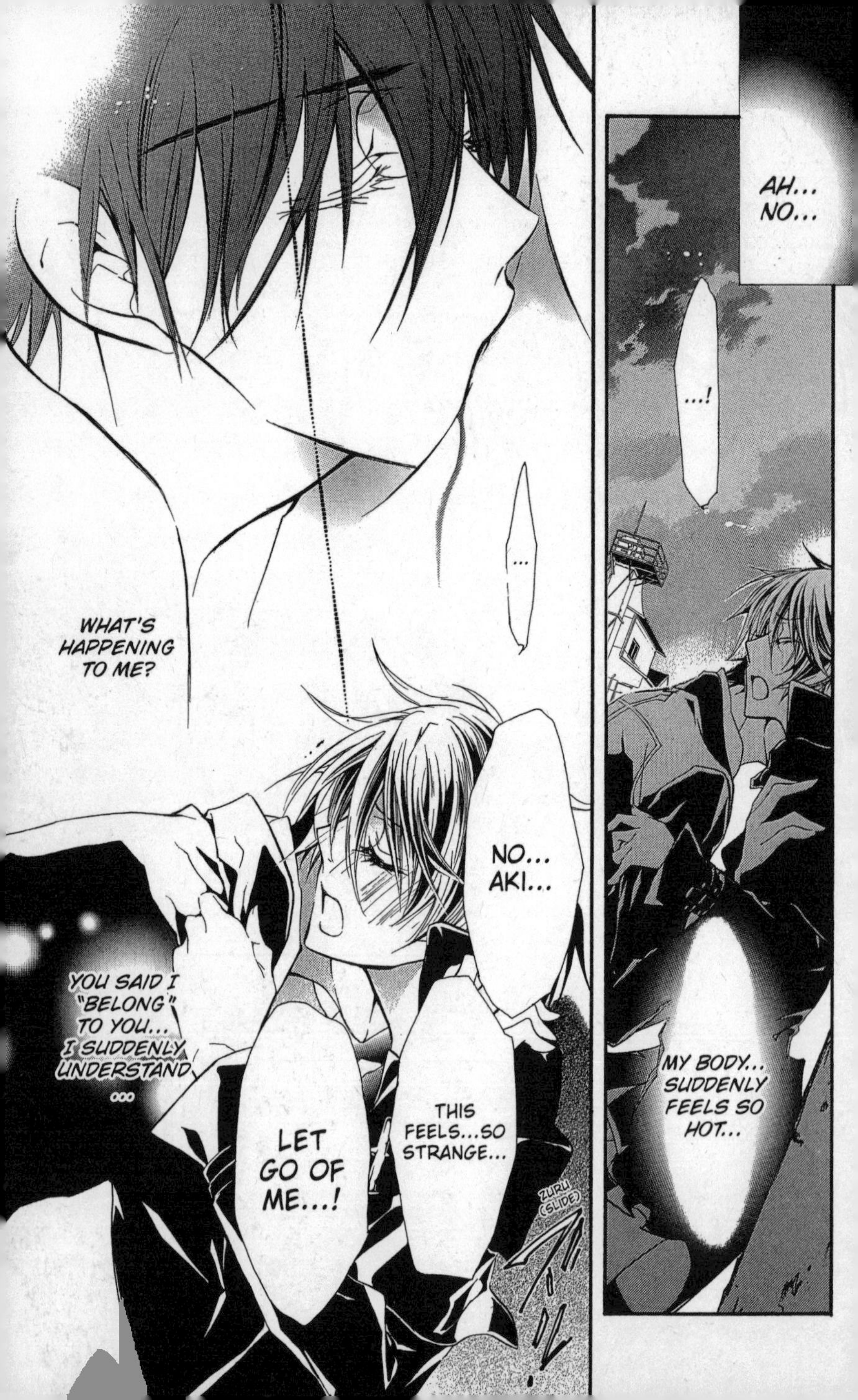
AH... NO...
...!
MY BODY... SUDDENLY FEELS SO HOT...
...
WHAT'S HAPPENING TO ME?
NO... AKI...
THIS FEELS...SO STRANGE...
ZURU (SLIDE)
LET GO OF ME...!
YOU SAID I "BELONG" TO YOU... I SUDDENLY UNDERSTAND ...

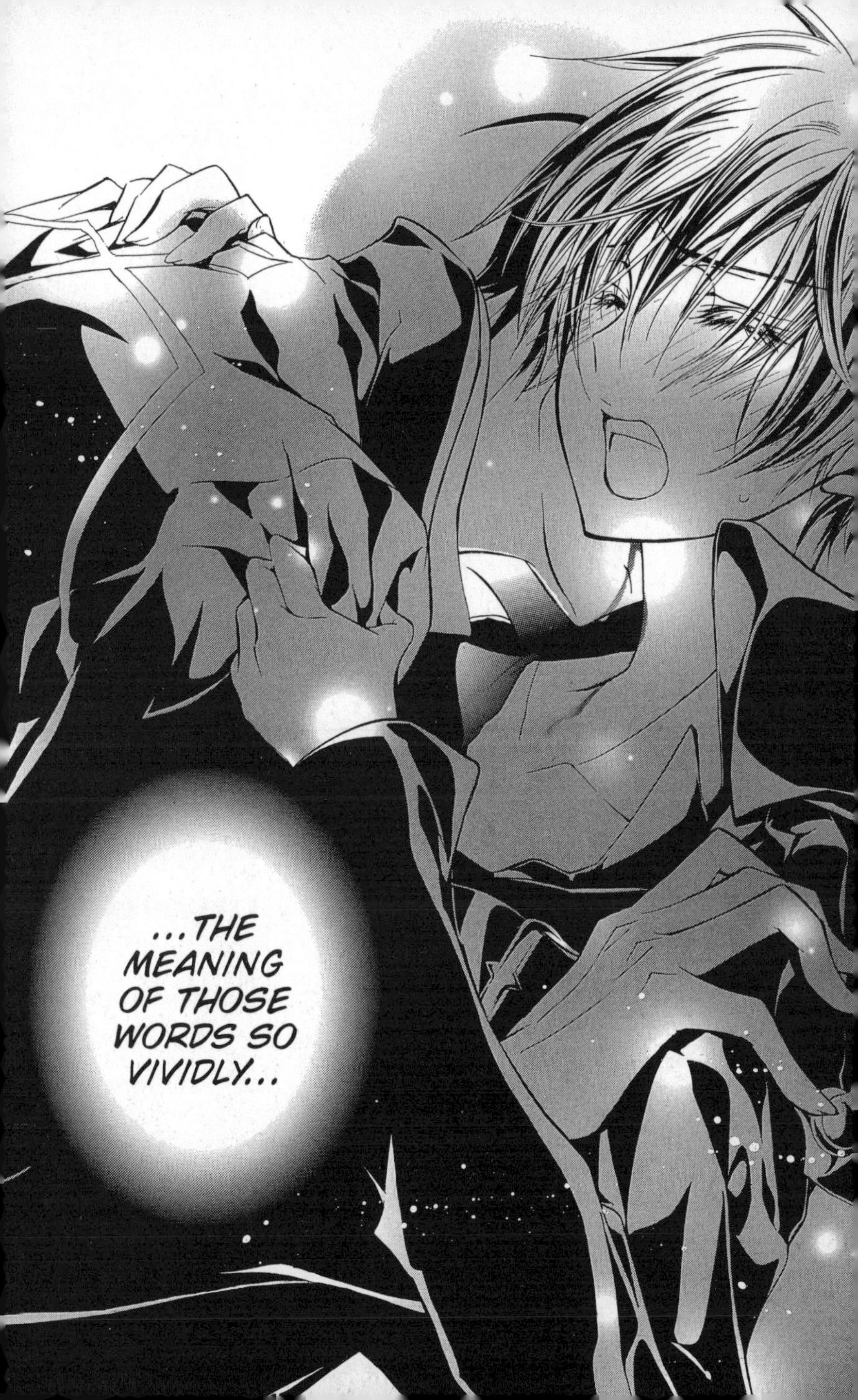
...THE MEANING OF THOSE WORDS SO VIVIDLY...

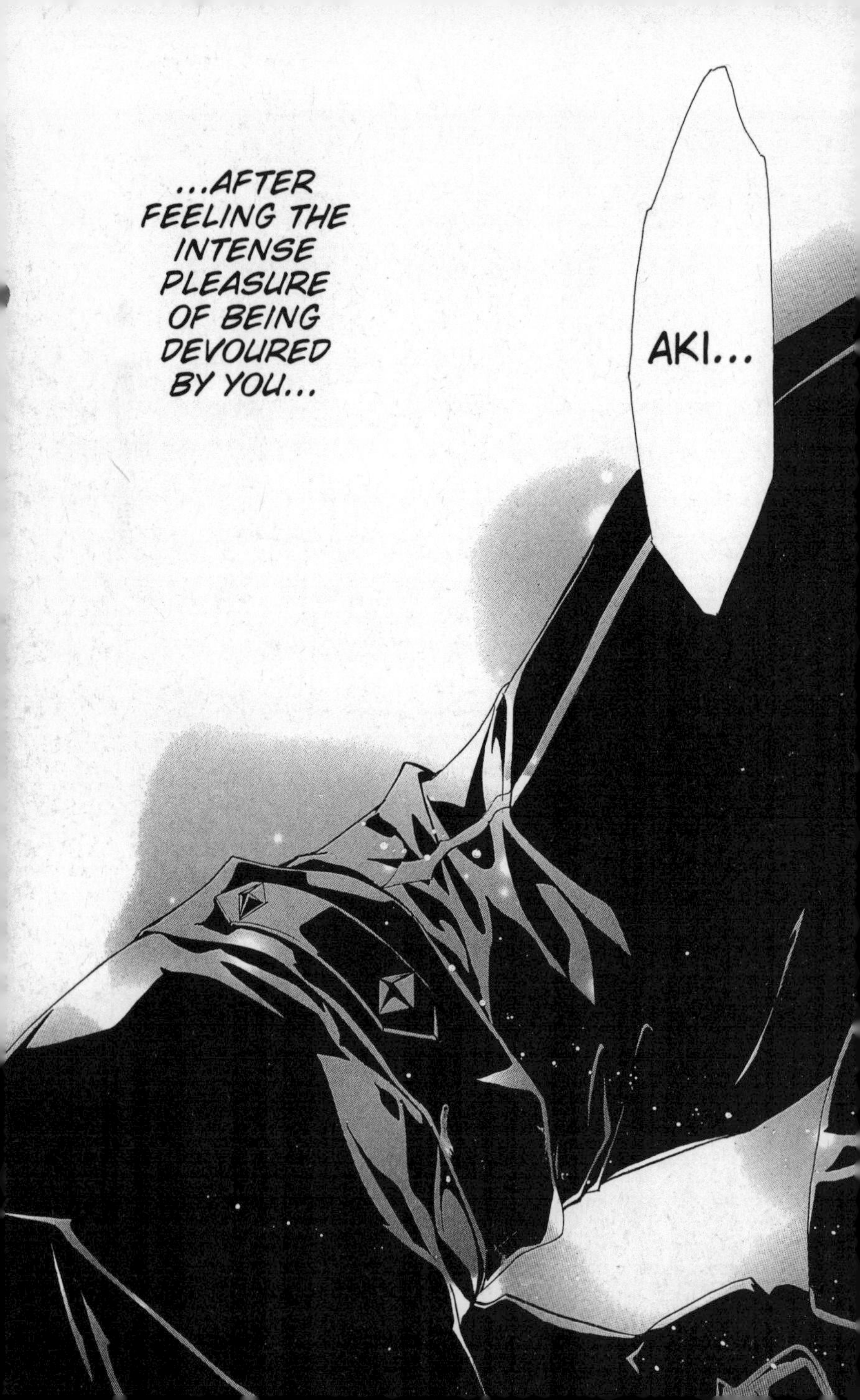
AKI...
...AFTER FEELING THE INTENSE PLEASURE OF BEING DEVOURED BY YOU...

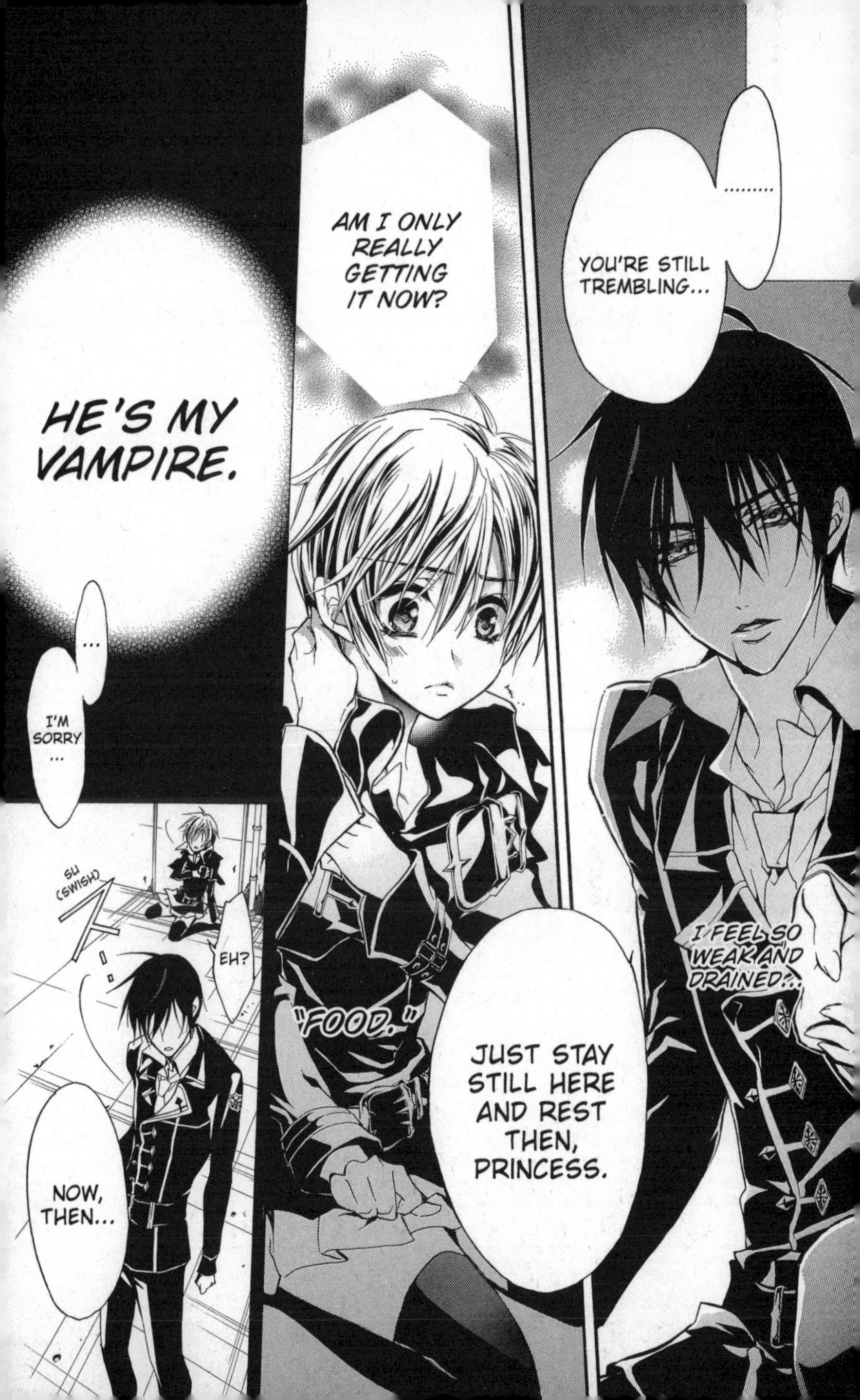
....
YOU'RE STILL TREMBLING...
I FEEL SO WEAK AND DRAINED...
AM I ONLY REALLY GETTING IT NOW?
"FOOD."
JUST STAY STILL HERE AND REST THEN, PRINCESS.
HE'S MY VAMPIRE.
...
I'M SORRY ...
SU (SWISH)
EH?
NOW, THEN...

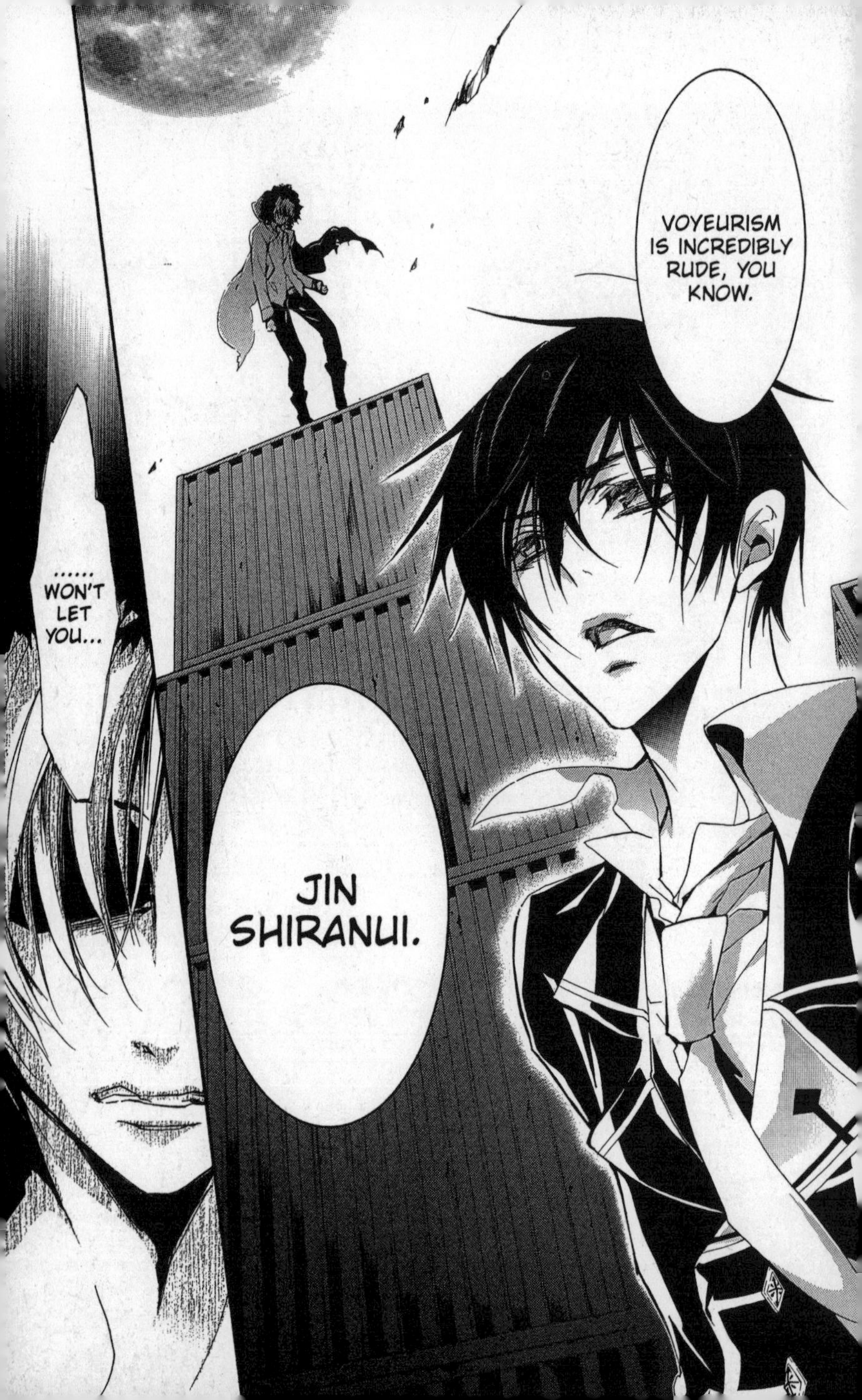
VOYEURISM IS INCREDIBLY RUDE, YOU KNOW.
JIN SHIRANUI.
...... WON'T LET YOU...

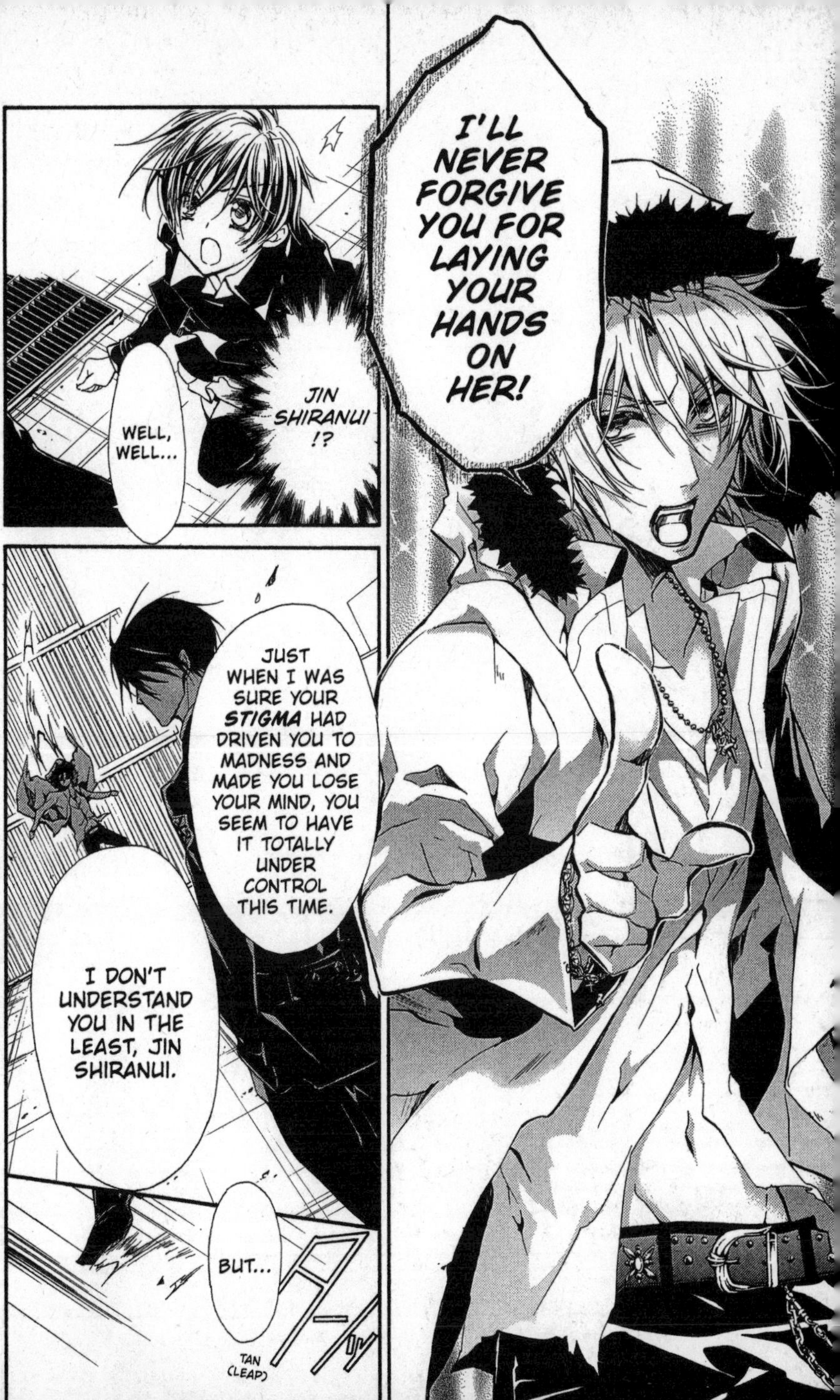
I'LL NEVER FORGIVE YOU FOR LAYING YOUR HANDS ON HER!
JIN SHIRANUI!?
WELL, WELL...
JUST WHEN I WAS SURE YOUR *STIGMA* HAD DRIVEN YOU TO MADNESS AND MADE YOU LOSE YOUR MIND, YOU SEEM TO HAVE IT TOTALLY UNDER CONTROL THIS TIME.
I DON'T UNDERSTAND YOU IN THE LEAST, JIN SHIRANUI.
BUT...
TAN (LEAP)

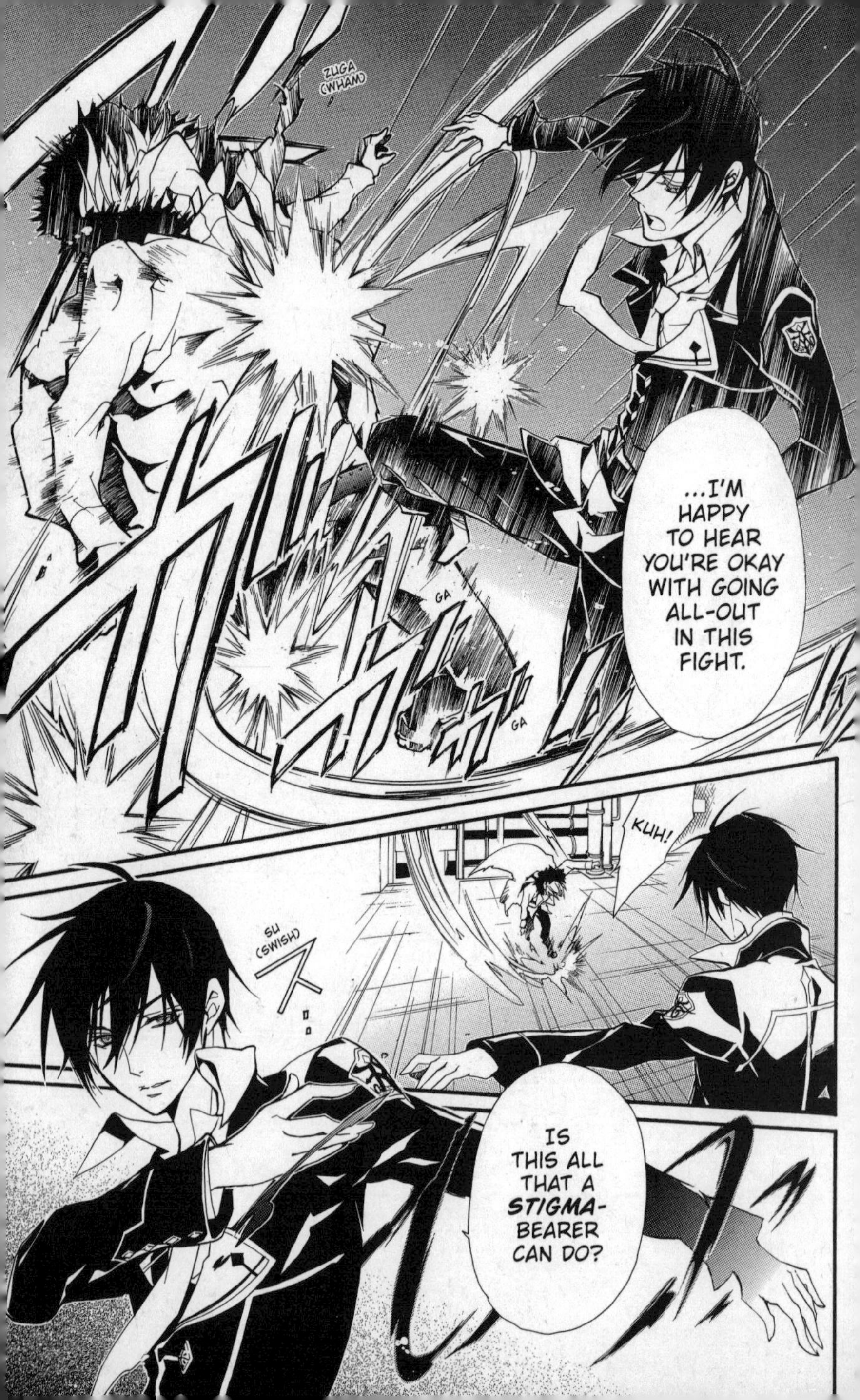
ZUGA (WHAM)
...I'M HAPPY TO HEAR YOU'RE OKAY WITH GOING ALL-OUT IN THIS FIGHT.
GA
GA
KUH!
SU (SWISH)
IS THIS ALL THAT A STIGMA-BEARER CAN DO?

BAS-
TARD!
DO
(BAM)
GUAAAH!
GA
(WHACK)
GA
GA
GA
OH, COME ON... CAN'T YOU MAKE THIS HUNT AT LEAST A LITTLE MORE ENTERTAINING FOR ME?

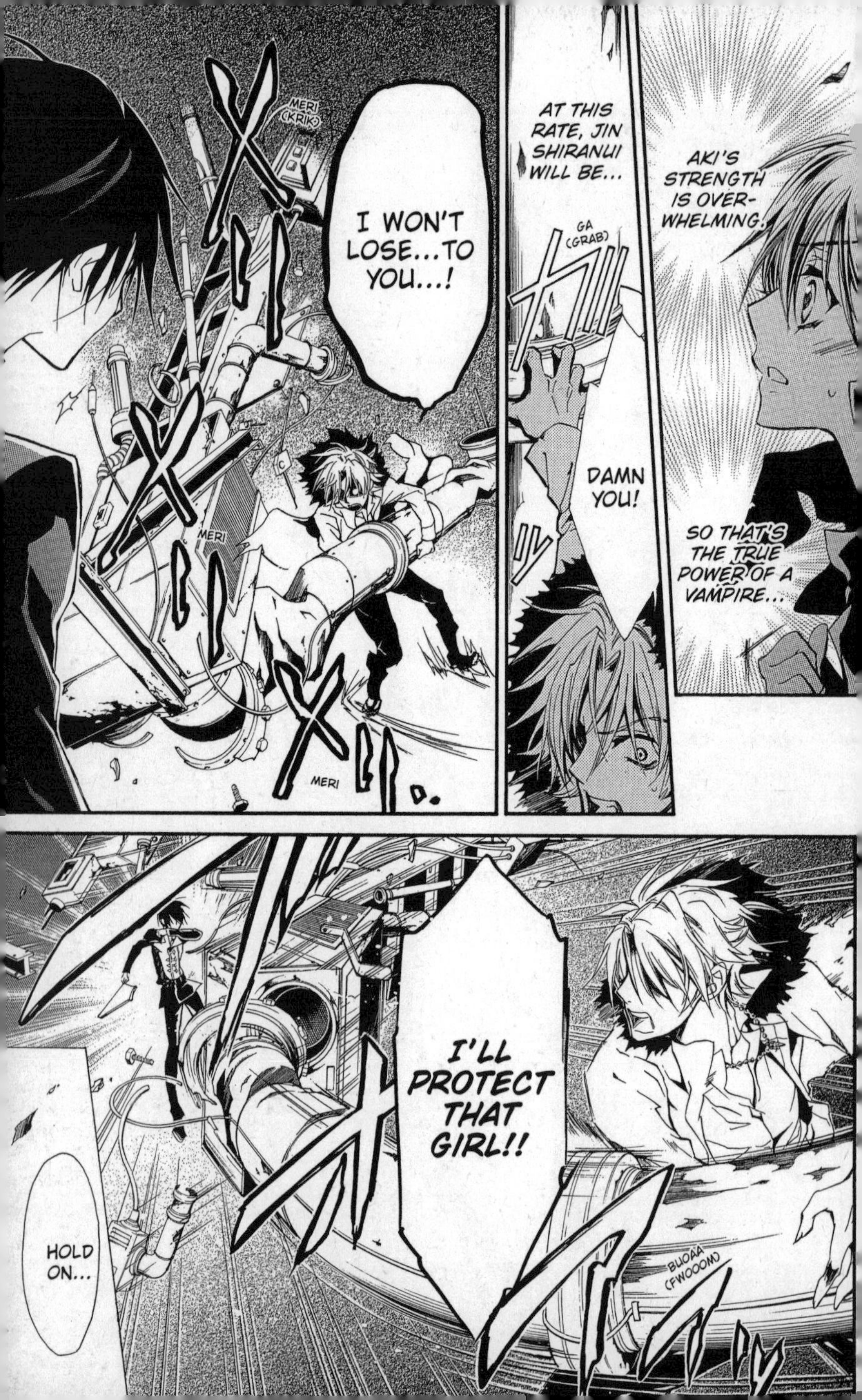
AKI'S STRENGTH IS OVER-WHELMING!
SO THAT'S THE TRUE POWER OF A VAMPIRE...
AT THIS RATE, JIN SHIRANUI WILL BE...
GA (GRAB)
DAMN YOU!
I WON'T LOSE...TO YOU...!
MERI (KRIK)
MERI
MERI
I'LL PROTECT THAT GIRL!!
BUOAA (FWOOOM)
HOLD ON...

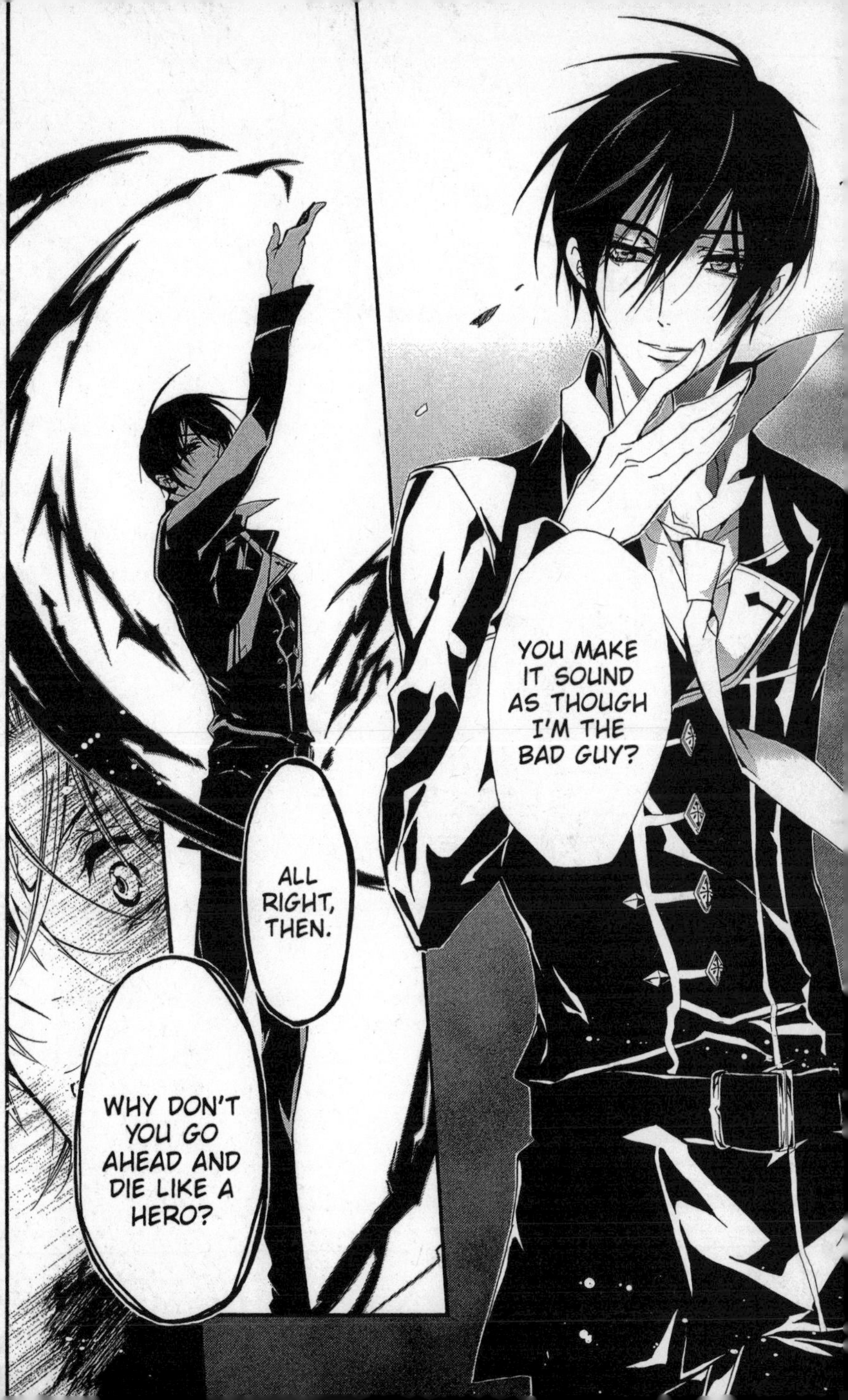
YOU MAKE IT SOUND AS THOUGH I'M THE BAD GUY?
ALL RIGHT, THEN.
WHY DON'T YOU GO AHEAD AND DIE LIKE A HERO?

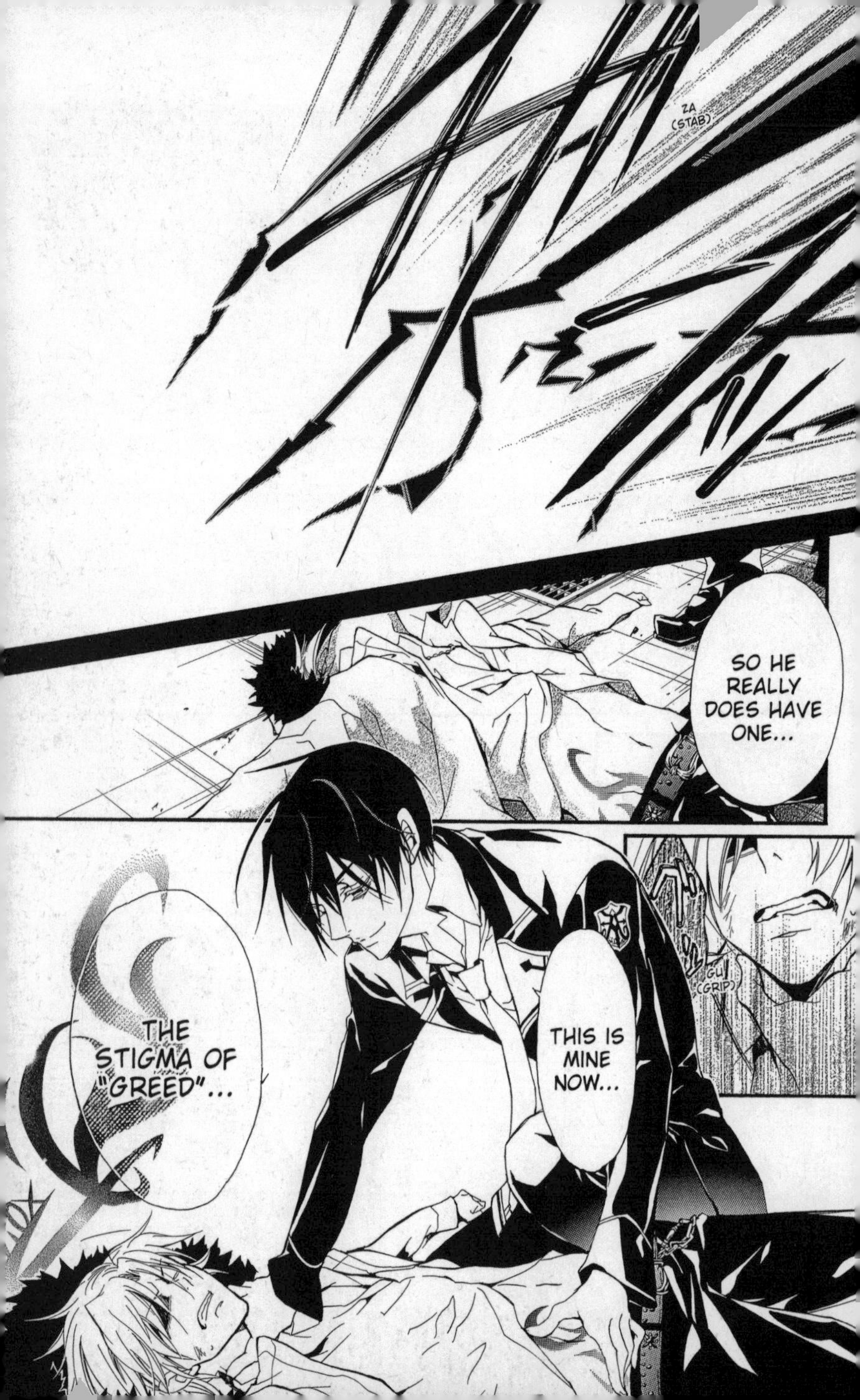
ZA
(STAB)
SO HE REALLY DOES HAVE ONE...
GU
(GRIP)
THIS IS MINE NOW...
THE STIGMA OF "GREED"...

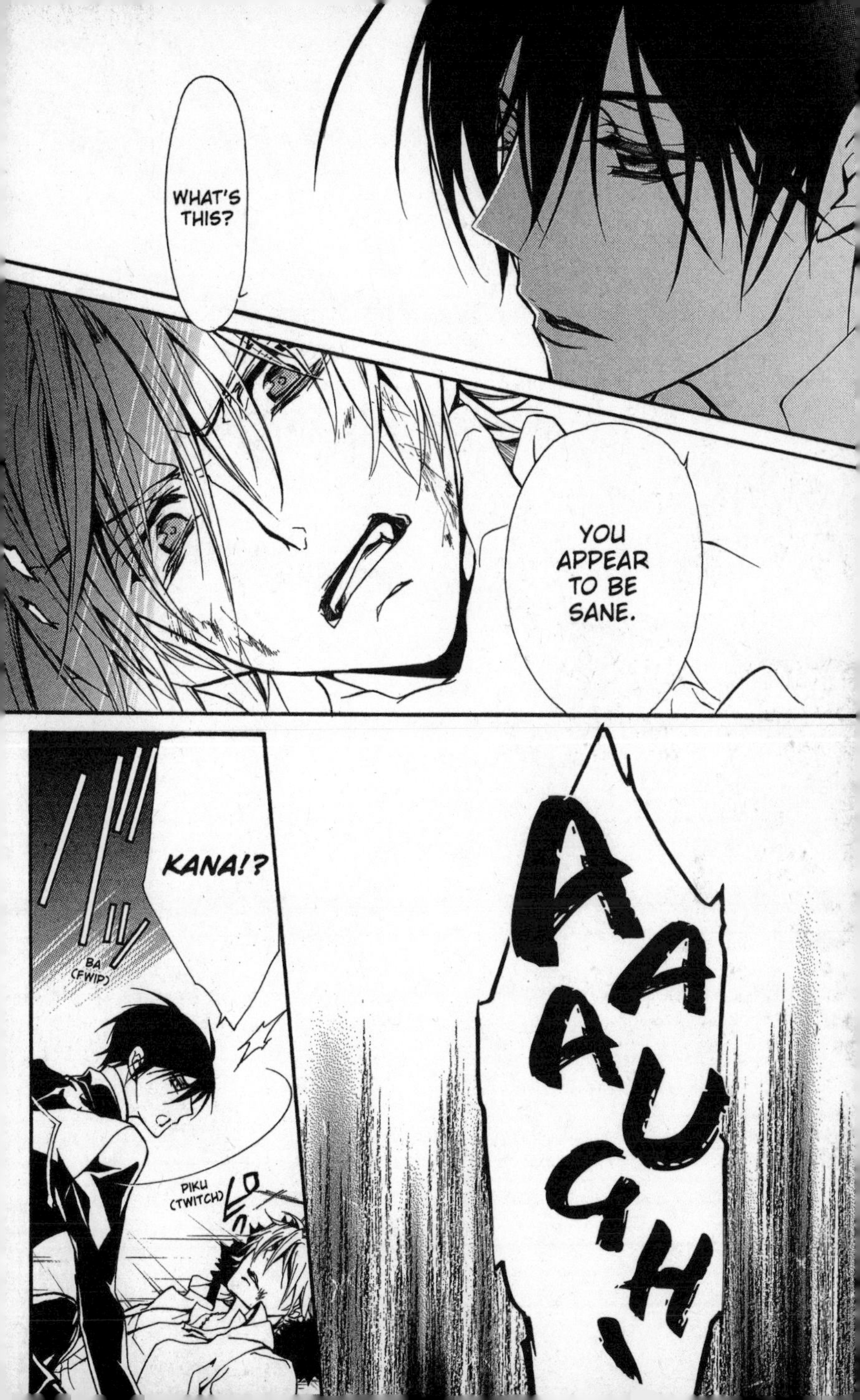
WHAT'S THIS?
YOU APPEAR TO BE SANE.
AAAAUGH!
KANA!?
BA (FWIP)
PIKU (TWITCH)

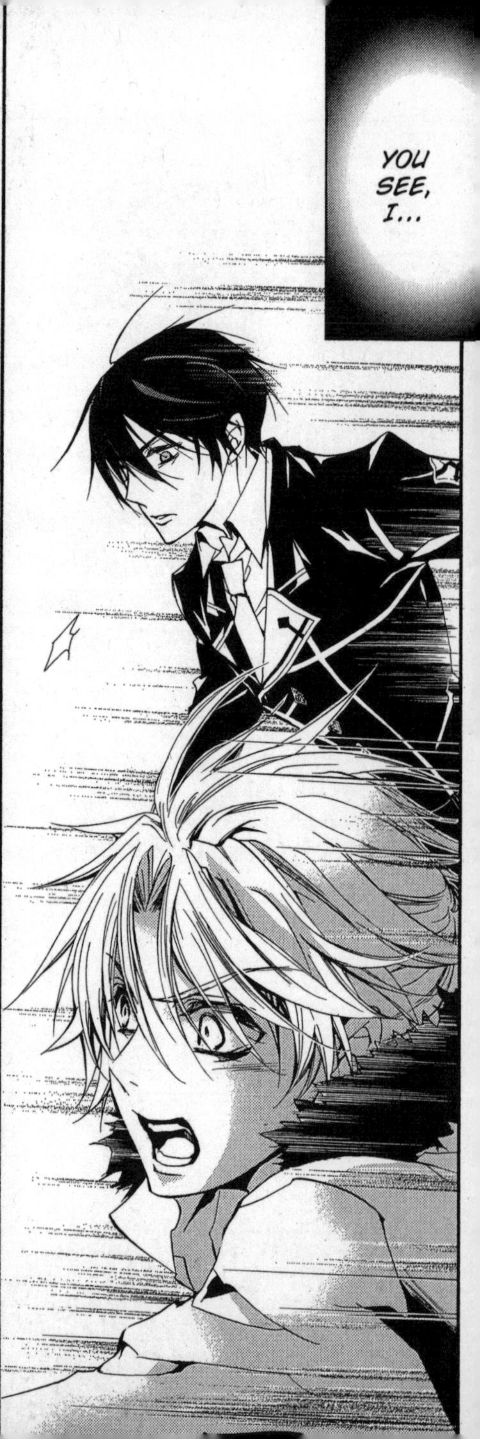
YOU SEE, I...

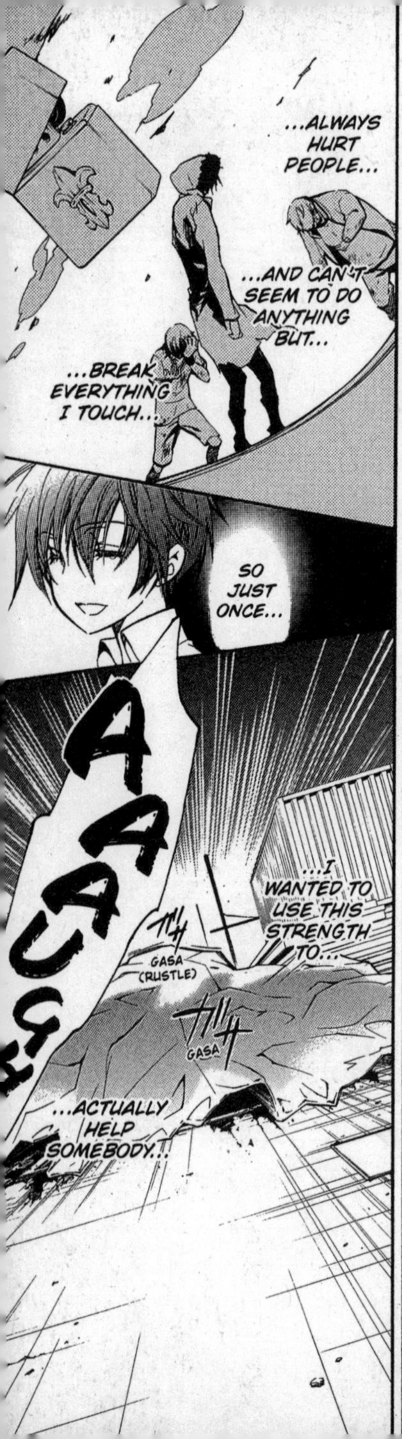
...ALWAYS HURT PEOPLE...
...AND CAN'T SEEM TO DO ANYTHING BUT...
...BREAK EVERYTHING I TOUCH...
SO JUST ONCE...
AAAUGH
...I WANTED TO USE THIS STRENGTH TO...
GASA (RUSTLE)
GASA
...ACTUALLY HELP SOMEBODY...

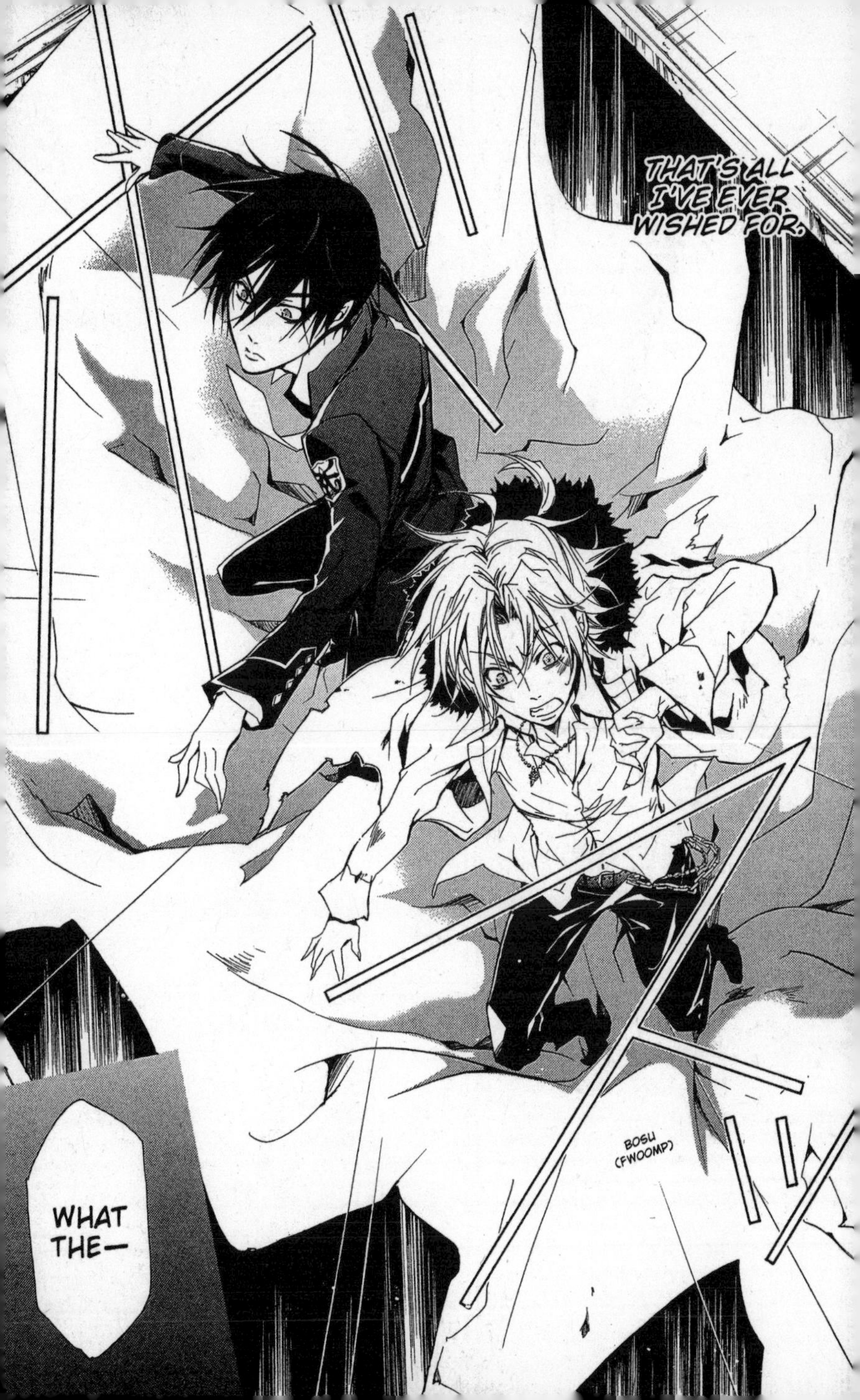
THAT'S ALL I'VE EVER WISHED FOR.
BOSU (FWOOMP)
WHAT THE—

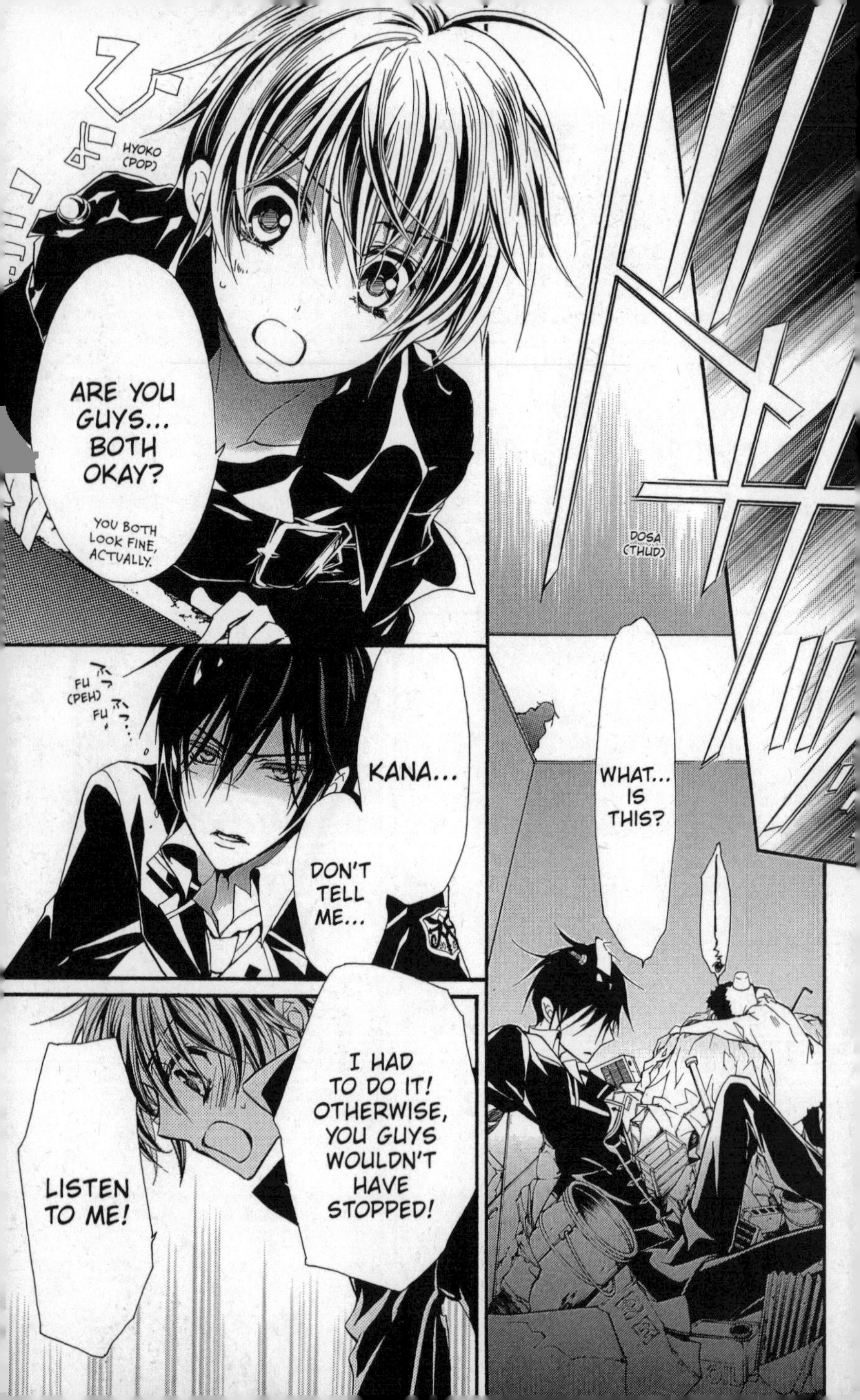
DOSA (THUD)
WHAT... IS THIS?
HYOKO (POP)
ARE YOU GUYS... BOTH OKAY?
YOU BOTH LOOK FINE, ACTUALLY.
FU (PEH) FU
KANA...
DON'T TELL ME...
I HAD TO DO IT! OTHERWISE, YOU GUYS WOULDN'T HAVE STOPPED!
LISTEN TO ME!

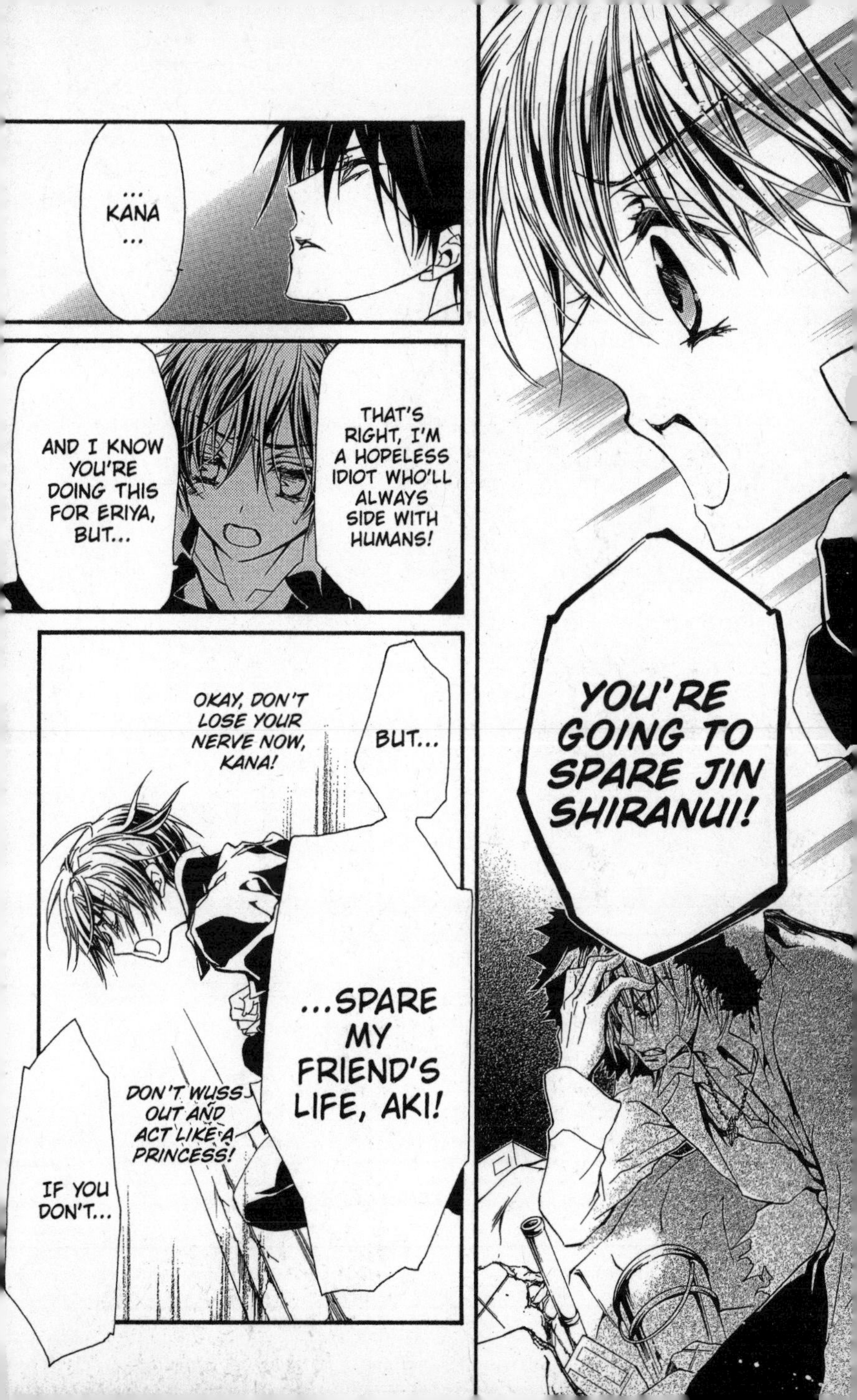
YOU'RE GOING TO SPARE JIN SHIRANUI!
...KANA...
THAT'S RIGHT, I'M A HOPELESS IDIOT WHO'LL ALWAYS SIDE WITH HUMANS!
AND I KNOW YOU'RE DOING THIS FOR ERIYA, BUT...
BUT...
OKAY, DON'T LOSE YOUR NERVE NOW, KANA!
...SPARE MY FRIEND'S LIFE, AKI!
DON'T WUSS OUT AND ACT LIKE A PRINCESS!
IF YOU DON'T...

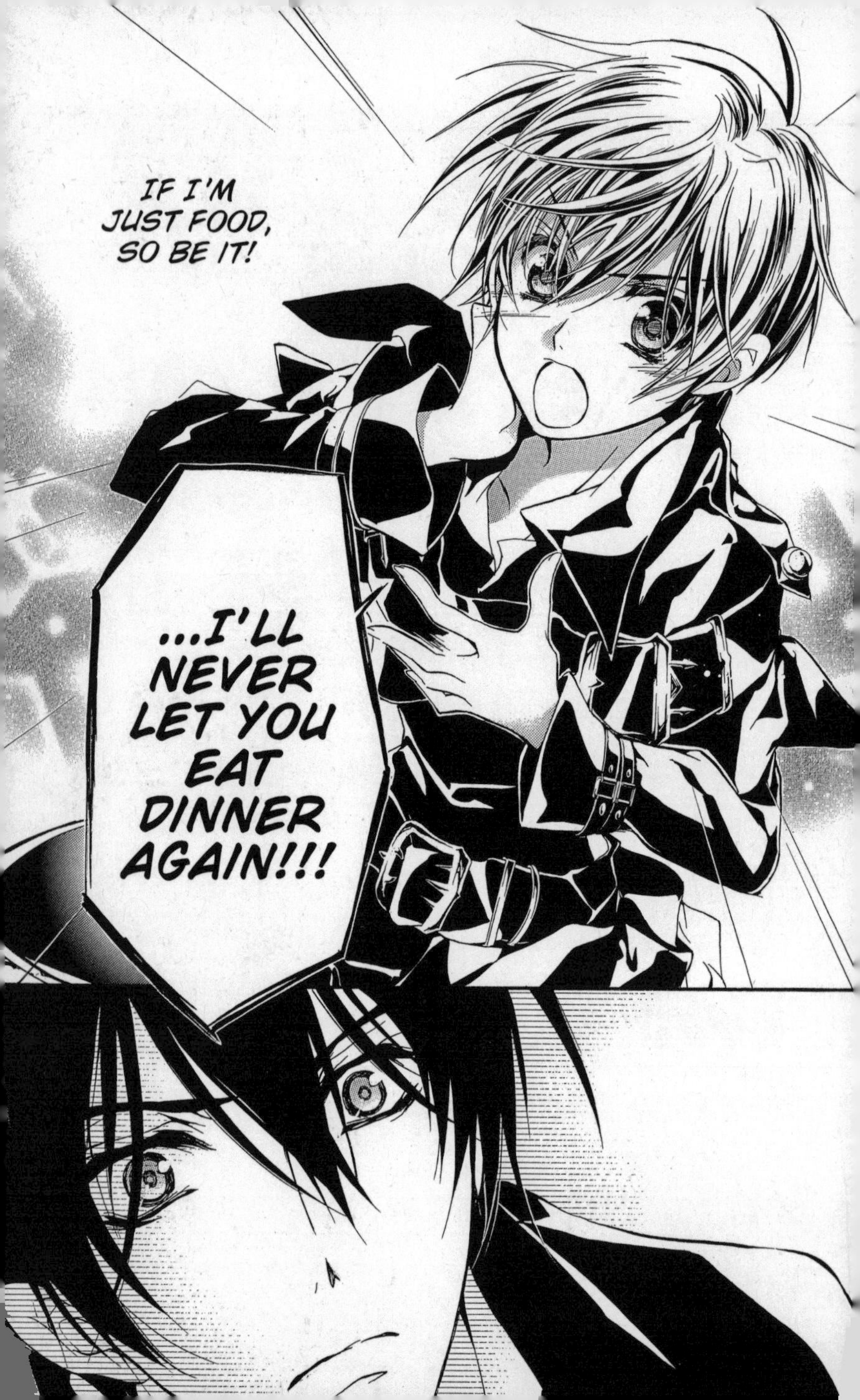
IF I'M JUST FOOD, SO BE IT!
...I'LL NEVER LET YOU EAT DINNER AGAIN!!!

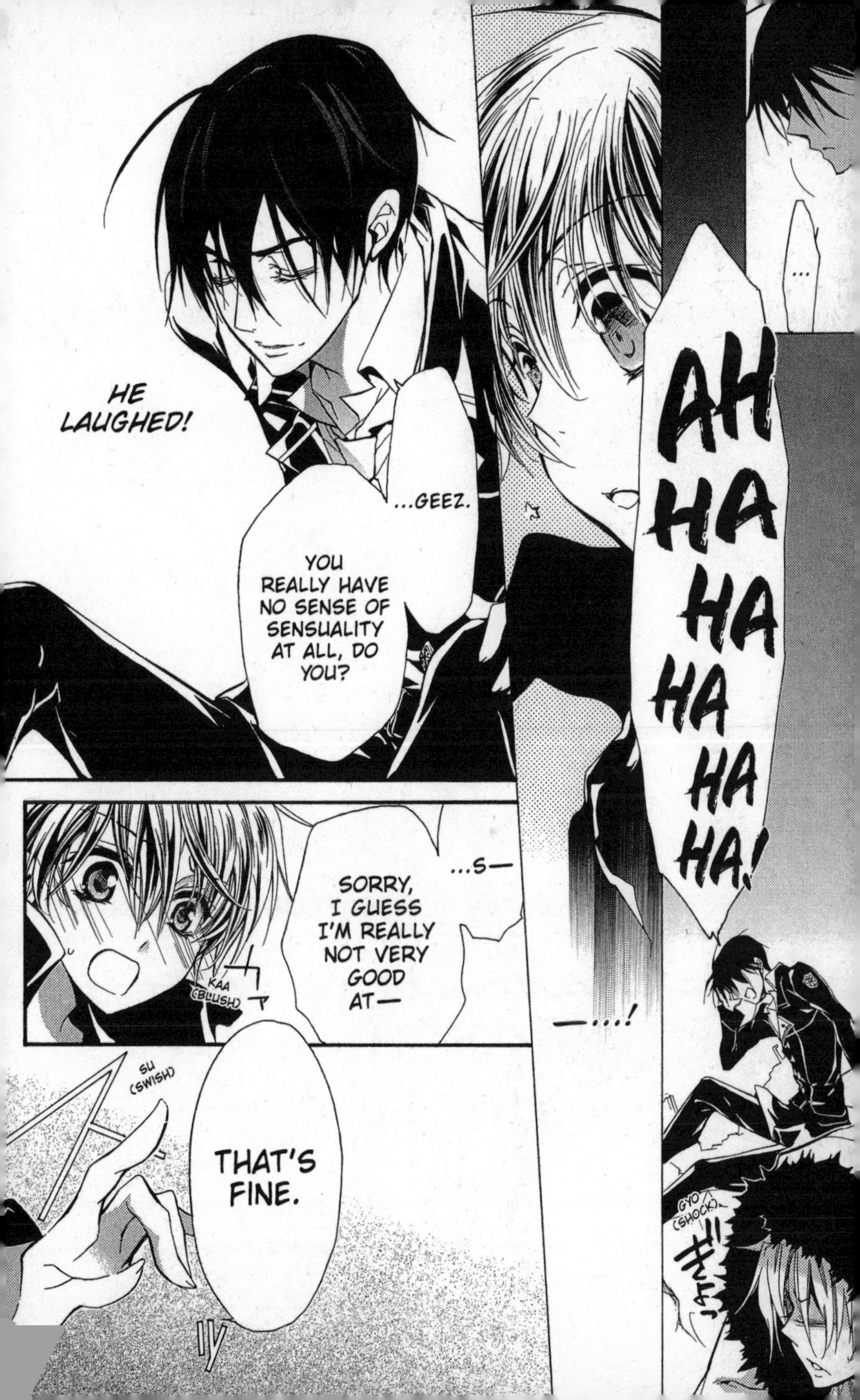
...
AH HA HA HA HA HA HA HA!
—...!
GYO (SHOCK)
HE LAUGHED!
...GEEZ.
YOU REALLY HAVE NO SENSE OF SENSUALITY AT ALL, DO YOU?
...S—
SORRY, I GUESS I'M REALLY NOT VERY GOOD AT—
KAA (BLUSH)
SU (SWISH)
THAT'S FINE.

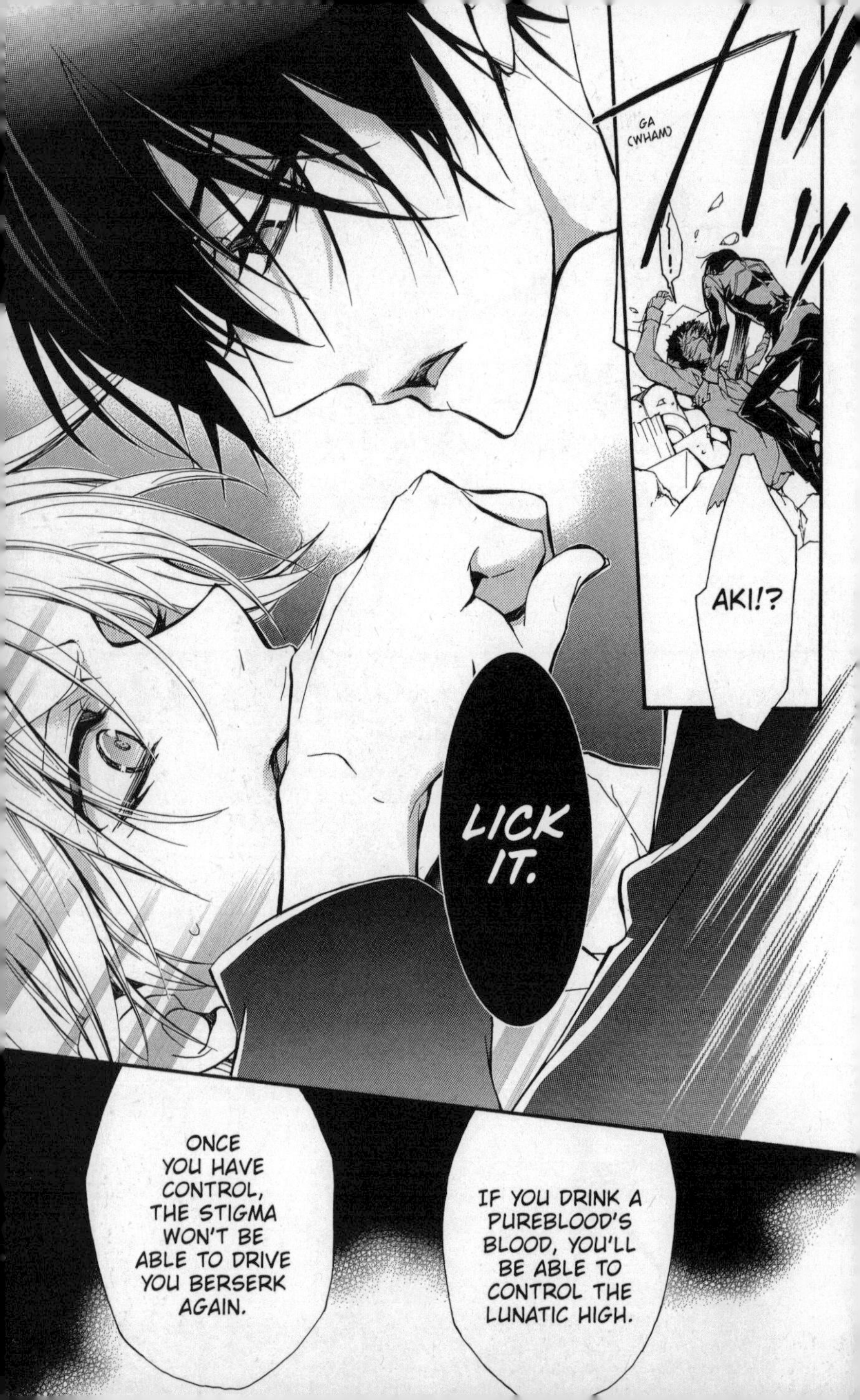
GA (WHAM)
!
AKI!?
LICK IT.
IF YOU DRINK A PUREBLOOD'S BLOOD, YOU'LL BE ABLE TO CONTROL THE LUNATIC HIGH.
ONCE YOU HAVE CONTROL, THE STIGMA WON'T BE ABLE TO DRIVE YOU BERSERK AGAIN.

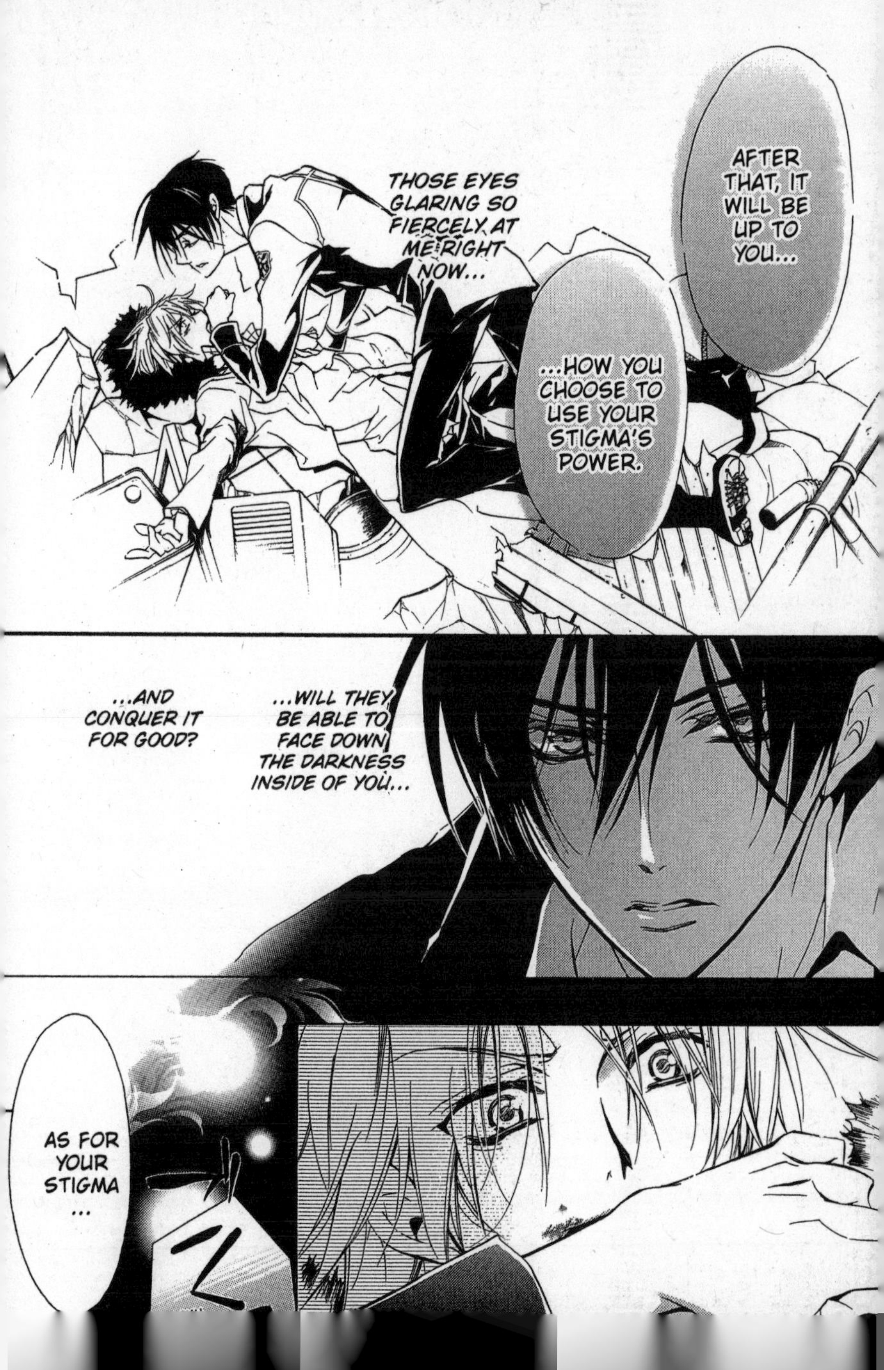

AFTER THAT, IT WILL BE UP TO YOU...
...HOW YOU CHOOSE TO USE YOUR STIGMA'S POWER.
THOSE EYES GLARING SO FIERCELY AT ME RIGHT NOW...
...WILL THEY BE ABLE TO FACE DOWN THE DARKNESS INSIDE OF YOU...
...AND CONQUER IT FOR GOOD?
AS FOR YOUR STIGMA ...

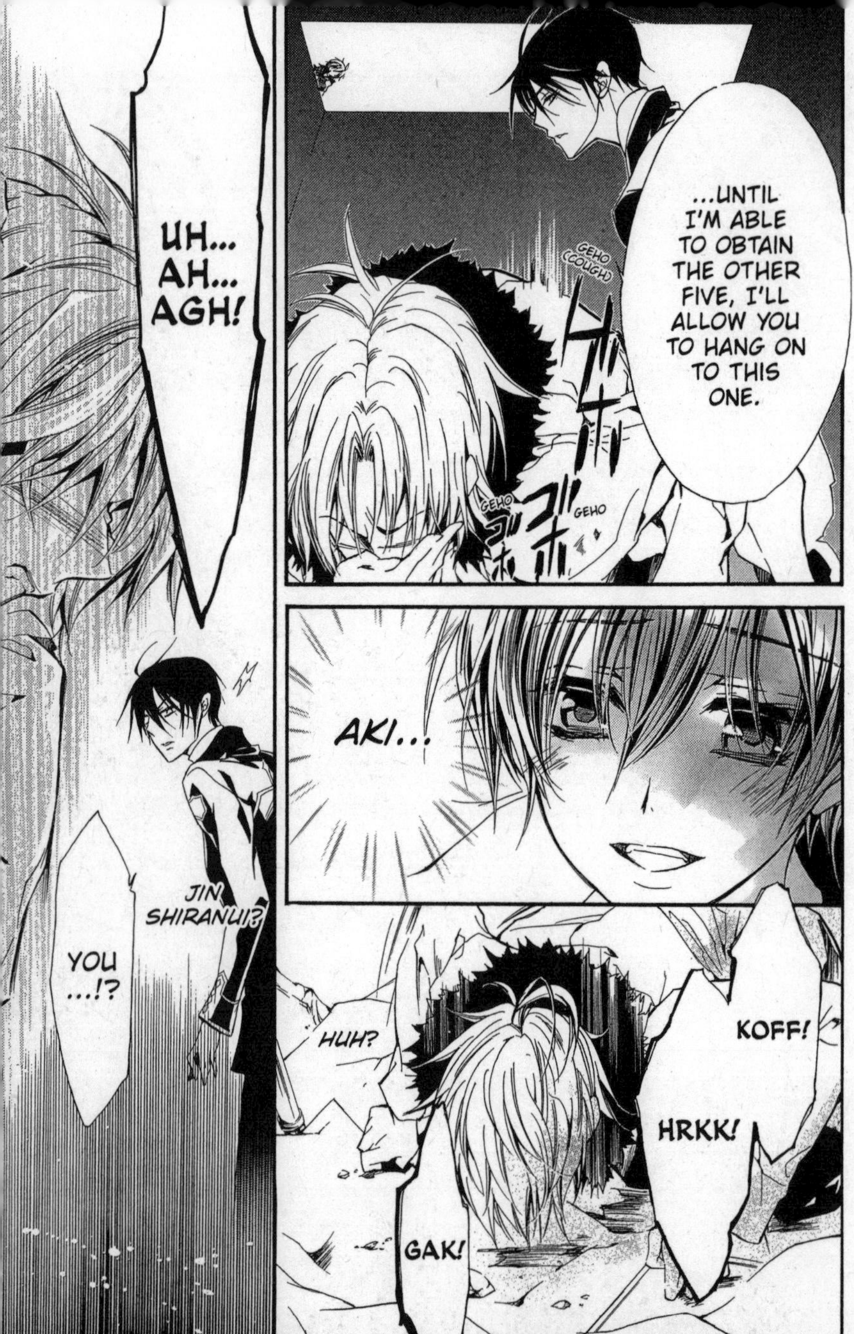
...UNTIL I'M ABLE TO OBTAIN THE OTHER FIVE, I'LL ALLOW YOU TO HANG ON TO THIS ONE.
GEHO (COUGH)
GEHO
GEHO
AKI...
KOFF!
HRKK!
HUH?
GAK!
UH... AH... AGH!
JIN SHIRANUI!?
YOU ...!?

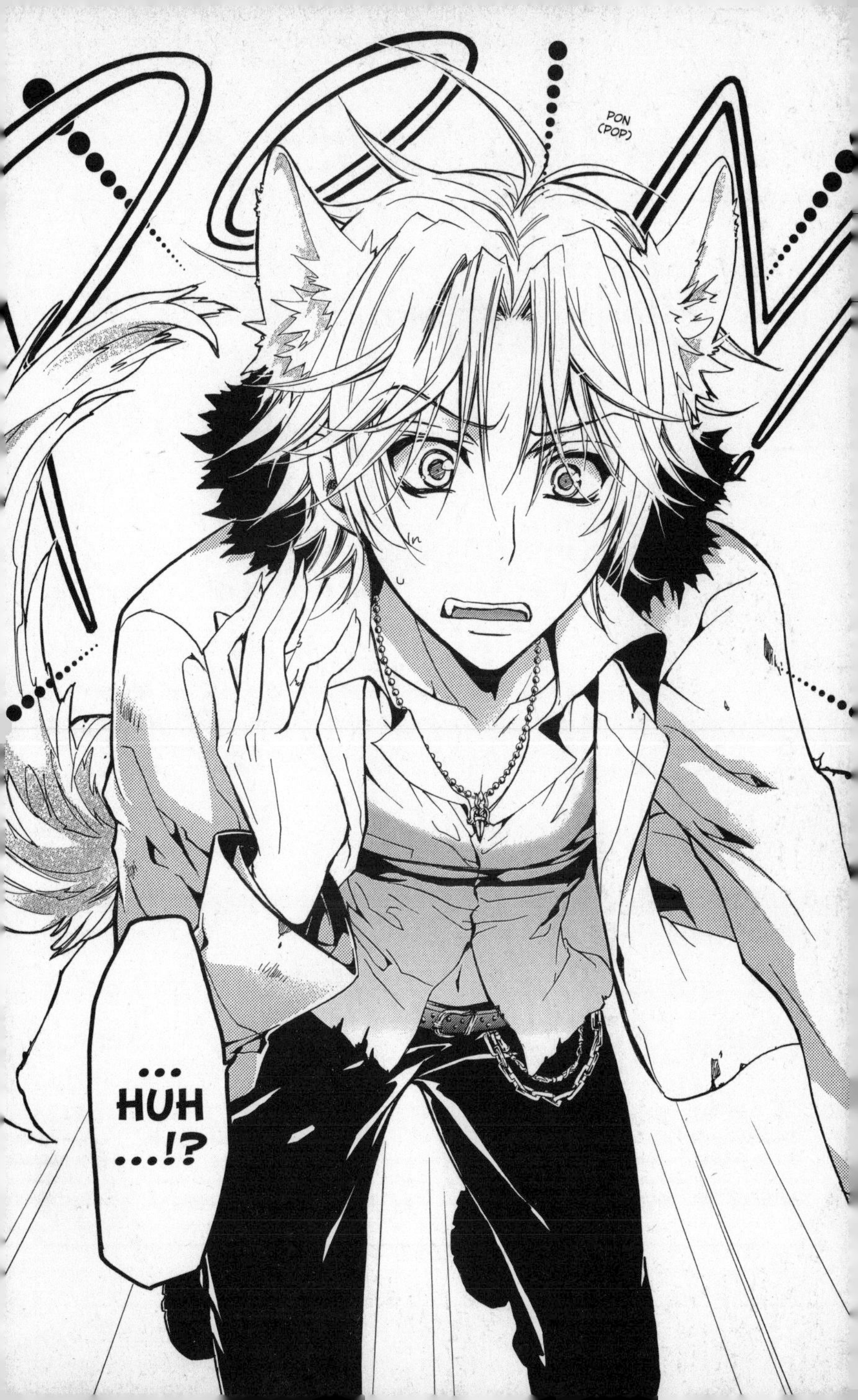
PON
(POP)
...HUH...!?

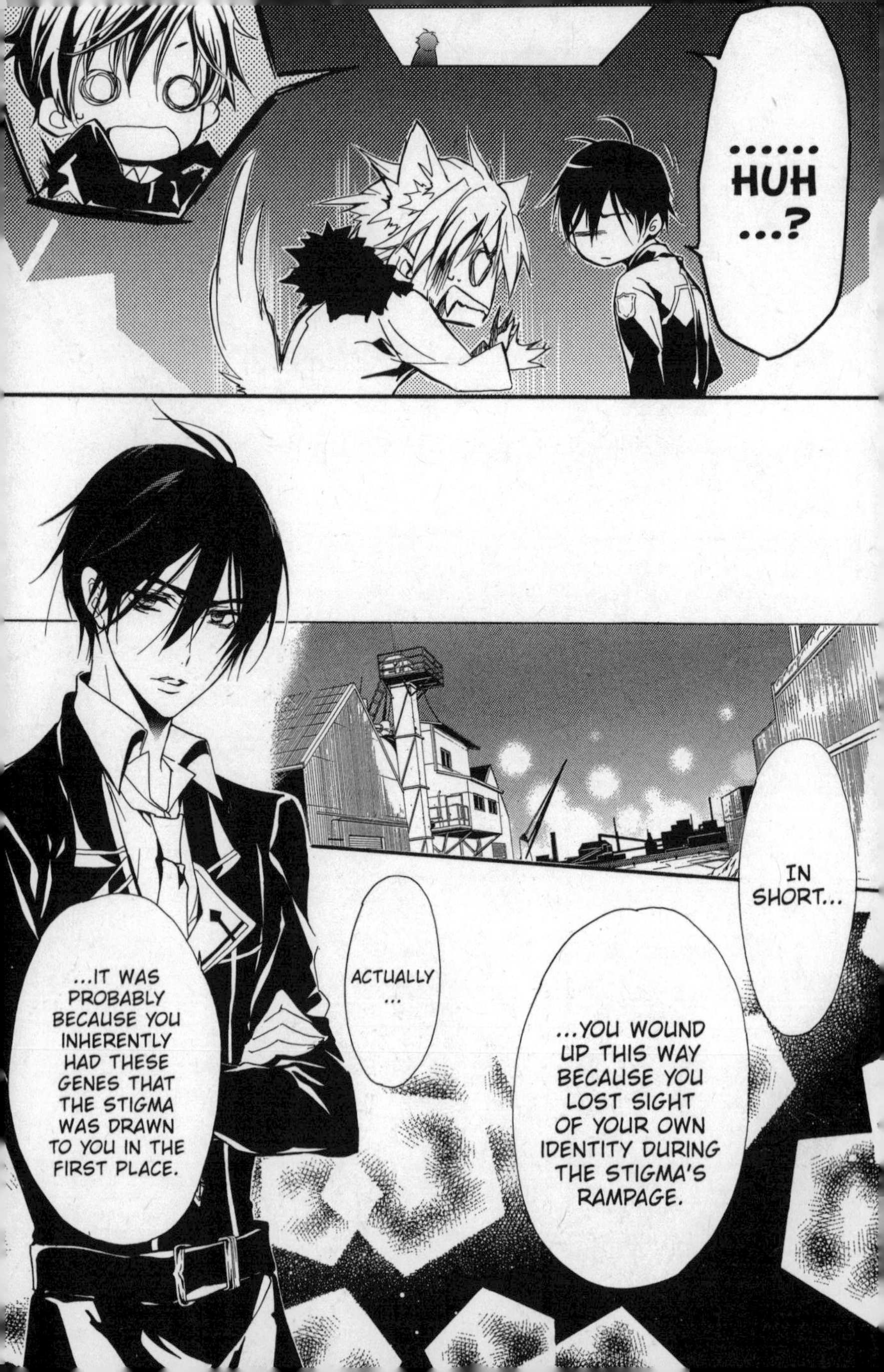
......HUH ...?
IN SHORT...
...YOU WOUND UP THIS WAY BECAUSE YOU LOST SIGHT OF YOUR OWN IDENTITY DURING THE STIGMA'S RAMPAGE.
ACTUALLY ...
...IT WAS PROBABLY BECAUSE YOU INHERENTLY HAD THESE GENES THAT THE STIGMA WAS DRAWN TO YOU IN THE FIRST PLACE.

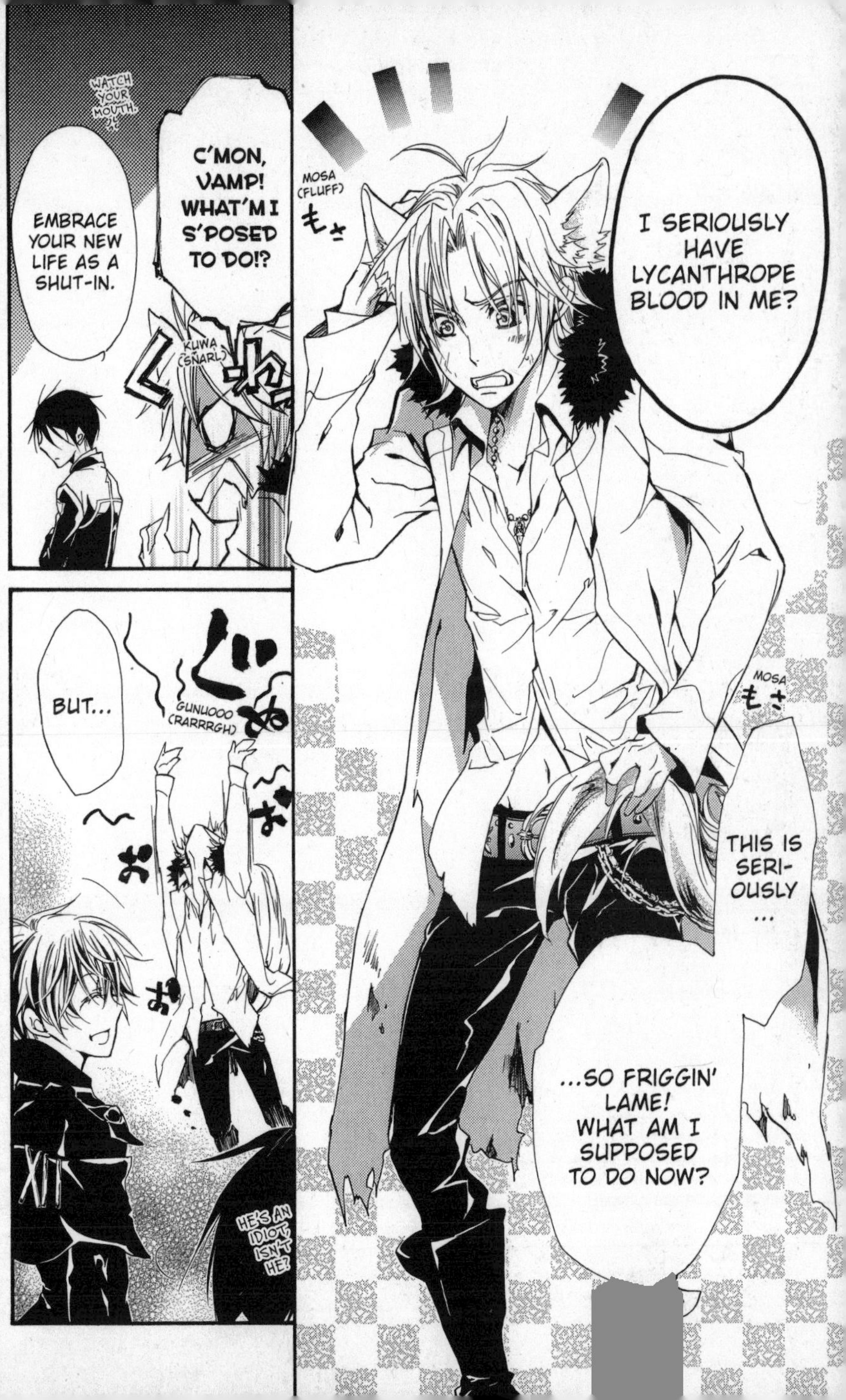
I SERIOUSLY HAVE LYCANTHROPE BLOOD IN ME?
MOSA (FLUFF)
もさ
MOSA
もさ
THIS IS SERI-OUSLY ...
...SO FRIGGIN' LAME! WHAT AM I SUPPOSED TO DO NOW?
C'MON, VAMP! WHAT'M I S'POSED TO DO!?
WATCH YOUR MOUTH.
EMBRACE YOUR NEW LIFE AS A SHUT-IN.
KUWA (SNARL)
GUNUOOO (RARRRGH)
BUT...
HE'S AN IDIOT, ISN'T HE?

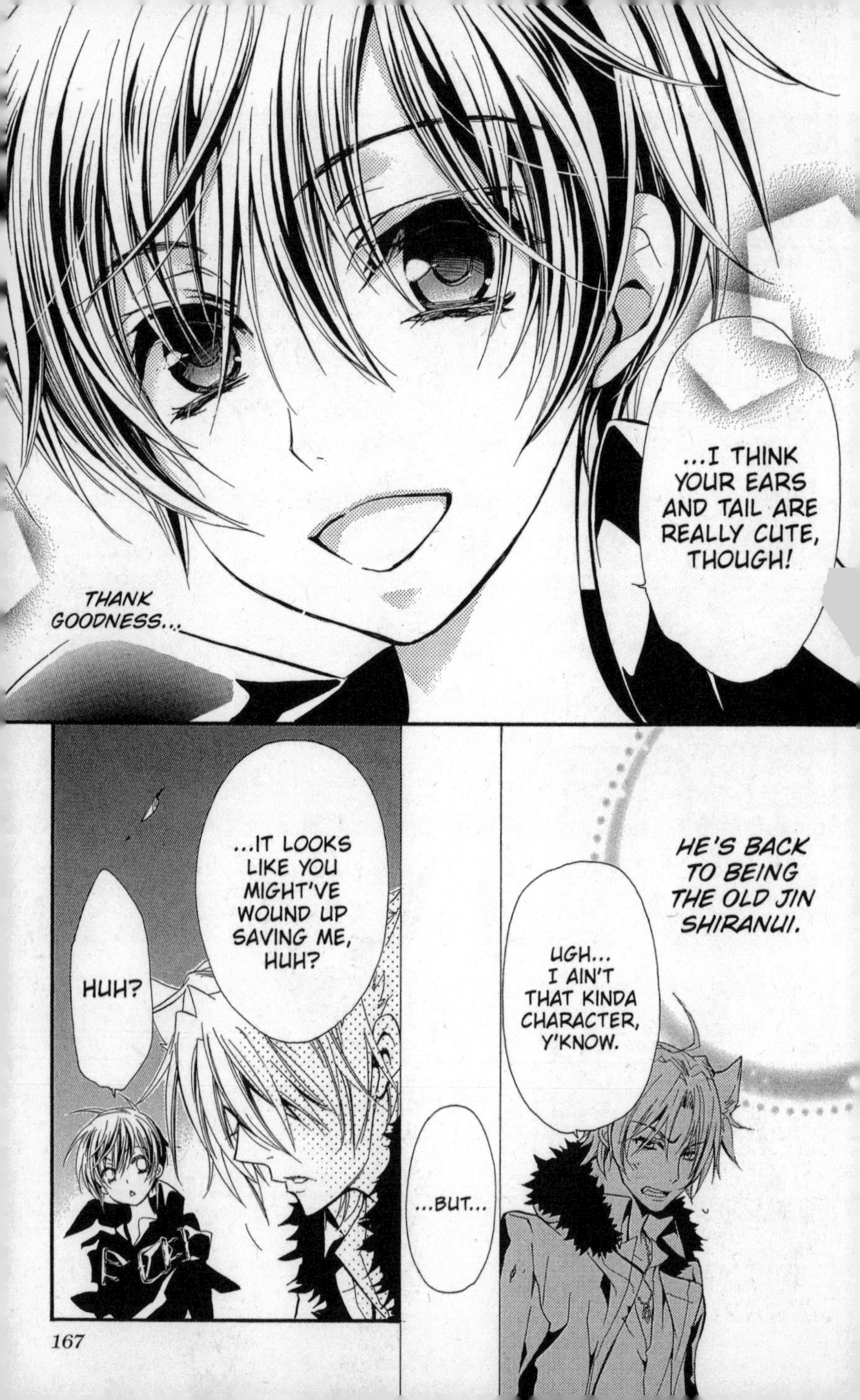
...I THINK YOUR EARS AND TAIL ARE REALLY CUTE, THOUGH!
THANK GOODNESS...
HE'S BACK TO BEING THE OLD JIN SHIRANUI.
UGH... I AIN'T THAT KINDA CHARACTER, Y'KNOW.
...BUT...
...IT LOOKS LIKE YOU MIGHT'VE WOUND UP SAVING ME, HUH?
HUH?

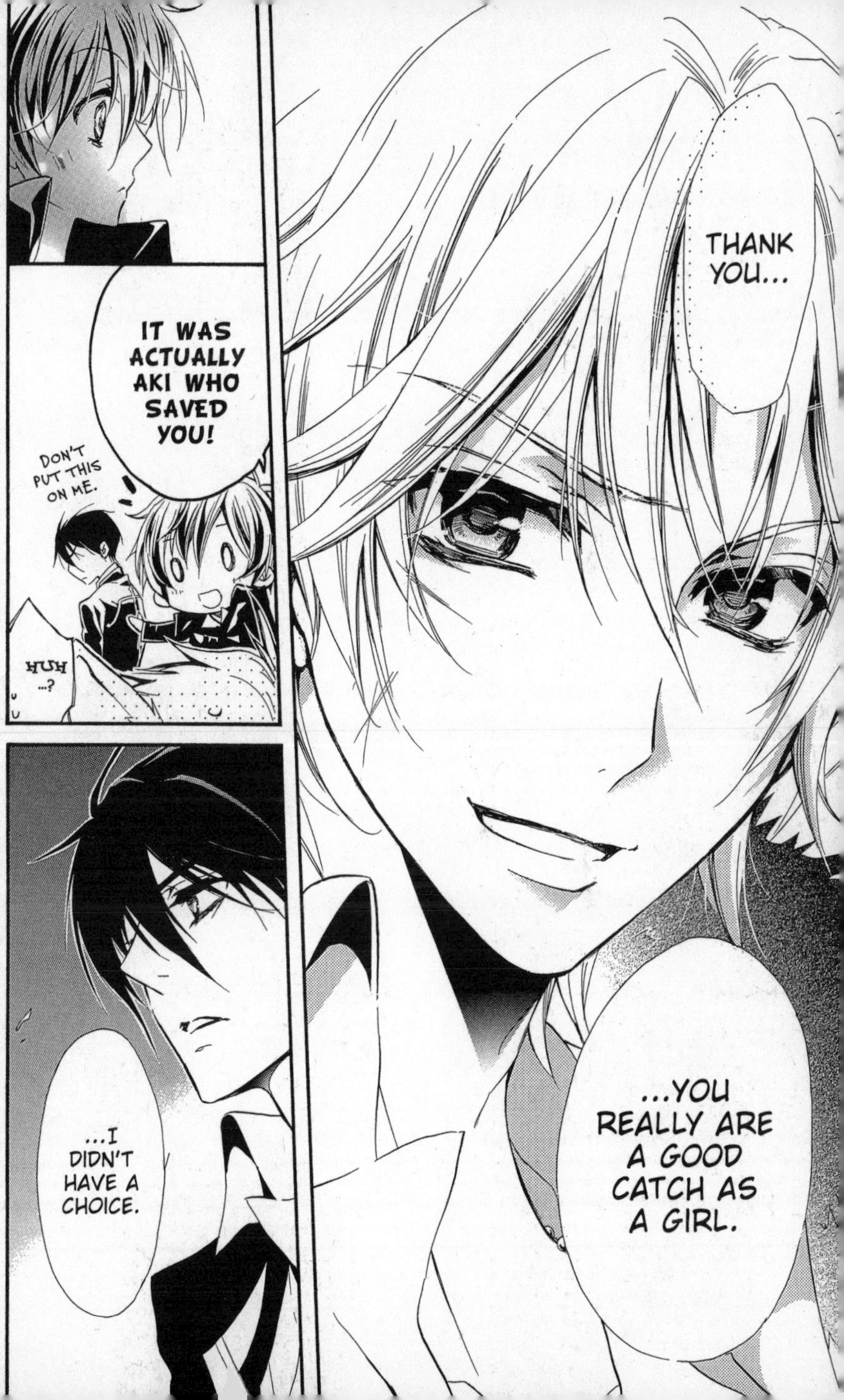
THANK YOU...
...YOU REALLY ARE A GOOD CATCH AS A GIRL.
IT WAS ACTUALLY AKI WHO SAVED YOU!
DON'T PUT THIS ON ME.
HUH ...?
...I DIDN'T HAVE A CHOICE.

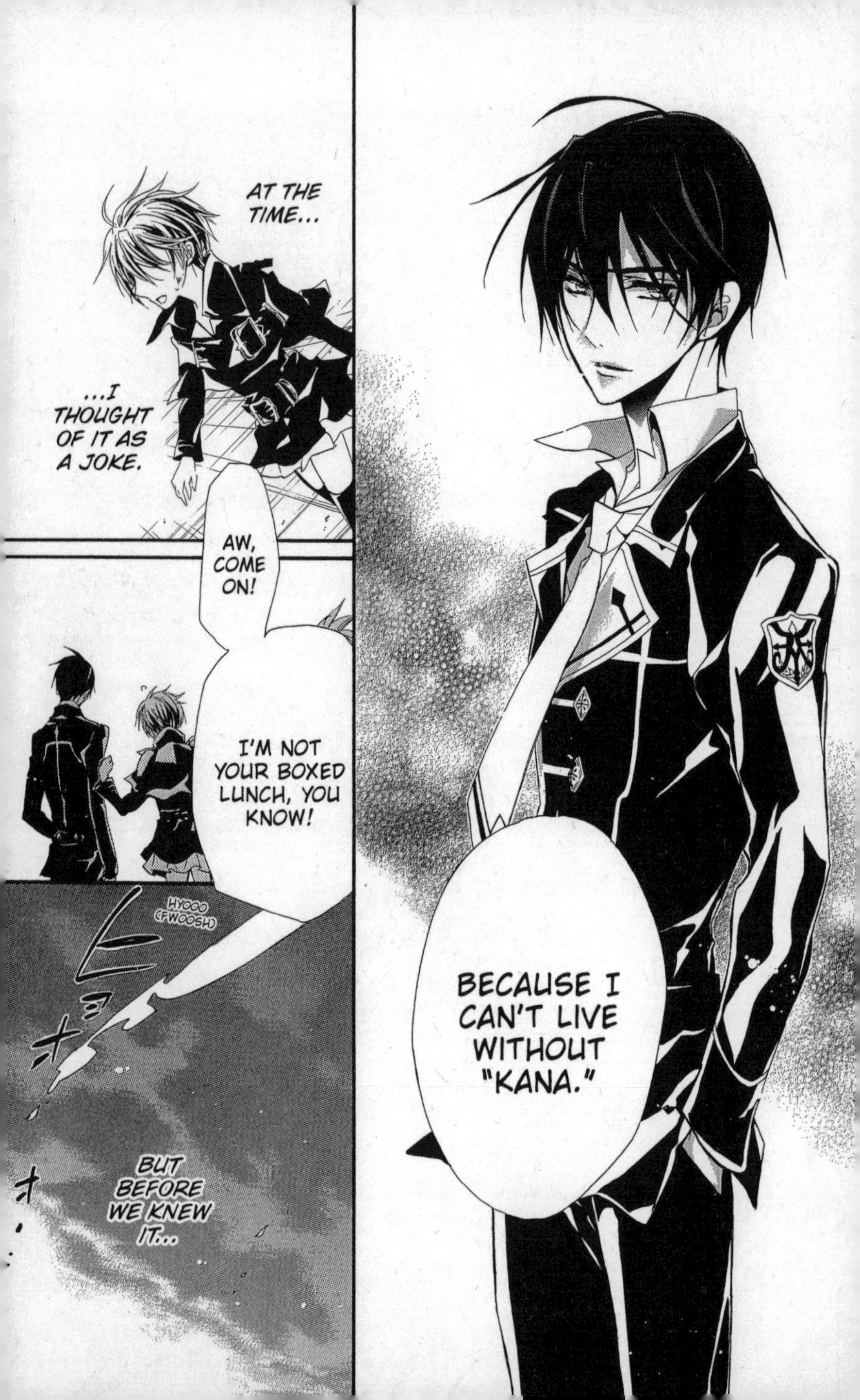
BECAUSE I CAN'T LIVE WITHOUT "KANA."
AT THE TIME...
...I THOUGHT OF IT AS A JOKE.
AW, COME ON!
I'M NOT YOUR BOXED LUNCH, YOU KNOW!
HYOOO (FWOOSH)
BUT BEFORE WE KNEW IT...

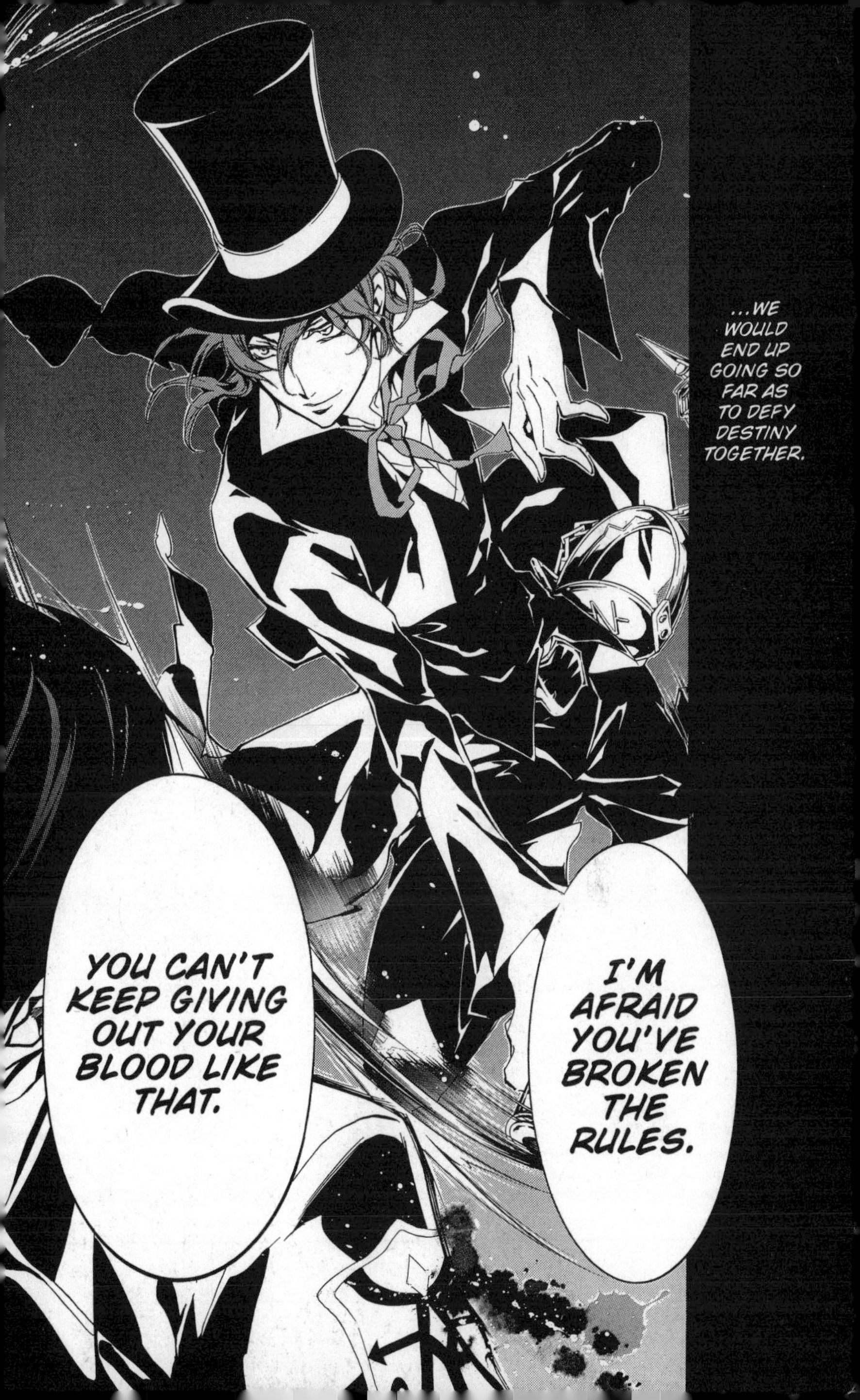
...WE WOULD END UP GOING SO FAR AS TO DEFY DESTINY TOGETHER.
I'M AFRAID YOU'VE BROKEN THE RULES.
YOU CAN'T KEEP GIVING OUT YOUR BLOOD LIKE THAT.

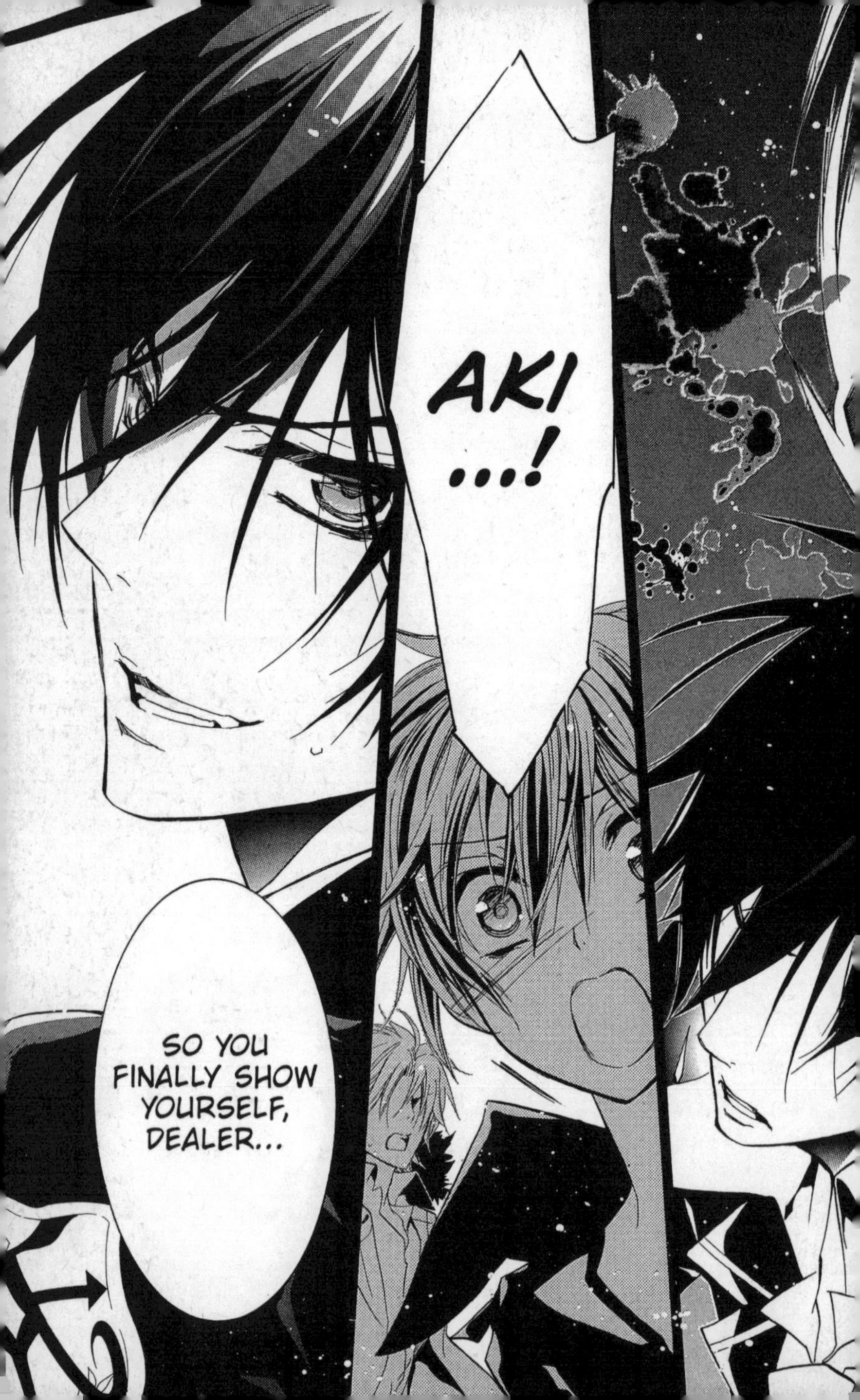
AKI ...!
SO YOU FINALLY SHOW YOURSELF, DEALER...

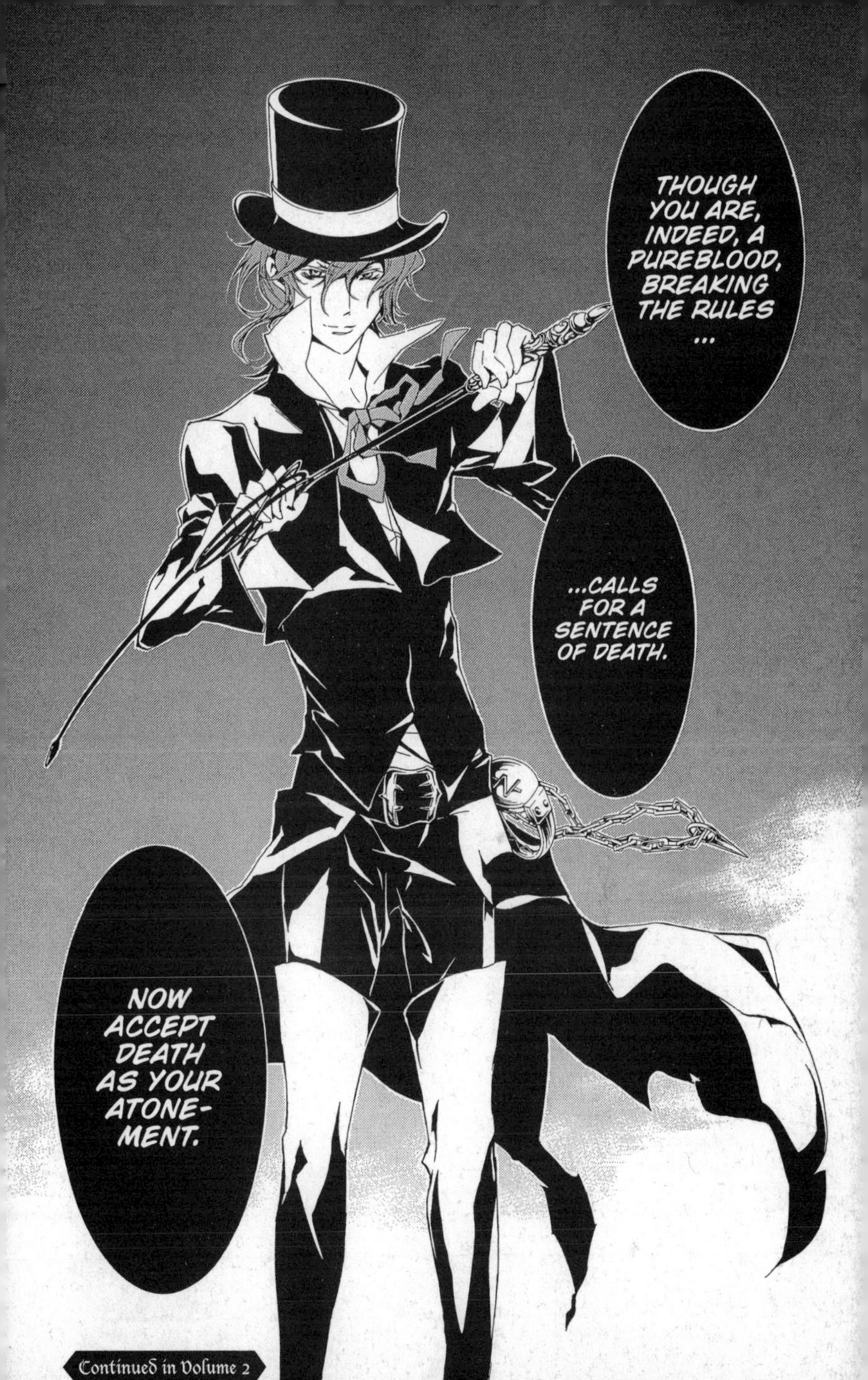
THOUGH YOU ARE, INDEED, A PUREBLOOD, BREAKING THE RULES ...
...CALLS FOR A SENTENCE OF DEATH.
NOW ACCEPT DEATH AS YOUR ATONE-MENT.

Continued in Volume 2

He's my only vampire
Aya Shouoto

HELLO, EVERYONE. IT'S NICE TO MEET YOU ALL. MY NAME IS AYA SHOUOTO.

MY HANDWRITING IS TERRIBLE, BUT I'LL DO MY BEST HERE! THANK YOU SO MUCH FOR READING HE'S MY ONLY VAMPIRE VOLUME 1!!

I BEGAN THIS SERIES WHEN MY EDITOR K-SAN ASKED ME, "HOW WOULD YOU FEEL ABOUT WRITING A VAMPIRE STORY?" [QUITE A DIFFICULT (IMPOSSIBLE?) TASK FOR ME!] AS A VERY MAINSTREAM PERSON, I FOUND VAMPIRES ATTRACTIVE BUT ALSO HAD ALL SORTS OF MISTAKEN IDEAS ABOUT THEM!

AFTER THIS POINT, MORE NEW CHARACTERS WILL KEEP SHOWING UP IN THE MANGA. THE NEW MALE CHARACTERS WILL FOLLOW THE "PUREBLOOD" THEME. (THOUGH I MAY TURN THAT ON ITS HEAD AND MAKE SOME OF THEM CONTRARY OR THE ANTI-PUREBLOOD TYPE. LIKE RIE...SORTA.) SO I HOPE YOU'LL LOOK FORWARD TO SEEING SOME PRINCELY "PUREBLOOD BOYFRIEND" TYPES ACTING LIKE LITTLE KIDS!

LET'S MEET AGAIN IN VOLUME 2!!

硝音あや 2011.
Aya Shouoto xxx.

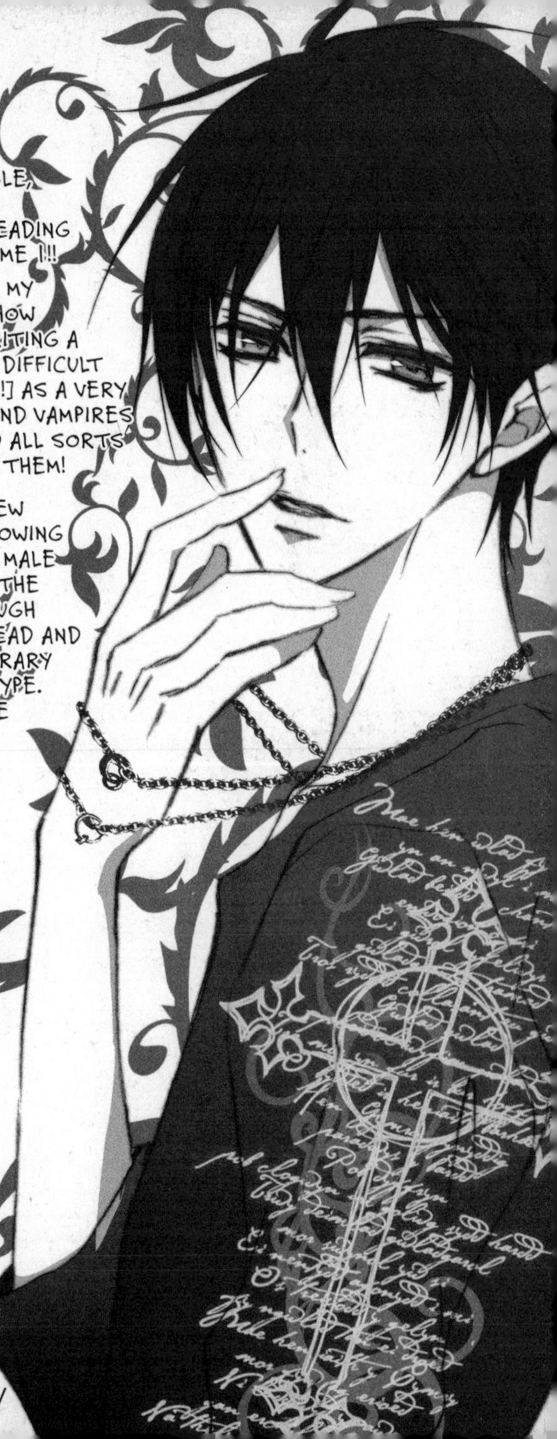

SPECIAL THANX

NORIE OGAWA
AYA NAKAMURA
MAIKO YOSHISE
AYA MAEDA
RIKA KASAHARA
KANAE SAITOU
YURIKA HONDA
KOU HIYOCO
and YOU

ttp://www.kashi.jpn.org/w/

Pure Blood Boyfriend In The House

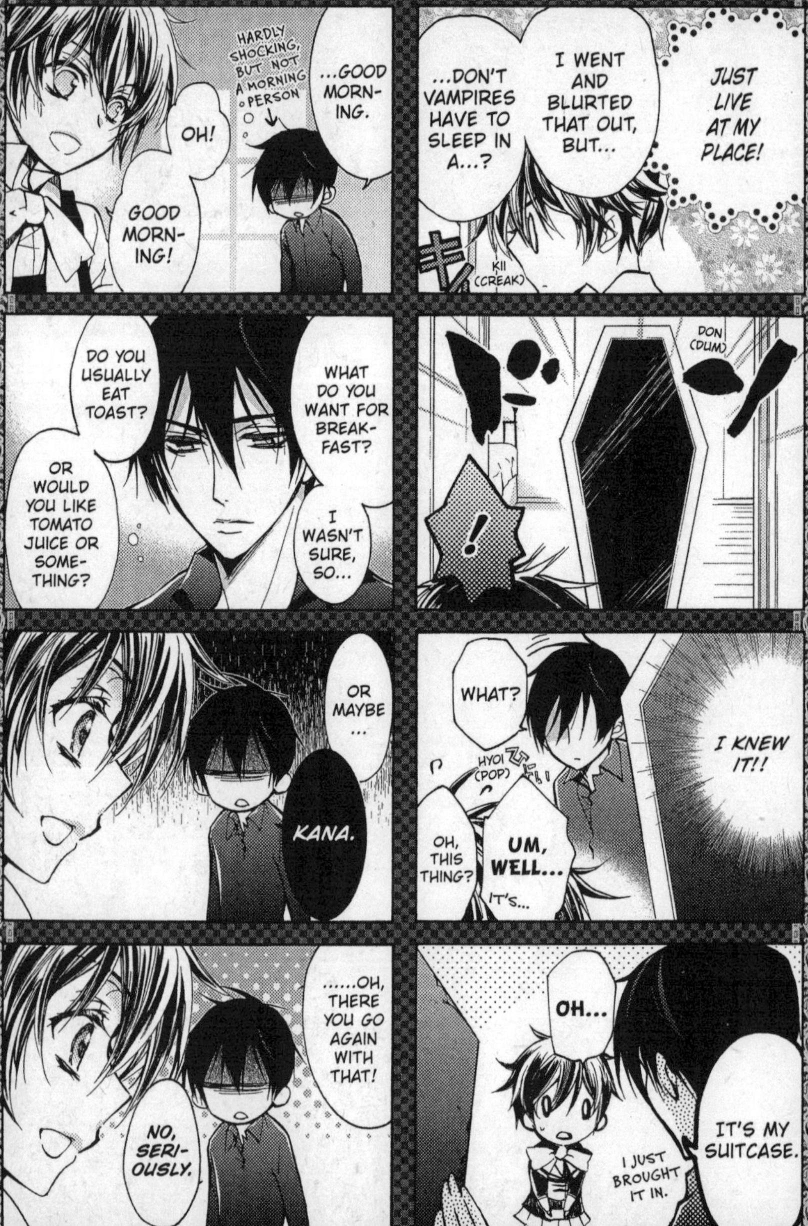
JUST LIVE AT MY PLACE!
I WENT AND BLURTED THAT OUT, BUT...
...DON'T VAMPIRES HAVE TO SLEEP IN A...?
KII (CREAK)
DON (DUM)
!
I KNEW IT!!
WHAT?
HYOI (POP)
UM, WELL...
IT'S...
OH, THIS THING?
IT'S MY SUITCASE.
OH...
I JUST BROUGHT IT IN.
AN UNEXPECTEDLY STYLISH SUITCASE...
...GOOD MORNING.
HARDLY SHOCKING, BUT NOT A MORNING PERSON
OH!
GOOD MORNING!
WHAT DO YOU WANT FOR BREAKFAST?
I WASN'T SURE, SO...
DO YOU USUALLY EAT TOAST?
OR WOULD YOU LIKE TOMATO JUICE OR SOMETHING?
OR MAYBE ...
KANA.
......OH, THERE YOU GO AGAIN WITH THAT!
NO, SERIOUSLY.
HOW SERIOUS, THOUGH?

Aya Shouoto

Next Story

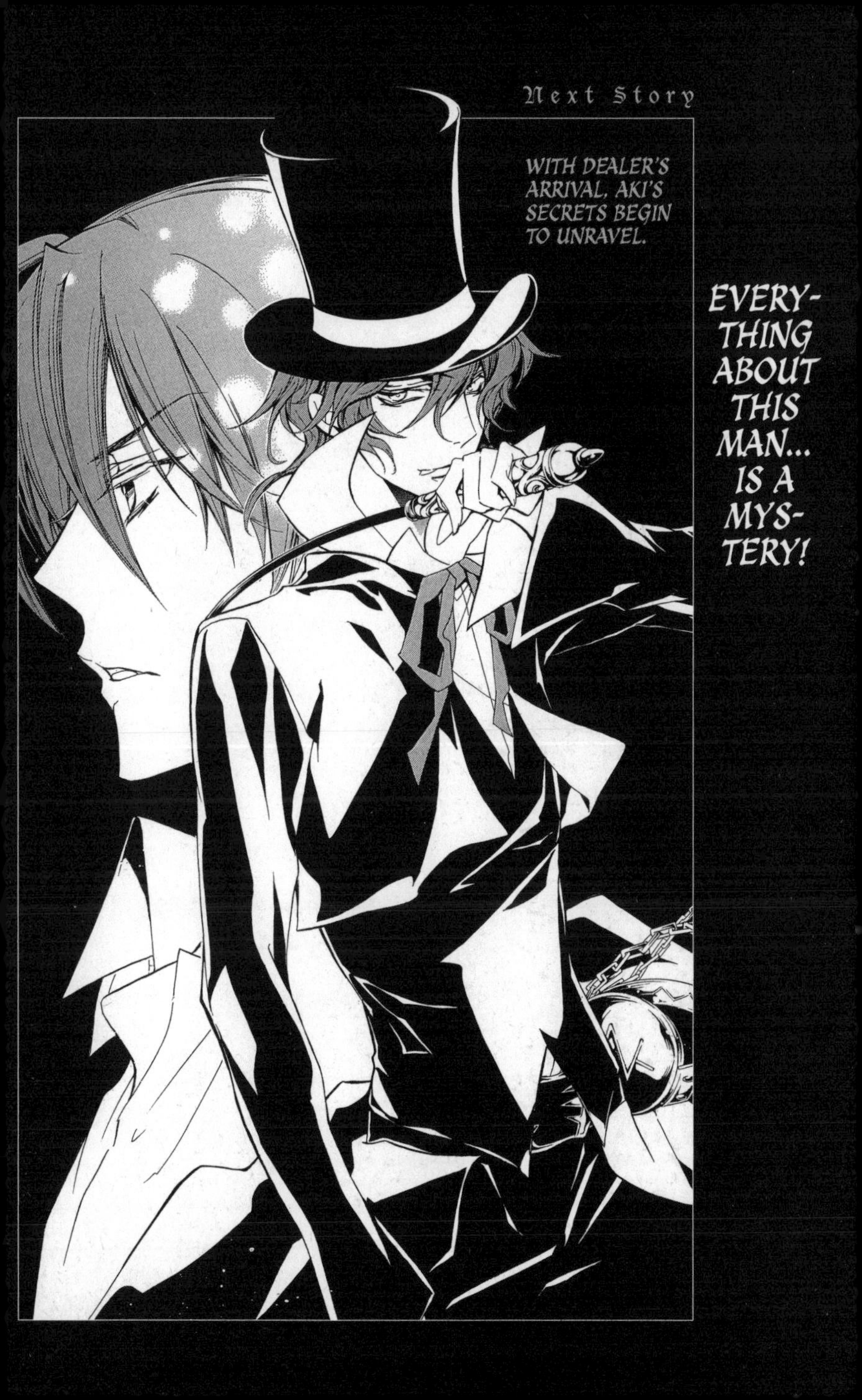
WITH DEALER'S ARRIVAL, AKI'S SECRETS BEGIN TO UNRAVEL.

EVERY-THING ABOUT THIS MAN... IS A MYS-TERY!

He's My Only Vampire 2

EVER MORE STYLISH!! —— COMING IN MARCH 2015!!

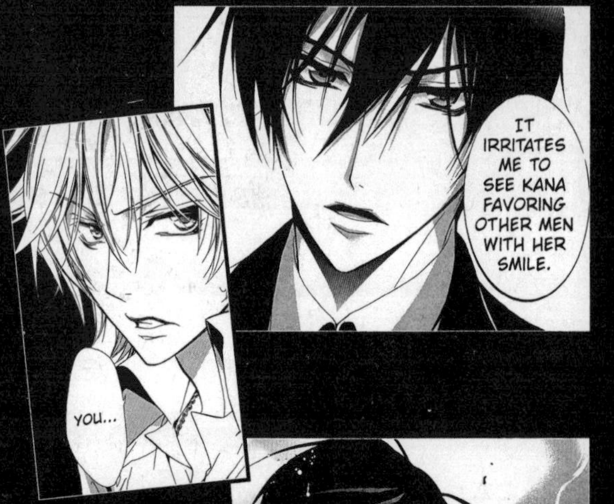
IT IRRITATES ME TO SEE KANA FAVORING OTHER MEN WITH HER SMILE.
YOU...

AKI, JIN, AND KANA GRADUALLY DRAW CLOSER TO ONE ANOTHER ...!?

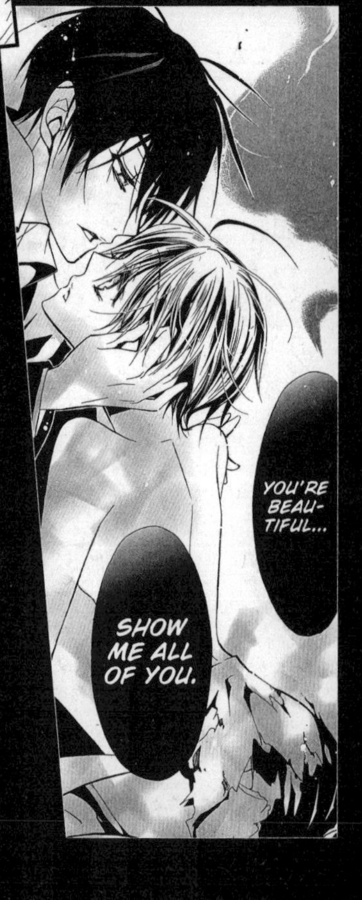
YOU'RE BEAU-TIFUL...
SHOW ME ALL OF YOU.

He's My Only Vampire ◆1

Aya Shouoto

Translation: Su Mon Han † Lettering: Alexis Eckerman

HE'S MY ONLY VAMPIRE Volume 1 © 2011 Aya Shouoto. All rights reserved. First published in Japan in 2011 by Kodansha Ltd., Tokyo. Publication rights for this English edition arranged through Kodansha Ltd., Tokyo.

Translation © 2014 by Hachette Book Group, Inc.

Yen Press
Hachette Book Group
1290 Avenue of the Americas, New York, NY 10104

www.HachetteBookGroup.com
www.YenPress.com

Yen Press is an imprint of Hachette Book Group, Inc. The Yen Press name and logo are trademarks of Hachette Book Group, Inc.

First Yen Press Edition: December 2014

ISBN: 978-0-316-33666-6

10 9 8 7 6 5 4 3 2 1

BVG

Printed in the
United States of America

c o n t e n t s

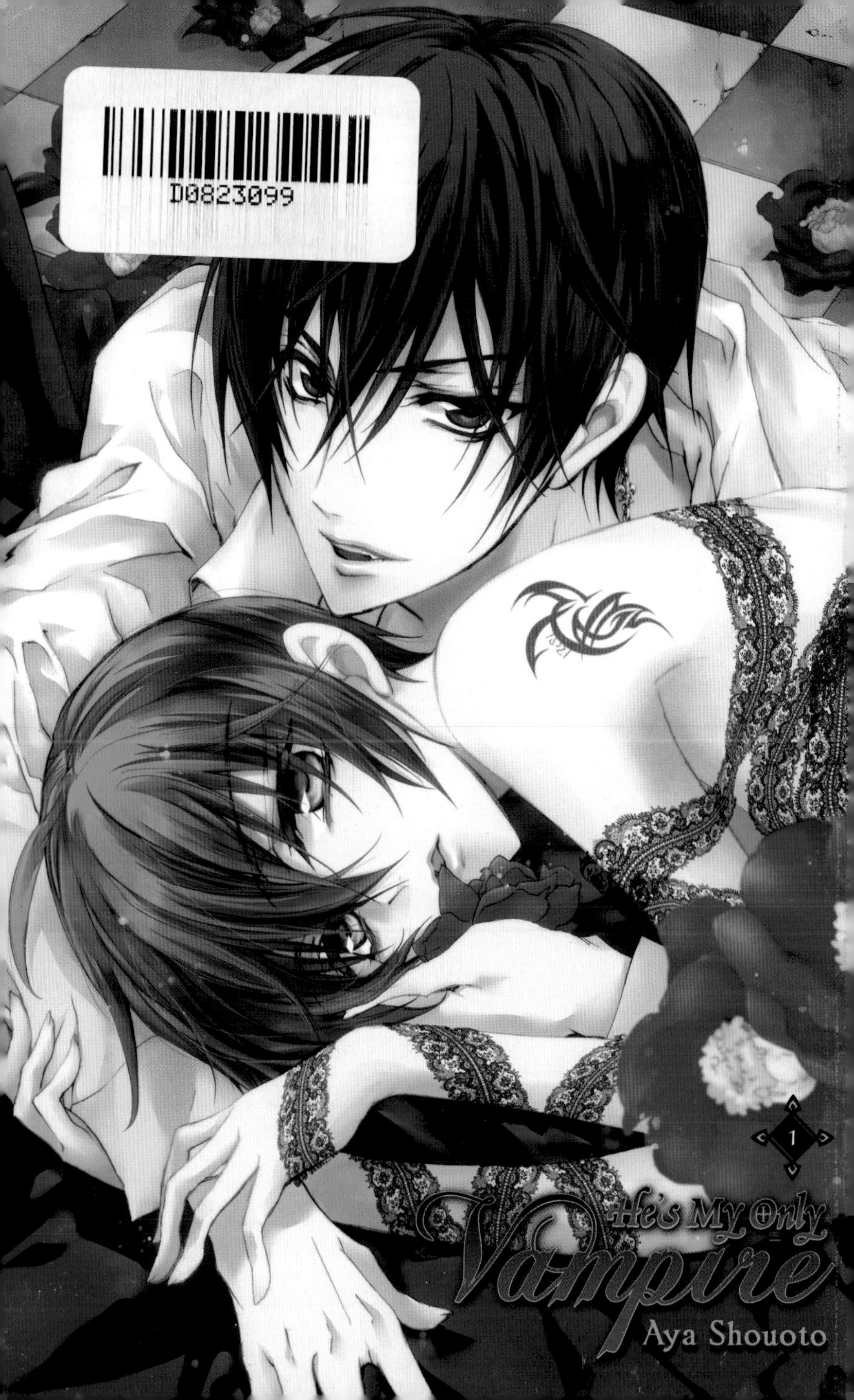

1
He's My Only Vampire
Aya Shouoto